THE MESSAGE AND MINISTRY OF JESUS

An Introductory Textbook

David A. Fiensy

University Press of America, Inc.
Lanham • New York • London

Copyright © 1996 by

University Press of America,® Inc.
4501 Forbes Boulevard, Suite 200
Lanham, Maryland 20706

3 Henrietta Street
London, WC2E 8LU England

Library of Congress Cataloging-in-Publication Data

Fiensy, David A.
The message and ministry of Jesus : an introductory textbook / David
A. Fiensy.
p.   cm.
Includes bibliographical references and indexes.
1. Jesus Christ--Biography. 2. Jesus Christ--Teachings. I. Title.
BT301.2.F52 1996   232.9'01--dc20   96-34221 CIP

ISBN 0-7618-0505-2 (cloth: alk. ppr.)
ISBN 0-7618-0506-0 (pbk: alk. ppr.)

⊖™The paper used in this publication meets the minimum
requirements of American National Standard for information
Sciences—Permanence of Paper for Printed Library Materials,
ANSI Z39.48—1984

DEDICATION

To Our Daughters

Amanda and Jeannie

With the belief that little girls seldom know how much they
are loved

Contents

List of Maps and Plans

List of Tables

Abbreviations

Aland	K. Aland, *Synopsis of the Four Gospels*
ABD	*Anchor Bible Dictionary*
ANF	*AnteNicean Fathers*
b.	Babylonian Talmud
BAGD	Bauer, Arndt, Gingrich, Danker, *Greek-English Lexicon*
BAR	*Biblical Archaeology Review*
BDB	Brown, Driver, Briggs, *Hebrew and English Lexicon*
Danby	Danby, *The Mishnah*
Hennecke	Hennecke, Schneemelcher, Wilson, *New Testament Apocrypha*
IDB	*Interpreter's Dictionary of the Bible*

ISBE o.s.	*International Standard Bible Encyclopedia* (old edition)
JE	*Jewish Encyclopedia*
LCL	Loeb Classical Library
LSJM	Liddel, Scott, Jones, McKenzie, *Greek Lexicon*
m.	Mishnah
OCD	*Oxford Classical Dictionary*
OTP	Charlesworth, *Old Testament Pseudepigrapha*
par.	Parallel(s)
1QH	Thanksgiving Scroll from Qumran
1QM	War Scroll from Qumran
4QpHab	Habakkuk Pesher
1QS	Community Rule from Qumran
11QT	Temple Scroll fromQumran
S-B	Strack and Billerbeck, *Kommentar zum neuen Testament aus Talmud und Midrasch*
SVM	Schuerer, Vermes, Millar, Black, *The History of the Jewish People in the Age of Jesus Christ*
t.	Tosephta

TDNT	Kittel, et al. eds., *Theological Dictionary of the New Testament*
Vermes	Vermes, *The Dead Sea Scrolls in English*
WHJP	*World History of the Jewish People*
y.	Jerusalem Talmud

Preface

As the subtitle indicates, this monograph is an attempt to introduce the beginning student to the academic study of the Gospels. In keeping with this purpose, I have not attempted striking innovations. My conclusions are conservative and traditional. This work may therefore disapoint some who have become use to the recent fascination with shocking copy. As teaching tools, however, more traditional works have longer value.

This introduction was written to be used alongside K. Aland's *Synopsis of the Four Gospels.* Nevertheless, I have attempted to give not only the section numbers from Aland but also the scriptural references in discussing specific passages. In addition an index of Aland sections with corresponding scriptural references can be found at the end of the book. Thus the text could be used with another synopsis or Gospels' harmony or simply with a New Testament to refer to. It goes without saying that the student should continuously refer to the biblical text while reading this monograph.

All scripture quotations in this volume are the author's own translation unless otherwise stated.

No long project is accomplished without the help of others. I wish to thank Mr. John Dundon, Executive Vice President of Kentucky Christian College, for his support in this endeavor. I also wish to thank Mr. Ryan Shellabarger for his helpful computer assistance. Finally, I wish to thank my wife, Molly, whose love and friendship enable me to do many things that I could not do without her.

Chapter 1

Geography and History of Palestine

Geographical Introduction

Bibliography: Y. Aharoni and M. Avi-Yona, *The MacMillan Bible Atlas*; Y. Aharoni, *The Land of the Bible*; M. Avi-Yona, *The Holy Land*; R.C. Foster, *Studies in the Life of Christ;* J. Klausner, *Jesus of Nazareth*; J. Monson, *Student Map Manual*; idem., *The Land Between*; M. Nun, "Cast your Net Upon the Waters" *BAR* 19/6 (1993) 46-56, 70; J.A. Thompson, *Handbook of Life in bible Times*

Israel (or Roman Palestine) is a small land in comparison with many modern countries. It is only slightly larger than our state of Vermont. From the city of Dan to the city of Beersheba (the Old Testament border) it is 150 miles. Its width is 54 miles in the south and 28 miles in the north. Yet in this tiny area are four different topographical regions and two different climates.

The western strip of Palestine is the narrow strip of coastal plain called the Plain of Sharon. It is very flat with sandy soil. There was in antiquity a major travel route up the Palestinian coastal plain which turned east through the Megiddo pass, went through the Great Plain (also called the Valley of Jezreel and Plain of Esdraelon), turned northward running along the western side of the Sea of Galilee and up along the upper Jordan river. This very important trading route connected Egypt with the Mesopotamian cities and with Syria.

Moving toward the east we come to the low hills (the Shephelah)

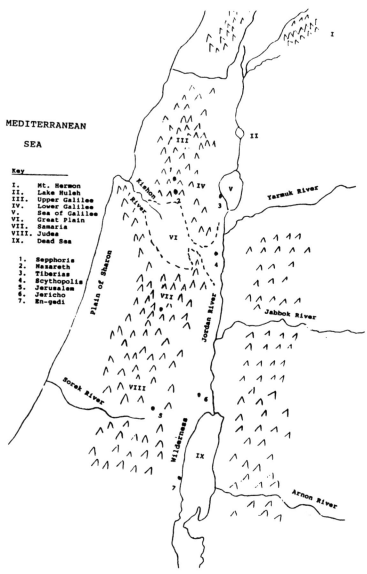

MEDITERRANEAN

SEA

Key

I.   Mt. Hermon
II.   Lake Huleh
III.   Upper Galilee
IV.   Lower Galilee
V.   Sea of Galilee
VI.   Great Plain
VII.   Samaria
VIII. Judea
IX.   Dead Sea

1. Sepphoris
2. Nazareth
3. Tiberias
4. Scythopolis
5. Jerusalem
6. Jericho
7. En-gedi

Map 1.1
Topographical Map of Israel

which give way soon to mountains or hill country. None of the mountains in Israel are very high except for Mt. Hermon which reaches 9000 feet. The hill country in Galilee--consisting especially in the northeast of black basalt, volcanic rock--climbs to about 4,000 feet and that of Samaria and Judea climbs to around 3,300 feet. Judea like Samaria consists of white limestone rock.

Farther east we find the Jordan rift, a huge geological fault which begins in Syria, goes through the Gulf of Aqaba and ends in east Africa. The Jordan River which runs along this fault has its head waters at the base of Mt. Hermon and falls to 700 feet below sea level by the time it empties into the Sea of Galilee. The Sea of Galilee is about 6 miles wide at its widest and around 12 miles long. It is a fresh water lake teeming with fish of many varieties (see M. Nun).

Exiting the Sea of Galilee from the south, the Jordan then falls to around 1,300 feet below sea level by the time it reaches the Dead Sea. The Dead Sea is 11 miles across and 50 miles long and reaches a depth of 1,250 feet. This body of water is so salty that no living thing, except microorganisms, inhabits it. It was, however, a rich source of bitumen in antiquity.

Israel is a land between the Mediterranean Sea on the west and the desert on the east. These two realities control Israel's climate. The western side of the hill country receives adequate rainfall and cooling summer breezes from the ocean. The area east of Jerusalem and running south all along the Dead Sea is desert. Here in this place of isolation and intense heat Jesus came to be tempted (Mt 4:1-11).

From the east comes, beginning in April, the scorching wind from the desert called the *sirocco* or *khamsin*. This dry wind lasts only a few days but withers the vegetation. Israel has a rainy season and a dry season. From April until October not a drop of rain falls. In the fall it may or may not rain but by winter (mid-December) the cold rain begins and it may occasionally snow. Yet the grass and other vegetation become green and the flowers bloom.

R.C. Foster has an interesting chapter on the influence of weather upon the ministry of Jesus. He notes that Jesus' ministry at Sychar (Jn 4:35) must have been in the winter because of the words, "Yet four months and then comes the harvest" (the harvest of grains in Israel comes in June). Again Jesus is pictured in John's Gospel in a winter scene. John 10:22 speaks of Jesus' preaching in the temple at the feast of Dedication or Hanukkah which takes place in December: "And it was the feast of

Dedication at Jerusalem, for it was winter, and Jesus was walking in the temple in Solomon's portico." Foster then indicates to us how often Jesus must have traveled and preached in inclement weather:

> When we picture Jesus traveling from place to place in his eager, but patient, ministry, we seldom think of His going through rain and cold, buffeted by the elements. . . (but) thus the gospel was preached, whether in fair weather or in foul, whether to many or to few. What an example this is to us! (p. 57)

The crops produced in the coastal plain included especially wheat, wine, and figs. Many were also engaged in fishing the Mediterranean. Also since an international travel route ran up the coast, trade flourished in the coastal plain. These people because of the frequent contacts with outsiders always were considered more sophisticated and worldly than those living in the hill country.

Galilee, Judea and Samaria produced the main three crops of all peasants: wine, olive oil and grain. There were also sheep and goats and the Gentile towns raised pigs. Many were employed as fishermen around the Sea of Galilee. The Jordan Valley, especially around Jericho and En-gedi raised balsam plants which produced a salve considered very valuable by the ancients. These centers also produced dates. The salty soil evidently was excellent for raising the tastiest dates.

Many of course were employed in crafts, especially those living in the cities. Villages also had their craftsmen. Sometimes whole villages specialized in one craft. The Talmud refers to two villages in Galilee (Kefar Hanania and Sikhnin) that were well known for their pottery. Villages in a southern area of Judea known as Darom were given to the purple dying trade and consequently everyone in these villages had purple hands.

Avi-Yonah estimated that the population of Palestine in the New Testament period was 2.5 million. But this figure seems to be his estimate of the number of Jews living in Palestine. We know there were also many Gentiles. The cities of the Decapolis (Scythopolis, Hippos, Gadara, Philadelphia, Abila, Pella, and Gerasa among others) were mostly inhabited by Gentiles. In addition were new cities like Caesarea Maritima, Tiberias, Sepphoris and Caesarea Philippi which had a majority of Gentiles. Even Jerusalem had some Gentiles. Thus we should perhaps increase the total to 3.5 million persons.

Palestine From Judas Maccabeus to the Bar Kosiba War

History of Rome: 146 BC to AD 68

Bibliography: E.M. Blaiklock, *The Century of the New Testament*; J. Buchan, *Augustus*; *Cambridge Ancient History*, Vols, VIII, X, XI; M. Carey, *History of Rome*; J. Carpopino, *Daily Life in Ancient Rome*; A Garzetti, *From Tiberius to the Antonines*; M.T. Griffin, *Nero*; H. Mattingly, *Roman Imperial Civilization*; M.C. Tenney, *New Testament Times*.

The Roman political situation changed quickly in the second and first centuries BC. By 146 BC the three Punic wars (against Carthage) and the three Macedonian wars had been fought and Rome controlled most of the Mediterranean world. These territories were organized into provinces which paid Rome taxes in money and produce. The city of Rome had now mastery of an empire.

But the empire brought wealth only to a few people. In 133 BC an altruistic senator named Gracchus tried to redistribute government land to the urban poor but was assassinated by a group of senators. Ten years later his brother tried to install a welfare system for the poor but was eventually driven to suicide by his enemies. Marius, a political and military leader also tried reforms for the poor but failed and resigned from office in 99 BC. There clearly was a clas struggle developing.

A civil war was brewing and needed only an incident to boil over. When Sulla, the consul--the highest political leader--left Rome to lead an army into battle in Asia Minor (85 BC), a man from the lower class was elected to replace him. When Sulla returned to Rome, the first civil war began with Sulla and his allies victorious. After the war was over, the victors effected a terrible vendetta with thousands of people murdered and families disenfranchised from their property.

In 62 BC Pompey, a former lieutenant of Sulla (and the conqueror of Palestine in 63 BC) made a pact with Julius Caesar, a relative of Marius. Together with another important man, Crassus, the wealthiest man in Rome, they formed the first Triumvirate ("rule of the three"). The alliance was actually illegal according to Roman republican law but it was hoped it would prevent another civil war. The alliance kept the lid on the boiling pot for only a short time. In 50 BC a second civil war began between Pompey and Caesar.

In 46 BC Caesar was victorious over Pompey and was elected dictator for ten years. At last, many thought, peace and stability have arrived. Caesar reinstated the programs of helping the poor. But once more the world was convulsed when Caesar was assassinated in 44 by allies of Pompey, by some of disgruntled friends and by republican purists who lamented the deterioration of their system of government.

The two ring-leaders of the coup d'etat, Brutus and Cassius, were in turn defeated by the next Triumvirate: Mark Antony, Octavian (later called Augustus) and Lepidus. Antony and Octavian, when the dust had settled, divided up the emjpire. Antony received the east (Greece, Asia Minor, Syria and Egypt) and Octavian the west (Italy, Africa, Spain and Gaul).

As with the first Triumvirate, the second one fell apart and once again civil war ensued. Octavian was the ultimate victor in 31 BC and subsequently his unrivaled rule of the empire began an era of peace and stability. From this point on, historians dub the single leader of Rome the "emperor" although the Romans themselves called him *princeps* or "first citizen".

Thus Octavian became the first emperor of Rome. He was also given the name Augustus ("consecrated"), a title of divinity and indeed in the east he was worshipped in temples while he was yet alive. Only much later would emperor worship be practiced in the west. Augustus was a powerful political figure from the beginning but his power even increased with his reign as more and more of the responsibilities of the government--and with them, the authority--fell to him. By the end of his reign, he was an absolute despot and the Roman system of government was forever changed. Jesus was born during Augustus' rule.

Augustus 31 BC-AD 14	**Claudius AD 41-45**
Tiberius AD 14-37	**Nero AD 54-68**
Gaius Caligula AD 37-41	

Table 1.1

JULIO-CLAUDIAN EMPERORS

None of the rest of the Julio-Claudian emperors--all of whom were related either to Augustus or to his wife, Livia--possessed Augustus' political savvy. His immediate successor, Tiberius, however, was quite competent. Tiberius was emperor when Jesus was executed and is mentioned in Luke 3:1. Claudius was also a very competent administrator and is referred to in Acts 18:2. Gaius Caligula and Nero, on the other hand, are synonymous with madness and debauchery. They knew no moral restraint and possessed no respect for human life. Caligula almost touched off a Jewish war when he ordered (in AD 38) his statue to be erected in the Holy of Holies in Jerusalem. Nero ordered the first Christian persecution (AD 64) executing hundreds, perhaps thousands, of believers in the cruelest of fashions. Among those killed at that time were the apostles Peter and Paul.

The Hasmoneans 167 BC to 63 BC

Bibliography: E. Bevan, *Jerusalem Under the High Priests;* E. Bickerman, *From Ezra to the Last of the Maccabees;* G.H. Box, *Judaism in the Greek Period;* S. Cohen, *From Maccabees to Mishnah;* W. Foerster, *From the Exile to Christ;* J.A. Goldstein, *1 Maccabees;* idem., *2 Maccabees;* L.L. Grabbe, *Judaism from Cyrus to Hadrian;* M. Pearlman, *The Maccabees;* D.S. Russell, *The Jews from Alexander to Herod;* SVM; S. Zeitlin, *The Rise and Fall of the Judean State.*

The family of Mattathias of the clan of Hasmon stepped on to the stage of world history in the year 167 BC. Mattathias was of priestly (but not High Priestly) descent and lived in a small village called Modin which lay 17 miles northwest of Jerusalem. He would have gone up to Jerusalem to perform his priestly duties twice a year, but otherwise lived as a peasant farmer with his five sons: John, Simon, Judas (called Maccabeus, the "hammer"), Eleazar and Jonathan.

Rome had not yet gained control of Palestine. After the exile, Palestine was under Persian rule until Alexander the Great, the Macedonian king, conquered Persia. After his death, Alexander's generals divided up his empire. Palestine was at this time under the power of the Syrian king, Antiochus IV, a great admirer of Greek culture. Antiochus determined that he would "Hellenize" (or compell to accept Greek culture) all of his subjects. Therefore, he set in motion a program to do just that in

Palestine. In order to Hellenize his subjects, however, he thought it necessary to forbid certain of their religious practices such as circumcising infants, keeping food laws and observing the Sabbath.

Sometime in the year of 167 BC officers of Antiochus IV came to Modin to compell the residents to sacrifice to the Greek god, Zeus. Mattathias was asked to lead the way in this ritual. When he refused, another Jew in the village started to sacrifice. The irascible Mattathias then grabbed a sword from one of the officers standing nearby, killed the man attempting to sacrifice and then killed the officer. This incident began an irreversible and perhaps inevitible series of events that would lead eventually to Jewish independence.

Mattathias and his sons fled to the hills and others quickly joined them among whom were the Hasidim ("pious ones") who were said to be, "mighty warriors, everyone a volunteer for the Torah" (1 Macc 2:42). How long prior to this time the Hasidim had existed as a group we cannot know but it appears that they and perhaps others that were loyal to the Torah had only awaited a spark to ignite rebellion.

In every rebellion there is at first a convulsion of revenge. Now Mattathias and his band of rebels attacked and killed Hellenizing Jews and forced Jewish boys to be circumcised. They also tore down pagan altars and "drove the haughty before them" (1 Macc 2:47). Years of anger were vented in those first weeks.

The importance of this period for understanding the Gospels cannot be overly emphasized. The commitment to the Torah which cost some Jews their lives left a deep impression on subsequent generations. The pious *hasid* who maintained loyalty to Torah regardless of environmental or cultural influences became a heroic type.

Mattathias died shortly after the rebellion began and the leadership fell to his son, Judas Maccabeus. The choice was a felicitous one. Judas proved to possess a native fighting genius which harked back to the days of King David. He was daring, yet clever and he knew perfectly how to fight in the Judean hill country.

Judas' successes over the next few years in keeping at bay one of the most formidable armies in the ancient world was due to three factors: The first was his own genius as a tactician; the second was the recklessness of some of the Syrian military commanders; the third was the chaotic in-fighting of the Syrians after Antiochus' death.

But Judas was not invicible. Although Judas won a stunning victory in early 161 BC and negotiated a treaty with Rome, he met his end later that same year. In spite of the fact that his army had dwindled to only 800 men, he attempted a suicidal attack on a large Syrian force. He was struck down and his body carried to Modin to be buried with his father and his brother, Eleazar, who had earlier died in battle.

The leadership was now given to Jonathan. Jonathan was not the military champion his brother had been but he knew how to play off opposing sides. By killing all of the Hellenists he found in the rural areas by night and courting the favor of the populace by day, he soon established himself as the political power to be reckoned with. Soon Jonathan had accepted the High Priesthood. From then on--until the time of Herod the Great who would appoint and depose High Priests at will-- the Hasmonean ruler in Palestine would be the High Priest. This action infuriated and scandalized certain of the Jerusalem Jews because the Hasmoneans, although priests, were not of High Priestly lineage. This year probably marks the beginning of the Essene sect.

Jonathan died by treachery in 142 BC. His brother, John, had also died in battle just before this. Thus of Mattathias and his five sons only Simon was left.

Simon was able to secure through treaties and alliances complete political independence for Judah (or the southern part of Palestine). Not since the Babylonian defeat of Judah in 586 BC had Judea known the feeling of freedom. Simon also was elected to the position of High Priest.

In 134 BC Simon was assassinated by his ambitious son-in-law leaving his son, John Hyrcanus (ruled 134-104) to succeed him. His noteworthy actions were first his conquering the Idumeans to the south and forcing them to be circumcised and his annexation of Samaria. But he broke with the sect of the Pharisees--which is mentioned here for the first time in Josephus--and favored the Sadducees.

Hyrcanus' eldest son, Aristobulus, only reigned one year before he died of a disease. His brief reign is marked by his annexation and forced circumcision of the residents of Galilee. The other notable event in Aristobulus's reign was his open assumption of the title of king, the first Jewish king since Zedekiah in 586 BC (see 2 Kings 24).

Alexander Jannaeus (reigned 103-77 BC), the brother of Aristobulus, was a man of war and violence. His unpopularity with the masses and his hostility toward the Pharisees led to conflicts, riots and eventually civil war. Once while sacrificing during the feast of Tabernacles--for he was not only king, of course, but High Priest--the crowd began to pelt him with their citrons--part of the required articles for Tabernacles. His soldiers took revenge by slaughtering many in the crowd. Later, after a failed attempt at revolution, Alexander took revenge on the leaders, many of whom were Pharisees. He executed 800 men along with their wives and children. At that time 8000 of Alexander's enemies fled from Jerusalem. Many historians believe a sizable part of this group went to Qumran to join the Essene community.

When Alexander Jannaeus died he left the throne to his wife, Alexandra (77-68 BC). Since she could not also be High Priest, she appointed her eldest son, Hyrcanus II, to that office. Her reign was characterized by peace and consolation. Syria was becoming ever weaker and was thus in no position to bother with Palestine. At home, Alexandra reconciled with the Pharisees and even made them leaders in her government.

Hyrcanus II was Alexandra's rightful heir but his younger brother, Aristobulus II, quickly deposed him and managed to rule for some five years (68-63 BC). His reign was cut short, however, by the coming of the great Roman general, Pompey.

In 66 BC Pompey defeated Mithridates of Armenia and in 64 he ended the Seleucid monarchy in Syria. While staying in Damascus, Pompey received both Hyrcanus II and Aristobulus II each of whom argued he should be king instead of the other. There was also an embassy of Jews requesting that neither remain as king. Pompey put off his decision but later when Aristobulus seemed to be preparing for war, Pompey pursued him and put him into prison. Aristobulus' followers fled to the Temple for refuge. Pompey laid seige and took the Temple in three months. He subsequently reinstalled Hyrcanus as High Priest--but not king--under the authority of the new Roman governor of Syria and took away much of the territory the Hasmoneans had acquired.

The importance of this period--from Mattathias' uprising in 167 BC to the coming of Pompey in 63--for the study of the New Testiment cannot be exaggerated. It witnessed the rise of the three most important religious-political sects: Pharisees, Sadducees, and Essenes. It produced a taste for freedom and a tradition of armed resistance against foreign foes from which later groups, in the middle of the first century AD, would gain inspiration. The Hasmonean illegal assumption of the High Priesthood left a desire for religious reform just as their acceptance of the title "king" strengthened the yearning for a Davidic king or Messiah. Finally, the personal danger which loyalty to the Torah had involved, resulted in an often extreme fanaticism. Neglect of the Torah was viewed by some groups as the worst of crimes. This 100 year era, then, shaped the Jewish religious and ideological soul which we find in the time of Jesus.

The Herods

Bibliography: M. Avi-Yonah, *The Herodian Period*; R.J. Bull, "Caesarea Maritima--The Search for Herod's City" *BAR* 8/3 (1982) 24-41; *Cambridge Ancient History* Vol. X; H.W. Hoehner, *Herod Antipas*; A.H.M. Jones, *The Herods of Judea*; E. Netzer, "Searching for Herod's Tomb" *BAR* 9/3 (1983) 30-51; R. Otto, "Herodes" *Pauly-Wissowa*; S.H. Perowne, *The Life and Times of Herod the Great*; idem., *The Later Herods*; S. Sandmel, *Herod: Profile of a Tyrant*; A Schalit, *Herodes*; SVM; Y. Yadin, *Masada*

Although Hyrcanus II was stripped of his formal political power by Pompey, a certain amount of political influence always accompanied religious power in the Middle East. By virtue of his being the High Priest he was still a powerful man in Jewish society. But the weak Hyrcanus was "helped" in wielding power by the opportunist, Antipater of Idumea.

The people of Idumea--a territory just south of Judea--had been subdued and circumcised by compulsion under Hyrcanus' grandfather, John Hyrcanus. The Idumean family of Antipater begins to find mention in Josephus after Pompey's conquest of Palestine when Antipater became advisor and confidant to Hyrcanus II. Later when Antipater joined forces with Caesar to defeat Ptolemy of Egypt--to wrench the throne from Ptolemy in favor of his sister, Cleopatra--Caesar was so pleased he gave Antipater Roman citizenship along with the title of "finance manager" (Gk: *epitropos*) of Palestine and later the title of governor of southern Syria.

The wily Antipater now had his claws on all of Palestine and he never let go for Hyrcanus ruled in name only. Antipater's two sons, Phasael and Herod, managed the country in Jerusalem and Galilee respectively. When Caesar was assassinated in 42 BC, Antipater's son, Herod, won the favor of Mark Antony, who along with Octavian (Augustus) divided up the empire. Soon thereafter, Herod's brother, Phasael, was killed leaving Herod alone to rule Palestine.

Herod was granted the title of king by Rome and ruled over the territories of Idumea, Judea, Samaria, Galilee, Perea and Gaulanitis from 37 to 4 BC. Herod, now firmly in control of Palestine, was free to build the kind of kingdom he envisioned. He made Jerusalem a magnificent city with his own palace, an amphitheatre, a hippodrome, a new military guard house called the Tower of Antonia (named after Antony) and especially by a newly built temple. The latter structure, begun in 20 BC, was finished well after Herod's lifetime and only a few years before the great war against Rome in AD 66.

Herod also built new cities such as Antipatris, Caesarea Maritima (see R.J. Bull) and Sebaste and strengthened and lavished fortified palaces such as Masada (see Yadin), Machaerus and Herodium (see Netzer). In addition he gave gifts of money to various Greek cities. Such building required a huge income. Most historians have concluded--from Herod's will--that his annual income was 1000 talents or 10,000,000 Attic Greek drachmas of silver.

Herod was a tyrant, cruel, morally profligate and greedy. He was closer to a mafia figure than a political personality. He often resorted to murder to eliminate opponents or even critics. He had murdered his wife and even three of his sons. The joke in Rome was that it was better to be one of Herod's pigs than one of his sons. Herod is the king of Matthew 2 that ordered the murder of all the babies in Bethlehem.

Shortly before his death, Herod gave orders to his government ministers to execute the most distinguished men in his kingdom on the day of his death. His rationale for such an order was that he wanted there to be great lamentation at his death. The order was never carried out, however. He died in 4 BC and was buried at Herodium. Though archaeologists have excavated at Herodium, his tomb has not yet been discovered.

Herod left his kingdom mainly to three of his sons: To Archelaus he bequeathed Idumea, Judea and Samaria and the title of king. Rome later changed his title to ethnarch (leader of a nation). To Antipas he left Galilee and Perea and to Philip he willed Gaulanitis, Batanea, Trachonitis and Auranitis. Antipas and Philip were called tetrarchs (literally, leaders of a fourth but meaning here leaders of a territory). According to the expected annual income, Archelaus received the greatest wealth, Antipas the next and Philip the least.

Archelaus ruled his territories from 4 BC to AD 6. He was a brutal and ruthless ruler like his father. The emperor of Rome, Octavian--now called Augustus--finally banished him to Gaul where he remained until his death. After him--except for a brief time under Agrippa I--a Roman procurator under the authority of the Syrian proconsul governed these regions

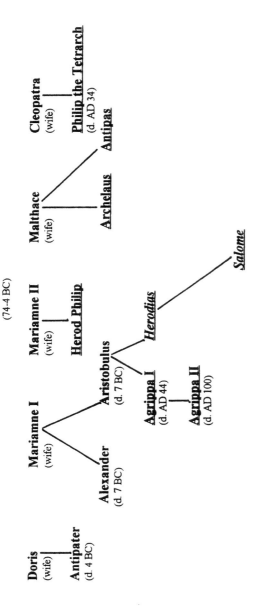

Table 1.2

HEROD'S FAMILY

(Italics indicate a daughter; those underlined are referred to in the New Testament. See Josephus, *Ant.* 17.1.3 and *War* 1.28.4.)

Antipas ruled from 4 BC to AD 39. He possessed evidently the cunning of his father, Herod, because Jesus called him on one occasion, "that fox" (Lk 13:32). Antipas scandalized the Jews by casting off his first wife, the daughter of Aretas, king of Arabia, and marrying Herodias, his brother's wife. Aretas would later defeat Antipas in battle (in AD 36) partly out of anger over the treatment of his daughter.

Antipas is best known for his execution of the prophet, John the Baptist. The Gospels (Mk 6:17-28) indicate that John who was already imprisoned by Antipas was beheaded at the prodding of Herodias (and her daughter Salome) because John condemned Antipas' marriage. Josephus writes that Antipas executed John because he feared he was becoming too popular. The truth is political leaders seldom act out of only one motive. Doubtless both considerations played a role in Antipas' decision.

Antipas, like his father Herod, was a builder. His two greatest achievements were the cities, Tiberias and Sepphoris, both in Galilee. The latter city called "the ornament of all Galilee" by Josephus, lay only three miles from Nazareth.

Antipas incurred the displeasure of emperor Caligula in AD 39 when the emperor heard a series of accusations made against him. He therefore exiled Antipas in Gaul, as Archelaus before him, and gave his territories to Herodias' brother and Herod the Great's grandson, Agrippa I.

Philip enjoyed a long reign (4 BC-AD 34) over the territories of northeast Palestine. Not much is known about him except that he built the well decorated city of Caesarea Philippi. When he died, Agrippa I received his territories as well

The Procurators

Bibliography: F. F. Bruce, *New Testament History*; W.R. Farmer, *Maccabees, Zealots and Josephus*; D.A. Fiensy, *The Social History of Palestine in the Herodian Period*; idem., *New Testament Introduction*; M. Hengel, *The Zealots*; R.A. Horsley and J.S. Hanson, *Bandits, Prophets, and Messiahs*; D. Rhoads, *Israel in Revolution*; S. Safrai and M. Stern, *The Jewish People in the First Century* I.1; SVM; E.M. Smallwood, *The JewsUnderRoman Rule*; M. Smith, "Zealots and Sicarii, Their Origins and Relation" *Harvard Theological Review* 64 (1971) 1-19; W. Stenger, *Gebt dem Kaiser was des Kaisers ist.*

The Roman procurators (see Table), who governed Judea until AD 41 and after AD 44 governed all of Palestine, began in violence and ended the same way. These administrators had three main duties: military (command a standing arming in Judea), judicial (serve as the supreme court), and fiscal (administer the finances). They resided at Caesarea Maritima but made occasional visits to Jerusalem.

Coponius	AD 6-9
Amvivibus	AD 9-12
Rufus	AD 12-15
Gratus	AD 15-26
Pilate	AD 26-36

Table 1.3
The Roman Procurators of Judea AD 6-36
(After SVM)

The first procurator, Coponius, immediately made a census of the population. Rome always sized up her expected income from a new land at the very beginning of its rule. Censuses were common in Egypt every fourteen years and presumably Syria would have done the same. Every male between the ages of 14 and 65 and every female between 12 and 65 was expected to pay a poll-tax in Syria. The average amount of the poll-tax for the poor was, according to Stenger, probably around one denarius per person (Mk 12:13-17). But in addition, an assessment would have been made of the agricultural potential of Judea to assess the tax on the soil, usually around 12% per year.

The Jews were outraged by this census and one Jewish scholar, named Judas--did he see something significant in his name?--decided the situation was intolerable. He said only cowards would submit to these taxes after serving God alone and that his fellow Jews should not tolerate men as their masters. From the vantage point of hindsight, Judas seems unreasonable. Certainly the Jews had paid taxes to Herod and his heirs, but they were regarded as (quasi) Jews. In the Jewish thinking God really was the owner of the land (Lev 25:23) and the king was his viceroy. But now a new god, Caesar, was demanding taxes as if he owned the land (see Hengel).

Judas formed a movement--called a "philosophy" by Josephus--which actively and violently opposed the census. Although Coponius rather quickly disposed of him and the disturbance, it was only the beginning of a series of violent clashes between Jewish idealists and Roman procurators, clashes that ultimately in AD 66 developed into total war.

The effect of Judas' uprising is now difficult to assess. Some historians (e.g. Hengel) speculate that a secret society, the Zealot movement, began at this time and was active behind the scenes until the war broke out. Others (e.g. M. Smith) argue that the Zealots did not exist as a movement or party until the war began. In the main one can say that the continental scholars follow Hengel (and Schuerer before him) but a growing number of Americans follow M. Smith (e.g. Rhoades, Horsley). At least one can say that the bitter memory of that encounter remained vivid and played a role in fanning flames later.

The next procurator of note was Pontius Pilate who not only executed Jesus of Nazareth but aroused the ire of the Jews in a number of ways. First he attempted to put in Jerusalem a flag or standard which had a figure of the Roman emperor (Tiberius) on it. This action obviously angered orthodox Jews who saw in it a transgression of the second commandment (Ex 20:4). A protest and riot in Caesarea over Pilate's activities resulted in the slaughter of a great many Jews.

Pilate provoked yet another riot when he appropriated temple funds to pay for an aquaduct for Jerusalem. From Pilate's perspective, the Jews should pay for this aquaduct themselves and where else could he get the money but the temple treasury? But to pious Jews he had committed sacrilege by robbing the temple. Many Jews also died in this riot in Jerusalem.

Finally, after Pilate's murder of a band of Samaritans which was traveling to Mt. Gerizim, he was dismissed as procurator.

The procurators ruled Judea, except for three years (AD 41-44) under Agrippa I, until AD 66 when the great war with Rome began. The war was caused in part by the greedy and inept procurators but other factors played a role too. Religious motives accounted for the intense zeal demonstrated by many of the Jewish combatants. Socio-economic reasons also influenced the Jews for many of the most desperate fighters came from the destitute classes. And of course in a climate such as this many imposters and deceivers could be found who would promise their followers kingdoms on earth in order to win popularity.

When the war finally ended, after defeat in Galilee in AD 68, after the destruction of Jerusalem in AD 70, and after the fall of Masada in AD 73 (or 74), Palestine was without its temple and the nature of Judaism was greatly altered.

The Time Between the Wars

Bibliography: J. Neusner, *A Life of Yohanan ben Zakkai*; idem., *First Century Judaism in Crisis*; P. Schaefer, *Geschichte der Juden in der Antike*; SVM; E.M. Smallwood, *The Jews Under Roman Rule*; S. Zeitlin, *The Rise of the Judaean State*.

The Great War of A.D. 66-73(74) left the Jewish nation decimated and the Jewish religion without a center. Schaefer estimates that one third of the Jewish population of Palestine died in the war. Jerusalem was a leveled ruin and the temple was completely demolished. A standing army--the Tenth Legion--would from now on guard against insurrection. The land now belonged to the emperor (Vespasian) and the peasants on it became his tenants. Since the temple was gone, the temple tax now went to the Roman god, Jupiter Capitolinus, in Rome.

It was a time of physical and emotional devastation. Some coped by turning to visions. The apocalyptists, especially 4 Ezra and 2 Baruch promised that God would soon rebuild the temple and smite the Romans. The anguish in these two writings is obvious.

The Sadducees disappeared from history. Without the temple as their power base, the mostly priestly Sadducees had no reason to exist as a group. Thus the destruction of the temple meant the end of this way of living as a Jew.

The scribes and Pharisees turned from the temple to theTorah. Their spiritual descendants, the rabbis, now focused on making the Torah the center of Jewish religious life and applying and interpreting its precepts. Post 70 Judaism, thus, became in the main rabbinic Judaism, the Judaism of Torah. The temple was not needed to study the Torah, thus rabbinic Judaism could survive.

The leader of the rabbinical movement was Johanan ben Zakkai. Born in Galilee, at some point he wound up in Jerusalem where he studied and taught Torah. During the Roman seige of Jerusalem he urged the Jews to make peace with Rome. When he saw the futility of his pleading, he decided to escape the city by stealth. His five disciples carried him from the city in a coffin and he immediately went before Vespasian where he combined flattery and chutzpah and won from the emperor the right to start an academy in the coastal town of Jamnia.

Johanan and his disciples were soon joined by other scholars and thus the Jamnia council began. Over the course of the following years and under Johanan's successors as head of the academy--Gamaliel II and Eleazer ben Azariah--they reorganized Judaism. The liturgy was standardized, various legal rulings were emended, a new Greek translation of the Old Testament was made by a Jewish proselyte named Aquila, and the canon of the Old Testament was debated. The period at Jamnia is formative for the direction Judaism would take after the Great War.

There was also further violence from A.D. 115 to 117, from the end of Emperor Trajan's reign to the beginning of Hadrian's. Jews lashed out in violence in Egypt, Cyrene, Cyprus, Mesopotamia and probably to some extent also in Palestine. The causes of the violence are unknown but it left great slaughter and destruction. Rome of course dealt extremely harshly with the insurrectionists and had all of them subdued within a few months after Hadrian began to reign as emperor.

The Bar Kosiba War

Bibliography: G. Alon, *History of the Jews in Palestine in the Period of the Mishnah and the Talmud*; Y. Harkabi, *The Bar Kokhba Syndrome*; H. Mantel, "The Causes of the Bar Kokba Revolt" *Jewish Quarterly Review* 58 (1967-68) 224-42; P. Schaefer, *Der Bar Kokhba Aufstand*; SVM; Y. Yadin, *Bar Kochba*.

It is one of the misfortunes of history that the second great Jewish rebellion, which lasted from AD 132 to 135, had no story teller like Josephus to record the events. Consequently we are left with only bits and pieces from several sources and these sources often contradict one another. Another consequence of this paucity of information is the relative lack of attention this war has received as if it were only a minor conflict. But as Schuerer has concluded (SVM), this war was at least as violent and destructive as that of AD 66. In terms of human lives, it may have been more costly.

Most historians cite two causes for the war: Emperor Hadrian's prohibition of circumcision and his plans to rebuild--perhaps already begun when the war broke out--Jerusalem as a Gentile city called Aelia Capitolina (named after himself, Aelius Hadrian). Hadrian believed circumcision was barbaric and should not be practiced within the empire. Jews were not the only practitioners of circumcision, of course. Some parts of Egypt and Arabia practiced it as well. But to the Jews this seemed like an attempt to destroy their religion, not unlike the attempt of Antiochus IV.

Further, the plan to build a pagan city and to erect a temple to Jupiter on the same location as the destroyed temple of Yahweh was an obvious sacrilege which few Jews could tolerate. Hadrian intended to do what Antiochus IV had failed to do. The result was predictable.

Y. Harkabi suggests that the rebels prepared for years before they began the revolt. How long these preparations took is not clear. It is also not clear whether or not the preparations began before Hadrian's decree about circumcision. If so, then a certain segment within Palestinian Judaism acted out of additional motives--desire for freedom? Messianism? socio-economic reasons?--to plan for war.

The leader of the revolt was Simon bar Kosiba. His name "son of Kosiba" was changed by his followers to bar Kochba, "son of the Star" (Num 24:17) a Messianic title. He was hailed as the Messiah by many Jewish leaders, among them, Rabbi Akiba, one of the great scholars of the Torah. The newly discovered documents from Bar Kosiba's time-- including some of his own correspondence--indicate that the Jews saw his leadership as beginning a new era. These documents date themselves, "year one of the freedom of Israel", that is the first year of the new era. He had coins minted--indicating political independence--and on one side of the coins was the picture of palm branches, a Messianic symbol. Other coins have a picture of a star standing over the temple. Christian sources (Justin Martyr) indicate that Jewish Christians were persecuted by Bar Kosiba because they would not accept him as Messiah.

Bar Kosiba was followed not only by the great rabbis of his day but also by Eleazar the Priest who it seems was his second in command. The new government, it has been suggested, intended to rebuild the temple with Eleazar as High Priest. This suggestion is undoubtedly true since no Jewish freedom movement could have forgotten about the temple.

Violence broke out in AD 132 but never developed into an all-out battle. Bar Kosiba's strategy was to wage guerilla war, hiding in caves and striking by ambush. At first Bar Kosiba must have been successful. He probably controlled much of Judea and may even have recaptured the ruins of Jerusalem.

The Romans under general Julius Severus were content to fight a war of attrition. Gradually their superior numbers and better supplies and arms wore down the Jews.

The major fighting seems to have taken place in Judea. Galilee either participated not at all or in a minor way. The Romans destroyed almost one thousand villages in Judea and killed close to 600,000 people--perhaps one half of the Jewish population of Palestine. Judea was practically depopulated of Jews.

Most historians conclude that the Romans also received heavy casualties in the war, though the numbers are not given by ancient sources. The war was a blood bath on both sides.

The last stronghold to fall to the Romans was Bethar, a few miles southwest from Jerusalem. Here in AD 135 Bar Kosiba was killed along with thousands of others. Many of the great rabbis, including Akiba, had already been martyred. It was a sad end and bitter disappointment for the Jews.

Hadrian did build his city, Aelia Capitolina, and his pagan temple to Jupiter. He forbade Jews to enter the city on penalty of death and maintained the prohibition against circumcision. Emperor Antoninus Pius in AD 138 rescinded the ban on circumcision but not until the fourth century under Constantine were Jews once more allowed to enter the holy city.

Excursus: Josephus as an Historical Source

Bibliography: P. Bilde, *Flavius Josephus Between Jerusalem and Rome*; S.J.D. Cohen, *Josephus in Galilee and Rome*; G. Cornfeld, *Josephus: the Jewish War*; L.H. Feldman and G. Hata, eds., *Josephus, the Bible, and History*; T. Rajak, *Josephus*; H. St. John Thackery, *Josephus, the Man and the Historian*.

Josephus ben Mattathias (AD 37-100?) Was born of a priestly family. His mother was of Hasmonean descent. At a young age (16) he studied the main Jewish sects and then became for three years a disciple of a desert hermit named Bannus. He claims that later he joined the Pharisees but some recent scholars doubt it.

He was swept up into the war in AD 66 and given the command of Galilee. After losing Jotapata, he surrendered and was accepted bv Vespasian as a mediator and interpreter during the remainder of the war.

He wrote an account of the war in Aramaic shortly after it ended and it was subsequently translated into Greek. Twenty years later he wrote his most extensive work, the *Antiquities*, which tells the story of Jewish history from the patriarchs to the start of the war. To this latter work he attached his own biography. Last of all, he wrote the *Against Apion*, a defense of Judaism against the calumnies of a pagan named Apion.

Josephus has been maligned as a historian for the past two hundred years. Scholars have alleged that he often flatters Vespasian and his son, Titus, he defends Judaism and mostly he justifies himself. But while it is true that Josephus does all of these things, that does not necessarily destroy his basic credibility as a historian. Archaeological and other literary evidence have helped to confirm his history and modern scholars are concluding that Josephus' biases are not as strong as some have claimed in the past. Thus Josephus' works are a major historical source for this period.

Chapter 2

Jewish Institutions

The Temple

Bibliography: M. Ben-Dov, *In the Shadow of the Temple*; A. Buechler, *Die Priester und der Cultus im letzten Jahrzehnt des Jerusalemischen Temples*; idem., *Das Synedrium in Jerusalem und das grosse Beth-din in der Quaderkammer des Jerusalemischen Temples*; A. Edersheim, *The Temple*; D. Gowan, *Bridge Between the Testaments*; J. Jeremias, *Jerusalem in the Time of Jesus*; J. Juster, *Les Juifs dans L'Empire Romain*; H.G. Kippenburg and G.A. Wewers, *Textbuch zur neutestamentliche Zeitgeschichte*; P. Levertoff, "Sanhedrin" in *ISBE* (o.s.); E. Lohse, *Umwelt des Neuen Testaments*; J.S. McLaren, *Power and Politics in Palestine*; H. Mantel, *Studies in the History of the Sanhedrin*; S. Safrai, "The Temple and the Divine Service" *WHJP*, Vol. 7; E.P. Sanders, *Judaism: Practice and Belief 63 BCE-66 CE*; E.M. Smallwood, "Highpriests and Politics in Roman Palestine" *Journal of Theological Studies* 13 (1962) 114-34; M. Stern, "Aspects of Jewish Society: The Priesthood and Other Classes" in S. Safrai and M. Stern, eds. *The Jewish People in the First Century* I.2; W.F. Stinespring, "Temple of Jerusalem" *IDB*.

It is difficult for us now to appreciate the importance of the temple in the life of Judaism in the first century AD. Certainly synagogues had appeared in most Jewish villages and cities, but these never replaced the role of the temple. The temple and the land gave Judaism its center and focus. The Torah was important but not yet as central as the other two elements.

Judaism was still a religion of sacrifice and offering, holy place and priest. Each day bloody offerings of animals were made in the temple. People made regular pilgrimages from various parts of Palestine and even outside of Palestine to worship in its sacred precincts. Nearly every Jew paid the yearly temple tax as well as tithes to priests and Levites. The temple was the glue that held all Jews together.

The structure in the first century AD was magnificent. Herod the Great had disassembled the beggardly temple of Zerubabbel to build one more in line with his taste for extravagance. The work, begun around 20 BC, was essentially completed in a few years (eight years to gather materials and three years to assemble them), but certain of the embellishments and trimming were only completed a short while before the temple was destroyed in AD 70.

By all accounts, Herod's temple was something to behold. It consisted of, first, a sacred precinct--also called the court of the Gentiles--a platform which Herod had built up around the upper part of the mountain on which the temple stood. The platform, much of which is still there (see Ben-Dov), measures 910 feet at its southern wall and 1,575 feet along its western wall (the eastern wall is somewhat shorter). The sacred precinct was then a trapezoid. The retaining walls of this platform in antiquity rose to a height of 98 feet or about equal to a ten story building but today only a few feet of the original Herodian stones remain. The retaining walls were built of massive stones that were quarried in the vicinity of Jerusalem. Most of them are two to five tons in weight but some weigh ten tons or more. Some colossal blocks have been discovered at the foundations of the walls weighing 50 tons or so a piece. One stone is 40 feet long, ten feet high, 13 feet thick and weighs 400 tons according to Ben-Dov. In this area Jews and Gentiles alike could gather for prayer, study, or exchanging money and buying sacrificial animals (see Plan 2.1).

The temple precinct was entered by pilgrims through the Hulda Gates on the south. A triple gate on the eastern side was for entering and a double gate on the western side was for exiting. A monumental staircase rose to these gates from the streets below. Archaeologists have discovered both the staircase and the gates. Inside the gates were lavish ornaments and decorations in stone with geometric and floral motifs.

The court of women marked the dividing point between Jews and Gentiles since no Gentile could cross beyond that point. This area (200 x 200 feet) was the location for public worship for all Israelites. Here the High Priest read the Torah on the Day of Atonement. Women could not proceed beyond this area.

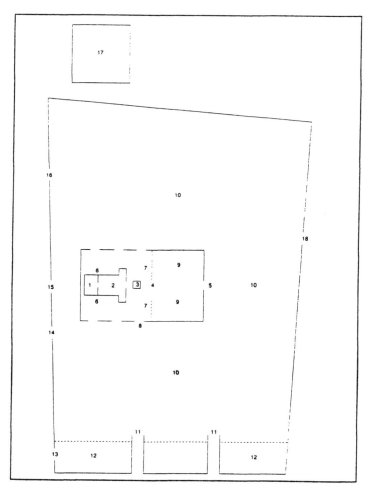

1 Holy of Holies	7. Court of Israel	13. Robinson's Arch
2. Holy Place	8. Hall of Hewn Stone	14. Wilson's Arch
3. The Altar	9. Court of Women	15. Warren's Gate
4. Nicanor's Gate	10. Court of Gentiles	16. West Gate
5. Gate Beautiful	11. Huldah Gates (tunnels)	17. Tower of Antonia
6. Court of the Priests	12. Solomon's Portico	18. Golden Gate

Plan 2.1
The Temple
(After Safrai and Steinspring)

The inner court, consisting of the court of Israel for all male Israelites, and the Priests' court was the locus of most of the temple ritual. The Levites stood to sing in the priests's court. Here the altar of sacrifices stood and the laver for purification of the priests and their sacrifices. Within this area also stood the sanctuary itself, which measured 150 feet long, 105 feet wide and 150 feet high. The sanctuary was divided into two parts, the Holy Place and the Holy of Holies with a curtain between the two chambers. In the Holy Place stood the Golden Altar (for incense), the Golden Table of Shewbread, and the Golden Candelabrum. Only the priests could enter the Holy Place. In the Holy of Holies stood, in place of the lost Ark of the Covenant, a stone. Only tne High Priest entered this chamber and then only on the Day of Atonement to sprinkle blood (originally on the Ark but now on the stone). Nothing remains today of the temple itself except a large rock inside the present mosque called the Dome of the Rock which allegedly stood in the Holy of Holies.

The temple officials consisted in the main of priests and Levites. The non-aristocratic priests--i.e. those not of a High Priestly family--were divided into twenty four divisions and served in the temple for one week at a time--thus about twice a year. The rest of the time they might engage in a craft or farming. Many lived outside Jerusalem in Judea and Galilee.

During their week of duty in Jerusalem, the priests offered the sacrifices and burned the incense in the temple. They kept themselves in a state of ritual purity by washing in the *mikvaoth*--ritual baths--in the temple and wore white garments as symbolic of their purity. They determined their various duties of the day by casting lots in the morning (m. Tamid 3:1).

The Levites were mainly involved as gate-keepers and singers/instrument players. As gate-keepers they insured that no one unclean could enter the temple area. As singers they sang the special Psalms during sacrifices and feast days and played lyres, harps, and cymbals. They too were divided into twenty four divisions and served one week at a time in the temple.

Over the entire procedure of the temple stood the High Priest. From the time of Herod the Great until the destruction of the Temple, the High Priesthood was controlled by four powerful, extremely wealthy, aristocratic families (see Table): the houses of Boethus, Hanan, Phiabi, and Kimchi.

1. **Ananel 37-36 B.C. and 34 B.C.**
2. **Aristobulus III (the last Maccabean) 35 B.C.**

3. @Jesus ben Phiabi 35-22 B.C.
4. *Simon ben Boethus 22-5 B.C.
5. #(?) Mattaiah ben Theophilus 5-4 B.C.
6. Joseph ben Elan 5 B.C.
7. *Joezer ben Boethus 4 B.C.
8. *Eleazar ben Boethus 4-? B.C.
9. #Jesus ben See ?-A.D. 6
10. #Annas A.D. 6-15
11. @Ishmael ben Phiabi I A.D. 15-16
12. #Eleazar ben Annas A.D. 16-17
13. +Simon ben Kimchi A.D. 17-18
14. #Joseph Caiaphas A.D. 18-37
15. #Jonathan ben Annas A.D. 37
16. #Theophilus ben Annas A.d. 37-41
17. *Simon A.D. 41-?
18. #Matthias ben Annas ?
19. # (?) Elionaius ben Kathros A.D. 44
20. +Joseph ben Kimchi ?
21. Ananias ben Nebedaius A.D. 47-55
22. @Ishmael ben Phiabi II A.D. 55-61
23. +(?) Joseph Kabi A.D. 61-62
24. #Ananus ben Ananus A.D. 62
25. Jesus ben Damnaius A.D. 62-65
26. Joshua ben Gamaliel A.D. 63-65
27. #(?) Matthias ben Theophilus A.D. 65-67
28. Pinhas of Habta A.D. 67-70

Table 2.1

The High Priests from 37 BC to AD 70

(After Jeremias and Stern)
House of Boethus=*; House of Hanan=#; House of Phiabi=@; House of
Kimchi=+

The High Priest during the ministry of Jesus, Joseph ben Caiaphas along with his father-in-law, Annas, was from the house of Hannan.

The High Priest permanently resided and worked in Jerusalem but did not usually conduct the sacrifices except on Sabbaths and feast days. His prestige as religious head of the nation and his wealth as recipient of tithes and probably owner of large tracts of lands made him the second most powerful man in Palestine, after the political ruler. In addition to presiding over the temple cultus, the High Priest was president of the Sanhedrin.

Second to the High Priest in authority was the captain of the temple (called *Sagan* in Hebrew). He is mentioned not only in the Mishnah but in the New Testament (Acts 4:1, 5:24-26). He was also a member of the ruling High Priestly family and evidently was responsible for the daily routine of the temple.

The temple opened and closed each day with the offering of a lamb and the recitation of the *shema* (i.e. Deut 6:4). In addition were the feast day ceremonies: the water procession at Tabernacles, the lamb slaying at Passover, the release of the Red Heifer and the blood sprinkling on the Day of Atonement, and so forth. The ritual for each of these feasts is described in the Mishnah and is presumably in the main correct.

But the people would bring sacrifices in addition to these. They might bring sin offerings or guilt offerings to expiate some offense or they could give free will offerings out of thanksgiving. Some of these offerings were holocausts and thus the entire animal--except for certain parts going to the priests--was burned. Most offerings were only partially burned on the altar with the rest eaten by the pilgrim and his party in a solemn meal.

Such daily ritual required a good supply of sacrificial animals as well as a supply of salt (Lev 1:13) since most sacrifices had to be accompanied with it. Obviously the temple needed a great quantity of wood for the altar and a quantity of water as well for washing down the area and for the purification of the participants, for blood was splattered everywhere.

Another important function connected with the temple and presided over by the High Priest was the Sanhedrin. The Sanhedrin was a body of 71 distinguished justices which judged civil and criminal cases[1]. On the council were members of the High Priest's family, scribes--i.e. experts in the Old Testament Law--and so-called elders or aristocratic laymen, with the High Priest as chief justice. Men both of the Sadducean and Pharisaic parties served on the Sanhedrin but the Pharisaic party was probably in the minority. Presumably the High Priest appointed the members of the court.

The origin of this court is shrouded in silence, but it is likely that it began under the Ptolemies and Seleucids. We read about a "council" (Gk.: *gerousia*) which decided important matters at that time (1Macc 12:6; 2 Macc 1:10, 4:44) although it is not called a Sanhedrin.

The Sanhedrin met in the Hall of Hewn Stone adjacent to the temple (see Plan) usually during the time of daily sacrifice but not on Sabbaths or feast days. The members sat in a semicircle to enable them to see one another and the accused stood in the middle. The court was evidently prohibited by the Romans from deciding capital cases, except in the case of a Gentile's desecrating the temple. Jesus was probably tried there at some point although it is possible the Sanhedrin met in the mansion of Caiaphas (see Aland 332).

Finally, we must mention the temple treasury and bank. The temple had its own treasury funded by the yearly temple tax of one half shekel on all male Israelites. This fund paid for the upkeep of the temple buildings, purchased the daily offering as well as, no doubt, financing the Sanhedrin- -although presumably most members of this body were wealthy. From time to time the treasury also paid for repairs and buildings throughout the city of Jerusalem. The temple tax is referred to in Matthew's Gospel (17:24-27).

In addition the temple may have served as a bank or currency exchange. Money could be exchanged from one currency--Tyrian, Attic, Roman, etc.--to another for a fee. This exchange was both for the temple, since one could only pay the temple tax in Tyrian coinage, and for business in general. It was these money changers that Jesus drove out of the temple (see Aland 273)

The main reason anyone came to the temple in Jerusalem of course, was to celebrate the feasts. The most important feast, Passover, was celebrated for seven days in the Jewish month of Nisan (see Table of Months). Passover included eating the passover lamb, unleavened bread, and bitter herbs in Jerusalem to commemorate the exodus from Egypt. The lamb would first have to be slaughtered in the temple precincts, then taken to a place of residence to be roasted (see Ex 12:1-13:16). The Passover is referred to often in the New Testament (e.g. Jn 2:13, 6:4, 12:1; Acts 12:3).

The feast of Weeks or Pentecost was a one day feast, kept in the month of Sivan. It marked the end of the grain harvest (Lev 23:15-21). It was during Pentecost that the church began (Acts 2:1).

The feast of Tabernacles took place in the month of Tishri and lasted seven days. It commemorated Israel's wandering in the wilderness for forty years when they lived in tents or tabernacles (Lev 23:33-43, Num 29:12-32). This feast is mentioned in John 7:2.

1. **Nisan (March-April)**
2. **Iyyar (April-May)**

3. **Sivan (May-June)**
4. **Tammuz (June-July)**
5. **Ab (July-August)**
6. **Elul (August-September)**
7. **Tishri (September-October)**
8. **Marcheshvan (October-November)**
9. **Chislev (November-December)**
10. **Tebeth (December-January)**
11. **Shebat (January-February)**
12. **Adar (February-March)**

Table 2.2

Jewish Months

In addition to the three main feasts found in the Old Testament Law, Judaism had added two more by the New Testament period. The feast of Dedication or Hanukkah celebrated the dedication of the temple after it was liberated by Judas Maccabeus (see 1 Maccabees 4:52-59). This feast is referred to in John 10:22 and was celebrated in the month Chislev.

The second new feast, Purim, was celebrated in the month Adar. It recalled the deliverance of the Jews from Haman by Esther and Mordecai (Esther 9:24-28). This feast is not alluded to in the New Testament unless John 5:1, which mentions an unidentified feast, is referring to it.

In addition to the feasts there was one fast, Yom Kippur or the Day of Atonement, held in the month Tishri. This was a day of repentance and expiation (see Lev 23:26-32; Num 29:7-11). The Day of Atonement is mentioned in Acts 27:9 and Hebrews 9:7.

All of these special days required presence in the temple in order to celebrate them. Thus most Jews living at some distance from Jerusalem celebrated them irregularly. Yet at feast time the city would swell with thousands of pilgrims.

The Synagogue

Bibliography: I. Elbogen, *Der juedische Gottesdienst in seiner geschichtlichen Entwicklung*; D.A. Fiensy, *Prayers Alleged to be Jewish*; J. Heineman, *Prayer in the Talmud* ; K. Hruby, *Die Synagogue*; L.I. Levine, *Ancient Synagogues*

Revealed; J. Mann, *The Bible as Read and Preached in the Old Synagogue*; S. Safrai,"The Synagogue" in *The Jewish People in the First Century*; S. Sandmel, *Judaism and Christian Beginnlngs;* H. Shanks, *Judaism in Stone.*

The second great Jewish institution was the synagogue. Although it seems reasonable that the synagogue began during the exile as many of the older scholars have maintained, this assumption is by no means proven. All that we can say with certainty is that regardless of when synagogues began appearing--during the exile or after the exile--they were very wide spread by the first century AD, existing throughout Palestine and the Diaspora.

The name synagogue comes from the Greek word, *sunagoge,* "assembly", which was normally used to designate the institution. But the Greek term *proseuche,* " (house of) prayer", was also used. The Hebrew term was *bet ha-knesset,* "assembly house."

While the temple was run by priests, the synagogue was operated by the general populace.[2] They selected a head of the synagogue (m. Sotah 7:7; Lk 13:14) who administered its services. He would have been a fairly well educated man who could judge the abilities of the Torah readers and preachers who might be at hand for Sabbath services. The head of the synagogue was usually a man of some financial means and thus was not paid for this service but enjoyed the honor of it.

The synagogue had two main functions: prayer and study. It was first and foremost a house of prayer. They would recite the *shema* (Deut 6:4) as in the temple but in addition there gradually developed a rather fixed set of prayers called the Eighteen Benedictions. Though the final form of these prayers was not set until a century later, the prototypes of these Eighteen Benedictions were already present.

One of the prayers that probably was recited in the first century synagogue is as follows: "Blessed are you, O Lord our God, and God of our fathers, God of Abraham, Isaac and Jacob. . . Blessed are you, O Lord, Shield of Abraham."

Another prayer emphasizes belief in the resurrection: "Blessed are you, O Lord, who makes the dead alive."

Another prayer reflects language from Isaiah 6 to extol the greatness of God: "Holy, holy, holy, Lord of Hosts, all the earth is full of your glory. . . There is no God beside you. Blessed are you, O Lord, the holy God."

The prayers were recited while standing with someone appointed to lead the congregation, perhaps the head of the synagogue or an assistant.

The second main function of the synagogue was study both for children and adults. Younger children were taught to read Hebrew and older children the content and exposition of the Old Testament. The teacher in this would have been a scribe employed by the village or perhaps paid by tuition fees. Most scholars agree that Jewish children generally were taught to read, but one must not assume that there were not many exceptions. Children from extremely poor families probably had to work.

Girls were most likely not invited to the synagogue school. Although there are references to female Torah scholars, they were apparently few in number. One famous rabbi is supposed to have declared, "There is no wisdom for a woman except at the spindle" (see Safrai).

Adults continued their study of Torah during Sabbath worship. In addition to the prayers said on Sabbath, someone would read a selection of scripture from the Torah scroll which was kept in a chest and unrolled with great ceremony. At a later time, the lectionaries were standardized so that the entire Torah/Pentateuch would be read every three years. It is not certain, however, if that sort of standardization existed in Palestine in the first century. In addition to reading the Torah passage someone would read from the prophets. After the Torah was read from the Hebrew text, someone would translate it--usually in a paraphrase rather than literally-- in the local vernacular. In Palestine therefore one translated the text into Aramaic. These Aramaic paraphrases also became standardized and were later written down as the Targums. In most parts of the Diaspora on the other hand a Greek version was used, at first the Septuagint, later Aquila's version. After the translation, someone--often a scribe, but anyone who wished and whom the head of the synagogue approved--made comments about the text or preached a sermon on it. Thus Jesus was invited at the synagogue in Nazareth to preach on the text from Isaiah (Lk 4:16-30).

It is not clear whether most synagogues in the first century had a special building for their meetings or if other public buildings were used. The ruins of most of the oldest synagogues found in Palestine indicate they were built in the latter part of the second century AD. Synagogue ruins from the first century, however, have been found at Masada, Herodium-- both of which were in Herodian fortresses and not village synagogues-- and at Gamala. In addition, some archaeologists believe the synagogue building in Capernaum, which is from the second century, rests on foundations from Jesus' time. Thus surely some synagogue buildings did exist in the first century but many villages probably met on the Sabbath in private houses or perhaps in other public buildings.

fellowship:

Notes

1. The Rabbinic sources describe a council, *beth-din*, which was led by Pharisees and decided religious matters as well. Whether there were two deliberative bodies, a criminal court and a religious court--which is doubtful--or only a criminal court, we cannot certainly decide. One must always be cautious, however, in using the Talmud uncritically as a historical source. McLaren has recently challenged the existence of the Sanhedrin as a continuous entity. He maintains that this deliberative body was only an *ad hoc* court. That is, it was only convened as a special need arose and the members were chosen anew each time.

2. The frequent assertion that Pharisess presided over the synagogue is untenable. It would have taken extraordinary organization and intercommunication for one religious party to control the thousands of synagogues.

Chapter 3

Jewish Sects

The Essenes

Bibliography: R.T. Beckwith, "The Pre-History and Relationships of the Pharisees, Sadducees, and Essenes: A Tentative Reconstruction" *Revue de Qumran* 11 (1986) 3-46; F.F. Bruce, *Second Thoughts on the Dead Sea Scrolls*; J.H. Charlesworth, "The Origin and Subsequent History of the Authors of the Dead Sea Scrolls: Four Transitional Phases among the Qumran Essenes" *Revue de Qumran* 10 (1979-81) 213-233; J.J. Collins, "Essenes" in *ABD*; F.M. Cross, *The Ancient Library of Qumran*; P.R. Davies, *Behind the Essenes*; A.D. Crown and L. Cansdale, "Qumran: Was it an Essene Settlement?" *BAR* 20/5 (1994) 24-35; N. Golb, *Who Wrote the Dead Sea Scrolls?* ; D. Gowan, *Bridge Between the Testaments*; G. Jeremias, *Der Lehrer der Gerechtigkeit*; K. Kohler, "Essenes" in *JE* (a pre-Qumran article); W.S. LaSor, *The Dead Sea Scrolls and the New Testament*; J. Murphy-O'Conner, "The Essenes and their History" *Revue Biblique* 81 (1974) 215-144; H. Ringgren, *The Faith of Qumran*; H. Shanks, "The Qumran Settlement--Monastery, Villa or Fortress?" *BAR* 19/3 (1993) 62-65; L.H. Schiffman, "The Significance of the Scrolls" *Bible Review* (October, 1990); idem., "New Light on Insights from the Dead Sea Scrolls" *Bible Review* (June 1992); idem., *From Text to Tradition*; J.E.H. Thompson, "Essenes" in *ISBE* o.s.(a pre-Qumran article); J.C. Vanderkam, *The Dead Sea Scrolls Today*; R. De Vaux, *Archaeology and the dead Sea Scrolls*; G. Vermes and M.D. Goodman, *The Essenes*; G. Vermes, *The Dead Sea Scrolls*; idem., *The Dead Sea Scrolls in*

English; B.Z. Wacholder, *The Dawn of Qumran.*

There has never been unanimity about the Essenes.[1] In the older works (before 1947) scholars wrestled with the discrepancies found among the classical sources (Josephus, Pliny, Philo and Hippolytus) and sometimes came to very different conclusions about the origin and nature of this Jewish sect. Then in 1947 the Dead Sea Scrolls were discovered at Qumran near the Dead Sea and things have only gotten more confused. To make matters worse (or better) new documents are now being published after long years of waiting. As these new documents are analyzed by the scholarly world, no doubt many innovative hypotheses will be posited.

At this point we can only present what the consensus has been among the "moderate" scholars and await the further developments. One can certainly find disagreements with virtually everything we will present below. But for the most part the leaders in Qumran research would accept this description. The writings of Vermes with some modifications from Jeremias, Davies and VanderKam can represent what has been agreed upon rather broadly and perhaps will even remain the commonly accepted view after the newer documents are more carefully considered.

First, the community at Qumran described in the Dead Sea Scrolls and whose material remains have been left behind in the settlement at Qumran were Essenes. Too much evidence exists--the similarity in theology and practice between the scrolls and what the classical sources say--to conclude otherwise. True, there have been suggestions that the settlement at Qumran was nothing more than the villa of a wealthy person, a military outpost or a commercial warehouse (see the articles by Shanks and by Crown and Cansdale). But few have so far been convinced by the arguments for these suggestions. It is also true that there are differences between what the archaeologists find in the material remains of the settlement and what the classical sources tell us about the Essenes. But these differences do not outweigh the similarities. Thus one can (cautiously) use certain of the scrolls in combination with the classical sources to construct the history and characteristics of the Essenes.

Second, the origin and history of the Essenes were as follows: Sometime after the exile, probably in the early second century BC, the sect began. The early Essenes followed an interpreter of the Torah who laid down new *halacoth* (legal precepts) about marriage, the calendar and other rules. At some point this charismatic teacher/interpreter--called the Teacher of Righteousness--arose in the community. He was of High

Priestly, Zadokite, lineage and thus opposed someone known in the scrolls as the "Wicked Priest."[2] Sometime later (about 150 BC) the Essenes led by the Teacher of Righteousness went into the desert to Qumran and pronounced the temple cultus in Jerusalem invalid (because its High Priest was of improper lineage). But not only did the Essenes live at Qumran but in many villages and apparently one group lived near the southwest gate of Jerusalem (near the site of the Upper Room mentioned in the Gospels and Acts). Philo reported that there were 4000 Essenes in Palestine in his day.

Third, the practices of the Essenes were as follows:

1. A one year, followed by a two year probationary period were required for one to become a member of the sect.

2. Only adult males were admitted to the sect though children were taken in to educate.

3. The members were celebate except for one sub-group within the Essenes that practiced marriage.

4. The members surrendered all of their possessions to the community and lived in personal poverty.

5. They forbade the practice of slavery.

6. They forbade the use of oaths (as did Jesus).

7. They bathed in cold water before each meal.

8. They wore white robes like the priests in the temple.

9. The eating of a meal together as a community was considered highly important. The priests of the community prepared the meal according to their purity rules, they took their ritual bath and then they assembled for the meal. No uninitiated person could participate.

10. They practiced healing and cultivated the knowledge of medicinal herbs.

11. Essenes also believed they had prophetic gifts and Josephus offers several examples of their prophecies that came true.

Essene beliefs are best discovered in the Dead Sea Scrolls. Their theology begins (Ringgren) with belief in the absolute providence and sovereignty of God. Everything that happens is predestined or "appointed" by God. This predestination includes nature, history and individual actions and thoughts. God has created two spirits or powers: good and evil. Man's behavior depends on belonging to the domain of one of these spirits. Those belonging to the domain of the good are called, "sons of light" and those belonging to the bad, "sons of darkness."

God's plan, his predestination for the universe, is a secret or mystery (Aramaic: *raz*). He has appointed a time for evil to predominate and then it will be destroyed. These mysteries are partly in the Old Testament but one must interpret it properly to see the mysteries. Thus God has given insight to the Teacher of Righteousness and has caused him to know the secrets. God has, then, made his esoteric teaching known to his elect through the Teacher of Righteousness.

Jesus and the Essenes

Bibliography: M. B.ack, *The Scrolls and Christian Origins*; J.H. Charlesworth, ed., *John and Qumran*; idem., *Jesus and the Dead Sea Scrolls*; R. Eisenman, *Maccabees, Zadokites, Christians and Qumran*; D. Flusser, *Judaism and the Origins of Christianity*; W.S. LaSor, *The Dead Sea Scrolls and the New Testament*; K. Stendahl, *The Scrolls and the New Testament*; B. Thiering, *Jesus and the Riddle of the Dead Sea Scrolls*; J.C. Vanderkam, *The Dead Sea Scrolls Today*.

The Essenes are never mentioned in the New Testament but that has not prevented speculation about their influence. Various scholars allege that John the Baptist and Jesus as well were Essenes, were reared by Essenes or were influenced by Essenes. Still others see Jesus as refuting specific Essene ideas (see especially the Sermon on the Mount) or they surmise that the Gospel of John opposed Essenism. This is not to mention the unusual and bizarre theories that the Dead Sea Scrolls have inspired (see the survey of some of these works by LaSor and the recent monographs of Eisenman and Thiering).

What we can say with confidence about the Essenes and the New Testament is as follows: Certainly Jesus and John the Baptist knew Essenes. Essenes were too numerous for them not to have known them. But if John the Baptist and Jesus ever had been Essenes (see especially Chapter 7) they were no longer so by the time we encounter them in the Gospels. John and Jesus invited sinners freely to repentance and Jesus even ate with them. Both of these actions are very unlike Essenes.

The Pharisees

Bibliography: L. Baeck, *Pharisees*; S. Cohen, *From Maccabees to Mishnah*; W.D. Davies, *Introduction to the Pharisees*; L. Finkelstein, *The Pharisees*; D. Gowan,

Bridge Between the Testaments; R.T. Herford, *The Pharisees*; G.F. Moore, *Judaism*; J. Neusner, *From Politics to Piety*; idem., *Rabbinic Traditions About the Pharisees Before 70*; E. Rivkin, *A Hidden Revolution*; A.J. Saldarini, *Pharisees, Scribes, and Sadducees*; E.P. Sanders, *Judaism, Practice and Belief 63 BCE-66 CE*; SVM; L.H. Schiffman, *From Text to Tradition*; G. Stemberger, *Pharisaeer, Sadduzaeer, Essener.*

The name Pharisee means "separated." That much is agreed upon. But scholars debate from what this group separated itself. Did the Pharisees separate themselves from the common folk, from the Hasmoneans, from the Sadducees or from the Hasidim? Further, were the Pharisees a political party or a religious sect? The answers to these questions depend on how one constructs the history of this sect.

The historical reconstruction of Neusner is still probably the best and most of the other recent attempts to understand the Pharisees borrow from or interact with him. Thus we will offer his view of the history of the sect.

We first meet with the Pharisees in Josephus at the time of the High Priesthood of John Hyrcanus (ruled 134-104 BC) when he dismissed them from his government because of a remark made at a banquet (*Antiquities* 13.288-98). Instead of Pharisees as the dominant political party, Hyrcanus now installed the Sadducees. This hostility was reversed under Queen Alexandra (ruled 77-68 BC) who reinstated the Pharisees in government. This series of events leads us to conclude that the Pharisees were originally a "political action group" (Saldarini's term) which competed with other like groups, especially the Sadducees, for power within the government. Naturally, the Pharisees were also concerned with religious matters--In a government in which the High Priest was also the king how could they not have been?--but political power was the main item on their agenda. Moreover, they seem to have been, usually, the dominant party.

Under Herod the Great this emphasis changed. This was the era of one of the greatest Pharisees named Hillel. Neusner concludes that Hillel changed the direction of the group from political party to pietiest sect. Herod would hardly countenance medling in his political affairs by a troublesome group of religionists bent on having its way. Thus the group retired from politics and devoted itself entirely to matters of *halacah*. The Pharisees became a "table-fellowship sect." They moved from "politics to piety," where they remained until the Jewish war of AD 66. After the war, the Pharisees emerged again as the politically dominant party within

Judaism. Thus during the Herodian period (37 BC-AD 70) the time of
Jesus and the early church, the Pharisees were a quietist sect concerned
with table fellowship, purity laws and tithing. In Josephus' day the sect
numbered 6000 members.

During the reign of Herod the Great, two great Pharisees, Hillel and
Shammai, became the founders of rival schools. The two schools debated
the issues dearest to Pharisees (laws of purity, Sabbath, festivals and table
fellowship) almost always disagreeing with one another. Yet in spite of
their many disagreements, they apparently did not split into two separate
sects but remained merely two schools of interpretation within
Pharisaism.

Many of the stories told about the founders of the schools are probably
legendary but they may indicate at least something about the two schools.
Hillel was said to be less strict and more progressive; Shammai was
known as strict and conservative. A Gentile allegedly once told Shammai
that he would convert to Judaism if Shammai could explain the Torah to
him while he (the Gentile) stood on one foot. The irascible Shammai
drove him away with a carpenter's stick. When the same Gentile
approached Hillel, the great Pharisee responded, "Do not do to others
what is hateful to you. This is the Torah and all the rest of commentary"
(cf. the words of Jesus in the Sermon of the Mount, Mt 7:12).

The many references in the Mishnah to the two schools demonstrate
that Pharisaism was not always the same. It changed not only as it moved
through history but as one moved from one school to the next. Thus it is
erroneous to characterize all Pharisees as agreeing on all matters of the
Torah. Yet we can indicate a few general similarities among this group:

1. Primary among their characteristics was the belief in and devotion
to the oral Torah. Both Josephus (*Antiquities* 13.297, 408) and the New
Testament (Mk 7:3) refer to the "traditions" (Greek: *paradoseis*) that the
Pharisees followed and which were handed down from their forefathers.
The Mishnah (m.Hagigah 2:2; m. Aboth 1:1-18) and the Tosephta (t.
Hagigah 2:8) give lists of tradents who passed on the oral Torah to the
next generation. This oral Torah, which the rabbis claimed originated
with Moses on Mt. Sinai, was actually an interpretation of the written
Torah (the Pentateuch) and a supplementation of it. The adherence to the
oral Torah was the main point of contention between Pharisees and
Sadducees. One could, with certain caveats, point to the Mishnah as the
repository of the oral Torah which was eventually written down around
AD 200. Much material in the Mishnah, however, originates later than
AD 70.

2. The Pharisees taught the general resurrection of the dead and the retribution of the wicked after death, doctrines the Sadducees rejected (*War* 2. 163; *Antiquities* 18. 16; Mk 12:18).

3. They believed in the existence of angels and spirits which the Sadducees denied (Acts 23:8).

4. Josephus writes something about divine sovereignty and freewill which is not totally comprehensible. It appears, however, that the Essenes believed in total predestination and absolute divine sovereignty, the Sadducees rejected these doctrines and that the Pharisees were somewhere in between. God is sovereign, but humans also have free will according to Pharisees (*War* 2.163).

5. The Pharisees concerned themselves much about dietary and purity laws and about tithing. They wanted to be in a state of ritual purity or cleanness like the priests in the temple and so were meticulous about what rendered the hands and garments unclean and the washing of hands (m. Yadaim 4:6; m. Hagigah 2:7; Mk 7:3). Likewise, they ate not only kosher food but only grain from which the proper tithes had been already given (m. Demmai 6:6; Mt 23:23).

6. The Pharisees were, according to Josephus, the most popular of the Jewish sects. They had the complete confidence of the masses (*Antiquities* 18.15-17).

7. Finally, we must say a word about the common assumption that all Pharisees were hypocrites, inwardly evil, while appearing outwardly to be pure. Jesus' denunciation of the Pharisees (Mt 23) should not be taken as applying to all Pharisees (nor by extension to all Jews). The Pharisees were in the main a pious sect seeking to live out the will of God as best they could. That Jesus strongly disagreed with some of them is clear but he also seems to have been friends with others of this sect (see Lk 7:36; 14:11).

We can now answer the questions we raised above. From whom did the Pharisees separate themselves? Undoubtedly they separated themselves from the Sadducees (as Rivkin maintains). A group as popular as this could not have separated itself from the masses (as the Essenes did). Were they a political party or a religious sect? Although politics and religion were closely intertwined in ancient Palestine, and even at times inseparable, one can say that the emphasis was on politics before the time of Herod the Great but on religious matters after that.

The Sadducees

Bibliography: S. Cohen, *From Maccabees to Mishnah*; D. Gowan, *Bridge Between the Testaments*; J. Le Moyne, *Les Sadduceens*; A.J. Saldarini, *Pharisees, Scribes, and Sadducees*; SVM; M. Simon, *Jewish Sects at the Time of Jesus*; G. Stemberger, *Pharisaeer, Sadduzaeer, Essener*; J. Wellhausen, *Die Pharisaeer und Sadducaeer*.

The origin of the Sadducees is even more mysterious than that of the Essenes and Pharisees. Virtually nothing is known about it. Further, although we have the Dead Sea Scrolls, which presumably represent some of the Essenes, and the Mishnah, which represents at least the descendants of the Pharisees, we have no literature from the Sadducees at all. None of the sources which refer to them are sympathetic or positive. Thus we are even more in the dark in describing this sect.

The name Sadducee undoubtedly derives from the name Zadok, the priest (1 Kings 2:35; Ezek 40:46). The Sadducees saw themselves as the true sons of Zadok, the true priests. They were closely affiliated, then, with the priesthood. But some priests were Pharisees and many belonged to no sect at all. Thus the group of priests was certainly not equal to the Sadducees. Since Josephus indicates that they were aristocrats, we should probably think of the Sadducean influence especially among the High Priestly families. They were a group of wealthy High Priests, relatives of the High Priests and friends of the High Priests. They also had many differences from the Pharisees in interpreting the written Torah and differences in theology.

The characteristics of the Sadducees were as follows:

1. They were aristocrats. Josephus wrote that they could persuade only the rich to their point of view (*Antiquities* 12.298). One is tempted to add that they only wanted to persuade the rich. Aristocrats are seldom concerned about increasing membership. Thus one should think of a rather small, but disproportionately powerful, politico-religious group.

2. They rejected the oral Torah of the Pharisees (*Antiquities* 13.297). Only the written regulations (i.e. the Pentateuch) were considered binding. It is probably not true, however, that the Sadducees rejected the prophetical books of the Old Testament, as the early church writers sometimes alleged. Josephus does not mention that and it would have been very unusual for any Jew to have done so (The Samaritans did so, however.).

3. In penal laws the Sadducees were usually severe and strict, keeping the letter of the law, and the Pharisees were lenient, even putting up legal roadblocks to harsh punishments (*Antiquities* 20. 199; m. Yadaim 4:7; but see by way of contrast m. Makkoth 1:6).

4. The Sadducees did not believe in the resurrection, the immortality of the soul or life after death (*War* 2.165; *Antiquities* 18.16; Mk 12:18, Acts 23:8). They thus denied penalty and reward after death. Here the Sadducees were adhering to the older theological strain of the Old Testament. Only in Isaiah 26:19 and Daniel 12:2 is there clear teaching concerning the resurrection (though other passages may hint at it).

5. They denied the existence of angels (Acts 23:8) again based on the older traditions of the Hebrew Bible.

6.   Finally, the Sadducees denied entirely the operation of predestination on the will of mankind. Men and women, they taught, are completely free to choose their own conduct (*War* 2. 164).

The Sadducees continued to wield enormous power over the life of the Jewish community until the destruction of the Temple in AD 70. After that, with the power base of the High Priesthood gone, the sect had no unifying symbol and no source of authority and thus ceased to function.

Zealots, Fourth Philosophy and Sicarii

Bibliography: S.G.F. Brandon, *Jesus and the Zealots*; D. Gowan, *Bridge Between the Testaments*; W.R. Farmer, *Maccabees, Zealots and Josephus*; M. Hengel, *The Zealots*; idem., *Was Jesus a Revolutionist?*: R.A. Horsley and J.S. Hanson, *Bandits, Prophets and Messiahs*; R.A. Horsley, "The Zealots" *Novum Testamentum* 28 (1986) 159-192; D.M. Rhoads, *Israel in Revolution: 6-74 C.E.*; M. Smith, "Zealots and Sicarii, Their Origins and Relation" *Harvard Theological Review* 64 (1971) 1-19.

The so-called Fourth Philosophy (Josephus' term) began with Judas of Galilee in AD 6. The Sicarii arose to prominence in the fifties and sixties of the first century and the Zealots are mentioned by Josephus in connection with their activities in AD 67-70. We will describe each of these movements below and then determine if they were related to each other in any way.

The Fourth Philosophy, by which Josephus meant the fourth Jewish sect (after the Essenes, Pharisees and Sadducees) began with Judas the

Jesus Said obey the leaders !!!

Galilean or Gaulanite. In AD 6 when Quirinius, proconsul of Syria, assessed Judea for taxation, Judas incited many Jews to rebel. He took a hard line in his devotion to Yahweh alone as Master and Lord. If Jews paid this tax, he maintained, it would be cowardice and apostasy from their commitment to God (see Chapter 19 below).

Judas is called a sophist (sage, teacher or scholar) by Josephus. Thus he was no poor man from the masses but a well educated teacher of the Torah. He was aided by a man named Zaddok, a Pharisee, and Josephus writes that this sect agrees with Pharisaism in other respects but adds to these teachings a passion for liberty and for serving God alone as master. The adherents of the Fourth Philosophy thought nothing of submitting to death themselves or seeing their relatives and friends die in the service of their cause.

Judas' armed uprising was apparently defeated and he was killed by Quirinius (Acts 5:37) but his Fourth Philosophy continued its influence. His sons, James and Simon, were executed later by the procurator, Alexander, for their seditious activities. Another relative (called a "son" by Josephus) of Judas, Menahem, was one of the leaders of the Jewish revolt in AD 66. Still another kinsman, Eleazar, led the sicarii that held Masada until AD 73 (74). Furthermore, Josephus says that Judas and his sect sowed the seeds of rebellion which led eventually to the war in AD 66-73 (74). Finally, the fact that Josephus calls Judas' movement a philosophy and sect indicates that it lasted beyond Judas' lifetime as an organized group.

The sicarii arose under the procurator, Felix (AD 52-60) and were especially troublesome by the time Festus began as procurator (AD 60-62). They were so named because of the dagger (called *sica* in Latin) which they concealed under their garments in order to carry out assassinations. They later participated as regular soldiers in the Jewish war and remained bitter enemies of Rome to the very end. The resistance fighters on Masada were mainly sicarii.

The Zealots were first mentioned by name in connection with the Jewish war. We meet them initially in Josephus when the High Priest, Ananus, a moderate (i.e. neither pro-Roman nor fanatically in favor of war) hopes to delay in prosecuting the war and thus possibly turn the fanatical Zealots to a wiser course. The Zealots are always represented as bent on slaughter and killing, unyielding in their lust for war with Rome and feared by any of the Jews that might wish to surrender to Rome.

Were these three groups in some way related? Were they actually the same group? It has been common in continental Europe and among

Israeli scholars to conclude that they all were more or less the same movement or sect. But recent American scholars have cautioned against that conclusion. Morton Smith, followed especially by R. Horsley, has argued that these groups must be kept separate. Smith and Horsley resist the earlier conclusions which saw a continuous Zealot movement from Judas the Galilean until the end of the war. Thus there were no Zealots, maintains Horsley, in the days of Jesus. Jesus was not interacting or debating with Zealots in any of his discussions.

Smith and Horsley are correct in demanding less speculation about this movement but they have perhaps overstated their case as well. Although we should not necessarily see a continuous Zealot movement and underground resistance in the first century AD, surely they did not spring up suddenly as the war began. An organized group with a name for itself surely argues for a history prior to AD 67. Second, Judas' sect certainly seemed to have existed beyond his lifetime as we affirmed above.

The three groups were probably not the same sect or movement. There may have been many such movements beginning and ending through the first century. Thus, although the typical Zealot historical construction (e.g. by Hengel) is not accurate, it does capture the atmosphere of what it was like to live in first century Palestine, a place infested with freedom movements of varying degrees of fanaticism and violence. Jesus may not have had the actual Zealots in mind in any of his teachings or debates but he almost certainly had a group or groups in mind which resembled them.

Boethusians

Bibliography: J. Le Moyne, *Les Sadduceen*; E. Rivkin, *A Hidden Revolution*; A.J. Saldarini, *Pharisees, Scribes and Sadducees*; G. Stemberger, *Pharisaer, Sadduzaeer, Essener*.

The Boethusians are always closely associated with the Sadducees in the Rabbinic sources. They possibly were so named after the House of Boethus which gave three High Priests to Judaism (see Table 2.1 in Chapter 2). Although the Boethusians appear to have been very similar to the Sadducees, both Le Moyne and Saldarini refuse to conclude that they were identical. The preservation of the difference in name must have been for a reason. Thus the Boethusians were probably a sub-group within the Sadducees. The characteristics that distinguished the

Boethusians cannot now be determined.

Haberim

Bibliography: G.F. Moore, *Judaism*; A. Oppenheimer, *The Am Ha-Aretz*; A.J. Saldarini, *Pharisees, Scribes and Sadducees*; R. Sarason, *A History of the Mishnaic Law of Agriculture*; G. Stemberger, *Pharisaer, Sadduzaeer, Essener*.

The Mishnah and Tosephta refer to a group of *Haberim* ("associates") which is very strict about purity laws and tithing. The group appears to have been similar to the Pharisees, so much so that earlier scholars identified the two groups. More recently, however, this view is changing. The Haberim were probably either a sub-group within Pharisaism or totally independent yet very similar to the Pharisees. Several such groups interested in purity and tithing may have existed in antiquity.

The Haberim marked themselves off sharply from the *Am Ha-Aretz* ("people of the land"). The latter were not meticulous about purity and tithing, often refusing to contribute anything more than the wave offering (1/40 to 1/50 of the crop), thus ignoring the first and second tithes found in Deuteronomy 14:22-27 and Numbers 18:20-32. Thus no Haber (the singular of Haberim) could deal with the Am Ha-Aretz because their produce was always under suspicion of not having been properly tithed. Not only that, but the Haber would not even accept the hospitality of one of the Am Ha-Aretz nor would he receive him as his guest.

To become a Haber one had to go through stages of initiation similar to those among the Essenes. Thus they formed an organized group with rules of entry and definite social boundaries. If anything, they were even more zealous than the Pharisees to keep the priestly purity laws and the tithes.

Other Sects

Bibliography: J.J. Gunther, *St. Paul's Opponents and Their Background*; C.H. Kraeling, *John the Baptist*; C. Scobie, *John the Baptist*; M. Simon, *Jewish Sects*; J. Thomas, *Le mouvement baptiste en Palestine et en Syrie*.

Some Christian writers living several years to a century after the events in first century Palestine have given lists of other Jewish sects not given in Josephus, the New Testament or the Talmud. The accuracy of these lists is uncertain but they should be presented for the sake of completeness:

A. The Galileans: This sect was perhaps either the followers of Judas the Galilean or early Christians.

B. Baptists (masbothei): This group (or these groups) required ritual water immersion of its new members. John the Baptist may have been the intentional or unintentional founder of all of these groups or he may have been only one baptist practitioner among many others. The medieval and modern sect called the Mandaeans is descended from this movement.

C. Hemerobaptists: This sub-group within the Baptists required baptism (or ritual bathing?) of its members everyday.

D. Genistae: These were to the second century AD rabbis heretics or nonconformists. Their doctrines are unknown.

E. Meristae: The "separatists" seem to have made distinctions in scripture, accepting only certain parts as authoritative.

F. Nasaraioi: Epiphanius (a third century AD Christian writer) maintained that this sect was not identical to the Nazarenes (Palestinian Christians) but was pre-Christian. They dwelt among the Jordan river, practiced circumcision and observed the Sabbath and other Jewish feasts. They believed that Moses had been given the Torah by God but denied that it was the Pentateuch of our present Old Testament. They refused to offer sacrifices or to eat meat of any kind. If they had a Bible, it must have had large sections missing which are in our present Old Testament. They may also have had extra esoteric books as M. Simon suggested. Simon thinks that the Nasaraioi later accepted Jesus as Messiah and became the Ebionites, a second century AD Christian heresy.

The Samaritans

Bibliography: F.M. Cross, "Aspects of Samaritan and Jewish History" *Harvard Theological Review* 59 (1966) 201-211; D. Gowan, *Bridge Between the Testaments*; H.G. Kippenberg and G.A. Wewers, *Textbuch zur neutestamentliche Zeitgeschichte*; J. MacDonald, *The Theology of the Samaritans*; J.A. Montgomery, *The Samaritans, The Earliest Jewish Sect.*

The next two groups we will consider, the Samaritans and scribes, were not, strictly speaking, Jewish sects. The Samaritans had a separate ethnic identity and different religious history. The scribes were more a guild than a sect. Nevertheless, the two groups are usually discussed in relation to the sects and it is convenient to do so here.

The Samaritans were the racial and religious descendants of the ten northern tribes which were conquered by the Assyrians in 722 BC. The aristocrats and the elite were sent by the Assyrians into exile and other conquered peoples were resettled in the Samaritan cities. But the country folk, the villagers, remained mostly untouched by the changes. The Samaritans of Jesus' day represented then the first century version of those members of the ten tribes left behind. They practiced in a way an older form of Yahwism which was not influenced by the Babylonian exile of Judah.

But Samaritanism too had made its changes by the first century. The Samaritans had their own High Priesthood and their own account of the origin of this priesthood which differed markedly from the biblical account (cf. 2 Kings 17:24-41 with the Samaritan Chronicle). This priestly succession has continued down to the present day. A small group of Samaritans still exists with its priests in modern Israel.

The Samaritan points of doctrine are as follows:

1. They believe in Yahweh as the only God and are thus fiercely monotheistic (not somewhat paganistic as some have alleged).

2. They accept the five books of Moses only (the Pentateuch), rejecting the prophets and the writings.

3. They too once had a temple which was destroyed in the Jewish War of AD 66-73 (74) just as the Jewish Temple in Jerusalem was destroyed. The Samaritans also took part in the Jewish War. Josephus records that 11,600 of them were massacred on Mt. Gerizim in Samaria when their temple was leveled. Samaritans still perform sacrifices on the mountain even though the temple is no longer standing.

4. They believe in a coming day of vengeance and recompense (in other words, a judgement day).

The animosity between Jews and Samaritans is clear both from Josephus and the New Testament. But both Jesus and the early church showed great interest in evangelizing the Samaritans. Jesus portrayed the Samaritans in a favorable light (Lk 10:33) and the early Christian community welcomed them into the church (Acts 8:5-17).

Scribes

Bibliography: M. Black, "Scribes" *IDB*; G.F. Moore, *Judaism*; A.J. Saldarini, *Pharisees, Scribes and Sadducees*; E.E. Urbach, "Class-Status and Leadership in the World of the Palestinian Sages" *Proceedings of the Israel Academy of Science and Humanities* 2 (1968) 38-74.

A scribe (Greek: *grammateus*; Hebrew: *sopher*) was one learned in the Torah and other wisdom. Saldarini rightly traces the history of this profession from the Old Testament pre-exilic period. They were highly educated government ministers and personal secretaries. Scribes were present in the Maccabean era and one of them, Eleazar (2 Maccabees 6:18), died a martyr's death for the Torah. The apocryphal book written by one Jesus ben Sirah (c. 180 BC), who was himself a scribe, describes how one trained for this profession (38:24-39:11). It required knowledge of wisdom, parables and the Torah and it necessitated travel to other lands to gain insight. The scribe was of course, according to Ben Sirah, a very devout Yahwist. Josephus also referred to scribes, both high level officials of the government and village scribes of low status (*War* 1.479). Likewise, the New Testament depicts scribes as Torah scholars. They seem to have been located mainly in Jerusalem but were also present in villages.

Saldarini speculates that the village scribe probably could read and write and knew how to compose letters, contracts and petitions for the villagers. At the middle level of the social ladder were the scribes with positions in the government. These latter were educated bureaucrats. At the highest level would have been the highly educated and well-trained scribes described by Ben Sirah. These last scribes were the highest level government ministers.

The scribes then were not a religious, a political party or a social class. They were a profession. No organization or group formation can be detected though they may have had guilds. They could be wealthy or poor, politically powerful or insignificant. They were often highly educated but may at times have known only how to write and compose official documents.

Although scribes were not a religious sect, they could belong to one. Some belonged to the Pharisees (Mk 2:16; Acts 23:9) and presumably others were Sadducees. We encounter the scribes often in the Gospels (e.g. Mt. 2:4; 5:20; 7:29; 9:3; 12:38).

Conclusion

The numerous Jewish sects indicate that Judaism was very pluralistic in antiquity. Pharisaic Judaism apparently won the competition for popularity after AD 70 and so made Judaism thereafter more normative and uniform. But before that came about, Palestine had many different groups vying for power, influence and attention. Many theologies and practices competed for followers. We have listed fourteen diffrerent sects--not counting the Samaritans and scribes--but there were probably many more. How many sects perhaps had only a handful of members? How many groups were so secretive that almost no one outside the sect knew of their existence? One can only guess how large the iceberg is by looking at its tip.

Notes

1. The various suggestions as to the meaning of the term Essenes are: the pious ones, the healers, the doers of the Law, the seers and the silent ones.
2. The Wicked Priest is usually identified with Jonathan the High Priest (ruled 161-143 BC).

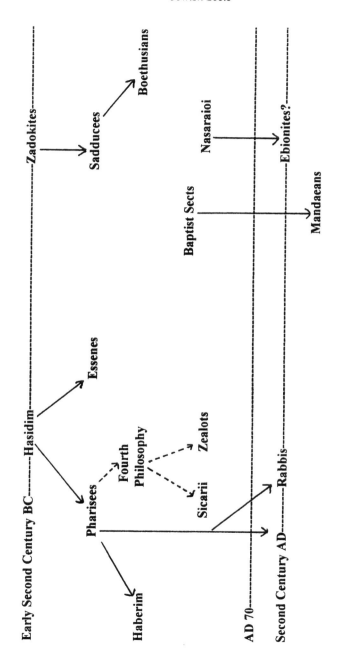

Table 3.1

Jewish Sects

Chapter 4

Sources for the Life of Jesus Outside the Canonical Gospels

Bibliography: F.F. Bruce, *Jesus and Christian Origins Outside the New Testament*; idem., *The New Testament Documents: Are They Reliable?*; J.H. Charlesworth, *Jesus Within Judaism*; J.D. Crossan, *The Historical Jesus*; G.H. Dalman, *Jesus Christ in the Talmud, Midrash, Zohar, and the Liturgy of the Synagogue*; R.C. Foster, *Studies an the Life of Christ*; G.R. Habermas, *Ancient Evidence for the Life of Jesus*; R.T. Herford, *Christianity on Talmud and Midrash*; R.J. Hoffmann, *Jesus Outside the Gospels*; J. Jeremias, *Unknown Sayings of Jesus*; J. Klausner, *Jesus of Nazareth*; J. McDowell and B. Wilson, *He Walked Among us*; J. Price, *Interpreting the New Testament*; A. Schweitzer, *The Quest of the Historical Jesus*; W.D. Stroker, *Extracanonical Sayings of Jesus*

Some critics are accustomed to asserting that the four Gospels of the New Testament are hopelessly biased about Jesus and therefore untrustworthy. These scholars are of course correct about the first part of their contention.   The writers of our Gospels were biased.   That is, they believed that Jesus was the Messiah, the Son of God.   But such reasoning is faulty in two ways.   It assumes that other sources about Jesus are not biased.   Every source is biased as is every critic, even modern historians.

Second, such reasoning assumes that a biased person cannot tell the truth.   Therefore, some scholars conclude that since these early Christians believed in Jesus they fabricated things about him.   But if we used such arguments in a court of law, we would never allow the testimony of any witnesses. The truth is, the early Christians had seen such wonderful things in the life of Jesus that they did not need to fabricate anything. They went to their own deaths giving testimony that Jesus had been raised from the tomb.

Yet it is useful to give here testimony about Jesus that comes outside the four Gospels. Over a century ago a German scholar named Bruno Bauer maintained that Jesus had never lived at all (see Schweitzer). Since then there have been a few who have tried to follow in Bruno Bauer's footsteps (see Charlesworth's summary pp. 97f). Therefore, we want to demonstrate first that non-Christian sources confirm that Jesus was an actual historical figure. Second, we want to show that the Jesus that emerges from these sources is essentially the same as the one from the New Testament.

Pagan Witnesses of Jesus

The first pagan author, as far as is known, to mention Jesus was Thallus who wrote, according to F.F. Bruce, around AD 52. Thallus published a chronological work in three volumes from the Trojan War up to his own time and he may have been a freedman of emperor Tiberius (see A.H. McDonald, in *OCD*). He is extant today only in a few fragments. The fragment which bears on Jesus was quoted in a work by the Christian philosopher, Sextus Julius Africanus who lived in the early third century AD. Africanus (*Chronography* 18.1) refers to the darkness that accompanied Jesus' crucifixion (Mt 27:45) and notes that Thallus had tried to explain the darkness rationalistically by claiming it was an eclipse of the sun. This explanation is unreasonable, writes Africanus (because at the time of the Passover there is a full moon and thus an eclipse of the sun is impossible). This reference indicates, however, that the story of Jesus was known to a pagan writer, who lived presumably in Rome, only twenty or so years after the crucifixion.

Another historian, Phlegon, who wrote in AD 140 a massive work of at least fourteen books, also alludes to Jesus' crucifixion and the darkness and earthquake that accompanied it. He is cited by two Christian writers, Julius Africanus (*Chronography* 18.1) mentioned above and Origen (early third century AD, *Against Celsus* 2.33).

The next author is Mara Bar Serapion who lived sometime after the first century AD, probably in the second or third century. In a letter intended to give encouragement to his son he refered to three famous martyrs: Socrates, Pythagoras, and Jesus. Of Jesus he wrote: "What advantage did the Jews gain from executing their wise King? It was just after that that their kingdom was abolished. . . The Jews, ruined and driven from their land, live in complete dispersion."[1]

Again the date of Mara Bar Serapion is uncertain but the text shows that the story of Jesus was widely dispersed to pagan circles. From his name we would expect that the author was from Syria.

Easily the most important reference to Jesus is found in the writings of Tacitus, the Roman historian who wrote at the end of the first century AD. Tacitus wrote an account of Rome from Augustus to his own time. In his handling of Nero's emperorship (AD 54-68) he described the great fire of Rome. Nero was accused of setting the fire and consequently tried to fix the blame on the Christians who were then rounded up and executed in barbaric ways. The story of this persecution leads Tacitus to explain who founded Christianity:

> But no human aid, no largesse from the Emperor, no supplications to heaven, did anything to ease the impression that the fire had been deliberately started. Nero looked around for a scapegoat, and inflicted the most fiendish tortures on a group of persons already hated by the people for their crimes. This was the sect known as Christians. Their founder, one Christus, had been put to death by the procurator Pontius Pilate in the reign of Tiberius.[2]

Since, as F.F. Bruce asserted, Tacitus probably got his information about Jesus' execution in Palestine from official government sources, his information is of utmost significance. He testifies that Jesus really lived, that he was executed and that he died when the Gospels say he did.

The final author we will quote is Lucian of Samosata who lived in the second century AD in Syria. He authored a host of satirical works, among them the *Death of Peregrinus*. In this dialogue Lucian wrote contemptuously of both Jesus and Christians:

> The Christians, you know, worship a man to this day--the distinguished personage who introduced their novel rites, and was crucified on that account. . .it was impressed on them by their original lawgiver that (Christians) are all brothers, from the moment that they are converted, and deny the gods of Greece, and worship the crucified sage, and live after his laws.[3]

Lucian confirms that Christians worship Jesus and that he has given new teachings. Because of these new teachings he was crucified.

Thus the testimony that these and other[4] pagan sources offer confirms that Jesus was no figment of the imagination of a few Galilean disciples. The sources give an outline of Jesus' story: his life as a teacher, his death and his resurrection.

Jewish Sources

The rabbinic sources refer to Jesus rather often.   Most of these references, however, are confused and full of vituperation. He is often called Jesus ben Pandira (or Pantera). The meaning of this term is not clear but probably is a slander on his birth. Pandira (Pantera) may be a cacophemism (meaning "son of the panther") on the Greek word *parthenos* which means "virgin". In other words instead of calling him the son of the virgin, he is called the son of the panther, for whatever reason. Jesus is villified in other ways as well: He practiced sorcery, having brought spells from Egypt (b. Shabbath 104b; cf. b. Yoma 66b and t. Yebamoth 3:3-4); he led Israel astray and practiced magic (b. Sanhedrin 107b); he was a deceiver who was taken to trial and stoned (t. Sanhedrin 10:11); Jesus had five disciples, Matthai (=Matthew), Neqai(=Nicodemus?), Netzer (Nazarene?), Buni (=Boanerges or sons of thunder, i.e. James and John?), and Thodah (=Thaddeus) (b. Sanhedrin 43a); Jesus was excommunicated by the rabbis (b. Sanhedrin 107b); Jesus gave ridiculous legal arguments (b. Avodah Zarah 16b-17a).

The most important text from the Talmud relating to Jesus describes his death:

> On the Eve of the Passover Yeshu was hanged. For forty days before the execution took place, a herald went forth and cried, 'He is going forth to be stoned because he has practised sorcery and enticed Israel to apostasy. Any one who can say anything in his favour, let him come forward and plead on his behalf.' But since nothing was brought forward in his favour he was hanged on the eve of the Passover![5]

The evidence of the Talmud although late (AD 200-500) actually harmonizes well with the Gospels. J. Klausner, a Jewish scholar, has summarized the Talmudic statements about Jesus: Jesus was a rabbi who beguiled Israel and mocked the words of the wise. He expounded scripture like the Pharisees and gathered disciples. He practiced sorcery. He was finally hanged (i.e. crucified) on the eve of the Passover, but his disciples continued to heal in his name.

These statements are really only a negative way of saying what the Gospels say.[6] Beguiling Israel is a slanderous way of saying Jesus had a large following. Mocking the words of the wise indicates Jesus had strong and basic disagreements with the scribes. Practicing sorcery is a negative way of reporting that Jesus performed miracles. The charge of sorcery was a strategy already attempted in Jesus' lifetime (Mk 3:22).

The evidence of the Talmud is weak because the Talmud is a late source. But the evidence of Josephus is very important. Josephus grew up in Palestine. He was descended from a line of priests and came from a wealthy family that owned lands near Jerusalem. He fought in the Jewish war of AD 66-73 (74?) and after the war settled in Rome to write his account of the war, his autobiograghy, his refutation of Apion and his history of Judaism. He is thus a very significant witness.

The first reference to Jesus we will quote is accepted by most as authentic: "(Ananus the High Priest) convened the judges of the Sanhedrin and brought before them a man named James, the brother of Jesus who was called the Christ." (*Antiquities* 20.200).[7] Thus Josephus demonstrates that Jesus was known to the Jewish authorities and that James was his brother (see Gal 1:19).

The longest and most controversial reference to Jesus has undoubtedly Christian interpolations in it. At some point in the transmission of the manuscripts of Josephus' works a Christian has slipped in some words of faith. The passage is as follows with the supposed interpolations in italics:

> About this time there lived Jesus, a wise man, *if indeed one ought to call him a man.* For he was one who wrought surprising feats and was a teacher of such people as accept the truth gladly. He won over many Jews and many of the Greeks. *He was the Messiah.* When Pilate, upon hearing him accused by men of the highest standing amongst us, had condemned him to be crucified, those who had in the first place come to love him did not give up their affection for him. *On the third day he appeared to them restored to life for the prophets of God had prophesied these and countless other marvellous things about him.* And the tribe of the Christians, so called after him, has still to this day not disappeared. (*Antiquities* 18.63f)[8]

Since Josephus was not a Christian as far as anyone knows, scholars assume he would not have written the words above in italics. But in addition to removing the italicized words one should probably rephrase a few places. F.F. Bruce[9] and Morton Smith[10] have published revised texts of Josephus based on the suggestions of previous scholars. We will give them in Table 4.1 along with the newer find of an Arabic text[11] of Josephus which could possibly be free of interpolations. We may be reasonably confident that Josephus wrote something like that given in the table. He confirms that Jesus really lived, that he was a teacher and had a large following, that he claimed to be the Messiah, that he was crucified by Pilate and that he was seen resurrected and continues to be followed by disciples.

The non-Christian sources are surprisingly harmonious with what we find in the Gospels and no one can claim that these sources are biased in favor of Jesus. As R.C. Foster wrote: "The scattering references of hostile writers establish Jesus as a historical figure, and are not able to shake the testimony of the Gospels as to details" (p. 31).

Christian Sources Outside the New Testament

The sayings attributed to Jesus which are not recorded in our Gospels (called *agrapha* "unwritten" in Greek, i.e. not written in the Gospels) were first collected by A. Resch in 1889. Resch gathered from: a) the rest of the New Testament (see e.g. Acts 20:35 "It is more blessed to give than to receive"); b) from additions and variants in the Gospel manuscripts (e.g. number 1 below); c) from the Apocryphal Gospels (e.g. number 2 below below); d) from the church fathers (e.g. numbers 3 and 5 below); e) from Gnostic texts; f) from the Talmud (two sayings, see e.g. footnote 5 above);g) and even from Muslim sources. In all he could point to 145 sayings many of which he thought could be genuine sayings of Jesus which had not been recorded in the Gospels. In addition, since his time many papyri dating from the second through the fifth centuries AD have been found in Egypt containing sayings of Jesus (e.g. number 4 below).

How could so many sayings have escaped our Gospels? We must understand that during the first decades of the growth of Christianity the stories and sayings of Jesus circulated mostly orally with perhaps a few small written collections. Only as the faith began to spread all over the world was there a need for a comprehensive and coherent account of Jesus' life and words. We should not be surprised then that many of Jesus' sayings that circulated orally simply were left out of our written Gospels. The Gospels never claimed to give us all of Jesus' words and deeds but only what we need as believers to understand salvation (see especially Jn 20:30-31).

Probably not all of Resch's sayings are authentic. J.H. Ropes in 1896 and more recently J. Jeremias in 1963 published analyses of Resch's work eliminating most of these as genuine sayings of Jesus. Ropes left 28 agrapha and Jeremias left only twenty sayings. Yet surely Jeremias overlooked many authentic agrapha. The most complete collection of these sources in recent years is by W.D. Stroker (published in 1989) who gives the text and translation of 286 sayings. Many of these repeat what is already in our four Gospels but with a few slight additions or alterations. Some sayings are vaguely reminiscent of ideas in the canonical Gospels. Others are totally new.

We will quote here only a few examples so that the reader may experience the flavor of these sayings:

> 1. On the same day he saw a man working on the Sabbath and said to him: Man, if you know what you are doing, you are blessed. But if you do not know, you are accursed and a transgressor of the law.[12]
>
> 2. Jesus said: Whoever is near me is near the fire (i.e. the fire of persecution?), and whoever is far from me is far from the kingdom (cf. Lk 12:49).[13]
>
> 3. No man can obtain the kingdom of heaven that has not passed through temptation (cf. Lk 22:28, 31).[14]
>
> 4. Lift up the stone and you will find me there; split the wood and I am there (cf. Mt 18:20).[15]
>
> 5. As you are found (at the second coming?) so will you be led away hence (Mt 25:1-12).[16]

These are interesting, even intriguing, sayings most of which have parallels in our canonical Gospels. Yet they really add very little to our knowledge of what Jesus was like. Jeremias has summarized well:

> The real value of the tradition outside the Gospels is that it throws into

sharp relief the unique value of the canonical Gospels themselves. If we would learn about the life and message of Jesus, we shall find what we want only in the four canonical Gospels. The lost dominical sayings may supplement our knowledge here and there in important and valuable ways, but they cannot do more than that (p. 121).

Yet the hoard of agrapha does strongly point to one conclusion. Such a large amount of oral teaching surely means there was an originator of the sayings. It would be very difficult to explain all of these sayings in all of these sources outside the New Testament if Jesus had never lived. It would even be difficult to explain them if he had lived differently than the four Gospels say he did.

New Testament Sources for the Life of Jesus (Outside the Gospels)

One of the oldest documents witnessing to the life of Jesus is Paul's first letter to the Corinthians, written in AD 54. At two points in the letter Paul reminded the Corinthians what he had "delivered" to them (1 Cor 11:23-26; 15:3-11), namely accounts of the Lord's Supper and Jesus' resurrection. The phrase "What also I delivered to you" (*ho kai paredoka hymin*) refers specifically to transmitting teaching to students. Paul also said it was teaching he "received" (1 Cor 15:3) that is from the earliest Christian community in Jerusalem and Galilee. Thus the terminology Paul used indicates these accounts came from eye-witnesses.

And what do the accounts indicate? They substantiate the narratives of the institution of the Lord's Supper in the Gospels (Mt 26:17-30; Mk 14:12-26; Lk 22:7-23; Aland 308, 310, 311). Paul says that Jesus instituted the Lord's Supper on the night he was betrayed and that he declared the emblems of the passover (unleavened bread and wine) to be emblems now of his body and blood, signs of the new covenant. His body and blood are being given "for you." Jesus saw his death as something given for his disciples.

Paul's testimony about Jesus' post resurrection appearances is also similar in character to those of the Gospels (Mt 28:1-10, 16-20; Lk 24:13-53; Jn 20:10-21:21; Aland 352-67). Paul says, as do the Gospels, that Jesus appeared to Peter and the Apostles, but then he adds that Jesus also appeared to James, his brother, who was at that time an unbeliever (Jn

7:5). Highly significant is Paul's statement that Jesus had appeared to a group of over 500 brethren at one time, many of whom were still (i.e. in AD 54) alive and could verify the account.

Also important are the indications that these accounts were being passed on from eye witnesses with a great deal of care and accuracy. First Paul used the terminology often employed in Jewish circles for a careful transmission of teaching from master to student.[17] Second, he indicated that people who were eye witnesses continued throughout their life times to serve as living Gospels.   Third, Paul's own narratives agree substantially with those of the New Testament Gospels.

The Epistle of the Hebrews also substantiates the Gospels. Probably writing sometime around AD 64, the author indicates that his witness to Christ was given him "by those who heard him (i.e. Christ)" (Heb 2:3). The author affirms on the basis of the eyewitness testimony he has received that Jesus lived as a man, endured temptations and suffering unto death, that he sought relief through "strong weeping" (a reference to Gethsemane, see Aland 330) that he died by crucifixion "outside the gate" of Jerusalem and that by all these trials he learned perfect obedience (Heb 2:10, 14, 18; 5:7, 8; 12:2; 13:12).

Likewise Peter, who was an "eyewitness", attests to the authenticity of Jesus' transfiguration (Aland 161) in his second letter (2 Pet 1:16-18, written around AD 65).

Thus the nonbiblical sources, both pagan and Jewish, confirm the outline of what the four Gospels tell us about Jesus. Further, the New Testament indicates that eyewitnesses and reliable teachers and transmitters of the events of Jesus' ministry were taking great care to report these events accurately.   The narratives in Paul's epistle to the Corinthians confirm those of the Gospels. Thus the Gospels should be accorded the highest respect as historical documents.

Notes

1. The translation is by Bruce, *Jesus and Christian Origins Outside the New Testament*, p.31.   The text is a Syriac ms in the British Museum.
2. The translation is by D.R. Dudley, *The Annals of Tacitus*, pp. 353f and is in Tacitus, *Annals* 15.44.
3. The translation is by H.W. Fowler and F.G. Fowler, *The Works of Lucian of Samosata*, Vol. 4 (*The Death of Peregrinus*, 11-13).

4. There are two other pagan authors whose statements we might mention. They say more about early Christianity than about Jesus himself. Suetonius, a Roman biographer who lived about the same time as Tacitus, refers twice to Christianity. In his life of Claudius he wrote: "Because the Jews at Rome caused continuous disturbances at the instigation of Chrestus, he expelled them from the city." (*Claudius* 25, translation in R. Graves, *The Twelve Caesars*, p. 202). Suetonius refers to the expulsion of Jews and Jewish Christians from Rome, due at least partly to disagreements about Christ. He mistakenly assumed that the historical Christ was actually in Rome

In the life of Nero Suetonius also describes, but very briefly, the fire and subsequent persecution of Christians: "Punishments were also inflicted on the Christians, a sect professing a new and mischievous religious belief." (Tranlation in Graves, p. 221).

Pliny the Younger, the governor of Bithynia, who wrote in the early second century AD also refers to Christians: "They were in the habit of meeting on a certain fixed day before it was light, when they sang in alternate verses a hymn to Christ, as to a god, and bound themselves by a solemn oath, not to any wicked deeds, but never to commit any fraud, theft, or adultery, never to falsify their word, nor deny a trust when they should be called upon to deliver it up; after which it was their custom to separate, and then reassemble to partake of food--but food of an ordinary and innocent kind." (Translation by W. Melmoth,_*Letters of Pliny*, Vol. 2 and is found in Pliny X. 96). Pliny gives us an intriguing glimpse of an early Christian worship service and notes that they worship Christ as "a god."

5. The translation is in I. Epstein , *The Babylonian Talmud*. Another important Talmudic passage is a version of Mt 5:17 in Aramaic. This text is found in b. Shabbath 116a-b.

6. Another Hebrew document, called *Toledot Yeshu* or the "generations of Jesus", is of interest here. The date of this text is somewhere between AD 500 and 1000 but may be based on an earlier text or texts. The *Toledot Yeshu* (summaries of it may be found in both Klausner and Hoffmann) is a detailed perversion of the Gospels with most of the features we have already cited from the Talmud. Again if one reverses the negative tone, the events of the Gospels are confirmed.

7. The translation is from L.H. Feldman, *Josephus*, (LCL).

8. The translation is in Feldman, ibid.

9. This revision of Josephus is in Bruce, *The New Testament Documents*, p.110. Another revision is given, that of R. Eisler, in Feldman, *Josephus* (LCL) Vol. 9, p. 48.

10. The revision is in Morton Smith, *Jesus the Magician*, p. 46.

11. The translation of the Arabic version of Josephus is by S. Pines and is quoted in Charlesworth, p. 95. There is also a Slavonic version of Josephus. But the text about Jesus is greatly expanded and embellished and apparently not helpful for our purposes. A translation of the Slavonic version on Jesus can be found in Bruce.

12. Translation in Stroker, p. 22 of Codex D after Lk 6:4 (a manuscript addition). For information about the New Testament manuscripts see D.A. Fiensy, *New Testament Introduction*, pp.353-358. For a general analysis of all of these sources (although the present author does not agree with all of his conclusions) see J.D. Crossan, *The Historical Jesus,* pp. 427-66.

13. Translation in Stroker, p. 194 of the Gospel of Thomas

14. Translation in Jeremias, p. 73 of Tertullian, *de Baptismo* 20.

15. Translation in Stroker, p. 193 of Papyrus Oxyrhynchus 1.27-30.

16. Translation in Jeremias, p. 83 of the Syrian *Liber Graduum.*

17. See the equivalent terms used in Hebrew in the m. Pirke Aboth 1:1: "receive" *qibbel* (Heb) = *parelabe* (Gk); "deliver" *masar* (Heb) = *paredoke* (Gk).

Revision of Greek Text (Bruce)	Arabic Text	Revision of Greek Text (Morton Smith)
And there arose about this time a source of new troubles, one Jesus, a wise man. He was a doer of marvelous deeds, a teacher of men who receive strange things with pleasure. He led away many Jews, and also many of the Greeks. This man was the so-called Christ. And when Pilate had condemned him to the cross on his impeachment by the chief men among us, those who had loved him at first did not cease; for he appeared to them, as they said, on the third day alive again, the divine prophets having spoken these and thousands of other wonderful things about him: and even now the tribe of Christians, so named after him, has not yet died out.	At this time there was a wise man who was called Jesus. His conduct was good, and (he) was known to be virtuous. And many people from among the Jews and the other nations became his disciples. Pilate condemned him to be crucified and to die. But those who had become disciples did not abandon his discipleship. They reported that he had appeared to them three days after his crucifixion, and that he was alive; accordingly he was perhaps the Messiah, concerning whom the prophets have recounted wonders.	At this time there lived Jesus, a man (who was a sophist), if it is proper to call him a man. For he was a doer of¹ miracles, a teacher of men who receive (impiety) with pleasure. And he led (astray) many Jews and many of the Greeks (who said that) this (fellow) was the Christ. And when, on accusation by our leading men, Pilate condemned him to the cross, those who formerly loved (him) did not cease (to do so), for (they asserted that) he appeared to them on the third day, again alive, while (pretended) prophets kept saying these and ten thousand other incredible things about him. And to the present (time) the tribe of Christians, named after him, has not disappeared.

Table 4.1
Josephus' Testimonia About Jesus

Chapter 5

The Infancy Narratives
(Aland 2-11)

The Virgin Birth
(Aland 3,7)

Bibliography: T. Boslooper, *The Virgin Birth*; R. Brown, *The Birth of the Messiah*; D.R. Cartlidge and D.L. Dungan, *Documents for the Study of the Gospels*; M. Connick, *Jesus, the Man, the Mission, and the Message*; C.E.B. Cranfield, "Some Reflections on the Subject of the Virgin Birth" *Scottish Journal of Theology* 41 (1988) 177-189; J.E. Crouch, "How Early Christians Viewed the Birth of Jesus" *Bible Review* 7.5 (1991) 34-37; W.D. Davies and D.C. Allison, *The Gospel According to Saint Matthew*; J. Fitzmyer, *The Gospel According to Luke*; J.G. Machen, *The Virgin Birth of Christ*; J. Orr, *The Virgin Birth*; J. Schaberg, *The Illegitimacy of Jesus*; J.S. Spong, *Born of a Woman*; V. Taylor, *The Virgin Birth*; B. Thiering, *Jesus and the Riddle of the Dead Sea Scrolls*; B. Witherington, III, "The Birth of Jesus" *Dictionary of Jesus and the Gospels*.

Without Question one of the most controversial issues today is the debate over the virginal conception of Jesus. Luke's Gospel says (1:34) when the angel announced to Mary that she would have a child that Mary responded: "How will this happen since I do not (sexually) know a man?" The angel responded to Mary: "The Holy Spirit will come upon you and the power of the Most High will over shadow you." This certainly sounds like Mary will conceive by a miracle by the power of the Holy Spirit and not by human agency. Matthew's Gospel also makes it clear that the birth was entirely miraculous. Matthew writes (1:18): "Before (Joseph and Mary) had consummated their marriage, Mary became pregnant through the Holy Spirit." Then Matthew quotes (1:23) the Greek (Septuagint) version of the Old Testament prophet Isaiah (Isaiah 7:14): "Behold a virgin (Gk: *parthenos*) will become pregnant and will have a son and you will call his name Emmanuel."

Yet some doubt the virgin birth. We will here outline the main arguments against this miracle together with our analysis to be followed with those arguments in favor of it.

Arguments Against the Virgin Birth

1. Some who dispute the virginal conception of Jesus maintain that the verses quoted above were not originally in the texts of Matthew and Luke. The verses were, it is maintained, inserted by later copyists. Yet there is not a single manuscript that indicates such a thing. V. Taylor has convincingly shown in his carefully argued monograph that the verses quoted above fit smoothly with the narratives.

A variation of this first approach is to maintain that while the literal meaning of the birth narratives is that Jesus was born of a virgin, we must look beyond the literal to find a hidden meaning. Thus J. Schaberg claims that Mary was actually raped and that such a conclusion is clear to anyone that reads these narratives with a feminists perspective. B. Thiering claims that both Joseph and Mary were Essenes and that Mary was a kind of nun, which the Essenes called virgins. Before Joseph and Mary were wed they succumbed to temptation and conceived a child together. Therefore, writes Thiering, a virgin (by which she means a member of a female monastic order) conceived a child.

These conclusions may seem obvious to their proponents but they will not at all be obvious to most readers. Nowhere in the texts is there any hint at all that Mary was raped. Nor has Thiering or anyone else proven that Joseph and Mary were Essenes. She has only assumed it. But even if they were Essenes, the religious order of women that Thiering suggests Mary belonged to is nowhere alluded to in the ancient sources. It is a figment of her imagination.

2. Some argue from silence. The Gospels of Mark and John do not allude to the virgin birth and neither does the apostle Paul. Therefore, it is alleged, these authors either did not know about the virgin birth, did not

believe it or did not care about it. But arguments from silence are almost always suspect. Only if one can show that these authors must have referred to the virgin birth if they knew of it, can an argument from silence be valid. Mark does not begin his story about Jesus until Jesus' baptism. Mark is much less biographical than Matthew and Luke and simply says nothing at all about how Jesus was born. John begins by writing of Jesus' eternal pre-existence (see Aland 1). Then he jumps (in Jn 1:14) to the incarnation: "The Word became flesh and dwelt among us." The entire birth of Jesus is summarized in those few words. It is the fact that the eternal Word (*logos*) became flesh that matters. The events surrounding Jesus' birth are not important for John's immediate theological purpose. The infancy stories just do not fit with the purposes of Mark and John. Paul does not say anything about the virgin birth either but Paul actually says very little about the historical Jesus in general. Therefore, the arguments from silence are not convincing.

3. Some give credence to the Jewish slander about Jesus illegitimacy. We noted in chapter 4 that the Talmud and a source called the *toledoth Yeshu* ("origins of Jesus", see chapter 4, notes) claimed that Jesus was sired by a man named Panther (or Pandira or Pantira). In addition a pagan critic of Christianity named Celsus wrote a scathing attack on the Christian faith in AD 178 in which he maintained among other things that Jesus' father was a man named Panther (see Origen, *Against Celsus* 1.32). This he had undoubtedly learned from Jewish circles because he cites several Jewish calumnies against Christianity in his treatise. We gave in chapter 4 the customary explanation for the origin of the name Panther. It is probably a sarcastic joke on the Greek word, *parthenos*, "virgin."

Schaberg is convinced that the Jewish slanders about Jesus' birth--which may have begun during his lifetime, see Jn 8:41--are true. But for modern critics like Schaberg to give credence to silly stories that most Jewish scholars do not even believe (see e.g. Klausner) is ridiculous. This is tantamount to believing the later absurd pagan allegations that Christians were cannibals.

4. Some scholars point to the similarities between the birth narratives of Matthew and Luke and accounts of conceptions by pagan gods. It is often affirmed that many famous people were reportedly born of a virgin. But we have only to quote an example of one of these alleged parallels to see the difference. The begetting of the Greek hero Herakles (or Hercules) was allegedly done by the pagan god, Zeus, through sexual union. (Zeus even enters the genealogy more than once!)

They say that Perseus was the son of Danae, who was the daughter of Akrisios and Zeus. Andromeda, Kepheos' daughter, lay with him (Perseus) and bore Elektryon; then Euridike, daughter of Pelops cohabited with him (Elektryon) and gave birth to Alkmene. Alkmene was taken by Zeus, through a deceit, and she bore Herakles. . . The excellence begotten in Herakles is not only seen in his great acts, but was known before his birth. When Zeus lay with Alkmene, he tripled the length of the night, and, in the increased length of time spent in begetting the child, he foreshadowed the exceptional power of the child who was to be begotten. (Diodorus Siculus, *Library of History* 4.9.1-10; trans. in Cartlidge and Dungan).

One cannot emphasize enough the essential difference between this narrative and either one of our Gospels' birth narratives. The Gospels' narratives simply relate that Mary will conceive by the power and might of the Holy Spirit. The carnal stories of the Greeks are not at all similar to the Gospels, as the sound works of Machen and Orr have shown us.

The closest accounts to our virgin birth narratives are, as R. Brown has argued, Biblical stories of miraculous births. God gave Abraham and Sarah a son even though they were quite elderly and Sarah was past menopause (Gen 18:10-11; 21:1-7). Manoah's wife was sterile and childless but an angel appeared to her and announced that she would give birth to Samson the judge (Judges 13:1-5). Hannah, who was also barren, prayed for a son and gave him in service to the Lord (1 Sam 1:1-28). And finally, John the Baptist himself was born by a miracle. His mother, like Sarah, had been barren and was now quite elderly. Yet an angel announced that Elizabeth and Zechariah would have a son (Lk 1:5-25, 57-66). In all of these stories God intervened miraculously to grant a child to a couple that was childless. These events are similar to the events behind Jesus' birth but the birth of Jesus was unique in that Mary was not barren but a virgin.

Arguments in Favor of the Virgin Birth

The arguments against the virgin birth are not convincing. They are either inherently illogical (arguments from silence), pure speculation (Schaberg's and Thiering's allegations), simplistic parallelomania (the comparisons with pagan myths) or the kind of attacks that one would expect from a competing religion (the slanders about illegitimacy).

But what is the evidence for the virginal Conception of Jesus? There are two main lines of argument:

1. The virgin birth is narrated in two accounts: that of Matthew and Luke.[1] The reader should note: a) These accounts are not identical. They both say Jesus was born of a virgin but they say this in quite different ways. This means that the two accounts are independent of one another. Neither has copied from the other. Thus we have two separate traditions about the birth of Jesus. b) The idea of a virginal conception is not one that is found in Jewish sources (see Brown and Witherington). The accounts of the annunciation of the coming birth of Jesus in both Matthew and Luke are, as we noted above, literarily most like the Old Testament accounts of miraculous births. Yet none of the women in the Old Testament was ever said to have been a virgin. We further noted that the pagan myths are worlds apart from the Gospels' birth narratives. Therefore one is compelled to ask where did a Gospel writer ever get the idea to affirm that Jesus was born of a virgin, if as some maintain the author created the story? This question is even more pointed when we consider that it is not one Gospel writer that has stated that Jesus was born of a virgin but two. That two different authors independently would create a story so out of character with Judaism is difficult to swallow. This evidence strongly suggests that the authors are reporting not creating the story of Jesus' virginal conception. c) These stories are told briefly and simply with no attempt to explain details or embellish. Such a writing style suggests that the stories were already well known in the Christian communities for which Matthew and Luke wrote their Gospels. If we date the Gospels of Matthew and Luke at AD 55 and 60 respectively as we are inclined to do, then the traditions about Jesus' birth are quite early since the traditions behind the birth narratives must predate the composition of the Gospels by many years. Even if we date the Gospels in the 80's or 90's as many scholars do, the traditions cannot be only recently accepted by the authors. They seem to be a standard part of the story of Jesus as told in their churches.

2. Early Christian tradition affirms belief in the virgin birth. Ignatius, bishop of Antioch who wrote in AD 110, expressed belief in the virgin birth as if it were done by everyone: "For our God Jesus Christ was conceived by Mary by the dispensation of God. . .and the virginity of Mary, and her giving birth were hidden from the Prince of this world. . ." (Ephesians 8:2-9:1; trans. in K. Lake, LCL).

Justin Martyr who wrote around AD 140 defended the virgin birth at great length in his *Dialogue with Trypho*. Aristides, who also lived in the second century, affirmed the virgin birth.

The virgin birth is affirmed in the earliest creeds, that is, the old Roman creed (c. AD 150) and that in Hippolytus, *Apostolic Tradition* (c. AD 200). The old Roman Creed was composed in the second century from the oldest traditions of the doctrines of the church. They did not admit new or strange doctrines into these creeds. The Roman Creed begins as follows:

> I believe in God the Father almighty; and in Christ Jesus His only Son, our Lord, Who was born from the Holy Spirit and theVirgin Mary. . . . (Trans. in J.N.D. Kelly (*Early Christian Creeds*)

One should emphasize that the Christian thinkers of the second century did not seek to accept new beliefs about the faith. They valued old traditions that had been handed down by word of mouth.

The virgin birth on the other hand was denied by the Ebionites, a heretical group that also denied the deity of Jesus. In addition the arch-heretic, Cerinthus--said, by the way, to have been the theological opponent of John the apostle--denied the virgin birth (see Irenaeus, *Against Heresies* 1.26 for the Ebionites and Cerinthus). Both Cerinthus and the Ebionites were condemned universally by the early church. No group of leaders among orthodox Christians denied or called into question this doctrine.

The evidence is ancient and sound that the earliest Christians believed that Jesus was conceived by the virgin Mary. Arguments to the contrary are not convincing. If one can admit the possibility of miracles, nothing prohibits accepting this event.

The Hymns in Luke's Infancy Narrative (Aland 4, 5, 8, 9)

Bibliography: R. Brown, *The Birth of the Messiah*; J. Ernst, *Das Evangelium nach Lukas*; J. Fitzmyer, The Gospel According *to Luke*; I.H. Marshall, *Commentary on Luke*; H. Schuermann, *Das Lukasevangelium*.

Scattered throughout Luke's birth narrative are four hymns Semitic in style which are attributed to Mary, Zecharias (John the Baptist's father), the angels, and to Simeon (an elderly man who met the infant Jesus in the temple). The hymns have been given Latin names based on the Vulgate translation. The *Magnificat* of Mary (Lk 1:46-55) was sung or spoken by Mary in response to Elizabeth's blessing of Mary. The *Benedictus* by Zecharias (Lk 1:67-79) was uttered upon the birth of John. The *Gloria in Excelsis* (Lk 2:13-14) was the song of the angels to the shepherds. Finally the *Nunc Dimittis* (Lk 2:29-32) was sung by Simeon who had waited for years to see the Messiah.

Space does not allow for an analysis of all of these hymns but we can say a word about the Magnificat. This sublime poetic prayer exhibits clear Hebraic poetic parallelism. Hebrew poetry in the Psalms, Proverbs, and most of the prophetic writings is arranged in parallel lines. The second line may repeat in an esthetically pleasing way the first line (synonymous parallelism) or it may say the opposite of the first line (antithetic parallelism). Much of the poetry, however, advances the idea further (synthetic parallelism). Verses 46-47, 51, and 55 are synonymous and verses 52 and 53 of the Magnificat are antithetical. The other verses are synthetic. This hymn was probably composed originally then in Aramaic or Hebrew.

The Magnificat is also similar in style and content to the hymn of Hanna, Samuel's mother (1 Sam 2:1-10). See especially verses 1, 4, 5, and 7 of the poem in 1 Samuel. Did both Mary and Hanna utter these hymns spontaneously? That is certainly possible since the Holy Spirit gave them inspired utterance. It is also possible that these hymns were composed over a longer period of time by these women. There is nothing that requires us to conclude that the hymns were uttered without any forethought in composition.

The Magnificat is a beautiful statement of God's care and love of the downtrodden and poor, a theme also common in Jesus' teaching. God brings down the proud and mighty but exalts a poor handmaiden. Mary, a humble peasant girl who nevertheless was favored by God as the mother of the Messiah, is the symbol of all the lowly whom God chooses (cf. 1 Cor 1:26-30).

The Census of Quirinius (Aland 7)

Bibliography: R. Brown, *The Birth of the Messiah*; F.F. Bruce, *The New*

Testament Documents, Are They Reliable?; J. Fitzmyer, The Gospel According to
Luke; I.H. Marshall, Commentary on Luke; W.M. Ramsay, The Bearing of Recent
Discovery on the Trustworthiness of the New Testament; P.H. Schmitz, "Census:
Roman Census" in ABD; A.N. Sherwin-White, Roman Society and Roman Law
in the New Testament; M. Stern, "The Province of Judea" in S. Safrai and M.
Stern, The Jewish People in the First Century; SVM; B. Witherington, III, "The
Birth of Jesus" in-J.B. Green and S. McKnight, eds., Dictionary of Jesus and the
Gospels

Luke records for us events surrounding the birth of Jesus as follows:
"And there went out in those days a decree from Caesar Augustus to make
a census of the entire (Roman) world. This was the first census of
Quirinius, governor of Syria." (2:1-2)

Schurer, Vermes and Miller point out five problems with this statement:

1) No where else in the ancient sources is there a reference to a general
imperial census in the time of Augustus.

2) Normally a person would not have been required to travel to his
home town.

3) A Roman census would not have been carried out in Palestine
during the time of Herod.

4) Josephus says nothing about a Roman census in Palestine during the
reign of Herod.

5) A census done by Quirinius could not have taken place in the time
of Herod because Quirinius was never governor of Syria during Herod's
lifetime.

Many scholars have concluded therefore that Luke made a mistake and
erroneously thought that the census of AD 6 (see chapter 1) really
happened in around 5 BC. But such a conclusion is not necessary. Since
Luke has been shown to be very accurate with regard to minute details[2],
we should search for a way to understand this statement without
attributing errors. As F.F. Bruce has pointed out, none of the problems
listed above is insurmountable. One can point to examples of people
returning to their home towns in order to be enrolled in a census (see
Ulpian, 50.4.2; and P. Lond. 904). The relationship between Herod the
Great and Augustus is fuzzy, especially in the few years before Herod's
death so Augustus might easily have ordered a census (see also Marshall
on this). In particular, an inscription (CIL XIV.3613) has been found in
Syria that may show that Quirinius was an imperial legate twice and that
his governorship in AD 6 was his second time in that office (see Ramsay).
Thus he could have ordered for Augustus a census twice.

B. Witherington suggests that we translate the verse in Luke: "This was the census prior to that of Quirinius." In this case Quirinius has nothing to do with the birth of Jesus. Luke was merely trying to differentiate the census of Jesus' birth with the later census of Quirinius.

At any rate, Luke's historical accuracy elsewhere should make us hesitant to conclude that he erred in this instance.

The Genealogies (Aland 6 or 19)

Bibliography: R. Brown, *The Birth of the Messiah*; W.D. Davies and D. Allison, *The Gospel According to St. Matthew*; J. Fitzmyer, *The Gospel According to Luke*; M.D. Johnson, *The Purpose of the Biblical Genealogies*; R.R. Wilson, *Genealogy and History in the Biblical World*.

Matthew begins his Gospel with a genealogy of Jesus while Luke offers his genealogy after Jesus' baptism. Luke's genealogy includes 77 names[3] and Matthew's offers three sets of 14 names (but only 41 names are given by him).

Genealogies were more important in the Old Testament than most of us can now realize. They showed Israelites how they were related to the great heroes of the past; they connected them with the spiritual and cultural history of their people; and they gave kinship legitimacy to the rule of a king or the office of a priest. The book of Genesis contains several genealogies (e.g. Gen 5; 6:9-12; 10; 11:10-32; 25:12-20; 36:1-43; 37:2-4) and there is an important genealogy also in 1 Chronicles 1-9.

Genealogies were also kept after the exile (Ezra 2:62, Nehemiah 7:5). In the rabbinic work, Genesis Rabbah, a midrash or commentary on Genesis, it states that a geneaological scroll was found in Jerusalem that showed that Hillel descended from David, that R. Hiyya descended from Shephtaiah, that the house of Kalba Shabua came from Caleb, and so forth (Gen Rabbah 98.8). A tractate of the Mishnah (m. Yebamoth 4:13) reads: "R. Simeon ben Azzai said: I found a family register in Jerusalem and in it was written, 'Such-a-one is a bastard'. . . ." (trans. in H. Danby, *The Mishnah*).

Genealogies showed ones prominence according to family lineage. A statement in the Mishnah illustrates this:

> Ten family stocks came up from Babylon: the priestly, levitic, and Israelitish stocks, the impaired priestly stocks, the proselyte, freedman, bastard, and Nathin stocks, and the shetuki and asufi stocks (m. Kiddushin 4:1; trans. in Danby).

The Mishnah passage quoted above then proceeds to discuss which stocks or families can intermarry. Clearly then they kept track of lineage.

Finally, Josephus writes that he could trace his lineage. He is proudly giving his noble lineage in his biography when he adds: "With such a pedigree, which I cite as I find it recorded in the public registers, I can take leave of the would-be detractors of my family" (*Vita* 6; trans. in H. St. J. Thackeray, LCL). Thus Josephus mentions "public registers" which contain people's lineage.

Luke's and Matthew's genealogies are not identical. The names seem to match rather well early on (and they match rather well with the genealogy of 1 Chron; see Fitzmyer) but the closer they get to Jesus the more they diverge. This can be because of gaps in the generations. That is, evidently Matthew jumps from grandfather to grandson or even to great grandson. In the Old Testament they could refer to someone's grandfather or distant ancestor as his father (2 Sam 9:7, 2Kings 14:3)[4]. Matthew wants to make the genealogy equal a multiple of 7, a very Jewish thing to do since Jewish sources often favor the number 7 (see Mt 1:17).

The genealogies show that Jesus descended from Abraham and thus was a Jew; that Jesus descended from David and thus was in the royal line; and that (see Matthew's genealogy) four women of Gentile origin and perhaps suspect morally were in his family line. The latter is especially interesting. The only women in the genealogies (Tamar, Rahab, Ruth, and the wife of Uriah, i.e. Bathsheba) were Gentiles. Thus the Messiah also has Gentiles in his family. He is the Messiah for the whole world. In addition, the women at one time had questionable morals. They have become prototypes of the kind of people that Jesus will call to follow him: the tax collectors, prostitutes and other sinners.

The Visit of the Magi
(Aland 8, 10)

Bibliography: R. Brown, *The Birth of the Messiah*; W.D. Davies and D. Allison, *The Gospel According to St. Matthew*; G. Delling, "*magos*" in *TDNT*; A. Edersheim, *The Life and Times of Jesus the Messiah*; J. Finegan, *The Archaeology of the New Testament*; D. Hagner, *Matthew*; A.H. McNeile, *The Gospel According to St. Matthew*; M. Smith, *Jesus the Magician*

Joseph and Mary went to Bethlehem to be enrolled in the census and there Jesus was born in a stable because the inn was full. The Church of the Nativity has a fair chance of being the actual place where Jesus was born (Finegan). The grotto (now in the basement of the church) was revered for centuries before Constantine in the fourth century built a church over it. But if this is not the actual place where Jesus was born, it probably typifies the place.

Nearby the village of Bethlehem shepherds were watching their flocks when angels announced that the Messiah had been born. The shepherds subsequently walked to Bethlehem to see the child.

The date of Jesus' birth was probably sometime around 5 BC[5] since it was in the days of Herod the Great (Lk 1:5; Mt 2:1). Herod died in 4 BC apparently not too long after Jesus' birth.

At some point--a few days or a few months?--after Jesus' birth some wise men (Gk: magoi)--how many we do not know--came to Jerusalem to see who the new king of the Jews was. They had come from the east when they saw his star. The word *magos* (see Delling) can mean: a) a member of a special caste in Media, b) in general one who possesses supernatural knowledge, c) a practicer of the magical arts, or d) a quack/deceiver. The latter two definitions probably are out of the question in this context. The caste of magi in Media and Persia was a very strange group of priests and dream interpreters. For some reason they deemed it their duty to kill every living thing they could, except dogs and men (Herodotus, 1. 101, 132, 140; 7.37). Probably the second definition of *magos* is meant here. These were men who were considered knowledgeable through learning and some kind of religious experience.

Since the wise men or magi came from the east, many have supposed that they came from Babylon, though Media and Arabia have also been suggested. Babylon seems likely for two reasons. In the first place that locality was especially known for its study of astrology (the wise men had seen the star). Second, there was since the exile a considerable body of Jews in Babylon who could have informed these magi of Jewish hopes for a Messiah.

Although it may seem odd that magi would come so far to see an infant, similar events in antiquity demonstrate that their actions were not uncommon. In the first place we have an account in three different sources of one Tiridates from Armenia, who is called a magos by Pliny the Elder, who journeyed to Italy to pay homage to Nero. Dio Cassius even reports that Tiridates said to Nero: "I have come to thee my god, to worship thee as I do Mithras." (Dio 63.5, trans. in E. Cary, LCL; see also Pliny *Natural History*, 30. 14-17; and Suetonius, *Nero* 13). Of course Nero was a grown man and already the emperor of Rome not an infant in a stable in a tiny village of Judea. Further, Tiridates wanted to flatter Nero in order to get a kingdom from him.

Yet there does also seem to have been about this time rumors going around pagan circles that a king would come out of Judea. Suetonius reports concerning Vespasian's time (c. AD 69): "An ancient superstition was current in the East, that out of Judaea at this time would come the rulers of the world." (*Vespasian* 4; trans. in R. Graves). Tacitus (*History* 5.13) and Josephus (*War* 6. 312) also refer to this "superstition". How far this idea had spread we cannot know but it shows that there were reasons to be interested in a Jewish king.

We also cannot know what sort of star the wise men saw. There were some unusual alignments of stars and planets about this time (see Brown; Was it a comet? A supernova? A planetary conjunction? An entirely miraculous light? An angel?). We can know, however, the effect such cosmic signs had on the ancients. Tacitus (*Annals* 14.22) reports the coming of a comet for example, which signaled to people everywhere that there would be a new king: "At this time (c. AD 60) a comet blazed in the heavens, which popular opinion regards as betokening a change of kings." (trans. in D.R. Dudley). Similar astral phenomena were said to have appeared at the births of Mithridates IV (c. 120-63 BC) and Emperor Alexander Severus (reigned AD 222-235; see Davies and Allison). Thus virtually everything the wise men did can be shown to have been done by others.

Jewish sources also connect a star with the coming Messiah, mainly because of Numbers 24:17. Thus the Testament of Levi 18:3 says the Messiah's star will rise in heaven and the Damascus Document (CD 7:18-26) also interprets the passage in Numbers to refer to the Messiah. The reader should also recall (see Chapter 1) that Bar Kosiba changed his name to Bar Kochba (son of the star). Thus if the wise men came from Babylon with its large Jewish population, their interest in coming to Jerusalem the capital city of Judea to seek the new king of the Jews is even more understandable.

The wily and paranoid Herod could not of course tolerate any competitors for the throne. Did he believe the wise men and subsequently the Jewish scribes who quoted Micah 5:2 (Mt 2:6) to show where the Messiah would be born? At least he was ruthless enough to take no chances. Human life meant very little to him. He would order the slaughter of all infants that were anywhere near the age of this potential rival. Thereby he would assure himself that his heirs would maintain control of his kingdom after his death. Herod was, as Josephus informs us, suffering from a terrible disease at this time that would eventually end his life. He would soon be in great pain and discomfort and no remedy would bring him relief (*Antiquities* 17.168170). This illness seemed to make him even more ruthless. But he was always notoriously bloodthirsty. He had ordered already the murder of two of his sons (*Antiquities* 16.394) and would soon give the word to execute a third (*Antiquities* 17.187). He had in a fit of jealousy had his wife, the Hasmonean princess Mariamne, murdered (*Antiquities* 15.236). As he would in a few months lie dying, he would order that upon his death all the prominent officials of his kingdom be rounded up and executed so there would be great lamentation (*Antiquities* 17.174-179). To kill a few babies, then, would not bother Herod very much. Yet as in the days of Pharoah at the time of the Exodus, the will of a ruthless despot is thwarted by the power of God. The savior is rescued although Herod must have thought that surely he had been one of the infants killed.

The infancy narratives have a compelling verisimilitude.[6] They fit well with what we know of the ancient world and with what we know of the characters involved. The only question that remains is the census of Quirinius but we must await the discovery of further evidence. The accuracy of Luke elsewhere is convincing that he should be given the benefit of the doubt here.

The wise men were warned in a dream not to return to Herod with information as to the infant's whereabouts. Later Joseph is also warned to flee to Egypt which had become at that time a place of refuge for Jews. Soon after learning that Herod had died Joseph took his family and returned to Palestine to their former village of Nazareth. Jesus the new savior of Israel and of the world had retraced the steps of Israel's first salvation, that from Egypt. Therefore Matthew can apply the words of Hosea 11:1 to Christ: "Out of Egypt I have called my son."

Notes

1. The story is referred to also in the Gospel of the Hebrews (see Chapter 16), a text that some date in the first century.

2. On Luke's historical accuracy see the brief survey of scholars in D.A. Fiensy, *New Testament Introduction*, pp. 158-

3. Some manuscripts, however, give 76, some 78, and some 79 names.

4. Compare the book of Daniel that calls Belshazzar the son of Nebuchadnezzar (Dan 5:2) and the Black Obelisk of Shalmaneser (text in J.B. Pritchard, *Ancient Near Eastern Texts*) that refers to the Israelite Jehu as the son of Omri.

5. How can Jesus have been born in the fifth year Before Christ? The calendar has throughout the centuries had many corrections and changes. Denys le petit in the sixth century assigned two different eras to calendrical reckoning calling them "before Christ" and "in the year of our Lord". Denys calculated that Christ was born 753 years after Rome was founded. But today scholars would say that Christ was born from around 747 to 749 years after Rome was founded. Thus Christ was born in the BC era by our reckoning.

6. One is struck with the sober restraint of Matthew and Luke in describing Jesus' infancy. Compare the legendary exaggeration that gathers around the births of other religious leaders such as Buddha (see H. Smith, *Religions of Man*). The canonical Gospels even contrast strikingly with the Christian apocryphal gospels.

Chapter 6

The Youth of Jesus in the Light of Archaeology

Bibliography: R.A. Batey, *Jesus and the Forgotten City*; E.M. K. Beyer, *The Aramaic Language*; Blaiklock and R.K. Harrison, *The New International Dictionary of Biblical Archaeology*; G.W. Buchanan, "Jesus and the Upper Class" *Novum Testamentum* 7 (1964) 195-209; A. Burford, *Craftsmen in Greek and Roman Society*; S.J. Case, *Jesus, A New Biography*; V. Corbo, "Capernaum" in *ABD*; idem. *The House of St. Peter at Capernaum;* D.A. Fiensy, "Jesus' Socio-Economic Background" in J.H. Charlesworth, ed., *Hillel and Jesus;* idem., *The Social History of Palestine in the Herodian Period*; J. Finegan, *The Archeology of the New Testament*; R.C. Foster, *Studies in the Life of Christ*; Y. Hirschfeld, "Tiberias--Preview of Coming Attractions" *BAR* 17.2 (1991) 44-51; J.C.H. Laughlin, "Capernaum from Jesus' Time and After" *BAR* 19.5 (1993) 54-61; P.E. McGovern, "BethShan" in *ABD*; E.M. Meyers, E. Netzer, and C.L. Meyers, *Sepphoris*; idem. "Sepphoris, Ornament of All Galilee"*Biblical Archaeologist* 49.1 (1986) 4-19; E.M. Meyers and J.F. Strange, *Archaeology, the Rabbis and Early Christianity*; M. Nun, "Cast Your Net Upon the Waters" *BAR* 19.6 (1993) 46-61; J.A. Overman, "Who Were the First Urban Christians" *SBL 1988 Seminar Papers*, pp. 160-168; D.C. Pellett, "Nazareth" in *IDB*; J. Strange and H. Shanks, "Has the House Where Jesus Stayed in Capernaum been Found?" *BAR* VIII.6 (1982) 26-37; J. Strange, "Bethsaida" in *ABD*; idem., "Nazareth" in *ABD*; idem., "Sepphoris" in *ABD*; idem., "Tiberias" in *ABD*.

"And (Jesus) increased in wisdom, in stature, in favor with God and man"

(Lk 2:52).

What did Jesus do from his return to Nazareth as a toddler until he began his ministry? The apocryphal gospels (see chapter 16) are full of fantastic and ridiculous stories about Jesus that represent him as a kind of Superboy. He can use his powers to create toys for himself and to overcome his childhood playmates. Jesus and his playmates make clay animals which Jesus miraculously causes to fly, eat and drink. Jesus can correct Joseph's carpentry work miraculously when Joseph makes an object too large or too small. He is even alleged to have stricken children dead that annoyed him at play. These stories are more the imagination of an overly active mind (see Foster).

Jesus in the Temple at Age Twelve (Aland 12)

We have only one reference to the boyhood of Jesus and that is in Luke. There Jesus has gone with his family and other kinsmen from Nazareth to Jerusalem for the Passover. After the Passover his mother and father assume that Jesus is traveling with other relatives and do not discover until nightfall when they stop for sleeping that Jesus is not with anyone. They return to Jerusalem in a panic to look for their twelve year old son amid hundreds of thousands of pilgrims. After searching for three days, they find him in the temple listening to the scribes and asking them questions. His mother begins to reprimand Jesus, but Jesus answers: "Didn't you know that I have to be involved in the things of my father?" Meanwhile the "teachers", probably scribes, had become very impressed with Jesus' understanding of the Old Testament and other halacic and spiritual matters. He obviously seemed to them to be a very precocious child.

Many famous people in antiquity were said to have been precocious and to have amazed teachers at their brilliance. Josephus immodestly claimed this for himself (*Vita* 2). Cyrus the king of Persia was a prodigy (Herodotus, 1.114-115), as were Alexander the Great (Plutarch, *Alexander* 5) and Apollonius of Tyanna, the famous pagan teacher of morals and virtue (Philostratus, *Life of Apollonius* 1.7). The ancients were fascinated with child prodigies that became heroes or political leaders as adults.

Why did Jesus remain in the temple to ask so many profound questions of these scholars? Some interpreters have suggested that Jesus realized for the first time that he was the Messiah. Perhaps Mary told him during that Passover week about the events preceding his birth. Or perhaps he was normally curious and inquisitive anyway and the trip to Jerusalem along with seeing so many other Jews from many different lands, the temple, and the most brilliant scholars of Israel naturally excited his desire to learn.

But what did Jesus do back in Nazareth? What kind of life did he live ordinarily when he and his family were not traveling to feasts? We cannot know for sure but we can begin to get a good idea about the youth of Jesus by examining the ruins of the cities in Galilee. Let us then look briefly at what is known about the cities that would have been important to Jesus during his youth: Nazareth, of course, but also Sepphoris, Tiberias, Capernaum, and Magdala, cities in Lower Galilee.

Urbanization in northern Palestine

Nazareth was a small village probably with only about 480 people (Strange). The evidence from archaeology indicates that it was overwhelmingly engaged in agriculture. The village is just north of the Great Plain and thus close to the international trade route. It is 15 miles from the Sea of Galilee and 20 miles from the Mediterranean. It lies at an altitude of 1,300 feet above sea level. There is an ancient spring still to be viewed in the city today which is called the well of Mary and probably goes back to the time of Jesus. J. Finegan relates that archaeologists have found storage silos for grain, cisterns, olive presses and millstones from the time of Jesus. A great deal of pottery has been found there from the Roman period (63 BC-AD 323). Archaeologists have found also 23 Jewish style tombs.

Sepphoris was only around three miles from Nazareth. It revolted at the death of Herod the Great in 4 BC and was destroyed and burned to the ground. Herod Antipas, the son and successor of Herod the Great in the territory of Galilee, began immediately to rebuild the city. Evidently Antipas had his father's flair for building impressive cities for Josephus called Sepphoris "the ornament of all Galilee" (*Antiquities* 18.27). The city probably had around 50,000 inhabitants. It boasted a theater with a capacity of 3,000 people, Herod's palace, an upper and lower city with markets in each. Excavations have uncovered the theater, houses with magnificent mosaic floors and a large villa. According to Christian tradition Mary, Jesus' mother, came from Sepphoris.

Tiberias was also built by Antipas. He began construction around the year AD 20 and named the city in honor of the Roman emperor, Tiberius. The city is 15 miles to the east of Nazareth. Two miles north of Tiberias was the city of Magdala (also called Taricheae). One mile south of Tiberias were the famous hot springs (the Hammath). Antipas built a stadium, his palace, and a market. The city was probably about the same size as Sepphoris. It is mentioned in the Gospels at John 6:23.

Magdala did not begin in Jesus' life time but was apparently an older city. Yet it may have built important edifices during Jesus' youth. Magdala had its own athletic stadium. It had 40,000 inhabitants and was an important fishing center as its Greek name, Taricheae ("salted fish"), indicates. It was the home town of one of Jesus' most devoted followers, Mary Magdalene (Lk 6:2).

Capernaum was a fishing village of probably 1,000 people. Although it was not large, it was economically important since it was located on the crossroads of important trade routes and since it capitalized on the rich fishing available in the Sea of Galilee (see Nun). Capernaum was Jesus' base of operations during his ministry (Mt 4:13; Mk 2:1) where he taught in the synagogue (Lk 4:31-33, 38) and healed (Mt 8:5-13; Mk 1:21-26, 2:1-11; Jn 4:46-54). Archaeologists have found houses from Jesus' time. As a matter of fact some--especially V. Corbo--are convinced that they have found Peter's house since it was clearly a first century house that later became a meeting place for Christians and since graffiti on the wall may spell the name Peter. Not every one has accepted this evidence but it is at least plausible that one of the many houses discovered at Capernaum belonged to Peter and Andrew (Mk 1:29). In addition, a synagogue from the third or fourth century is still partly standing on the sight of Capernaum. The foundation of this synagogue may be from Jesus' era, however.

Bethsaida Julius was built by Philip, Herod the Great's son, who inherited the territories to the north east of the Sea of Galilee (see chapter 1). It had already existed before Philip's day but he enlarged its population and built in it among other buildings his own funeral monument. Excavating at this site is still underway. Excavators cannot yet tell how large this village was. Three of Jesus' disciples, Philip, Andrew, and Peter, came originally from this city (Jn 1:44). Here Jesus healed a blind man (Mk 8:22-26). Jesus condemned Bethsaida for unbelief (Mt 11:21).

Caesarea Philippi (to be distinguished from Caesarea Maritima or

Caesarea on the Sea) was also built up by Philip, although Herod the Great had already begun the process. Excavations are also in the beginning stages there but it appears that the city had a population of around 35,000. It was near here that Peter made his Good Confession: "You are the Christ, the son of the living God" (Mt 16:18).

The city of Scythopolis (called Beth-Shan in the Old Testament, Josh 17:11) was the only one of the Decapolis cities west of the Jordan river. It was predominately Gentile and covered some 240 acres. Its population, therefore, was probably about the same as that of Sepphoris and Tiberias, or around 50,000. Excavations have uncovered the streets from the Roman era, a theater, an amphitheatre (for viewing gladiatorial games), a hippodrome, a villa, and the city walls. Scythopolis, like Sepphoris, is never mentioned in the New Testament.

Lower Galilee, the tetrarchy of Philip, and the free city of Scythopolis then were very urban areas.

What language or languages did they speak in this area? Four languages played a major role in Palestine in the first century: Latin was the official language of the roman government. Greek was the universal language of the eastern Roman empire and the language of trade and business. Greek made significant inroads into the everyday life of Jews, especially Jews in Lower Galilee (where Nazareth was located; see Meyers and Strange). Hebrew was the academic language of the scribes and other scholars of the Old Testament as most of the Dead Sea Scrolls and the Mishnah indicate. But Aramaic--specifically "Jewish Old Palestinian Aramaic was the mother tongue (Beyer). Meyers and Strange affirm (p. 65): "Therefore, although Greek was becoming the *lingua franca* of the whole Near East, Aramaic continued both as a literary language and as the household language of most Jews." Although it is very likely that Jesus could speak Greek as a second language and possible that he debated with the scribes in Hebrew, he seems to have done most of his teaching in Aramaic (see Mk 5:41; 7:34; 14:36)..

Jesus as Carpenter

What kind of childhood would Jesus have had in this region? We need to take into account the fact that Jesus was a carpenter. Mark 6:3 quotes Jesus' home town crowd as saying of him,"Is not this the carpenter?" The parallel passage in Matthew (13:55) says,"Is not this the son of the carpenter?"

But Matthew's version is really saying the same thing as Mark's since virtually every craftsman in antiquity taught his craft to his son. Thus Jesus would have learned carpentry from his (adopted, earthly) father. Jesus came from the artisan class.

As a carpenter Jesus would have been skilled in fashioning wood products such as furniture, tools, agricultural implements, water wheels for irrigation, scaffolding for houses, and perhaps even ships. He would have known and used a wide assortment of tools, including axes, chisels, drills, saws, squares, hammers and plumb lines. His skills would have been not unlike those of carpenters of one hundred years ago.

But what sort of business would a carpenter in Galilee in the first century AD have done? The traditional concept is of a simple village carpenter who made mostly yokes and ploughs for the local peasantry but seldom if ever left the village.

The Greek historian Xenophon describes the work of a village carpenter and then compares it to the life of an artisan in a large city (evidently in a shoe factory). His text is pertinent enough for our inquiry to quote:

> For in the small cities the same people make chairs, doors, ploughs, and tables, and many times this same person even builds (houses) and he is contented if in such a way he can get enough employers to feed himself. It is impossible for a man skilled in many things to do all of them well. But in the big cities because many people need each trade, one skill can support a person. And many times (one needs) not even a complete skill, but one makes men's shoes, another women's (shoes). It is possible for someone to support himself by merely stitching shoes. One divides (the parts), another only cuts out shoe pieces, and another of these workers does nothing but putting the pieces together (Xenophon, *Cyropedia* 8.2.5, author's translation).

The differences between village artisans and city artisans could be great not only in terms of job description but also in terms of economic comfort. The traditional understanding of Jesus' background has usually been that of the small village artisan described by Xenophon. But did Jesus' skill as a carpenter ever take him out of the village and into the city where he learned about and participated in urban culture? If so could his urban employment have elevated somewhat his economic status? Was Jesus and his family a village woodworker or did they also work in the building trade?

Since S.J. Case an alternate view has existed regarding Jesus' background. Although Nazareth was probably indeed a small village, it stood only three or four miles from Sepphoris, one of the largest cities in Galilee. Case suggested that Jesus as a youth had worked in the reconstruction of Sepphoris and later on the construction of Tiberias. Sepphoris had been destroyed by the Romans in 4 BC and was then magnificently rebuilt by Antipas. Surely it would take many years to reconstruct a city such as Sepphoris, reasoned Case, and thus a carpenter's family could have found important and lucrative work there for a sustained period of time. R. Batey has more recently taken up Case's thesis, and supported it from his own experience in working on the excavation of Sepphoris.

That artisans in antiquity would travel from their home villages to work on large construction projects is well known. It is also quite plausible that Jesus and his family worked in other towns in Galilee, such as Tiberias, which began construction somewhere 20 AD and perhaps even in Jerusalem.

In the first place there are clear examples in the Mediterranean world of artisans' traveling to distant building sites. Building temples and other public works almost always required importing craftsmen from surrounding cities. There was in general a shortage of craftsmen in the building trades--carpenters, masons, sculptors--especially from the fourth century BC on. This shortage necessitated that craftsmen travel from city to city. A. Burford cites for example the case of the city of Epidauros in Greece which in order to build the temple of Asclepius (c. 370 BC) imported masons, carpenters, and sculptors from Argos, Corinth, Athens, Paros, Arcadia, and Troizen. Argos itself had to hire Athenian masons to complete its long walls in 418 BC. Athens also needed carpenters and masons from Megara and Thebes to rebuild its walls in the 390's BC.

This shortage of craftsmen was especially acute in the Roman period according to Burford. The cities of North Africa, Asia Minor, Persia and Palmyra imported craftsmen for their building projects with the local artisans contributing what they could. Burford affirms, "For unusual projects such as public works, no city, not even Athens had a sufficiently large skilled labor force to do the job by itself" (p. 63).

Since such was the case throughout the Mediterranean world, we should expect that in Palestine in the Herodian period artisans from surrounding cities and villages were used for large building projects. This expectation is confirmed by a passage in Josephus. Josephus relates that Herod the

Great (ruled 37 to 4 BC) made the following preparations to build his temple in 20 BC:

> He made ready 1000 wagons which would carry the stones. He gathered 10,000 of the most skillful workers. . . And he taught some to be masons and others to be carpenters." (*Antiquities* 15.390, author's translation)

Josephus' description of Herod's collection and training of carpenters and builders in preparation for building his temple implies there was a shortage of artisans in Jerusalem for this massive construction project. Furthermore, the temple was only completed in the procuratorship of Albinus (AD 62-64) which caused, Josephus reports, 18,000 artisans to be out of work (*Antiquities* 20.219f). Thus the temple required--though perhaps Josephus' figure is exaggerated somewhat--a large force of artisans throughout most of the first century AD.

The evidence from Josephus confirms that an extensive public works project like building the temple required recruiting and importing--and even training--artisans from distant cities and employing them over long periods of time. Surely the construction of Sepphoris, and Tiberias required a similar contribution of skilled labor. Given the urbanization of Lower Galilee--e.g. Sepphoris, Tiberias, Magdala, Capernaum, and Scythopolis--and also in the Tetrarchy of Philip--Caesarea Philippi, Bethsaida Julius--one can well imagine that an artisan in the building trade would be in demand. Since such was the case in the Greco-Roman world in general--causing artisans to move frequently from job to job--we should expect the same to have been true in Galilee. It is even possible that Jesus and his family worked on the temple in Jerusalem from time to time.

Batey's assertion that carpenters were necessary for construction of public works--erecting scaffolding, forms for vaults, cranes, and ceiling beams--also is confirmed not only by the examples from classical Greece listed above but also from Josephus. He celebrates the importance of carpenters for building Solomon's temple (*Antiquities* 7.66, 7.340, 7.377), Zerubbabel's temple (*Antiquities* 11.78), and Herod's temple (*Antiquities* 15.390). They also figure prominently in building city walls (*War* 3.173).

Therefore we can say with certainty that there were several continuous and massive building projects during Jesus' youth and early adulthood. Second, we can be reasonably confident that these projects would have necessitated the services of skilled carpenters, even from distant cities and villages. Jesus and his extended family could easily have worked in Sepphoris, Tiberias, in other Galilean cities, and even in Jerusalem. Opportunities were there for this family to have experienced urban culture and to have risen to a level of economic comfort.

Are there any indications in the Gospels that Jesus came from an upper level artisan family as opposed to a poor village artisan family?

Buchanan has noted that Jesus is found among well-to-do people rather often. He called to be his disciples James and John, sons of Zebedee, a fishing merchant who was wealthy enough to employ day laborers (Mk 1:19f). Levi, the tax collector, hosted a banquet for Jesus--in which they reclined at table, a mark of status and wealth--and became a disciple (Mt 9:9-11). A certain man "of the rulers of the Pharisees" invited Jesus to dine with him (Lk 14:1-6). Jairus, ruler of the synagogue at Capernaum and a certain unnamed Roman centurion approached him (Mk 5:22f, Mt. 8:5). Zaccheus, the chief tax collector, also gave a meal for Jesus (Lk 19:1-10). Lazarus (or Simon the leper) hosted a banquet for Jesus in Bethany (Mk 14:3; Jn 12:2). Joanna, the wife of a court official of Antipas, was a disciple of Jesus (Lk 8:3). Nicodemus, a member of the Sanhedrin, was a disciple of Jesus in secret (Jn 3:1f, 7:50, 19:39). Finally, Joseph of Arimathea, who buried Jesus' body and was a disciple is described as a member of the council and wealthy Mk 15:43; Mt 27:57).

That Jesus could so easily move among these wealthier people may suggest some experience in similar social situations and an earlier association with people of some economic means. Of course we should imagine the personality of the Son of God as drawing people to him both poor and rich. But it is also possible that some of these wealthy people knew Jesus before he began his ministry. It does not necessarily follow from these texts, however, that Jesus' family was therefore itself wealthy or members of the elite class. But an itinerant artisan who had experience in urban environments, working for wealthy patrons could easily have become familiar with such people.

Jesus was probably not economically destitute before his ministry. We should expect that he and his brothers worked at hard manual labor but did not want for the necessities of life. The massive building projects of Palestine, especially in Galilee, should have provided ample opportunity for work. It is even possible that his family was rather comfortable. Certain texts in the Gospels may incline us in that direction.

Did Jesus return to these urban centers after his ministry began to preach to them? We have hints that he did but did not spend much time there. He evidently preached in Magdala since Mary Magdalene became his disciple ((Mt 27:56, 61; Lk 8:2; Jn 19:25, 20:1,18). Further, Jesus apparently preached in Tiberias because Joanna, the wife of Chuza, one of Antipas' bureaucrats, became a disciple of Jesus (Lk 8:3). As an official of Antipas, Chuza and his family would have lived in Tiberias. Certainly Jesus preached and taught in Capernaum and Bethsaida as we noted above. There is no mention at all of Sepphoris, however. This omission is puzzling in light of the fact that this city lay closest to Nazareth (only 3 miles).

Yet the picture is fairly clear. Our Lord worked as an obedient son and loyal family member in the family business of carpentry. He would have traveled extensively throughout Galilee visiting the cities and towns that he later would minister to. His growth in stature and in favor with God and man was enhanced by his active travel and learning.

Chapter 7

John the Baptist, Jesus' Baptism and Temptation

The Life of John the Baptist

Bibliography: O. Betz, "Was John the Baptist an Essene?" *Bible Review* 6/6 (1990) 18-25; W.H. Brownlee, "John the Baptist in the New Light of Ancient Scrolls" in K. Stendahl, ed., *The Scrolls and the New Testament*; J. Danielou, *The Work of John the Baptist*; S.L. Davies, "John the Baptist and Essene Kashruth" *New Testament Studies* 29 (1983) 569-71; J. Ernst, *Johannes der Taeufer*; W.R. Farmer, "John the Baptist" in *IDB*; M. Goguel, *Au Seuil de L'Evangile Jean-Baptist*; P. Hollenbach, "John the Baptist" in *ABD*; C.H. Kraeling, *John the Baptist*; W.S. LaSor, "Discovering What Jewish Miqva'ot Can Tell Us About Christian Baptism" *BAR* 13/1 (1987) 52-59; J. Reumann, "The Quest for the Historical Baptist" in J. Reumann, ed., *Understanding the Sacred Text*; J.A.T. Robinson, "The Baptism of John and the Qumran Community: Testing a Hypothesis" *Harvard Theological Review* 50 (1957) 174-191; A. Schlatter, *Johannes der Taeufer*; C.H.H. Scobie, *John the Baptist*; J. Steinmann, *Saint John the Baptist and the Desert Tradition*; J. Thomas, *Le Mouvement Baptiste*; R.L. Webb, *John the Baptizer and Prophet*; W. Wink, *John the Baptist in the Gospel Tradition*.

The Sources

The main source for studying about John the Baptist is, of course, the New Testament. All four Gospels tell us something about his life and preaching. Mark and Matthew tell of his death.

Josephus also wrote of John the Baptist. His account will be quoted below at the appropriate points. Though he seems a bit muddled about baptism, Josephus nonetheless gives a report that harmonizes quite well with the New Testament.

A third source sometimes cited is the Mandaean literature. The Mandaeans are a quasi-Gnostic group that live in Iraq. Their literature was written in the eighth century AD but probably contains some old traditions. This group celebrates John the Baptist as a great prophet about the same way Muslims honor Mohammed. There are several statements scattered in their writings that parallel what our Gospels have to say about John. The value of these writings as sources for John's life and theology is dubious, however. They probably represent adaptations from the New Testament. Scobie gives a good summary of this literature.

John's Birth (Aland 2, 5)

Zechariah and Elizabeth were an elderly and godly couple that lived in the hill country of Judea (Lk 1:39), probably in a small village not far from Jerusalem. Zechariah was a priest and was serving his week in the Temple service (see Chapter 2) in Jerusalem when he was visited by the angel Gabriel who announced that his barren wife would have a son. Zechariah responded with doubt and the angel struck him dumb until the baby would be born. The angel declared that he must be named John and be raised like a Nazarite. That is, he could not drink wine (cf. Judges 13:1-5) like Samson. John's birth then was a miraculous one similar to those of Isaac and Samson in the Old Testament.

Elizabeth was somehow related to Mary the mother of Jesus (Lk 1:36) though in exactly what way we are not told. When Mary came to visit Elizabeth who was six months pregnant, the baby John within her womb leaped. As the angel said, he was filled with the Holy Spirit even in his mother's womb (Lk 1:15) and was already giving testimony about the Messiah.

When John was born, those who lived in their village wanted to name him Zechariah after his father but Elizabeth said his name would be John. After Zechariah confirmed her wish by writing the name, his speech came back to him and he uttered a hymn, the *Benedictus* (Lk 1:68-79). The story of John's birth ends with the unexpected statement: "And the child grew and became strong in spirit. And he was in the deserts until the day he became known to Israel" (Lk 1:80). Why would this son of a priest whose home village was in the Judean hill country have grown up in the desert?

An Essene Connection?

Many scholars (e.g. Betz, Robinson, Brownlee) have concluded that John's youth was in some way influenced by the Essenes of Qumran. Qumran is only a few miles from the Jericho area where John later stationed himself to preach and baptize. Qumran is in the Judean wilderness where Luke says John spent his childhood. The Qumran community was strongly associated with priests. Its founder, the so-called Teacher of Righteousness, was a priest and the literature of the Dead Sea Scrolls often refers to priests at Qumran. Thus a priestly family might have connections there. John preached (see Jn 1:23 and Aland 13) that he was the voice in the desert preparing the way of the Lord, a prophecy from Isaiah 40:3 as did the Qumran community (1QS 8:13-16). The Dead Sea Scrolls even mention eating locusts as suitable food (CD 12:14-15; cf. Mk 1:6). John's parents were already elderly when he was born (Lk 1:7) and therefore may have died while he was quite young. The Essenes often took in children to rear (*War* 2.120) so they could easily have given John a home at Qumran. His parents, though not Essenes themselves, may have admired the strict life style of the Essenes and asked for their son to be taken by this group when they saw their death approaching. They knew the Essenes drank no fermented wine and kept strict food laws and would thus rear their son as he was supposed to be reared (Mt 11:18; Lk 1:15). The hypothesis that John grew up at Qumran is certainly plausible.

Yet Betz's cautions are also worth noting. First John is never mentioned by the Dead Sea Scrolls. Second, John is never called an Essene either by the New Testament or by Josephus. Third, John had a great concern for the salvation of his fellow Jews. But the Essenes condemned all non-Essenes as sons of darkness and took an oath to hate them. They did not do missionary work.

Betz's suggestion is probably the best. John grew up in Essene circles, probably in Qumran (there were Essenes living other places besides Qumran). At some point he was called by God to be a prophet and left the Essene environment and repudiated many of their teachings. Thus John had the advantage of the strict moral upbringing of the Essenes and of the education in the Bible available at Qumran but he in the end went his own way--or rather we should say, he went the way the Lord led him.

His Dress and Diet (Aland 13)

John wore camel's hair clothing with a leather belt and ate (mostly? only?) locusts and honey. His clothes remind us of Elijah (1 Kings 1:8) and perhaps other prophets as well dressed this way in the Old Testament period (Zech 13:14). His food is the food of a desert man. Steinmann writes that the New Testament pictures John as a hermit living in the wilderness, dressed like the bedouin.

John's Message (Aland 13, 14, 15, 16)

John's preaching had two parts. First, he preached repentance and baptism for remission of sins. He was calling all Israel to repent and to submit to the purification of water immersion. Thus John believed by inspiration that Israelites were not saved merely by virtue of their being Israelites, as some Jews might have maintained. Nor did he believe that those that had not repented should be condemned and abandoned as the Essenes maintained. One must repent because the kingdom of God is near (Mt 3:2). Repentance is the only appropriate preparation for God's rule. So emphatic was John about repentance that once when people came to him wanting to be baptized, he refused until they demonstrated fruits of repentance. His stinging rebuke of these people ("You brood of vipers!") indicates the character of John's stern preaching and his stringent demands.

The second component of John's preaching was his messianic message. There is coming after John someone greater than he who will baptize not with water alone but with the Holy Spirit and fire. He is so much greater than John that John is not worthy to untie his sandals. John saw himself then as a forerunner. Jesus would later say that John was like Elijah, the one who must come before the Messiah (Malachi 4:5-6; Mt 11:14; 17:10-13) though John himself never understood this as far as we know (see Jn 1:21). The coming one, the Messiah, says John, will bring judgment.

John used an illustration for this: It is like when a person uses a winnowing fork to separate wheat from chaff. At harvest, they separate wheat and chaff on the threshing floor (a flat area) by treading on the grain. Then at the time of evening breezes they toss a few handsful of the wheat and chaff into the air with a winnowing fork or winnowing fan, an object like a tray. The wind blows away the chaff but the heavier wheat falls back to the winnowing fork. So the Messiah will separate the good from the bad.

John's ethics emphasized honesty and sharing with those less fortunate (Lk 3:10-14). Thus if one has two coats, he should give one of them to someone who has none and we should share our food.

We may here compare part of Josephus' account of John:

> But to some of the Jews the destruction of Herod's army seemed to be divine vengeance, and certainly a just vengeance, for his treatment of John, surnamed the Baptist. For Herod had put him to death, though he was a good man and had exhorted the Jews to lead righteous lives, to practice justice towards their fellows and piety towards God, and so doing to join in baptism. In his view this was a necessary preliminary if baptism was to be acceptable to God. They must not employ it to gain pardon for whatever sins they committed, but as a consecration of the body implying that the soul was already thoroughly cleansed by right behavior. When others too joined the crowds about him, because they were aroused to the highest degree by his sermons, Herod became alarmed. (*Antiquities* 18.116-117; Trans. In L.H. Feldman, LCL)

Josephus also emphasizes John's demand both for repentance ("he exhorted them to lead righteous lives" etc.) and baptism. Josephus also agrees with the Gospels that John was immensely popular with the multitudes (cf. Mk 1:5; Lk 3:7). Josephus writes about the crowds that, "they were aroused to the highest degree by his sermons." Thus the account of Josephus agrees substantially with the Gospels.

Baptism

John stationed himself for the most part at the fords of the Jordan (Mt

3:6), not far from where it joins the Dead Sea, and preached his message of repentance and baptism. He also preached and baptized at Bethany beyond the Jordan (Jn 1:28) and at Aenon near Salim (Jn 3:23).[1]

Why did John demand that people be immersed under water? The Gospels say it was for the remission of sins. Josephus' wording here is somewhat confused. He appears to have thought that John's baptism was little more than Jewish ritual immersion.

There were many Jewish antecedents to baptism. It would not have seemed very different to Jews at all. The Old Testament commanded ritual immersion when a person became unclean or impure in a cultic sense. One could become unclean due to touching unclean animals, by coming in contact with a corpse, through having a disease like leprosy, through menstruation or sexual intercourse (Lev 11-15; Num 19; Deut 23). One could become clean again--that is, able to go into the Temple or have a sacrifice offered for oneself--after a ritual immersion.

In this period ritual immersion on a regular basis became more and more popular. The Mishnah devotes an entire tractate to the subject (Mikvaoth or "baths"). Those who composed the Mishnah then were very scrupulous about how the ritual cleansing was done. The men of Qumran also practiced this ritual immersion (1QS 2:25-3:12, 5:7-20). The Dead Sea Scrolls refer to "water for impurity" (i.e. water for removing impurity) and "water of cleanness" which people who enter into God's covenant accept. In addition were all of those sects mentioned in Chapter 3 such as the Hemerobaptists that practiced daily ritual immersion for impurity.

Archaeologists have found numerous ritual bathing places or *mikvaoth* at Masada, Herodium, Qumran, Jericho and Jerusalem. Thus this practice was maintained even where there was not much water from natural sources (see LaSor).

Later there would develop a practice of baptizing proselytes to Judaism, that is, those Gentiles that converted to Judaism and were circumcised. Some scholars maintain that Jews practiced proselyte baptism already by this time. The sources for this practice, however, are all late first century and later.[2] Thus we cannot be sure that proselyte baptism was being done by John's time.

John's baptism had its parallels and similarities but it was not just another example of ritual bathing. John connected his baptism with remission of sins; he refused it to those that did not show fruits of genuine repentance; and it was part of his prophetic calling. He was called by God to proclaim his message and to baptize. What he did looked very Jewish but he was actually transforming ritual bathing into something new.

John's Death (Aland 144, 106)

Josephus records the death of John as follows:

> Herod became alarmed. Eloquence that had so great an effect on mankind might lead to some form of sedition, for it looked as if they would be guided by John in everything that they did. Herod decided therefore that it would be much better to strike first and be rid of him before his work led to an uprising, than to wait for an upheaval, get involved in a difficult situation and see his mistake. Though John, because of Herod's suspicions, was brought in chains to Machaerus, the stronghold that we have previously mentioned, and there put to death, yet the verdict of the Jews was that the destruction visited upon Herod's army was a vindication of John, since God saw fit to inflict such a blow on Herod (*Antiquities* 18. 118-119; Trans. In Feldman, LCL).

Josephus gives a political motive for Herod's execution of John. According to Josephus, Herod feared John's growing popularity. He might someday lead an uprising if left unchecked, reasoned Herod Antipas--a true son of Herod the Great!--and so he executed him to prevent what might happen some day.

John was held prisoner in one of Herod's fortresses, Machaerus, which is just east of the Dead Sea. From there John, who was evidently allowed communication with his disciples, sent word to Jesus who was now intensely involved in his ministry. John asked, "Are you the one who is to come or should we look for another?" (Lk 7:19). In other words, "Are you the Messiah?" Perhaps John's faith was wavering as he contemplated his death which he knew would come soon. John had witnessed the Holy Spirit descend on Jesus at his baptism (Jn 1:32) but now in such circumstances he wanted to be sure. At any rate, Jesus answered by both referring to his activities and by alluding to important Messianic prophesies: "Go and tell John what you have seen and heard: the blind see again, the lame walk, lepers are healed, the deaf hear, the dead are raised, the poor have the gospel preached to them" (Lk 7:22; cf. Isaiah 29:18-19, 35:5-6, 61:1-2).

Matthew and Mark have John dying because of more personal reasons. Antipas had abandoned his wife, the daughter of Aretas, king of Arabia.

In her place he had taken his niece, Herodias, the former wife of Herod Philip of Chalcis (see Table 1.2). John in his usual blunt manner denounced this sin. He feared no one, not even a king. Herod Antipas, however, was intimidated by John both because the people held John in such high esteem and because John's preaching and holy asceticism impressed him. Therefore, even though Herodias wanted John executed, Herod hesitated. The end for John came when Herodias' daughter, Salome, danced for Herod who was so pleased with this performance that he, in typical oriental fashion (and probably in a half-drunken state) made a lavish promise to her of anything up to half of his kingdom as reward.[3] Salome, coached by her mother, asked for John's head.

The accounts of Josephus and the Gospels tell of John's death from two different perspectives. But there is no reason to doubt the veracity of the Gospels' accounts. People usually do not do things out of only one motive. This is especially true of political figures. John was executed for several reasons. The one that tipped the scales of Herod Antipas' mind in favor of killing him was the request of Salome.

John had his own disciples who had been preaching alongside him and perhaps had gone out on their own missionary campaigns. Now these disciples came to claim his body for burial (Mt 14:12). So ended the life of a great man of God. The Gospels represent John as standing at the threshold of the kingdom of God. He marks the transition from Judaism to Christianity. As Jesus said: "The law and prophets were until John" (Lk 16:16).

Jesus' Baptism and Temptation (Aland 18, 20)

Bibliography: R. Brown, *The Gospel According to John*; W.D. Davies and D. Allison, *The Gospel According to St. Matthew*; J. Fitzmyer, *the Gospel According to Luke*; D. Hill, *The Gospel of Matthew*; W.L. Lane, *The Gospel According to Mark*; C.S. Mann, *Mark*; I.H. Marshall, *The Gospel of Luke*; A. Plummer, *The Gospel According to Luke*; E. Schweizer, *The Good News According to Mark*; idem., *The Good News According to Matthew*; V. Taylor, *The Gospel According to St. Mark*.

Jesus' Baptism

Large crowds were coming to John to be baptized. Both Josephus and the New Testament agree on this. At some point--probably in the year AD 28--a young man "about thirty years old" (Lk 3:23) also came to him for baptism. Why did Jesus come for baptism? In the Gospel of Matthew Jesus says that it is to fulfill all righteousness (Mt 3:15). Righteousness means doing the will of God (Mt 7:21), fulfilling the requirement of relationship with God. Jesus was baptized because he concluded that it was the will of God.[4] The first words Jesus spoke in the Gospels as an adult were words of obedience and submission to God.

Jesus has also come to the desert to reaffirm his spiritual commitment. John's baptizing in the desert would have meant, as Lane has aptly pointed out, a call of Israel to return to the wilderness as in the days of Moses. In those days the Israelites had to learn to trust completely in the Lord. Jesus has come to confirm his faith.

As Jesus was being baptized, the heavens were split or opened. God's revelation often was accompanied by such a heavenly sign (Ezek 1:1; Acts 7:56; Rev 11:19, 19:11). This was a moment then of great self-disclosure on the part of God.

In addition, as Jesus came up out of the water, the Holy Spirit descended on him like a dove. Was there an actual dove or is this only a simile to describe the gentle out-pouring of the Spirit? Luke's Gospel seems to indicate that there was an actual dove for he says it was "in bodily form." The dove as a symbol of the Spirit was known from the rabbinic literature (b. Hagigah 15a). There the hovering of the Spirit of God at creation (Gen 1:2) is said to be like the hovering of a dove. In addition, *bath qol* (literally: "daughter of a voice" or "echo") which is the usual designation in rabbinic literature for a heavenly voice, is sometimes said to be like the cooing of a dove (b. Beracoth 3a; see Davies and Allison).

Jesus' being anointed by the Holy Spirit is like the leaders of the Old Testament who were also set apart in such a way: Gideon (Judges 6:34), Samson (Judges 15:14), Saul (1 Sam 10:6). The prophets were also recipients of God's Spirit (Ezek 2:2; Isa 63:1) and they were called in a vision or audition to their ministries (Isa 6:9-10; Jer 1:5; Ezek 2:3). Jesus' experience also fulfilled the word of the Lord to King David: "I will be his father and he will be my son" (2 Sam 7:14). God affirmed at Jesus' baptism that he was his unique Son and therefore he was the King of Israel, the Messiah. Thus Jesus' baptism was also his call to prophetic activity and to Messiahship (cf. Isa 42:1).

Did Jesus know that he was the Messiah before his baptism? We cannot know of course what was in his mind. But at least at that moment he learned it. Perhaps he only up until then had felt a strong urgency to serve God in some fashion. He was coming to John the Baptist, the famous prophet, to begin that service. But his baptism showed him that he was to do far more than he had ever imagined. It is possible in other words that God gradually unfolded to Jesus who he was and what his mission was.

The Temptation

Immediately after Jesus' baptism, the Spirit led Jesus (Mark's Gospel makes the language sharper: "The Spirit drove him") farther into the wilderness. Compare the Spirit's leading and carrying prophets in the Old Testament (1 Kings 18:12; 2 Kings 2:16; Ezek 3:12, 14-15, 8:3, 11:24). There Jesus was tempted for 40 days. 40 as a period of testing is a common Old Testament length. The Israelites were tested for 40 years in the wilderness (Deut 8:2). Moses was on Mt. Sinai for 40 days during which time the Israelites were required to wait patiently (Ex 24:18, 34:28). 40 days were also the length of Elijah's flight in the wilderness from Jezebel (1 Kings 19:8).

Matthew's order of the temptations are somewhat different from Luke's. Temptation's two and three are reversed in Luke. Fitzmyer is probably correct when he speculates that Luke changed the order so the temptations could end in Jerusalem. This is geographical symbolism. This makes the temptation a foreshadowing of Jesus' crucifixion in Jerusalem some three years later.

The devil begins his temptation with the taunting words, "If you are the Son of God. . . ." He then refers to the baptism and Jesus' life-changing vision of God's purpose for his life. Now the devil seeks to exploit that experience.

The three temptations are as follows:

1. Use God for your own comfort. Attempt to manipulate God for your convenience ("Turn stones into bread").

2. Make a show of your religiosity. Be popular by doing great wonders ("Cast yourself down"). The devil even quotes scripture here in an attempt to look religious himself.

3. Gain the world--the Messiah's objective--by using the methods of Satan. Surrender your commitment to God and instead commit yourself

to Satan ("Fall down and worship me").

To each of these temptations Jesus replies by quoting from Deuteronomy (8:3, 6:16 and 6:13). These texts refer to Israel" testing in the wilderness. They look back to the exodus and wilderness wandering. On the one hand, Israel often did fail in precisely these areas. But Jesus stood fast.

Jesus would have discussed these temptations with his disciples perhaps on several occasions. Of course Jesus was tempted with many other temptations both in the desert and later. We should not assume that this was the only time Satan tempted him and that he used only these three temptations. But these three were especially difficult for Jesus. They are aimed precisely at his Messiahship. Thus he probably recalled especially these in his recounting the episode of his 40 days of intense testing in the desert.

Fyodor Dostoyevski's *The Brother's Karamazov* has a penetrating chapter in which these three temptations are examined. Dostoyevski maintained that history has witnessed that the church has often itself succumbed to one or more of these temptations. They therefore must be reflected upon not just as a bit of personal history in the life of Jesus but as painful reminders of how we, Jesus' disciples, have failed.

Notes

1. For Bethany beyond the Jordan, see J. Finegan, *Archaeology of the New Testament*, p. 9 who thinks the manuscript reading "Bethabara" is correct here instead of "Bethany." Bethabara is just east of the Jordan river and just above the Dead Sea. For Aenon near Salim see Finegan, pp. 12-13. Finegan places Aenon eight miles south of Scythopolis. See also Y. Aharoni and M. Avi-Yona, *the Macmillan Bible Atlas*, map 227.

2. See Epictetus, *Dissertations* 2.9; b. Yebamoth 47; and Gerim (an "extra-canonical" tractate of the Talmud dating AD 1300). See Scobie.

3. For another example of a lavish promise made by an oriental monarch, see Xenophon, *Anabasis* 1.7.18. Cyrus promised a certain seer that if his prediction came true, he would pay him ten talents of gold, a sizeable sum.

4. How does one refer to the relationship between Jesus and the Father? While Jesus as the eternal Word and Son of God was truly God, he was also truly man. As man, he was subservient to the will of the Father. Also as man he limited himself in knowledge (Mt 24:36).

John the Baptist

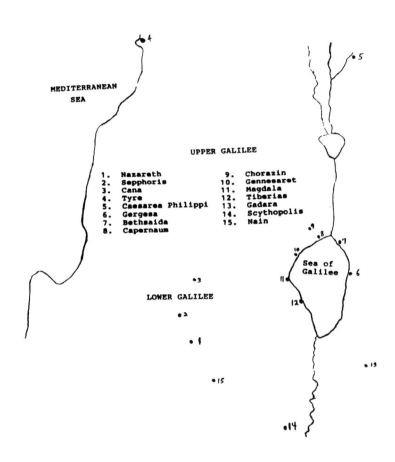

Map 8.1
Galilee

Chapter 8

The Galilean Ministry

Bibliography: R. Brown, *The Gospel According to John*; W.D. Davies and D. Allison, *The Gospel According to St. Matthew*; R. Gundry, *Matthew*; J. Fitzmyer, *The Gospel According to Luke*; R.C. Foster, *Studies in the Life of Christ*; D. Hill, *The Gospel of Matthew*; J. Jeremias, *New Testament Theology*; G.E. Ladd, *Jesus and the Kingdom*; W.L. Lane, *The Gospel According to Mark*; J. Lightfoot, *Commentary on the New Testament from the Talmud and Hebraica*; C.S. Mann, *Mark*; T.W. Manson, *The Teachings of Jesus*; I.H. Marshall, *The Gospel of Luke*; N. Perrin, *What is Redaction Criticism?*; A. Plummer, *The Gospel According to Luke*; E. Schweizer, *The Good News According to Mark*; idem., *The Good News According to Matthew*; V. Taylor, *The Gospel According to St. Mark*; B. Y. Young, *Jesus the Jewish Theologian*.

After Jesus' baptism and temptation, Jesus returned to the area where John was baptizing. There John gave witness that he had seen the Holy Spirit descend on Jesus and that he was the Lamb of God that takes away the sins of the world (Jn 1:29-36) and therefore some of John's disciples began to follow Jesus (Jn 1:37-51). But then Jesus decided to begin his own ministry and so departed for Galilee, taking some of his disciples with him (Jn 1:43; Mt 4:12; Lk 4:14; and Aland 30). Matthew and Mark indicate that Jesus went to Galilee shortly after John the Baptist was arrested and imprisoned. There in Galilee Jesus would begin his ministry though he would make several evangelistic trips to Judea (see Chapter 13).

Cana of Galilee (Aland 22)

Jesus probably returned to his home village to see his family. Then he went to a marriage feast in the tiny village of Cana (see Map 8.1). This action stands in stark contrast to John the Baptist. John was well known as an ascetic loner. For him to attend such a banquet would have been unheard of. As Jesus said, "John came neither eating (ordinary food) or drinking (wine)" (Mt 11:18). Jesus did, however, dine on ordinary food and even at banquets and he drank wine.

Was this the wedding of a relative of Jesus? We assume so but John's Gospel does not inform us. Jesus' mother, Mary, is also present which supports the view that this is a relative's wedding.

At some point the wine ran out and Mary quietly informed Jesus of the host's embarrassment. Jesus' response seems to our ears to be impolite ("Woman, what is that to me and you?"). The expression is common in the Hebrew of the Old Testament (e.g. 2 Kings 3:13) and means nothing more than, "That is not our concern."

Jesus' reference to his hour not having yet come (v. 4) introduces us to one of the common Johannine terms. In the Gospel of John the term hour means the time of his self-revelation, especially by the cross (12:23, 27; 13:1; 16:32; 17:1). Here it means he has not yet begun his ministry.

Jesus commanded the large jars to be filled with water and when they poured out the water, it had become wine. This was his first miracle (Jn 2:11) and the beginning of his self-disclosure and ministry. John again uses a favorite term: "He manifested his *glory*" (see 1:14; 5:41; 8:50; 11:40; 17:5), that is, he began to make his divine origin known.

Capernaum (Aland 23, 32, 35, 43, 46, 47, 116, 117, 118, 121, 119, 150)

Jesus' Teaching on the Kingdom of God

Jesus soon after the wedding at Cana traveled to Capernaum where he began his preaching ministry in earnest (Jn 2:12; Mt 4:13; Lk 4:31). This fishing town of about 2000 people will be his main base during the Galilean Ministry (see Chapter 6). He immediately began to preach: "Repent for the kingdom of God[1] has come near" (Mt 4:17).

The central theme of Jesus' preaching was the kingdom of God. The kingdom of God (Greek: *basileia theou*; Aramaic: *malkutha d'elaha*) as an expression and concept appeared in ancient Judaism as well but not to the extent that Jesus used it. Jesus' message is summarized also in Mark (1:15), Matthew (4:23), and Luke (4:43). Many of the parables begin: "The kingdom is like. . ." (E.g. Mk 4:26, 30). Finally, the word kingdom appears in many sayings and teachings.

The Aramaic word *malkutha* did not, as Jeremias explained, mean the same to the oriental that kingdom means to the westerner. For westerners, kingdom denotes a territory or spatial area over which a king rules. But in the Old Testament and later Judaism (see Manson) *malkuth* (Hebrew) or *malkutha* (Aramaic) meant the authority and power of the king which is always in process of being realized. Thus the concept is dynamic. That is, it describes action such as God's defending the poor or saving his people.

Jesus taught that God's reign was both present and would be manifested in the future in a final and all-encompassing way (see Ladd). Jesus clearly indicated that the kingdom was already present when he said (Mt 11:12): "From the days of John the Baptist until now the kingdom of Heaven (=God's reign) has been making its way with triumphant force." Compare Luke 11:20 and especially Luke 17:21, "They will not say, 'Look here!' or 'There!' for the kingdom of God is within you (God is reigning in your midst)."

On the other hand, Jesus also clearly taught that the kingdom was yet to come. Thus he says in his model prayer, "May your kingdom come" (Mt 6:10). He is especially clear when in talking about his second coming and the consummation of the age, he says, "There will be weeping and gnashing of teeth when you see Abraham, Isaac and Jacob in the kingdom of God (=in the sphere of God's reign) and you are cast outside" (Lk 13:28). Certainly if the three patriarchs are present, the general resurrection and the end of the age have come.

Entering the kingdom of God meant submitting to God's rule or entering the sphere of his rule. Jesus taught that nothing was more important in life than the kingdom. In the parables of the Pearl of Great Price and the Treasure Hidden in the Field (Mt 13:44-46) Jesus explained that the kingdom is worth the most priceless treasure. In the sermon on the Mount, Jesus admonished his disciples, "But seek first the kingdom and its righteousness" (Mt 6:23), that is, "Seek above all to submit to God's rule." Nothing must prevent ones commitment to the kingdom of God. That is why Jesus told the rich young ruler to sell all his possessions (Mk 10:17-22). We must be ready to give up everything, even our own lives if necessary for the kingdom (Lk 14:26).[2]

God in Jesus' teaching then is the king, the sovereign ruler of the universe. But God is no remote potentate. As Ladd notes, God seeks out sinners (Lk 15) and invites them to salvation which Jesus often pictures as a great banquet (e.g. Mt 22:1-14). It was Jesus' mission to issue God's invitation to his banquet of joy and celebration. Thus God as king does not withdraw into the corner of the universe and demand that men and women submit to his rule but he seeks them out and invites them to know the joy of his banquet.

But God is also the end-time or eschatological judge. For those who reject his loving invitation, there awaits everlasting punishment (Mt 25:41). Thus the decision one makes about the kingdom or rule of God determines ones destiny.

Controversies in Capernaum
(Aland 43, 46, 47, 150)

Jesus' teaching and healing in Capernaum did not go unchallenged. Most of his debates are over halacah, that is, proper observance of legal regulations such as washing the hands and keeping the Sabbath. The first controversy, however, (Aland 43) concerns Jesus' authority to forgive sins. This event scandalized the scribes and probably began a concerted effort on the part of some to discredit Jesus.

The scene is Peter's house in Capernaum. If indeed this house has been discovered,[3] it was a simple house of wadi stones with a stick roof. Into this small one room house were gathered many people with many more outside listening at the door. Why were so many people in the house? Perhaps it was winter and it was raining. At any rate, four men brought to Jesus a paralyzed man hoping that Jesus would heal him. When the crowd proved too great to get through to Jesus, they climbed up on the roof, detached some of it and lowered the man down by ropes. Jesus responded to the lame man by saying, "Your sins are forgiven." The scribes cried, "Blasphemy! Only God can forgive sins." Only then did

Jesus heal the afflicted man: "In order that you may know that the Son of man has authority on the earth to forgive sins. . . Get up, pick up your bed and go to your house" (Mt 9:6-7).

The second and third controversies (Aland 46 and 47) concern the Sabbath. Jesus and his disciples were walking through the grainfields on the Sabbath and out of hunger began picking the grain and eating it. The Old Testament provided for travelers and the poor to pick some of a person's grain for a snack (Deut 23:25). Thus this was not considered stealing though one could not of course harvest large amounts. The real legal or halacic problem was that one was not supposed to labor on the Sabbath. Exodus 34:21 forbids harvesting (*qatsir*) on the Sabbath. More specifically the Mishnah lists 39 prohibitions to be observed on the Sabbath:

> The main classes of work are forty save one: sowing, ploughing, reaping (Hebrew: *qotser*), binding sheaves, threshing, winnowing, cleansing crops, grinding, sifting, kneading, baking, shearing wool, washing or beating or dyeing it, spinning, weaving, making two loops, weaving two threads, separating two threads, tying (a knot), loosening (a knot), sewing two stitches, tearing in order to sew two stitches, hunting a gazelle, slaughtering or flaying or salting it or curing its skin, scraping it or cutting it up, writing two letters, erasing in order to write two letters, building, pulling down, putting out a fire, lighting a fire, striking with a hammer and taking out aught from one domain into another. (m. Shabbath 7:2; Trans. in Danby)

Thus the Pharisees were referring to the Old Testament and the prohibition of the oral tradition (that later was written in the Mishnah) in their condemnation of Jesus' plucking grain on the Sabbath. The difference between them is the Pharisees interpret *qatsar* as even plucking a few heads of grain for a snack but Jesus interpreted it as harvesting a field.

Jesus replied in a very rabbinic fashion, using the interpretive technique known as *qal vehomer* or from lesser to greater. If something is true of a lesser case, it surely is true of a greater case. Thus Jesus reminds the Pharisees that king David ate the bread of presence or shewbread (reserved for the priests only) in the tabernacle once[4] when he was hungry and, further, the priests do work in the Temple on the Sabbath. Both of these cases contravene Old Testament commands. They are necessary, however. If these people may do it (the lesser case), then surely the Son of man (the greater case) may do it for the Son of man is Lord of the

Sabbath.

The same kind of argument is used in the controversy over healing on the Sabbath (Aland 47). Jesus again argues *qal vehomer* to prove that it is lawful to help a sick man on the Sabbath.

But the impression that one gets from these texts is that Jesus did not consider Sabbath laws that which must be meticulously and scrupulously kept. He tended more toward the spirit of the law. His interpretation of the Old Testament, however, greatly angered the Pharisees who began to plot ways of discrediting him (Mt 12:14), even joining with adherents of the Herodian family (Mk 3:6).

The last controversy we will discuss (Aland 150) concerns another halacic topic: washing of the hands to remove ritual uncleanness. There is even an entire tractate devoted to it called Yadaim ("hands"). Hands could become unclean by touching anything in a house of a leper, from touching any of the scrolls containing the Old Testament and from handling unclean food (see m. Yadaim and Lightfoot). Allegedly Hillel and Shammai, the great sages of the first century BC, decreed the rules about washing hands (j. Shabbath 3:4). Although these rules are not in the Old Testament, one rabbinic sage was excommunicated from the group for casting doubt on the teaching about washing hands (m. Eduyoth 5:6). Thus, although the rules are not in the Old Testament, the sages valued them highly. The rules further stipulate how much water is required for each stage of uncleanness and how one is to pour the water over the hands (see m. Yadaim).

Jesus responds to the criticism that he does not ritually wash his hands with more than his usual rabbinic argumentation. He points out that the scribal loyalty to Pharisaic halacoth could potentially lead to contravening the Old Testament commandment to honor father and mother. One could hypothetically make a vow to declare his property *korban*, that is, a gift or offering to God (Mk 7:11). Korban is a Hebrew and an Aramaic term used commonly (see m. Maaser Sheni 4:10; m. Nedarim 1:2, 3, 4; m. Nazir 2:1, 2, 3; *Antiquities* 4.73; *Apion* 1.22)[5] in reference to a gift set aside for purely religious purposes. If a son declared his property korban to his parents, he would not necessarily give it to the Temple nor prohibit himself from using it but he would deprive his parents from it. If later he regretted his decision (see Lane) and desired to help his parents from his property, the scribes would have told him that he must honor his vow. Such was the legal thinking of the scribes. But in so doing they disobeyed the spirit of the law.

Finally, Jesus gives his view of the rules of ritual purity. Food, whether clean or unclean, merely becomes after it is eaten whether it is clean or not. What does make a difference is what is in ones heart. Evil thoughts defile a person morally; unclean hands and food defile one only in a ritual sense. Thus Jesus had also little use for laws of ritual purity, at least as they were interpreted by the Pharisees.

Opposition to Jesus' Ministry (Aland 116, 121, 117-118, 119)

Jesus, it has been said, was either liar, lunatic or Lord. Moderns are not the first to observe this. Those who knew Jesus had various opinions also. His own family at first thought he was crazy (Mk 3:19-20; 31-35; cf. Jn 10:20). John's Gospel informs us that Jesus' brothers (James, Joseph, Judas and Simon; (Mk 6:3) did not believe in him at first (Jn 7:5). They came to Capernaum and attempted to bring him home to remove a seeming embarrassment.

But the greatest opposition came from certain of the Pharisees. Some of them demanded a cosmic sign that Jesus was truly from God (Aland 119). Moses had done many wonders in Egypt and in the wilderness. Elijah and Elisha had also done their great and miraculous deeds. People would occasionally, especially in times of crisis, report having seen such things (*War* 6. 288-299) as war chariots in the sky or a sword-shaped star. Apocalyptic works often refer to cosmic signs that will accompany the end of the age (4 Ezra 4:51-5:13). The false prophets, Theudas and the Egyptian, promised their followers that they would part the Jordan river as Joshua had done and make the walls of Jerusalem fall as at Jericho (*Antiquities* 20. 97-98, 169-171). Now the Pharisees wanted such confirmation from Jesus.

Jesus responded to them that such a demand is carnal and unbelieving to begin with. The signs of the Old Testament did not assure that the Israelites would have faith. They could witness the parting of the Red Sea and then make a golden calf. An evil and adulterous people demand that God meet their expectations of what it means to reveal himself to them. The only sign he offered was his own death-resurrection, that is, the sign of Jonah who was a prototype of Christ in that he was "entombed" in a great fish for three days.

Far worse was the opposition that came from others of the Pharisees. All four Gospels report that Jesus was accused of performing miracles by the power of the devil (Aland 117). This charge was obviously an attempt to discredit Jesus. We must not think that all Pharisees were in on such a plot. There were around 6000 members of the Pharisaic party according to Josephus and probably no two of them were exactly alike.

Such a charge is of course a tacit admission that Jesus did perform miracles. There were no charges that his miracles were faked. If you have an enemy that is obviously doing miracles what else can you say?

Jesus gave four answers: First, it is absurd to suppose that Satan would empower someone to cast out demons. He would be opposing himself. That would be a house divided against itself. Second, if Jesus casts out demons by the power of the devil, how do other Jewish exorcists do it? That there were other Jewish exorcists in antiquity is well known (see *Antiquities* 8.46-47; cf. Testament of Solomon in *OTP*). Do the Pharisees condemn also "their sons" (i.e. other Jews)? If not, this is of the Spirit of God and thus the kingdom of God has come upon them. Third, Jesus told a parable about a robber (=Jesus) having to bind a strong man (=Satan) before he could plunder his house (=cast out demons). Finally, Jesus warned that the Pharisees were dangerously close to committing the blasphemy of the Holy Spirit. What is blasphemy of the Holy Spirit? Most would see this as a spiritual state brought about by repeated hostility toward God. This is not a statement made in anger or even rejection of the gospel. This state is a willful perversion of the Spirit which defiantly calls light, darkness. The soul thus raises a permanent barrier between it and God (see Taylor).

Thus Jesus' ministry in Capernaum had its opposition. Yet it had its victories to and to these we now turn.

Jesus Calls Disciples
(Aland 21, 34, 44, 49, 89)

Jesus had begun to collect a group of disciples about him while he was still in the company of John the Baptist (Jn 1:37-51). In the area of Bethany beyond the Jordan he called Peter, Andrew, Philip and Nathaniel. Then in Galilee in the Capernaum area Jesus again summoned Peter and Andrew to follow him in his ministry and added James and John, the sons of Zebedee, to be disciples. Later he called Levi (or Matthew) the tax collector, a move that angered his critics. At some point Jesus had twelve disciples (Aland 49) though the names of these disciples do not always seem to match. Thaddaeus, for example, is only listed by Matthew and Mark. It seems likely that Jesus intentionally kept in his circle twelve specially appointed assistants and students (or disciples) but some of his disciples did not remain with him throughout the entire three year ministry. These would have been replaced then by others.

We even have some examples of disciples that turned back and gave up their commitment to follow Jesus in a special way. Jesus encountered someone who promised him he would follow him anywhere (Aland 89) to which Jesus responded that unlike foxes and birds he had nowhere even to lay his head at night. Someone promised to follow him after he had buried his dead relative and Jesus said, "Leave the (spiritually) dead to bury their own (physically) dead" (Mt 8:22). The shock of such a statement to a pious Jew must have been severe because burying the dead was considered especially an act of piety.[6] Jesus' point was that not even pious acts must take precedence over service to the kingdom of God. Another would-be follower wanted first to bid his family good-bye but Jesus forbade it. These examples not only indicate that some disciples probably did not stick it out but also that Jesus attracted large numbers of people that wanted to be in his company and learn from him. He was a popular master or teacher.

While many sought out Jesus, he also sought out people as we saw in some of the cases above. Such an action was probably rare. At least in the Talmud it is usually the student that implores the master to instruct him ("Rabban Gamaliel used to say, 'Make for yourself a master/teacher.'" m. Aboth 1:17). That Jesus sought out his disciples, mirrors God the seeking father who calls back the wayward and seeks out the sinner. Jesus would not have merely waited for his students to come to him.

Jesus' Popularity
(Aland 35, 38)

Large crowds thronged about Jesus both to hear him teach and to bring relatives and friends for healing. He must have been enormously popular and famous in this area in spite of strong opposition from some quarters. Capernaum was in the main a place of success for his ministry.

Other Locations About the Sea of Galilee
(Aland 108, 115, 148)

We should conceive of Jesus' ministry in Galilee as primarily in the Sea of Galilee basin. He used Capernaum as his base and traveled often to locations on or near the sea. Travel by ship would have made these forays very easy and convenient. Evidently Jesus preached repeatedly in the towns of Chorazin and Bethsaida (Mt 11:20-24). They are mentioned in the same context as Capernaum and all three are upbraided for their general unbelief.

In addition, Jesus must have preached in the city of Magdala for Mary Magdalene (i.e. Mary from Magdala) was one of his most important female disciples (Lk 8:2; Mt 27:56; Jn 20:11-18). Jesus also preached in Tiberias as we know from another female disciple, Joanna, wife of Chuza an administrator in the government of Herod Antipas (Lk 8:3; 24:10). Since Tiberias was the capital of Galilee, Chuza and Joanna would have lived there. Finally, Jesus performed healings at Gennesaret, on the northeast coast of the sea. Thus he frequently sailed to the cities and towns around the sea in order to conduct evangelistic campaigns.

The Galilean Campaign(s)
(Aland 33, 39, 40, 86, 98, 99)

At some point in his stay at Capernaum, Jesus initiated a tour of Galilean villages in order to teach and heal. We possibly should even think of more than one campaign such as this. At any rate, we know of two of the villages he visited: Nain and Nazareth. Nain lay in the Great Plain or Valley of Esdraelon. As Jesus was entering the village, he encountered a funeral procession. He commanded the dead young man to get up from the bier and thus raised him from the dead. This is one of three times in which Jesus raised people from the dead (the other two are Jairus' daughter, Aland 95; and Lazarus, Aland 259).

Jesus' visit in Nazareth should have been characterized by jubilation and celebration for the growing popularity of their kinsman and neighbor. But this was not the case. Scholars are divided on whether Luke records a second visit to Nazareth after Jesus began his ministry or whether it is the same as the visit recorded by Matthew and Mark. There are some differences in the narratives but the three Gospels seem to this author to refer to the same event. Jesus entered the synagogue on the Sabbath and both read the scripture texts--there would have been readings from the

Law and from the prophets--and preached to them. At a later date, the readings were determined by a yearly cycle but we cannot be certain that this practice was in place in the first century. If so, then the prophet's reading of the day was providentially arranged by God for it was a Messianic prophecy. If not, then Jesus himself chose the text. The text was from Isaiah 61:1-2 (we are not told what the reading from the Law was). Jesus said that he was the fulfillment of this prophecy whereupon the hometown crowd was offended that a carpenter would try to teach them and almost killed him in a lynching action. Jesus, however, miraculously passed between the people in the lynch mob and went away marveling at their unbelief.

Probably toward the end of his preaching tour or possibly at one of those periods in which he was residing in Capernaum, Jesus sent out his disciples on their own evangelistic campaign (Aland 99). He gave them power over demons, told them to travel lightly relying on the providence of God and the generosity of he people to whom they preach and instructed them not to go among the Gentiles.

Jesus' Tour Among Gentile Cities (Aland 137, 151, 158-160)

At some point also Jesus made journeys into certain Gentile cities. He seems always to have envisioned a Gentile mission for his followers although he primarily himself preached to Jews. Yet we must not overlook the fact that he did minister to non-Jews. Jesus healed a demon possessed man near the city of Gergesa,[7] a Gentile area in which pigs were raised. He further made a trip into the area of Tyre and Sidon where he healed a demon possessed girl. Jesus even commended the faith of the little girl's mother.

The most significant trip was the one to Caesarea Philippi, the capital city of Philip's tetrarchy. It is now impossible to know at what point in Jesus' ministry this trip took place. The Gospels do not usually show concern for precise chronological information. At any rate, Jesus and his close disciples were journeying toward this city when Jesus asked them who people were saying he was. They replied that there were various opinions about him. Some thought he was John the Baptist resurrected; others thought he was Elijah who would come at the end-time; still others thought he was Jeremiah or one of the other prophets of old resurrected. When Jesus asked, "But who do you say I am?", Peter replied, "You are the Messiah."

Matthew alone records Jesus' response to Peter's confession. Jesus praised Peter's answer as coming not from flesh and blood but from God. Then Jesus says, "You are Peter and on this rock I will build my church" (Mt 16:18). What is the rock upon which Jesus will build his church? 1) The Catholic church says the rock was Peter himself. 2. Most Protestants maintain that the rock is the confession Peter made or Jesus himself who is confessed. 3) Gundry maintains that the rock (see Mt 7:24) is the words of Jesus. Which is correct? There seems to be a play on words. Jesus says, "You are *Petros* (a small stone) and on this *petra* (huge cliff) I will build my church." Thus Peter's confession is one small part of the millennia of confessing Christians. Yet there is also a certain sense in which the Catholic church was correct. Peter and the rest of the apostles as the first confessors of Christ are themselves foundational. It is really impossible to separate the two: the confession itself and the confessor. Both Catholics and Protestants should recognize the contribution of the other's position.

Next Jesus promised that he would give to Peter the keys of the kingdom of Heaven. "Whatever you bind on earth will have been bound in heaven, and whatever you loose on earth will have been loosed in heaven" (Mt 16:19). What is this binding and loosing? 1) Some think this refers to a declaration of what is sin and what is not sin and is similar to the rabbinic judgments about clean and unclean.[8] 2) Most think that Jesus was giving Peter (and the apostles) power to forgive and retain sin. Which is correct? First of all we should note that Jesus says the same thing to the apostles as a whole in Matthew 18:18 for there the verbs are in the plural. Thus this privilege was not for Peter only. Second, we should compare this passage with one in John's Gospel (20:23) in which Jesus tells his disciples--again using plural verbs--"The sins of anyone you forgive will be forgiven, of anyone you retain will be retained." In John's Gospel it is clear that Jesus was not talking about decisions concerning what is sin and what is not but rather actually forgiving and retaining them. How could the apostles do that? By preaching the Gospel which contains both salvation and judgment. They were the inspired proclaimers and interpreters of Jesus' message.

Peter has no sooner been praised for his faith when he gets himself into trouble. In the next scene Jesus predicts his death. Peter who has just confessed that Jesus is the Messiah seems scandalized by such talk. He even "rebukes" Jesus for speaking of death when he is the Messiah. Clearly Peter thought of the Messiah as someone like Bar Kosiba (see Chapter 1) that is, a military and political leader. Such a Messiah in Peter's view conquers; he does not voluntarily submit to death.

Jesus then says, "Get away from me, Satan! You are a stumbling block to me because you do not think godly things but carnal things." From being praised for his faith to being called Satan--such was the life of Peter. To be taken apart verbally by one you admire and believe in must be terribly painful. But Jesus had to teach him and the rest the carnal nature of their thinking.

This event is pivotal in the ministry of Jesus and in the disciples understanding of who he was. From here on, Jesus focuses on his coming death. The event is also pivotal for the organization of Mark's Gospel. Before this, Jesus is a wonder worker with amazing success. After this, the Gospel speaks less of Jesus as miracle worker and more of Jesus as the suffering one.

There would be two other similar confrontations between Jesus and his disciples over their misunderstanding of who he was and therefore what disciples should be. N. Perrin has shown that Mark 8-10 narrates three episodes in the life of Jesus using the following pattern:

	Mk 8	**Mk 9**	**Mk 10**
1. Jesus predicts his death.	8:31	9:31	10:33-34
2. The Disciples misunderstand	8:32f	9:32-34	10:35-41
3. Jesus teaches them.	8:34-38	9:35-37	10:42-45

Table 8.1
Prediction Pattern in Mark

Jesus' approaching death means that the servant of all gives his life as a ransom price for the sin of the world (10:45). The disciples of Jesus, then and now, must also learn humility and commitment even to the point of taking up the cross (8:34).

Notes

1. Matthew uses the expression "kingdom of Heaven" instead of "kingdom of God." Heaven is a circumlocution for God. This was a common practice among pious Jews to avoid any chance of using God's name irreverently. Thus in rabbinic literature we often find God referred to as "The Holy One", "The Name" or "The Place." For Heaven as a name for God see: m. Sanhedrin 10:1; m. Nedarim 10:6; b. Sanhedrin 99a; m. Aboth 1:11; 2:12; 4:4; 4:11, 12; 5:17.

2. Jesus' use of the word "hate" in this verse is of course, hyperbole.

3. See J. Strange and H. Shanks, *BAR* 8/6 (1982) 26-37.

4. Mark's Gospel indicates that David ate this bread when Abiathar was the High Priest. But the Old Testament says that David did this when Ahimelech, Abiathar's father, was the High Priest (1 Sam 21:16). Some assume that a manuscript copyist mistakenly inserted this reference (Mk 2:26) into the text of Mark. Lane suggests the most reasonable solution, however. He proposes that we understand the reference to Abiathar as a reference to the section of the Old Testament in which the story about David's eating of the bread occurs. In Mk 12:26, for example, another passage of the Old Testament is alluded to by the phrase, "in the passage concerning the bush." Thus these are ways of referring to Old Testament texts in a time when there were no chapter and verse divisions.

5. See especially J. Fitzmyer, "The Aramaic *qorban* inscription from Jebel Hallet et-Turi and Mk 7:11/Mt 15:5" in Fitzmyer, *Essays on the Semitic Background of the New Testament.*

6. See M. Hengel, *The Charismatic Leader and His Followers.*

7. The manuscripts are in disagreement over the name of this town. Some read Gadara, others Gerasa, still others Gergesa. We will handle this problem in Chapter 11.

8. See J.D.M. Derrett, "Binding and Loosing" *Journal of Biblical Literature* 102 (1983) 112-117.

CHAPTER 9

THE PARABLES OF JESUS

Bibliography: K.E. Bailey, *Poet and Peasant*; idem., *Through Peasant Eyes*; M. Connick, *Jesus, the Man, the Mission and the Message*; J.D. Crossan, *In Parables*; C.H. Dodd, *The Parables of the Kingdom*; D.R. Dungan, *Hermeneutics*; A. Feldman, *The Parables and Similes of the Rabbis*; P.W.J. Fiebig, *Die Gleichnisreden Jesu im Lichte der rabbinischen Gleichnisse des neutestamentlichen Zeitalters*; D. Flusser, *Die rabbinischen Gleichnisse und der Gleichniserzaeler Jesus*; F. Hauck, *"parabole"* in *TDNT*; A.M. Hunter, *Interpreting the Parables*; J. Jeremias, *The Parables of Jesus*; P.R. Jones, *The Teaching of the Parables*; A. Juelicher, *Die Gleichnisreden Jesu*; W.S. Kissinger, *The Parables of Jesus: A History of Interpretation and Bibliography*; E. Linnemann, *Jesus of the Parables*; H.K. McArthur and R.M. Johnston, *They Also Taught In Parables*; T.W. Manson, *The Teaching of Jesus*; L. Mowry, "Parable" in *IDB*; W.O.E. Oesterley, *The Gospel Parables In the Light of Their Jewish Background*; B. Ramm. *Protestant Biblical Hermeneutics*; A.M. Rihbany, *The Syrian Christ*; B.B. Scott, *Hear Then the Parable*; K.R. Snodgrass, "Parable" in J.B. Green and S. McKnight, eds., *Dictionary of Jesus and the Gospels*; R.H. Stein, *An Introduction to the Parables of Jesus;* D. Stern,

Parables in Midrash; D.O. Via, Jr., *The Parables*; C. Westermann, *The Parables of Jesus in the Light of the Old Testament*; B.H. Young, *Jesus and His Jewish Parables*

Preliminary Considerations

Before we discuss what parables are we should say a word about what they are not. A parable is not a fable. A fable is a story in which a plant or animal is given human qualities in order to illustrate some truth or moral. Aesop's Greek fables are good examples. The Old Testament has a famous fable in Judges 9:6-21, Jotham's fable, and the apocryphal book, 4 Ezra also contains one (4:13-18). Parables do not have the trivial or the make-believe qualities of fables.

Nor is a parable an allegory though at times they do have close similarities. An allegory is a story in which its several points refer to some other event or idea.[1] Some of the parables are given an allegorical interpretation by Jesus as we will see below and others have allegorical elements in them but in the main one should distinguish allegory from parable. Since A. Juelicher's seminal work on parables, most scholars have sought to find only one point in a parable (with the exceptions mentioned above) while an allegory makes many points.

Formerly most parables were interpreted as allegories. For example the great thinker, Augustine, interpreted the parable of the Good Samaritan (Aland   183) as follows: The man who went down to Jericho from Jerusalem represents Adam; Jerusalem is the city of peace from which Adam has fallen; Jericho represents mortality; the priest and Levite are the Old Testament era; the Samaritan represents Christ; the devil and his demons are the robbers; the inn in which the beaten man was housed is supposed to be the church; the innkeeper is Paul.

The allegorical interpretation of this parable has a certain appeal to it but we are left wondering if Jesus really meant for all of this to be found in his story. The story seems more to be about love, that is, living out the commandment to love your neighbor as yourself. When Jesus, himself, explicitly gives an allegorical interpretation to a parable as he did in the case of the parable of the Sower (Aland 122) then we are justified in this understanding. Otherwise we should probably usually heed Juelicher's advice and find only one point to the story. Nevertheless, no hard and fast rule can be given since some parables--e.g. the parable of the Prodigal Son--exhibit allegorical elements.

The word parable comes from the Greek *parabole* which means "something put alongside", that is, for comparison. A parable is then an expanded narrative metaphor or simile. The classical sources, especially Homer (e.g. *Iliad* 2.147; 3.222), Plato, and the Stoic-Cynic diatribe (e.g. Epictetus, *Dissertationes* 1.27.15-21; see Hauck) are rich in such illustrations. Yet they are not exactly like most of Jesus' parables in form or in content, especially Jesus' longer and more developed ones. In the *Phaedo* (87b) for example, Plato has Socrates compare a weaver and his coats to the body and soul. Socrates does not like the common argument that the soul outlasts the body although he does believe it:

> The analogy I will adduce is that of an old weaver, who dies, and after his death somebody says: --He is not dead, he must be alive;--see, there is the coat which he himself wove and wore, and which remains whole and undecayed. And then he proceeds to ask of someone who is incredulous, whether a man lasts longer, or the coat which is in use and wear; and when he is answered that a man lasts far longer, thinks that he has thus certainly demonstrated the survival of the man, who is the more lasting, because the less lasting remains. (Trans. by B. Jowett).

Epictetus, a Stoic philosopher, also used many illustrations. Here is one justifying his condemnation of certain immoral practices. Though the reprimanded person may object to the moral teaching, he will regret the results of his sin if he does not listen to the moral physician:

> (It is)as if a man should say to his physician who was forbidding him to bathe, "Why, but didn't I bathe just the other day?" If, then, the physician is able to say to him, "Very well, after you had bathed, then how did you feel? Didn't you have a fever? Didn't your head ache?" (*Diss.* 3.15.6-10; trans. by W.A. Oldfather in LCL).

These illustrations from the writings of Plato and Epictetus give us a good comparison with Jesus' parables. Jesus used usually more agrarian motifs; his parables, especially the longer ones, have a genuine plot; and of course his topic was the Kingdom of God. Yet the idea of putting some common occurrence or truth alongside the more abstract concept in order to clarify it is similar to Jesus' purpose. As a matter of fact Jesus himself used illustrations from clothing and a physician (Mt 9:12, 16; Lk 4:23).

The word *parabole* is used often in the Greek version of the Old Testament (the Septuagint version) to translate the Hebrew word, *mashal*. A *mashal* is a proverb, a simile, a sentence of ethical wisdom, or a prophetic figurative discourse (see BDB). The term is used in 1 Samuel 10:12 (of a proverb), in Ezekiel 17:2 (of a similitude, that is an extended simile) and in Numbers 23:7, 18 (of a prophetic figurative discourse). In each of these cases the word *mashal* is translated in the Septuagint Greek version of the Old Testament by the word *parabole*. But there is another Greek word used twice in the Septuagint for *mashal*; that word is *paroimia*, or "riddle, figure of speech, or dark saying". It is interesting that the Synoptic Gospels (Mt, Mk, and Lk) call Jesus' illustrations *parabole*, but the Gospel of John calls them *paroimia* (Jn 10:6, 16:25,29).

At any rate we can see from these passages from the Old Testament that a *mashal* is much broader than a New Testament parable   A *mashal* may not be a narrative at all but a proverbial saying. As a matter of fact although the Old Testament has several parables, we do not find any quite like Jesus' parables though some illustrations--like those of the Greeks--come close. Ezekiel's tale of the eagle (Ezek 17:1-10), Nathan's story for David (2 Sam 12:1-4), and the story of the vineyard in Isaiah (Isa 5:1-2) are the nearest to Jesus' parables and may have actually stirred his thinking.

We do not find any parables at all in the intertestamental literature. The book of 1 Enoch (e.g. chapters 37-71) has a group of visions which it calls parables but these are much different from the New Testament parables. The Dead Sea Scrolls have no parables.

The closest thing we have to Jesus' parables are in the rabbinic literature. There is only one parable in the Mishnah, the earliest of the rabbinic literature. Many more, however, are found in the Tosephta, the two Talmuds, and the Midrashim (see the glossary for these terms). We give three from the Tosephta, the earliest of the four latter sources (AD 250-400):

> (Gentiles, women and uneducated persons cannot be expected to understand the Law) They parable a parable. Unto what is the matter like? It is like a king of flesh and blood who told his servant to boil him some broth, though he had never boiled him broth in his life. The result was that he burnt the broth and provoked his master (t. Beracoth 7:18).

> When the luminaries are eclipsed, it is an ill omen to the whole world.

Unto what is the matter like? It is like a king who made a banquet and summoned guests. He became angry with them and bade the steward remove the lamp before them, so that they were all sitting in darkness (t. Sukkah 2:6).

They parable a parable. Unto what is the matter like? It is like a street that passes between two paths, one of fire and the other of snow. If one deviates this way, he will be burned by the fire; if he deviates that way, he will be frostbitten. It is profitable for a man to walk in the middle and not be deviating this way or that way (t. Hagigah 2:6). (Translations in McArthur and Johnston)

These are closer to Jesus' kind of illustrations. Thus we can use the rabbinic parables, even though they are late, to help us understand or clarify Jesus' illustrations.

Before we turn to the exegesis we must define parable. Connick's definition ("An earthly story with a heavenly meaning") is a good start. Scott's definition is a bit more scholarly but essentially the same: "A parable is a mashal that employs a short narrative fiction to reference a transcendent symbol." Jesus used ordinary occurrences, everyday events, as well as well-known people and happenings to construct his illustrations of theological points. He could also adapt commonly told folk tales to use in his teaching. One thing is clear: Jesus was a master story teller and a master teacher.

Parables clarify abstract ideas but they can also obfuscate. A parable is only a means of understanding and revelation if one is open to Jesus' message. For those hardened to God by sin Jesus' parables can be difficult to make sense of. They then separate those whose hearts are hardened (Mk 4:10-12).

Some parables are in three Gospels, some in two, others appear in only one Gospel. The Gospel of John has only two parables and one of these, the Vine, is not considered by some a true parable. Some of Jesus' parables are quite brief. Jones calls these very short parables, 'parabolic sayings". Most of these parabolic sayings are in Matthew (e.g. 5:13, 6:24). The parabolic sayings are most similar to the illustrations in the classical sources.

On the other hand, most of the very long and developed parables are in Luke (e.g. 12:16-21, 10:30-37). These latter parables are true narratives usually told in the past tense with an engaging plot that pulls the reader into the story.

There are some differences among scholars as to the exact number of parables in the Gospels. But these differences are minor. What follows is a fair representation of the consensus regarding the complete list of Jesus' parables:

Parables in Three Gospels (denotes Aland)

	Mt	Mk	Lk
Salt of the Earth (52)*	5:13	9:50	14:34-35
Light of the World (53)*	5:15	4:21	8:16
Physician and Sick (93)	9:12	2:17	5:31
Wedding Guests (94)*	9:15	2:19-20	5:34-35
New Cloth (94)*	9:16	2:21	5:36
New Wine (94)*	9:17	2:22	5:37-39
Sower (122)*	13:3ff	4:3ff	8:5ff
Mustard Seed (128)*	13:31ff	4:30ff	13:18ff
Wicked Husbandmen (278)*	21:33ff	12:1ff	20:9ff
Fig Tree (293)	24:32ff	13:28ff	21:29ff

Parables in Two Gospels

The Accuser (55)	5:25-26	12:58-59
The Lamp of the Body (65)	6:22-23	11:34-35
Speck and Log (68)*	7:3-5	6:41-43
Tree and Fruit (73)	7:16-20	6:43-45
House on the Rock (75)	7:24-27	7:47-49
Children in Market Place (107)	11:16-17	7:31-32
Return of Evil Spirit (120)	12:43-45	11:24-26
Leaven (129)	13:33	13:20-21
Blind Guides (150)	15:14	6:39
Signs (154)	16:2-3	12:54-56
Lost Sheep (169)	18:12-14	15:3-7
Faithful Servant (203)	24:45-51	12:42-46
The Pounds/Talents (266)	25:14-30	19:11-27
Great Supper (279)	22:1-14	14:15-24

Parables in One Gospel

A. Matthew:

City On a Hill (53)	5:14
Wheat and Weeds (127)*	13:24-30
Hidden Treasure (132)*	13:44

The Pearl (132)*	13:45-46
The Net (133)*	13:47-48
The Householder (134)	13:52
Unforgiving Servant (173)*	18:23-34
Laborers in Vineyard (256)*	20:1-15
Two Sons (277)	21:28-31
Wedding Garment (279)	22:11-13
Ten Virgins (298)	25:1-13
Sheep and Goats (300)	25:31-46

B. Mark

Seed Growing Secretly (126)*	4:26-29
Watchful Doorkeeper (294)	13:34-36

C. Luke

Two Debtors (114)	7:41-43
Good Samaritan (183)*	10:30-37
Friend at Midnight (186)*	11:5-8
Rich Fool (200)	12:16-20
Watchful Servants (203)	12:35-38
Barren Fig Tree (207)	13:6-9
Chief Seats (215)	14:7-10
Tower Builder (217)	14:28-30
King at War (217)	14:31-32
Lost Coin (220)	15:8-10
Prodigal Son (221)*	15:11-32
Dishonest Steward (222)*	16:1-8
Rich Man and Lazarus (228)*	16:19-31
Unprofitable Servants (232)	17:7-10
Unjust Judge (236)	18:2-5
Pharisee and Publican (237)*	19:12-27

D. John

The Good Shepherd (249)	10:1-18
The Vine and Branches (320)	15:1-6

Table 9.1
The Parables of Jesus
(*Denotes parables discussed in this chapter)

Exposition of Some of Jesus' Parables

The Nature of the Kingdom of God (Aland 94, 126, 128, 132)

A. Aland 94. In answer to the disciples of John on why Jesus and his disciples did not fast Jesus told three parables. In the first place, it is not appropriate to fast when the bridegroom is present answered Jesus. During a wedding the guests celebrate, not fast. Thus Jesus' disciples should celebrate while he is present with them. This first parable presents us with a theme common in Jesus' teaching: the joy of the kingdom of God. There should be celebrating and rejoicing in God's kingdom.

B. Next Jesus told two parables (also in Aland 94) to illustrate that something new was present. His disciples did not fast according to the traditions of the Jews because something new has come. It is a new era with the in-breaking of the Kingdom. That is like when a person makes wine. He does not put unfermented or new wine in an old wine skin or one that has already been stretched. If he does, the skin might burst. One should not try to mix old with new. Likewise, a person should not sew a new patch on an old garment. Otherwise when you wash the garment the new patch may shrink and tear it. Be careful in mixing new with old. Jesus' teaching is new. Accept it for what it is and do not try to force it into the mold of the old.

C. Aland 126 and 128. The Kingdom will grow; that much is sure. In the parable of the Seed Growing Secretly Jesus says that the Kingdom is like a seed that grows. We do not really know how it does that. We can water it and weed it but we cannot make it grow. It does that on its own. The Kingdom cannot really be advanced by our efforts. We can preach and teach as indeed we must, but only God can give growth. The Kingdom is like a mustard seed which is very tiny. The Kingdom begins in an apparently insignificant way but will grow to great size just like a mustard tree or bush which has large spreading branches and provides a home to many birds. The mention of the birds in this parable is probably only part of the scenery. Some have maintained that the birds represent the Gentiles or the nations but that interpretation seems forced.

D. Aland 132. The benefits of the Kingdom are worth all we have. In the parables of the Hidden Treasure and the Pearl Jesus tells of someone who sells all he has in order to acquire his treasures. He deems these treasures worth his life's fortune. The treasures represent clearly the Kingdom. It is more valuable than money or any other possession we have. Notice that the theme of joy in the Kingdom also enters the parable of the Hidden Treasure since the man joyfully sells all he has to acquire it.

Behavior in the Kingdom (53, 68, 173, 183, 186, 222, 237)

A. Aland 53. Many of Jesus' parables deal with the ethics of the Kingdom. How should one act in light of Jesus' presence which is ushering in God's reign? Two short parables--or parabolic sayings--found in the Sermon on the Mount urge the disciple to influence others. We should see ourselves as a light in a world of darkness or a lamp in a dark house. We should not try to hide what we are but let what we are becoming by the grace of God shine through.

B. Aland 68. Relating to the world, the disciple of Jesus should be a light. But with respect to other disciples how should we behave? One thing we must not do is judge others. When we judge others we often make mistakes which hurt people deeply. The worst mistake we make is in failing to see our own failings. We can so focus on others' faults that we ignore ours, even when ours may be much worse. In teaching these things Jesus employed what is in the Talmud a rather common saying: "Why do you see the speck in your brother's eye but do not see the huge log in yours?" (see b. Baba Bathra 15b; b. Arachin 16b). The expression must have been rather common in Palestinian Judaism.[2] At any rate the picture is quite humorous. A person with a gigantic log in his eye is carping at a speck of sawdust in someone else's eye. Such is often the ludicrous nature of judgmental people.

C. Aland 173. Another teaching regarding our relationship to others, especially our forgiveness of other disciples is found in the parable in Matthew 18. This story draws us into it much like the story of Nathan in the Old Testament referred to above. We feel amazement at the generosity of the king who forgave the main character in the story an enormous debt of 10,000 talents. When we realize that the entire annual income of Herod the Great was only 1,000 talents and of Agrippa I was only 1,200 talents, we begin to understand the hugeness of the debt and the awesomeness of the king's forgiveness. But then the main character unmercifully grabbed someone who owed him a sum of 100 denarii and had him thrown into prison. We must realize that the sum of 100 denarii was no paltry sum. It probably equaled one half year's wages for a day laborer.[3] But it pales in comparison: 10,000 talents would equal 100,000,000 denarii. Thus the wrongs people do against us are not insignificant but they pale when compared with our debt of sin to God. The main character was forgiven an enormous debt but would not forgive a man a normal debt. The story catches us and angers us at the injustice of the main character until in the last verse (35) we are told that we are the unforgiving person. Just like Nathan's parable in the Old Testament which engages the reader (as it engaged David) until Nathan pronounces: "You are the man!", so this story does not release us until we realize that it is about us.

D. Aland 183. Closely akin in content to the two preceding parables is the parable of the Good Samaritan. Jesus has just answered the question of a Biblical scholar, namely what is the greatest commandment. Jesus responded that there are two: love God with all your being and love your neighbor as yourself (Dt 6:5; Lev 19:18). The Biblical expert (or lawyer) then asked: "Who is my neighbor?" This question brought about the parable.

There was a debate in Judaism as to where one should draw the line for neighbor. What does the verse in Leviticus (19:18) mean by neighbor? The rabbinic literature excepted the *'am haaretz* or people of the land, that is those not meticulous about the law. The Essenes took an oath to hate all sons of darkness (i.e. by definition all non-Essenes), even fellow Jews.[4] Whom then must I love?

We perhaps should conclude that Jesus dismissed the question as invalid for the parable does not exactly answer it. We should not ask who is my neighbor, but how can I best be a neighbor? We should make ourselves neighbors instead of asking whom do I have to help.

The story takes place on the notorious 17 mile long road from Jerusalem to Jericho. This route leads through barren desert which is full of caves and other hideouts for robbers. Even in the days of J. Jeremias; in the early part of this century) there were robbers along this road. The victim was robbed, beaten and left to die. Why the priest and Levite did not stop to help is not said. We may presume that they worried about ritual uncleanness from touching a corpse (Lev 21:1). If so, this is a subtle jab at those who value ceremony over essence, being ritually pure over being inwardly pure. Perhaps Jesus only meant, however, to contrast Judaism's best representatives (priests and Levites) with a lowly Samaritan.

Samaritans (see Chapter 3) were those people that lived in the territory between Galilee and Judea. They were racially the same as Jews but religiously and politically had their differences that often led to violence. Pilgrims from Galilee traveling to Jerusalem were often attacked and sometimes killed (*War* 2.233-235). Jews retaliated in kind and thus the hatred developed over the years between these two Hebraic peoples. We might liken them to the Protestants and Catholics of Northern Ireland. They were racially the same and even religiously very similar, but had enough differences and enough history of violence to cause them to hate each other. Thus Jesus has a hated Samaritan act in a loving manner. This is a stinging rebuke against prejudice and at the same time the presentation of a model in loving the hurting. The Samaritan did not allow his own dislike of Jews to prevent him from doing an act of mercy.

E. Aland 186. This parable and another one somewhat similar to it (Aland 236) demonstrates to us the importance of not taking seriously too many of the details of most parables. Both parables are intended to teach us something about prayer. In this parable a man pesters his friend at midnight, when the family members are in their warm beds and fast asleep, to lend him some bread. The friend really does not want to be bothered at that hour but will grant the request just to get rid of the persistent borrower. The friend in bed clearly represents God in this story and the borrower is someone who prays. Now it is not true that God only answers prayers because people keep pestering him and because he only wants to end the importunity. He answers prayer because he is a gracious and compassionate God. But Jesus wanted his disciples to pray persistently. This parable illustrates the importance of persistent and trusting prayer.

F. Aland 222. This parable also makes clear to us that we should usually see the details of a parable as nothing more than part of the scenery. The story of the Unjust Steward has two problems. What did the steward actually do? What is the point of the parable? Some say the steward acted illegally throughout the whole story. Others say he acted legally in the end by reducing the debt of his master's debtors. He had increased the debt dishonestly in order to get himself some of the profits but in the end asked only for the rightful payment. But really we must point out that it does not matter exactly what the steward did, whether honest or dishonest. The steward, who represents the disciple, is not a role model for us in any way except one: using money wisely. We are naturally not to imitate his dishonest and roguish life. The point of the parable is then found in verse 9. Use your money wisely to secure for yourself a heavenly reward. Just as the steward saw catastrophe coming if he did not act wisely, so should the disciple use his/her money with the day of Judgment in view. Therefore use your wealth for the service of God.

G. Aland 237. The last parable to be considered under the heading of ethics of the Kingdom is the parable of the Pharisee and the Publican.

The Pharisee (see Chapter 3) was a very righteous man and the tax collector was almost a mafia-like figure. Yet when they prayed, the Pharisee was condemned because he did little more than brag to God about himself. Such pride is always condemned by God. On the other hand, although the tax collector was a sinful man, when he prayed a sincere prayer of humble repentance, he was justified or forgiven. His heart was not hardened by pride but was open to God. There are surprises when we examine hearts instead of externals.

The Judgment of the Kingdom (122, 127, 133, 228)

A. Aland 122 (and 124). One of Jesus' most famous parables is about the four soils. A sower sowed seed on four different types of soil with four different results. All the details so familiar from Israel are present in the parable: the path, the rocks, the thorns, the scorching sun, and the birds. This parable is one of only two parables that were actually interpreted by Jesus (the other is the Wheat and Weeds). Jesus declared (see Aland 124) that the four soils represent four kinds of people. Some hear the word of God and do not accept it at all because Satan (=the birds) snatches it away from them. Others hear the word and accept it but do not remain steadfast in persecution (=the heat of the sun). Still others accept the word but their faith is destroyed by the cares of everyday living (=the thorns). Finally some accept the word and remain steadfast bearing fruit.

Juelicher had maintained that Jesus did not allegorize his parables and therefore this interpretation (which is very allegorical) could not possibly be from him. Allegory is an interpretive technique of Greek speaking Jews like Philo of Alexandria and thus the interpretation of this parable must be from the later Greek Christian church, he affirmed. But we must note that the Palestinian rabbis employed allegory. Hunter quotes a good example of a rabbinic allegorical parable.[5] Rabbi Yishmael (early second century AD) also was wont to interpret the Old Testament Law allegorically.[6] There is even allegory in the Dead Sea Scrolls.[7] It is now being recognized more and more that we should not make sharp distinctions between Jewish Palestine and the Hellenistic dispersion. Palestine was by Jesus' day already quite Hellenized and would surely have been conversant with Greek allegorical interpretations.[8] The contention of Juelicher, based as it is on an antiquated view of Palestine, is untenable.

B. Aland 127 (and Aland 131). The Parable of the Wheat and Tares or Weeds is another parable for which an allegorical interpretation was given by Jesus. The parable and its interpretation tell about a time of judgment when all the evildoers will be gathered out of the Kingdom of God. Again a man sows seed which sprouts and produces good results. But an enemy sows weeds which also grow. The man sowing the good seed is Christ and his seed is his disciples. The enemy is the devil and his seed is his children. The workers (=angels) want to pull up the weeds, a practice that would have been normal. But the landowner forbade that to be done else they might make a mistake and pull up some wheat along with it. That will be done at harvest (=judgment) when the weeds will be burned with fire. Thus Jesus taught that judgment was an act which only God should do and in his time. Meanwhile we live among weeds sometimes not knowing for certain who the weeds are and who the wheat is, and allow God alone to judge. Jesus was both teaching that there will be a Day of Judgment and that we should not in the meantime be sectarian. We should eschew attempts to remove ourselves radically from our world. We must rather be a light within it. We should also be very cautious about rooting out the weeds of our churches. We might also throw out some wheat with it.

C. Aland 133. This is another parable of judgment. Just as fish are sorted out after the catch, with the good being kept and the bad ones being thrown away, so it will be at the Day of Judgment. Some will be accepted and others will be rejected.

D. Aland 228. The parable of the Rich Man and Lazarus is probably the best known story of judgment. Jeremias has correctly noted that this parable is very similar to a folk tale found in Egypt and in the Palestinian Talmud. The story in the Talmud is as follows:

> A rich and wicked tax collector named Bar Mayan died and was given a splendid funeral. Work stopped throughout the entire city to celebrate his funeral. At the same time a poor scholar (of the Bible) died and no one took any notice of his burial. Later one of the poor scholar's colleagues was allowed to see in a dream the fate of the two men in the next world. The poor scholar was in gardens of paradisal beauty, watered by flowing streams. Bar Mayan stood on the bank and tried to reach the stream but was unable to do so. (j. Sanhedrin 6.23c; in Jeremias)

This story certainly looks similar to our parable. Jesus probably formed his parables from many sources including: old tales that circulated in

Palestine such as this one; common expressions such as the speck and log expression we referred to above; everyday experiences such as planting a field; Old Testament stories such as Isaiah's parable of the vineyard (Isa 5:1-2); and historical occurrences in the Old Testament (see Aland 278) and in recent Palestinian history (see Aland 266 Lk 19:12, 14 and Archelaus). Of course Jesus was a creative genius in his own right and many of his parables are completely fresh creations. But he also adapted, as a master teacher should, the best illustrations already at hand. This procedure he hints at in one of his teachings (Mt 13:52).

The rich man in our parable--who unlike the folk tale quoted above is not named--has all the trappings of wealth: fine clothes, sumptuous dining, and a large mansion. But the poor man, Lazarus (an abbreviated form of the name Eleazar="God helps"), has all the associated evils of poverty: homelessness, hunger, and disease. The religious and ethical lives of the two are not described but from the fates of each of them after their death we must assume that the rich man was wicked and that Lazarus was a pious Jew. The point of the parable is that God does not honor what our world honors. Thus in the afterlife their situations are reversed. The rich man is horribly tormented and the poor man is in "Abraham's bosom" or paradise. God will not judge us the way the world judges us.

Is this an account of an actual event or just a fictional story to warn about what will happen to those that do not repent? The fact that there is a well-known folk tale so similar to this parable probably indicates that Jesus adapted the story from it. Further, although Jesus usually tells stories that have a basis in everyday experiences, he does not necessarily tell actual historical events. In other words, it is possible that enemies in Palestine did occasionally sow weeds in a man's field, but Jesus is not necessarily referring to a specific case of such criminal behavior. These are mere illustrations. Thus we should be hesitant to construct a theology of the intermediate state--that is, the state between death and the great Day of Judgment--based on this parable.

The God Who Reigns (221, 256)

A. Aland 256. The parable of the Laborers in the Vineyard tells a remarkable story about the God of grace and forgiveness. In the narrative a landowner goes out to hire workers five different times in a day, from early in the morning until the eleventh hour. Yet when he pays his day laborers they all receive a normal day's wage of one denarius.[9] Those who worked only one hour get the same pay even though they clearly do not deserve it. This story teaches about God's grace. Those who have contributed much to the Kingdom as well as those who contributed little are saved with the same reward.

Hunter quotes a very interesting parallel parable from the rabbis:

> It is like a king who hired many labourers. But one was outstanding in his work. What did the king do? He took him away and walked to and fro with him. When it was evening, the labourers came to receive their pay, and he gave him, with them, the full amount of his wage. Then the labourers murmured and said, We have worked the whole day, and this man has worked only two hours. Then the king said, This man has done more in two hours than you have done in the whole day. So has Rabbi Bun learned more in the Law in twenty-eight years than a clever student could have mastered in a life-time (S-B 4, 492-493).

As Hunter points out, the rabbinic parable is about works but the parable of Jesus is about grace. In the rabbinic parable the laborer received the same wage because he had done the same work even though he only worked two hours. He was that much better at his job than the others. In Jesus' parable the laborers who worked only one hour received the same wage because of the landowners generosity. One parable glorifies a worker; the other glorifies the master.

B. Aland 221. The parable of the Prodigal Son[10] is surely one of the great pieces of literature of the world. It is a masterpiece of story telling. The drama moves us from anger to disgust to joy when we see at last the homecoming of the wayward young man.

Jesus told this parable as part of a trilogy in answer to his critics who complained that he was associating with tax collectors and sinners. The parables of the Lost Sheep and Lost Coin serve as a kind of introduction meant both to help interpret the parable of the Prodigal Son and to build the drama.

K. Bailey's important insights are especially useful in interpreting a parable like this one. Bailey attempted to understand Jesus' parables in light of the Middle Eastern customs and attitudes. He notes that he made a survey from Morroco to India and from Turkey to Sudan to ask what people thought of the younger brother's demand to receive his inheritance from the father before the father's death. Invariably the conversation went as follows:

> Has anyone ever made such a request in your village? Never! Could anyone ever make such a request? Impossible! If anyone ever did, what would happen? His father would beat him, of course! Why? This request means--he wants his father to die!

To ask for your inheritance in the orient while the father is still alive is insulting in the extreme to the father. The book of Ben Sirach (33:20-24) strongly forbids anyone to give his property to his son, wife, brother, or friend during his lifetime. The Mishnah (Baba Bathra 8:7) allows for this to be done in a technical sense but the father continues to control the produce of the land until his death. The Talmud even discourages such a legal technicality (b. Baba Metzia 75b) since it will probably come to haunt the father sooner or later. But there is no provision for actually selling the land and giving the proceeds to a son which is what obviously happened in this parable. That would be unthinkable while the father is still alive.

The son not only demanded that the father be considered dead to him for all intents and purposes but he contravened an important village custom in the Middle East: he sold off the land of his ancestors. One just does not sell land in the region as if it were an investment and nothing more. Land is a perpetual family holding. The extended family and villagers would be appalled. The Talmud and other rabbinic sources refer to a village rite of excommunication to those that commit such as sacrilege (j. Ketuboth 2.10; Ruth Rabbah 7.11).[11]

So the younger brother really is lost. He has despised his father in a most shameful way and has thumbed his nose at his community. He must have his money immediately in order to live his life of debauchery. He journeyed into a far country and wasted his money in a wanton life. When he was broke a famine hit the country and he now descended into his own Hell. He could only find work feeding the horrible, unclean pigs. Their only food was a thorny pod which began to look appetizing to the starving younger brother.

The hardship and degradation brought him to his senses. He "came to himself" means he wised up, he snapped out of his deluded life of sin.[12] He now understood that it had all been a terrible mistake, that he had fooled himself into thinking that he could live such a life with no consequences, that he could live only for his own pleasure and care not a fig for the feelings of others, especially of his father.

So he would return home. He would ask to be a hired hand. Oesterley pointed out that a hired hand, unlike a bond servant, would not be a part of the estate but only an outsider that found temporary employment. The son realized that he had no more claim on the father.

The father had not beaten the son when he insolently asked for his inheritance so he could sell the land and waste the money on sin. Rather he had sadly complied. Now when he sees the son returning home--are we to imagine that the father was looking for him everyday?--he does a very undignified thing for an oriental elderly man: he runs to meet the son. Middle Easterners consider it humiliating for an aging patriarch to run (Bailey). So great is the father's love for the son he throws off any concern for his own dignity. Further, he orders a feast with a slaughtered sheep (cf. 1 Sam 28:24), a sign of great honor to a distinguished guest (Rihbany). The son receives a robe, ring, and sandals. The father accepts him as a full son, though in reality of course such a son had no more inheritance to receive. Yet he is forgiven all the terrible insults to his father. He was lost but now is found, dead but now alive.

The story grips one with the emotion of that scene: a father weeping for joy; a son weeping with repentance. We appreciate anew the message in John Newton's classic hymn:

> Amazing grace how sweet the sound,
> That saved a wretch like me.
> I once was lost but now am found,
> was blind but now I see!

The father of course represents God who seeks us and accepts us even when we have hurt him deeply by our sin. He heals us in our brokenness. All we like the prodigal must come to ourselves in repentance and humility before our heavenly father.

But the story does not end there. The older brother represents the Pharisees and scribes (Lk 15:2) that had complained about Jesus' association with unsavory people. The pride and sense of self-righteousness make him in many ways a character even more despicable than the younger brother. The younger brother has sinned and found repentance. The older brother is guilty of pride and lack of love for the sinner and does not realize that he is one of them.

Notes

1. Modern examples of lengthy allegories are Spenser's *Faerie Queene*, Swift's *Gulliver's Travels*, and Bunyan's *Pilgrim's Progress*.

2. See J. Lightfoot, *Commentary on the New Testament from the Talmud and Hebraica*; and S-B.

3. See D.A. Fiensy, *Social History of Palestine in the Herodian Period*.

4. See S-B II, 515-516; and 1 QS 1:10.

5. See Hunter's English rendering of S-B I, 665.

6. See H.L. Strack and G. Stemberger, *Einleitung In Talmud und Midrasch*, p. 38.

7. See J.H. Charlesworth, "An Allegorical and Autobiographical Poem by the *MOREH HASSEDEQ* (1QH 8:4-11)" in M. Fishbane and E. Tov, eds., *Studies in the Bible, Qumran and the Ancient Near East*.

8. See M. Hengel, *Judaism and Hellenism*.

9. See Fiensy, *Social History of Palestine*, pp. 85-90.

10. A papyrus letter found in Egypt and dated to the second century AD indicates that prodigal sons were not uncommon in antiquity: "Antonius Longus to Nilous his mother very many greetings. I pray always for your health; everyday I make supplication for you before the lord Serapis. I would have you know that I did not expect that you were going up to the metropolis; for that reason I did not come to the city myself. I was ashamed to come to Karanis, because I go about in filth. I wrote to you that I am naked. I beg you, mother, be reconciled to me. Well, I know what I have brought on myself. I have received a fitting lesson. I know that I have sinned. I heard from . . . who found you in the Aarsinoite nome, and he has told you everything correctly. Do you not know that I would rather be maimed than feel that I still owe a man an obol?. . . (Addressed) To Nilous his mother from Antonius Longus her son. (Trans. In A.S. Hunt and C.C. Edgar, *Select Papyri*, LCL)

11. See Bailey, p. 167 and Fiensy, *Social History of Palestine*, p. 8.

12. Compare a similar phrase in Xenophon, *Anabasis* 1.5.17.

CHAPTER 10

THE SERMON ON THE MOUNT

Bibliography: W.C. Allen, *The Gospel According to S. Matthew*; B.W. Bacon, *Studies in Matthew*; J.H. Charlesworth, ed., *Jesus and the Dead Sea Scrolls*; idem., *Jesus Within Judaism*; M. Connick, *Jesus, the Man, the Mission and the Message*; W.D. Davies and D. Allison, *The Gospel According to St. Matthew*; W.D. Davies, *The Setting of the Sermon on the Mount*; M. Dibelius, *The Sermon on the Mount*; J. Fitzmyer, *The Gospel According to Luke*; D. Flusser, *Judaism and the Origins of Christianity*; R.C. Foster, *Studies in the Life of Christ*; G. Friedlander, *The Jewish Sources of the Sermon on the Mount*; R.A. Guelich, *The Sermon on the Mount*; R. Gundry, *Matthew*; D. Hamm, *The Beatitudes in Context*; D. Hill, *The Gospel of Matthew*; J. Jeremias, *The Prayers of Jesus*; idem., *The Sermon the Mount*; W.S. Kissinger, *The Sermon on the Mount: A History of Interpretation and Bibliography*; P. Lapide, *The Sermon on the Mount*; I.H. Marshall, *The Gospel of Luke*; I.A. Massey, *Interpreting the Sermon on the Mount in the Light of Jewish Tradition as Evidenced in the Palestinian Targums of the Pentateuch*; T. Meistad, *To Be A Christian in the World: Martin Luther's and John Wesley's Interpretation of the Sermon on the Mount*; G.F. Moore, *Judaism*; D. Oakman, *Jesus and the Economic Questions of His Day*; J. Piper, *Love Your Enemies*; A. Plummer, *The Gospel According to Luke*; H. Schuermann, *Das Gebet des Herrn*; E. Schweizer, *Die Bergpredigt*; idem.,*The Good News According to Matthew*; G. Strecker, *The Sermon on the Mount*; H. Windisch, *The Meaning of the Sermon on the Mount*.

The Geographical and Literary Setting of the Sermon

Matthew (and perhaps Mark) notes that the sermon took place on a mountain (Mt 5:1; Aland 50). If the visitor today inquires about the Mount of the Beatitudes, he is led to a hill just west of Capernaum overlooking the Sea of Galilee. This seems as good a spot as any but no one can be certain about the location of a place such as this. There is an old church at the foot of this hill, however, which may commemorate the tradition of where the sermon took place.

Luke, who records a great deal of material similar to if not identical to Matthew's sermon, says explicitly that the sermon took place on a level place (6:17). But surely Jesus did not say these things only once, to only one crowd and in only one location. We should conclude that these are two different, albeit similar, sermons.

B.W. Bacon observed that Jesus' sayings in Matthew are for the most part--but not completely--collected into five great discourses:

Chapters 5-7	**The Sermon on the Mount**
Chapter 10	**Sending Out the Twelve Apostles**
Chapter 13	**Parables of the Kingdom**
Chapter 18	**Community Life**
Chapters 24-25	**Teaching on the End of the Age**

Table 10.1
The Structure of Matthew

Bacon maintained that Matthew was presenting Jesus as a second Moses who gave five collections of laws like the Old Testament five books of Torah given by Moses. This is an interesting thesis and may be correct but Matthew certainly did not make this obvious. What is clear is that Matthew stresses Jesus words.

The Interpretation of the Sermon on the Mount

How should we understand the demanding commands of Jesus in this sermon? Opinions have varied widely (see Kissinger and Connick):

1. Some say we should interpret the sermon literally. Thus we should always turn the other cheek to violence (5:39). But even the literalists would admit that Jesus words ("If your right eye offends you pluck it out") in 5:29 are figurative.

2. Others say that if we add certain explanatory clauses we can take these commands literally. For example: "If someone persecutes you because you are a Christian, turn the other cheek." Or: "Give to anyone who asks you (5:42) if he is a genuine seeker and not a tramp."

3. Still others say that Jesus spoke demandingly merely to dramatize his ethic. He never meant for us to take these commands literally.

4. The point in these strong demands is to change our attitudes not to cause us to do these things literally, say others.

5. Some in the Roman Catholic tradition have seen these rules for the spiritual elite (the saints) not for the ordinary Christian.

6. Martin Luther maintained that the rules apply only to the spiritual sphere of life. In the physical sphere we must live as anyone else.

7. Some liberal scholars (A. Schweitzer) have seen these commands as an "interim ethic" only to be in effect for a short time between the beginning of Jesus' ministry and the end of the age which Jesus (according to Schweitzer) mistakenly thought would come very soon in his life.

8. Modern premillennial dispensationalists see these ethics as reserved for the future kingdom of God on earth.

9. Others say the purpose of these commands is to teach us how sinful we are and thus to lead us to an attitude of repentance.

10. Finally, some say these are God's absolute will but we can only completely do them in heaven. We just do the best we can now.

Which view is correct? We would certainly lean toward number 10. A definitive conclusion can only be reached, however, as we interpret some of the individual pericopes of the Sermon.

Exposition of the Sermon

We will follow E. Schweizer in outlining the sermon as follows:

I. **God's Compassion on the Poor, Beatitudes (Mt 5:3-12)***
II. **Discipleship (Mt 5:13-16)**
III. **Fulfilling the Law (Mt 5:17-20)***
IV. **The New Righteousness, Antitheses (Mt 5:21-48)***
V. **Righteousness Before God (Mt 6:1-18)***
VI. **Freedom From Possessions (Mt 6:19-34)**
VII. **On Judging (Mt 7:1-6)**
VIII. **The Joy of Prayer (Mt 7:7-12)**
IX. **Dangers of Discipleship (Mt 7:13-23)**
X. **Right and Wrong Hearing (Mt 7:24-27)***

Table 10.2
The Structure of the Sermon
(*Denotes pericopes discussed in the chapter)

The Beatitudes (Aland 51)

The word beatitude comes from the Latin Vulgate translation *beatus* for "blessed". Thus all of the beatitudes are blessings. The beatitude form is found in the Old Testament, especially the Psalms (Pss 1:1; 84:5, 12; 128:1). Later Judaism also uses this form (Ben Sirach 25:7-10). Luke's version of the beatitudes also includes woes: "Blessed are the poor, but woe to the rich." The woes are found in the Old Testament and later Judaism as well (Isaiah 5:8-23; 2 Enoch 45 and 52, see OTP). Thus Jesus has taken a somewhat rarely used Jewish form and elevated it to an important part of his teaching.

"Blessed are the poor in spirit, for theirs is the kingdom of heaven." The parallel text in Luke 6:20 reads, "Blessed are you poor for yours is the kingdom of God." What is the difference between poor in spirit and poor? Some scholars have maintained that Luke gives us the actual words of Jesus while Matthew adapts Jesus' words for a wealthy congregation of Christians. Jesus, it is alleged, was an economic champion and spoke a message of deliverance to socially poor people. But Matthew wrote his Gospel in a congregation of wealthy Christians. Since none of them were poor, so it is argued, Matthew had to make Jesus refer to the emotionally poor or down hearted. This sounds somewhat plausible at first until one realizes that the expression "poor in spirit" is found commonly in Judaism, especially the Qumran texts but also in the Old Testament. If it is a common Jewish expression, then one cannot easily argue that Matthew is adapting Jesus' words.

As D. Flusser points out, Jesus has based his first three beatitudes (including blessed are those that mourn and are meek) on Isaiah 61:1-2 and 66:2 (and on Psalm 37:11 which is quoted almost verbatim in 5:5). In the first passage Isaiah looks forward to the time of the Messiah and predicts that the one anointed by the spirit will proclaim good news to the poor, will bind up the brokenhearted, and will comfort those that mourn. In Isaiah 66 the prophet declares that God esteems those of a contrite spirit. In these texts the poor and broken people are especially cared for by God. The Psalms also refer to the people of God as poor ones or paupers (Ps 12:5; 86:1). The meaning is those poor who nevertheless trust in God. Thus it takes on a spiritual meaning: down-trodden yet righteous.

The term is also found in the intertestamental literature: Psalms of Solomon 10:7, 15:1, 18:2 (see OTP). But the Qumran literature is especially replete with references to the people of God as the poor, the contrite, or the humble (CD 14; 19:4; 4QpPs 37:2; 1QM 11:10;13:12-14;14:6-7; 1QH 5:13-14; 4Q 434, 436, etc.). But as Flusser shows the passage in the Thanksgiving Scroll, 1QH 18:14-15, is especially significant:

> (The author thanks God) To [have appointed] me in Thy truth a messenger [of the peace] of Thy goodness, to proclaim to the *meek* the multitude of Thy mercies, and to let them *that are of contrite spirit* he[ar salvation] from [everlasting] source, and to *them that mourn* everlasting joy. (Trans. by Flusser).

Thus the author of this Qumran prayer/hymn also patterned it on Isaiah. All of these terms (poor in spirit, mourn, meek, contrite of spirit) mean about the same thing. These are the people of God who are oppressed and afflicted yet who are repentant and lowly before him. But what does the expression "poor in spirit" mean exactly? Flusser compares it with an expression in the Qumran scrolls (1QH 5:22): "paupers of grace". This expression, also used of the people of God, does not seem to mean that they have very little grace. It means that although they are paupers, they yet have the abundant grace of God or "poor yet with the (abundant) grace of God". Therefore, poor in spirit would mean that although the people of God may be paupers economically, they abound in his Spirit. "Blessed are the poor who have God's Spirit, for theirs is the kingdom of God." But all of us are paupers in some way in comparison with the abundant riches of God's spiritual blessings which he pours out on the believer. Thus even Matthew's wealthy Christian church--if indeed his congregation was wealthy--is poor before God.

The fourth Beatitude is also a Jewish expression. Matthew's "Blessed are those who hunger and thirst for righteousness" is paralleled by Luke's "Blessed are those who hunger now". Again some scholars have concluded that Matthew changed Jesus' original words from those of promise to the starving masses to a blander promise to wealthy Christians that were not physically hungry at all. The purely economic interpretation of Jesus' words has become popular in some circles (see Oakman, e.g.). But Flusser again shows that Matthew's phrase is quite Jewish. He quotes part of a *selihah* prayer (prayer of forgiveness) which is said on the evening of the Day of Atonement:

> Thy people and Thy heritage, who hunger for Thy goodness, who thirst for Thy grace and who long for "Thy salvation, will recognize and know that to the Lord our God, belong mercy and forgiveness. (Trans. by Flusser)

The *selihah* prayers are very old[1] and no doubt date from the time of Jesus if not before. Thus Matthew's version of the Beatitude is not a Matthean editing of Jesus' words but surely the actual words of Jesus. Luke's version is from another occasion.

Already the psalmist had used this expression in Psalm 42:1. "As the deer pants for the stream of water, so pants my soul for you, O God." To hunger and thirst for righteousness is to long to see God's salvation and judgment in the kingdom of God, the same as longing for God himself. The verbal imagery, however, describes a deep longing for God as the hungry or thirsty person who longs with all his being to be satisfied.

The rest of the beatitudes are also very Hebraic and based on Old Testament ideas. Purity of heart, for example, means purity of mind (Ps 24:4; 73:1). The heart in the Hebrew language was considered the place of thought, emotion, and will. The peacemakers are those that desire and work for peace among their neighbors and was considered a virtue among Jews (Psalm 34:14; m. Aboth 1:12; James 3:18).

The rewards for the faithful disciple, that is, those that demonstrate the characteristics of the beatitudes are: the kingdom of God, being comforted (Isa 61:2), inheriting the earth (Psalm 37:11; cf m. Sanhedrin 10:1), being filled, obtaining mercy, seeing God, and being called children of God. All of these results amount to the same thing. They refer to eschatological or kingdom rewards. The kingdom or rule of God is present in the ministry of Jesus, will be manifested especially in the founding of the church, and will be consummated at Christ's second coming. Thus these rewards will only be fully given at the second coming.

Fulfilling the Law (Aland 54)

"Do not think I have come to abolish the Law or the prophets," said Jesus. "I have not come to abolish but to fulfill." What did he mean by this? There are at least four interpretations of these words (see Gundry): 1. He has come to obey the Torah. But the word "fulfill" (Greek: *pleroo*) is not usually used for keeping the Torah or Law. 2. He came to teach in support of the Law. But why did he mention the prophets and why use the unusual word "fulfill"? 3. He came to accomplish the prophecies about him in the Old Testament. This seems closer but why would he also refer to the Law and why would he pose the alternative as "abolish" them? This interpretation also does not seem to fit exactly. 4. He came both to teach the Torah (Law) and to fulfill the prophecies. This is apparently his meaning. He has not come to annul, abolish or destroy the Old Testament but to support it by teaching it and fulfilling its prophecies.

Jesus continues to demand that the Law be kept. Not a yod (the tiny Hebrew mark for "I") or other minute markings in the Hebrew of the Law will pass away "until all things come about". That is, the Law must be observed until the kingdom of God comes in its consummation. The disciples' righteousness must exceed that even of the scribes (scholars of the Law) and Pharisees (the strictest interpreters of the Law). But we must understand how Jesus means this. He says twice (Mt 7:12; 22:37-40) that the entire Law and prophets are summarized in the love commandments (Deut 6:4-6; Lev 19:18). Thus keeping the Law and teaching the Law involves the greater righteousness of love. It is the essence of the Law that the disciple is responsible for. Jesus had little use, for example, for dietary regulations (Mk 7:18-23; see chapter 8).

The Six Antitheses (Aland 55-59)

The Antitheses have the recurring literary structure: "You have heard it said. . . but I say to you. . .". Thus in each case Jesus contrasts his teaching with a respected saying. With what does he contrast his teaching? 1) E. Schweizer maintains that Jesus strengthens commands from the Ten Commandments in the first two antitheses; that he abrogates commands from the Old Testament (but not from the Ten Commandments) in antitheses 3,5, and 6; and that antithesis 4 is somewhere in the middle. 2) J. Jeremias maintained that Jesus did not contradict the Old Testament but only scribal interpretations of the Old Testament. 3) R. Gundry affirms that Jesus did not contradict either the Old Testament or the scribal tradition but only carried further the tendency of the Old Testament. Gundry is closer to being correct but Jeremias' view as we will see is partly true.

Antithesis I (Mt 5:21-26). In this antithesis Jesus contrasts his teaching with one of the Ten Commandments (Ex 20:13). He builds his teaching on Leviticus 19:17, "Do not hate your brother in your heart." Jesus' point here is that anger, if left unchecked, can boil over into acts of violence. Anger and hatred in ones heart are internalized violence.

This reasoning is also found in the Tannaitic midrash on Deuteronomy called Sifre:

> "If any man hates his neighbor and lies in wait for him, and attacks him" (Deut 19:11). From there it was deduced: if a man has transgressed a light commandment, he will finally transgress a weighty commandment. If he transgressed: "You shall love your neighbor as yourself" (Lev 19:18), he will finally transgress "You shall not take vengeance or bear any grudge (Lev 19:18) and the (commandment) "You shall not hate your brother (Lev 19:17). . . until he will (finally) be led to bloodshed. (Trans. in Flusser).

Jesus then is demanding that the heart be right toward ones neighbor first. Jesus adds to the prohibition of anger the demand that we not harm people with our words. "Whoever calls his brother *raka* will be liable to the Sanhedrin, and whoever says to his brother 'You fool!' will be liable to the fire of Hell." *Raka* is an Aramaic word meaning empty head or idiot. It is found somewhat frequently in the rabbinic literature as a term of insult (b. Beracoth 32b; b. Baba Bathra 75a; see S-B). The term "fool" is found also in the rabbinic literature, especially between religious factions. The Pharisees called the Boethusians fools, for example (b. Menahoth 65a; S-B).[2] Jesus demanded that we not only not harm others physically but also not with our words. As G.F. Moore pointed out, Judaism, with its Middle Eastern sense of honor and shame,[3] was especially sensitive to the public humiliation of someone by insulting him.

Jesus then gives two examples of being reconciled with a brother. Reconciliation should be considered of utmost importance.

Jesus, then, strengthened one of the Ten Commandments but the seeds of what he said were already in the Old Testament and Judaism.

Antithesis II (Mt 5:27-30). In this teaching Jesus contrasts his word with another of the Ten Commandments (Ex 20:14). He makes not just the physical act of adultery sin but also the mental desire for adultery wrong.[4]

Antithesis III (Mt 5:31-32). Jesus contrasts his teaching with Deuteronomy 24:1-4. This passage says that a man may divorce his wife if he finds in her "something indecent" (Hebrew: *ervat dabar*). But how should one interpret this vague expression? The reader will recall that there were two rival factions within the Pharisees led by the two great Pharisees of the first century BC: Hillel and Shammai (see chapter 3). These two schools had different interpretations of the "something indecent". Shammai and his school thought it referred to sexual immorality; Hillel and his school thought it could refer to anything the husband did not like, even if the wife burned the dinner (m. Gittin 9:10; Sifre on Deut 24:13). One later thinker, Rabbi Aqiba (died AD 135) even said that one could divorce his wife if he found someone better looking (m. Gittin 9:10). Jesus agrees here with Shammai. The only allowable cause for divorce is adultery on the part of the spouse. Thus Jesus does not contradict the Old Testament here; he rather agrees with the interpretation of it of the school of Shammai.

It is interesting that only here and in Matthew 19:9, does Jesus allow divorce because of adultery (Aland 252). In the parallel passage in Mark 10:11 and in another passage in Luke 16:18 Jesus does not mention that divorce is permissible in cases of adultery. He simply says that divorce is not allowed. Some scholars say that Matthew has softened Jesus difficult complete prohibition of divorce by allowing one exception. But Matthew has not softened any of Jesus' other difficult sayings in the Sermon on the Mount (cf. Mt 5:29; 5:39). The Sermon on the Mount in Matthew is characterized by its strictness. Why would he then soften this one?

Jesus seems to have prohibited divorce in principle because in the beginning God made one man for one woman (see Mt 19:1-9). But he allowed divorce in exceptional circumstances such as adultery on the part of one of the spouses. The prohibition of divorce is like that against retaliation (5:39) and others. Its difficulty teaches us that our nature is sinful. If we fail in its demand, we must seek repentance and forgiveness.

Antithesis IV (Mt 5:33-37). This antithesis also strengthens one of the Ten Commandments (Ex 20:7) which prohibited taking the name of Yahweh in vain. That is, it prohibited lying after taking an oath in the name of Yahweh. Jesus prohibited any oaths at all whether in the name of Yahweh or by Jerusalem, etc. This prohibition by Jesus may have been in response to the Essenes who not only demanded oaths of allegiance to their sect but even required that one curse or swear against those not in the sect (see 1QS 5:7-20; 2:4-10 and Charlesworth in *Jesus and the Dead Sea Scrolls*).

Antithesis V (Mt 5:38-42). The Old Testament restricted unrestrained blood vengeance by requiring after a court trial the exact affliction for the guilty that they had perpetrated on the victim, thus an eye for an eye, etc. (Ex 21:24-25; Lev 24:19-20). It put a lid on punishing someone excessively yet demanded a just penalty. Therefore, Jesus' refusal of punishment for the guilty is quite striking. His teaching is apparently based on Leviticus 19:18: "Do not take vengeance or bear a grudge against any one, but you will love your neighbor as yourself." Jesus gives five examples or cases of how this rule is applied in real life. The first one would have been most shocking to people in this society. There were stiff penalties of law for such a thing:

> If a man cuffed his fellow he must pay him a sela. R. Judah says in the name of R. Jose the Galilean: One hundred zuz. If he slapped him he must pay him 200 zuz. If [he struck him] with the back of his hand he must pay him 400 zuz. (m. Baba Kamma 8:6; Trans. in Danby).

This legal ruling from the Mishnah illustrates the shame attached to striking one on the cheek. To overlook it and even to turn the other cheek to be struck as well is quite a challenging command for any society and in any age, especially first century Palestine. But Jesus' disciples must be committed to God not their own sense of honor.

Antithesis VI (Mt 5:43-48). Finally Jesus contrasts his teaching on love with some other teacher or group. He quotes Leviticus 19:18 but then adds that someone teaches "Hate your enemy." No such saying exists in the Old Testament, however. Nor is such a thing in the Talmud. To whom then does Jesus refer when he says, "You have heard it said. . . hate your enemy"?

J.H. Charlesworth is probably correct when he points to the Essenes. According to the Qumran text known as the Manual of Discipline or Community Rule (1QS) the Essenes took an oath to love all the sons of light (=Essenes) and to hate all the sons of darkness (=everyone else):

> That they may love all the sons of light, each according to his lot in God's design, and hate all the sons of darkness, each according to his guilt in God's vengeance (1QS 1; Trans. in G. Vermes).

Thus here Jesus is contradicting one of the basic teachings of the Essenes. We must by contrast love everyone, even our enemies.

The Lord's Prayer (Aland 62)

The Sermon next turns to the practice of everyday piety: almsgiving, fasting, and prayer (Aland 60-63). In general the disciple must be cautious of doing things only or even partly for show. He/she must not give alms, pray in public, or fast in order to impress people. That is the kind of thing the hypocrites do (6:2, 5, 16). The Greek term *hypocrites* means an actor. Thus the hypocrites are merely acting like they are pious.

In the course of instructing the hearers on prayer Jesus gives his model prayer or the Lord's Prayer. This prayer is also found in somewhat different form in Luke 11:2-4.

"Our father in heaven. . ." God was already addressed as father as Friedlander has shown (see as early as Ex 4:22). Two of the Jewish Eighteen Benedictions, recited on weekdays in the synagogue, contain addresses to God "our father" (Hebrew: *abinu*). Yet Jeremias has shown that Jesus' common way of addressing God was unusual. In the first place Jesus always addressed God in prayer as father,[5] a practice not found in Judaism. God was sometimes called father but more often other terms were used such as "our king", or "Lord" (but not spelled with the tetragrammaton). Jeremias affirms that Jesus must have also used the Aramaic term *abba* in reference to God. He clearly used it in Mark 14:36 for it is merely transliterated here. Further, the early church continued to call God *abba* in prayer as the Pauline letters show (Gal 4:6; Rom 8:15). They surely obtained this practice from Jesus. Now *abba* is the familiar

word in Aramaic for father (just as *imma* was the affectionate word for
mother). The Talmud says (b. Beracoth 40a), "When a child experiences
the taste of wheat (i.e. when it is weaned) it learns to say *abba* and *imma*
(i.e. these are the first sounds which it makes" (Trans. by Jeremias).
Theodore of Mopsuestia (a city in north Syria where Aramaic was also
spoken) wrote in his Commentary on Romans: "It is the practice of small
children to call their fathers *abba*." Thus Jesus, argued Jeremias, seems
to have addressed God in the most familiar and affectionate of terms and
to have taught his disciples to do the same.

"May your name be hallowed, may your kingdom come, may your will
be done on earth as it is in heaven. . ." All three prayer requests here
mean about the same thing. Praying for God's name to be hallowed or
sanctified is reminiscent of the prophet Ezekiel (36:20-23) who predicted
that the Gentiles would see God's acts and would sanctify or hallow his
name. Jesus is praying then for God to be glorified by all peoples. This
will happen when the kingdom of God is fully consummated at the second
coming. Praying for the kingdom to come was also a common practice
in the early church (Rev 22:20) and even done in Aramaic (1 Cor 16:22:
maranatha "come Lord!"). When Christ comes again, God's will will be
all in all (1 Cor 15:28). Many have noted the essential similarity between
this part of Jesus' model prayer and the Jewish Kaddish prayer:

> Glorified and sanctified be God's great name throughout the world
> which he has created according to his will. May he establish his
> kingdom in your lifetime and during your days, and within the life of
> the entire house of Israel, speedily and soon; and say, Amen. (Trans.
> in P. Birnbaum, *Daily Prayer Book*) .

This prayer which is also in Aramaic is quite old and may predate the
time of Jesus.

"Give us today our daily bread" (or: "the bread of tomorrow")[6] and
forgive us our debts as we forgive our debtors and lead us not into
temptation but deliver us from the evil one." The last three petitions
involve physical and spiritual needs. Disciples must lay their needs
before God their father in openness and honesty. The idea of being
debtors to God because of our sin is later made into a parable (Mt 18:23-
27; see Chapter 9). The last petition for protection from the devil is based
most. likely on an Aramaic causative (the aphel). This form in Aramaic
can mean "Do not allow us to enter into temptation (beyond our ability to
resist)". In other words Jesus wants his disciples to pray so that we will

not be overwhelmed by temptation.[7]

Conclusion of the Sermon (Aland 75)

Space does not permit us to discuss every pericope in the Sermon. Many of the sayings will be dealt with in Chapter 12. Jesus continues by giving teaching on anxiety, judging one another, producing fruit and other topics. Then he comes to the gripping conclusion.

The parable of the two house builders shows that there are two ways of responding to Jesus' words. Each way has its own result. One way leads to life; the other way leads to destruction. Several Old Testament texts might have suggested this parable to Jesus, such as Deuteronomy 28:30; Proverbs 10:25; 12:17. The best Old Testament parallel to Jesus' parable, however, is Proverbs 14:11-12:

> The house of the wicked will be destroyed, but the tent of the upright will flourish. There is a way which seems right to a man, but the end is the way of death.

The importance of doing good not just knowing good was stressed in Judaism. In particular the possibility of two ways, the way of obedience to God which brings life and the way of disobedience which brings death, was a recurring theme. An interesting parable occurs in the rabbinic literature that is somewhat similar to Jesus' parable:

> Elisha ben Abuya says: One in whom there are good works, who has studied much Torah, to what may he be likened? To a person who builds first with stones and afterward with bricks: even when much water comes and collects by their side, it does not dislodge them. But one in whom there are no good works, though he studies Torah, to what may he be likened? To a person who builds first with bricks and afterward with stones: even when a little water gathers, it overturns them immediately. (Aboth de Rabbi Nathan 24; trans. in Davies and Allison).

Jesus' words are not just interesting speculation or philosophical babbling. They are the words of life. To ignore them, to fail to heed them, is to build the house of ones life on the sand. R.C. Foster captures the emotion of Jesus' dramatic ending:

> Hear the wild, rushing roar of the storm as blinding lightning pierces

the night sky! See the swift destruction descending upon the heedless! Hear the crash of falling timbers and stones and the shrieks of those caught in the toils of their own folly! (p. 473).

Notes

1. See I. Elbogen, *Der Juedische Gottesdienst.*

2. See the collection of other insulting terms found in the rabbinic literature in S-B Vol. I, 280-282.

3. On honor and shame in the ancient world see B. Malina, *The New Testament World, Insights from Cultural Anthropology.* For an ancient text, see m. Aboth 3:15.

4. For verses 29-30 see Chapter 12.

5. See Mk 14:36 and par.; Mt 6:9 and par.; Mt 11:25 and par.; Lk 23:34, 46; Mt 26:42; Jn 11:41; 12:27-28; 17:1, 5, 11, 21, 24, 25.

6. The Greek word *epiousios* is variously translated. See BAGD.

7. The words at the end of the Lord's Prayer as it appears in the King James Bible ("For thine is the kingdom and the power and the glory forever, Amen") are not found in the oldest and best manuscripts and thus are omitted from all recent translations such as the NIV. Both the Sinaiticus and Vaticanus mss omit it.

CHAPTER 11

THE MIRACLES OF JESUS

Bibliography: P. Achtemeier, *Mark*; F.W. Beare, *The Earliest Records of Jesus*; O. Betz and W. Grimm, *Wesen und Wirklichkeit der Wunder Jesu*; B. Blackburn, *Theios Aner*; C. Brown, *Miracles and the Critical Mind*; R. Brown, *The Gospel According to John*; R. Bultmann, *The History of the Synoptic Tradition*; idem., *Kerygma and Myth*; J.H. Charlesworth, ed., *Jesus and the Dead Sea Scrolls*; M. Connick, *Jesus the Man, the Mission, and the Message*; J.D. Crossan, *The Historical Jesus*; W.D. Davies and D. Allison, *The Gospel According to St. Matthew*; J. Fitzmyer, *The Gospel According to Luke*; J. Fossum, "Understanding Jesus' Miracles" *Bible Review* 10.2 (1994) 17-23; R.C. Foster, *Studies In the Life of Christ*; R.M. Grant, *Miracle and Natural Law in Graeco-Roman and Early Christian Thought*; C. Holladay, *Theios Aner*; H.C. Kee, *Miracles In the Early Christian World*; J. Klausner, *Jesus of Nazareth*; W.L. Lane, *The Gospel According to Mark*; X. Le'on-Dufour, S.J., ed., *Les miracles de Je'sus*; C.S. Lewis, *Miracles*; S.V. McCasland, *By the Finger of God*; C.S. Mann, *Mark*; I.H. Marshall, *The Gospel of Luke;* J.P. Meier, *A Marginal Jew*; E.R. Micklem, *Miracles and the New Testament Psychology*; R.L. Murray, *Can I Believe in Miracles?*; F. Mussner, *The Miracles of Jesus: An Introduction*; A. Richardson, *The Miracle Stories of the Gospels;* C.F. Rogers, *The Case for Miracle*; A. Schweitzer, *The Quest of the Historical Jesus*; Morton Smith, *Jesus the Magician*; D. Strauss, *The Life of Jesus Critically Examined*; V. Taylor, *The*

Gospel According to Mark; W.M. Taylor, *The Miracles of Our Saviour*; F.R. Tennant, *Miracle and Its Philosophical Presuppositions*; G. Theissen, *The Miracle Stories of the Early Christian Tradition*; J. M. Thompson, *Miracles in the New Testament*; R.C. Trench, *Notes on the Miracles of Our Lord*; H. van der Loos, *The Miracles of Jesus*; G. Vermes, *Jesus the Jew*; J. Wendland, *Miracles and Christianity*; D. Wenham and C. Blomberg, eds., *The Miracles of Jesus*; C.J. Wright, *Miracle In History and In Modern Thought*.

The Modern Interpretation of Jesus' Miracles

For nearly eighteen hundred years the church believed that the miracles attributed to Jesus actually happened. Then in the nineteenth century under the influence of scepticism, some in the church began to doubt the authenticity of the miracles in the Bible and even the possibility of miracles in general.

The Rationalists

The first group to challenge the veracity of the miracles attributed to Jesus were the rationalists who tried to find some natural explanation for the alleged supernaturalistic occurrences (see Schweitzer's survey). H.E.G. Paulus believed that in the past people were impressed by miracles but that now we must seek rational explanations. The Biblical miracles, Paulus affirmed, were simply events for which causes were unknown. Thus Paulus explained healings in the Gospels as the cure of illness caused by psychosomatic effect. He claimed that most of the people healed by Jesus were not really sick at all from an actual physical disease. In addition he maintained that Jesus, when he supposedly raised people from the dead, actually brought them out of a coma.

But Paulus' explanations are difficult to swallow. Jesus is reported to have cured lepers, people lame from birth and blind from birth. These cannot have been psychosomatic. Further, are we to assume that the ancients could not tell if someone was dead? Rationalists have a distinct tendency to see the ancients as hopelessly ignorant and ready to believe just about anything.

Paulus explained the nature miracles as follows: Jesus' walking on the water was really a case of his walking on the shore in shallow water. He could calm the sea only because the disciples sailed out of the storm. He fed the 5,000 people by setting the rich an example of sharing. The transfiguration happened when Jesus and two friends were seen by his disciples with the sun at their backs. Jesus' resurrection was really his recovery from a trance or swoon. His ascension was only a cloud of mist that moved in when Jesus walked away.

And so goes the rationalistic explanations. Most of these are laughable. Would anyone be so slow witted as not to know that a person was walking on the sea shore? Further, one did not just sail out of storms on the Sea of Galilee. It is only six miles wide and thus storms usually cover the entire surface of the sea. The other alleged explanations are not worth commenting upon. Jesus' resurrection and the alleged swoon will be handled in a later chapter.

K.A. Hase, in typical rationalist fashion, also accepted the Gospel record as factual but explained the events as natural happenings. His explanations win the prize for hilarity. The voice of God that Jesus heard at his baptism was actually, affirmed Hase, a meteor that passed over head. Jairus' daughter whom Jesus raised from the dead was actually, maintained Hase, only asleep. Again, Hase like most of the representatives of this school of interpretation assumed that the ancient people of Palestine were abysmally stupid and gullible.

Many more recent interpreters such as Vermes, Thompson, McCasland, and Micklem also understand Jesus' miracles in this way.

Mythological Interpretation

Another way of viewing the miracles was proposed by David Strauss also in the nineteenth century and he has been followed by a twentieth century scholar, R. Bultmann. Strauss wrote that myth is the clothing in historic form of religious ideas. These ideas are shaped by the unconsciously inventive power of legend and embodied in a historic personality. Thus Strauss saw the miraculous events in the life of Jesus as follows: Jesus' baptism really happened but the part about the descent of the Holy Spirit is myth. This did not happen but was invented by the writers to express their conviction that Jesus was God's chosen one. His healings did not happened but were invented entirely by the authors to show that Jesus surpassed the Old Testament prophets. The feeding of the 5,000 did not happen but was composed based on Old Testament stories. The transfiguration also did not happen (Jesus and the disciples were not even on the mountain for that matter) but rather, maintained Strauss, is a myth created to point out that Jesus was the perfecter of the kingdom by narrating the appearance of the lawgiver (Moses) and the reformer (Elijah). The resurrection and ascension are also nothing but myths, created entirely by the pens of the Gospel writers. Strauss maintained that the essence of the Christian faith is independent of criticism and historical investigation. The Virgin Birth, miracles, resurrection, ascension and so forth are eternal truths but not historical facts. The early Christians were uneducated orientals who adapted and expressed their ideas only in concrete ways of fantasy as pictures and stories and not in abstract forms of rational concepts. Thus if the rationalists went to absurd lengths to explain by natural causes the extraordinary events recorded in the Gospels, Strauss explained them all by appealing to the imaginations of the writers. The rationalist would say that the transfiguration, for example, was a mistake made when the sun partially blinded Jesus' disciples and caused them to think he was being transfigured. Strauss would say nothing happened at all except in the fertile mind of the writer as he sat in his room and composed the story.

Strauss, however, forgot about all of the eye witnesses running around Palestine that could verify and refute the events recorded in our four Gospels (Lk 1:1-4; Heb 2:3; Jn 19:35). What would they have thought about such created stories? Further what of the fact that all four Gospels claim that Jesus did miracles? Does Strauss's explanation not mean that all of the Gospel writers created stories? Is it likely that all would do that? Finally, we have other sources beside the Gospels that indicate that Jesus performed miracles. Josephus seems to be referring to Jesus' miracles (*Antiquities* 18.63) when he says Jesus did "surprising feats." The Talmud (see Chapter 4) accuses Jesus of sorcery or performing miracles by magic as did Celsus the pagan (Origen, *Contra Celsus* 1.6). This is a negative way of admitting that Jesus did do miracles. If even his detractors admitted that he performed miracles, we must conclude that Strauss's explanations are without merit. The wholesale dismissal of all of the events considered miraculous is unwarranted.

The "Magician" School of Interpretation

More recently, Morton Smith (followed by Crossan) has asserted that Jesus certainly did do miracles (though his definition of the term is often unclear). The charge by the Pharisees and others that Jesus cast out demons because he himself was possessed by Beelzebub (Mt 12:22-29) is tantamount to an admission on their part observed Smith that Jesus did miracles. The Pharisees never claimed he faked miracles. They accepted that he actually did them, but claimed he did them by the power of the Satan. Smith agreed with the Pharisees that Jesus really was a practitioner of magic and went to great lengths to offer parallels with ancient magicians. Crossan has tried to place Jesus' miracles in the context of Mediterranean anthropological studies of shamans. Crossan seems to be more open to the supernatural element (p. 337) but he is reductionistic in classifying Jesus' "magic" as typical of every other "shaman" in the Mediterranean world. Not only is it inappropriate to term Jesus' miracles "magic" (see Meier), in the end both Morton Smith and Crossan are only rationalists with a new approach. Smith asserted that these healings were really only done by the power of suggestion and they worked because of "psychological reasons."

The Supernaturalistic View

It is the tendency of those denying the possibility of miracles to suggest that modern science has disproved them or made it impossible to believe in them. Science, it is maintained, has shown us that the universe operates according to certain rules or laws and these cannot be superseded. Such people often say or imply that only ancients, with their unscientific superstitions, could believe in miracles. This amounts of course to an *ad hominem* argument or argument "to the man". Such persons argue that only ignorant and unscientific ancient peoples (and their contemporary, out-of-touch heirs) can believe in miracles. But *ad hominem* arguments can always go both ways. Maybe the ancients, for example, were less biased against miracles and, therefore, could believe them more readily.

But is it true that science has proven the impossibility of miracles because they would be breaking the natural laws of the universe? C.S. Lewis responds:

> But mere experience, even if prolonged for a million years, cannot tell us whether the thing is possible. Experiment finds out what regularly happens in Nature: the norm or rule to which she works. Those who believe in miracles are not denying that there is such a norm or rule:

they are only saying that it can be suspended. A miracle is by definition an exception. How can the discovery of the rule tell you whether, granted a sufficient cause, the rule can be suspended? (chapter 7, *Miracles*).

Thus the denial of the possibility of miracles is illogical and a judgment of bias, not of science. In spite of such influential writers as C.S. Lewis, many who even profess to be Christians rule out the possibility of miracles. They have swallowed the line of the naturalist and still attempt to swim around in the pool of the believer.

The most honest and open minded position regarding miracles is to allow that they are possible. But we are not maintaining that we can or should be made to prove that every miracle or any of the miracles attributed to Jesus actually occurred. It is enough for this author that, given the possibility of miracles, the Gospels claim that Jesus performed them. Thus the acceptance of the miracles as authentic happenings is a matter of faith, as Richardson has maintained:

> Thus the answer to the question, Did the miracles (of Jesus) happen? is always a personal answer. It is not the judgment of an historian *qua* scientific investigator. . . It is the "Yes" of faith to the challenge which confronts us in the New Testament presentation of Christ--the only Christ we can know.

The Exegesis of Some of Jesus' Miracles

Miracles in One Gospel

	Mt	Mk	Lk	Jn
Water to wine				2:1ff
Lame man				5:1ff
Catch of fish			5:1ff	
Widow's son			7:11ff	
Blind-mute	12:22			
Two blind men	9:27ff			
Mute demoniac	9:32f			
Blind man		8:22ff		
Temple tax	17:24ff			
Blind man				9:1ff
Crippled woman			13:10ff	
Man with dropsy			14:1ff	
Lazarus raised*				11:17ff

Ten lepers		17:11ff	
Malchus' ear		22:49ff	
Catch of fish			21:1ff

Miracles in Two Gospels

Deaf-mute*	15:29ff	7:31ff	
Demoniac		1:23ff	4:33ff
Gentile girl	15:21ff	7:24ff	
4000 fed	15:32ff	8:1ff	

Miracles in Three Gospels

Centurion's boy*	8:5ff		7:1ff	4:46ff
Peter's mother-in-law	8:14ff	1:29ff	4:38f	
Leper*	8:2ff	1:40ff	5:12ff	
Paralytic	9:2ff	2:3ff	5:18ff	
Withered hand	12:10ff	3:1ff	6:6ff	
Storm calmed*	8:23ff	4:35ff	8:22ff	
Two demoniacs*	8:28ff	5:1ff	8:26ff	
Suffering woman	9:20ff	5:25ff	8:43ff	
Jairus' daughter	9:23ff	5:35ff	8:49ff	
Walking on water*	14:25ff	6:45ff		6:16ff
Epileptic boy	17:14ff	9:14ff	9:38ff	
Two blind men	20:29ff	10:46ff	18:35ff	

Miracles in Four Gospels

5000 fed*	14:15ff	6:35ff	9:12ff	6:1ff

Table 11.1
Jesus' Miracles
(*Denotes miracles discussed in this chapter)

We will divide the miracles of Jesus into five different categories[1]: 1) healings, 2) resuscitations, 3) exorcisms, 4) nature miracles, and 5) feeding miracles.

Healings (Aland 42, 85, 152)

The first healing miracle we will examine is found in Mark 1:40-45 and parallels (most of the miracles are narrated in greater detail in Mark). This is the account of Jesus' healing or "cleansing" a leper. Leviticus 13 details the procedure for one stricken with a skin disease that could be leprosy. The priest among other duties was supposed to be an expert in the symptoms of leprosy. If one were diagnosed as having the dreaded disease he had to stand outside the camp or outside the city and warn passers-by that he was infected by yelling, "Unclean!" (Lev 13:45). If someone were healed[2] of this disease he had to go through another procedure of cleansing (Lev 14:1-32) which included making a sacrifice of a lamb and a ritual bath. Thus leprosy was not just a disease it was ritual impurity and no Jew meticulous about ritual purity (like the Pharisees and Essenes) would associate with lepers. When one was "cured" of this disease, therefore, one had to go through a cleansing process in order to be admitted back into the camp of Israel and back in association with other practicing Jews.

The Essenes were especially concerned that nothing unclean would be in their villages and cities. They designated an area east of the city of Jerusalem, for example, (see the Temple Scroll, 11QT 46) as the place of residence of lepers. It is interesting that this location seems to coincide with the village of Bethany the home of Simon the leper whom Jesus also healed (Mk 14:3; see Charlesworth).

But notice in the healing of this leper that Jesus is not offended by his presence nor does he seek to avoid him in order to protect his own ritual purity. On the contrary, because Jesus is moved emotionally (Gk: *splangchnistheis*; Mk 1:41) he actually touches this wretchedly ill person. He volunteered out of compassion to make himself unclean. Jesus consistently put the needs of others ahead of the concerns of ritual purity, food laws, and even Sabbath laws.

Jesus' touch healed or cleansed the leper. He now charges the former leper to do two things: 1) Not to tell anyone what has happened (Jesus did not want to be known as merely a wonder worker but also as a teacher). 2) Report to the priest for the pronouncement of cleanness as Leviticus commanded.

The next healing is that of the Roman centurion/official's son/servant found in Luke 7:1-10 (and par. in Mt) and John 4:46-54. Many commentators consider the miracles in Luke (and par.) and in John to be different miracles (see e.g. Trench, Foster). But the details, though somewhat different, do not seem sufficient to conclude that these are two separate incidents. Both take place in Capernaum, are healings of a sick boy somehow related to or belonging to a man of prominence, and the miracles take place at a distance. R. Brown is correct to conclude that all three accounts concern the same event, though one must use one's imagination a bit to figure out how to harmonize them.

Was the boy the man's servant or his son? Perhaps he was a servant boy whom the centurion adopted. Such an occurrence was not at all uncommon in the ancient world.

The miracle is here not just that Jesus cured a very sick lad but that he did so from a distance without seeing the boy or even being in the vicinity of the boy. Elisha healed a Syrian king of leprosy (1 Kings 5:10-11) by sending word with his servant rather than coming himself to the king. Even more significant is the parallel in the Talmud. The great Rabbi Hanina ben Dosa to whom several miracles are attributed (see below), is supposed to have healed the son of Rabbi Gamaliel II from a distance. Emissaries came to Galilee to request prayer and Hanina ascended to his upper room. After returning, he announced that the boy had been healed in Jerusalem (b. Beracoth 34b). This story illustrates that people would send for help from quite a distance in the desperate search for someone to aid a sick child.

Matthew points out especially that the centurion--already a pious God-fearer who had built at least part of the synagogue in Capernaum (Lk 7:5)--had great faith in Jesus. This is contrasted with the comparative lack of faith in many of Jesus' Jewish contemporaries. Indeed at the Messianic banquet (Mt 8:11-12) Gentiles like the centurion will feature prominently while many of the supposed righteous leaders of Israel will be cast out.

Jesus did not preach and heal only within the borders of Galilee, Judea, and Perea, as we pointed out in chapter 8. Some of his most impressive miracles were in Gentile areas. That is true of the next healing miracle, the healing of the deaf mute (Mk 7:31-37 and par). Jesus has come into the region of the Decapolis (i.e. the ten Greek cities which were in a loose confederation with one another). In this case Mark records that Jesus touched the affected parts by putting his fingers into the man's ears and by spitting and touching the man's tongue with the spital (cf. Mk 8:23; Jn 9:6). These symbolic actions were to indicate to the sufferer that he was about to be healed. In addition, Mark gives us the exact Aramaic word that Jesus used in the healing, "*Ephphatha*". Although some Jews were planning ways to discredit and even kill Jesus, Gentiles were experiencing some great miracles. But even more important is the fact that Jesus was fulfilling Old Testament prophecies. Isaiah 35:5-6 predicted that the deaf would hear, the mute would speak, the blind would see, and the lame would walk.

Resuscitations (Aland 259)

We use the term resuscitation here to distinguish from resurrection. Only Jesus has been resurrected thus far, that is raised to a glorified, incorruptible body. The people Jesus raised from the dead were only temporarily given life in the body once more. Later they died a normal death. At the second coming we will be given a glorified body that will not decay.

Jesus raised three people from the dead according to the Gospels: the widow's son at Nain, a tiny village in Galilee (Lk 7:11-17); Jairus' daughter (Mk 5:21-43 and par.); and Lazarus of Bethany, a village just east of Jerusalem (Jn 11:1-44).

The raising of Lazarus is the seventh and greatest "sign" in the Gospel of John (see 2:1-11; 4:43-54; 5:1-15; 6:1-15; 6:16-21; 9:1-12 for the first six signs). It both caps the series of signs or miracles and introduces us to the Passion Narrative or the story of Jesus' death. Its point is to demonstrate the awesomeness of Jesus' power and to explain that death cannot overcome him.

Many scholars conclude that Lazarus of Bethany is the same as Simon the leper of Bethany (Mk 14:3) and that therefore Lazarus has died from leprosy. He is certainly not the same as the Lazarus of the parable in Luke (16:19-31) for in that parable--which is probably only a fictional story anyway, see chapter 10--Lazarus is a very poor man with no home or relatives to look after him. The Lazarus of Bethany is a man of some means who can afford a house and a tomb and has at least two sisters.

It is significant that all three of the names of this family--Lazarus, Mary and Martha--have been found in inscriptions in Palestine of this period and one tomb near Bethany indicates that three people by this name were buried in it.[3] This is important since some sceptics have maintained that the story is fictional and that the name Lazarus is purely symbolic.

Jesus clearly has known this family for some time and loves them all as if they were his brother and sisters (cf. Lk 10:38-42 and Jn 11:3, 5). They believe that Jesus is the Messiah, the son of God (Martha's confession is similar to Peter's. See 11:27) and therefore when Lazarus is near death they send word to him for help. Jesus delays in coming in order that Lazarus might die and that he might then raise him from the dead. This miracle will glorify God and himself (11:4). Jesus will be glorified not in that people will marvel at the miracle but because the miracle will lead to his own death (11:45-57). The chief priests and other leaders will plot

Jesus' death because of the raising of Lazarus. But their plans, though apparently successful at first, will fail because Jesus will conquer death. As Jesus declares of himself: "I am the Resurrection and the Life. He that believes in me, even though he should die, will live (eternally)" (11:25).

Exorcisms (Aland 91)

Jesus often encountered people possessed by demons. Some modern interpreters maintain that we should psychologize these demonic experiences. In other words, they want us to view the demon possessed people as people afflicted by psychological problems. But that is a conclusion that is based more on bias than evidence. In many of these encounters Jesus converses with the demons (e.g. Mk 1:24) and here in the example we will presently discuss the demons even give their name and beg not to be sent into the abyss (Lk 8:31). The New Testament authors clearly believed in the existence of such beings (e.g. Eph 2:2; Col 2:15).

There are many references to demons and demon possession in the ancient world. Those who claimed to be able to exorcise demons were also plentiful. The famous pagan healer, Apollonius of Tyana, is said to have cast out demons. The numerous Greek magical papyri also attest to the prevalence of magic texts which claimed to help in warding off demons.

But Jews also tried to cast out demons. The pseudepigraphical book, the Testament of Solomon (see OTP), demonstrates that Solomon of the Old Testament was considered the patron of exorcism among Jews. Josephus also relates the case of an exorcism performed by a certain Eleazar who lived in the first century AD and cast out a demon using secret knowledge he thought came from Solomon:

> He put a ring that had a root of one of those sorts mentioned by Solomon to the nostrils of the demoniac, after which he drew out the demon through his nostrils; and when the man fell down immediately, he abjured him to return into him no more, making still mention of Solomon, and reciting the incantations which he composed. (*Antiquities* 8.46-47; Trans. By W. Whiston)

How different Jesus' exorcisms were! Jesus merely had to speak and the demons obeyed. There were no elaborate procedures or rituals to seek to trick or coax the demons out of a person. The simple accounts in the

Gospels of Jesus' overpowering the forces of Satan by the word of his mouth stand in marked contrast to the stories found in other literature.

Without a doubt Jesus' exorcism of the man plagued by a legion of demons (Mk 5:1-20 and par.) is the most detailed narrative of an exorcism in the Gospels. Where did the miracle take place? The manuscripts read variously: Gerasa (a city some 30 miles southeast of the Sea of Galilee); Gadara (a city around six miles southeast of the Sea of Galilee); and Gergesa (a village on the eastern shore of the Sea of Galilee). The last one is a good candidate since there is a steep slope nearby (Mk 5:13) and some ancient tombs (Mk 5:2). Origen, the third century Christian writer, who also lived for a time in Caesarea Maritima, identified Gergesa as the location of this miracle. But as V. Taylor has shown, the miracle could have taken place in the territory of Gerasa, some of which bordered on the Sea of Galilee. The exact location is therefore unclear but must have been somewhere on the eastern shore of the Sea of Galilee.

There in that Gentile area Jesus encountered a man[4] horribly disfigured because of being tormented by a host of demons. The demons say that their collective name is "legion" (Mk 5:9). Normally a Roman legion has around 6000 men but we should not necessarily think that this poor fellow was tormented by so many demonic spirits. There were simply many of them. Imagine what a horrible life it was for this wretched victim who raved uncontrollably night and day and whose only companions were these Satanic minions and the corpses of the graves he inhabited!

Jesus immediately commanded the demons to depart whereupon they begged him not to send them to the abyss (the abode of Satan; Rev 20:3). Instead they requested to be sent into a herd of pigs which was grazing in this Gentile territory. Jesus complied with their request then caused the pigs to stampede into the sea and drown.

This incident like Jesus' miracles in general is interpreted variously. The rationalists (see Taylor) maintain that the man was only psychologically tormented and in his insane frenzy scared the pigs into stampeding into the sea and drowning. The mythological school (Bultmann) maintains that this is a borrowed story about a thwarted demon applied here to the life of Jesus. The whole thing is simply an old legend that the Gospel writers, they maintain, slipped into their Gospels. Again, we would say these views are more assumed than proven. The best conclusion is that Jesus really did cast out the demons because he is Lord is the cosmos, both of things seen and unseen. He sent the demons into the pigs to demonstrate the hostility of the demons and the forces of Satan (Lane).

The grateful victim wants to follow Jesus and become a disciple. He has no fear of Jesus, unlike the people of the nearby town, but merely wants to do some service for his new master. This is of course quite impossible since Jesus was preaching primarily among Jews who would have been even more incensed and offended at the prospect of a Gentile in his company. The Gentile mission would come but the time was not right for it.

Nature Miracles (Aland 90, 147)

The first of the nature miracles that we will consider is Jesus' calming of the storm on the Sea of Galilee (Mk 4:35-41 and par.). Storms arise quickly and furiously on this little body of water which is only twelve miles long and six miles wide at its widest point. If one of the small[5] fishing boats happens to be out in the water at the time, it can be quite dangerous.

The story bears some resemblance to the story of Jonah. Like Jesus, Jonah was sleeping--probably from exhaustion--while the storm raged (Jonah 1:5). Like Jesus' disciples, the other men on Jonah's ship awakened him with the urgent request that he pray to his God for safety (Jonah 1:6). The difference, as Trench pointed out, is that Jonah was the cause of the storm while Jesus was the deliverer from it.

Jesus first rebukes his disciples for their fear and their small amount of faith. The follower of Jesus should have trust and a measure of serenity even in the face of what appears to be imminent death. The disciples go in the story from fear of the storm to fear of Jesus. Yet neither fear is proper. Jesus was no mere wonder worker whose presence should have inspired awe. He was the savior who has come to give his life a ransom for us all.

Next Jesus rebukes the wind in the same way he had rebuked disease (Lk 4:39). At his word the winds obey just as illnesses are driven out. This is because the author of evil in our present world is Satan. Thus in calming the winds and delivering his disciples from death Jesus was rebuking Satan and his power.

As Trench rightly noted, the striking element in this miracle in comparison with Moses' parting the Red Sea is that Christ needed no instrument such as Moses' staff but his very word, "Peace!", sufficed to calm the raging storm.

The second nature miracle we will look at briefly is the walking on the water (Mt 14:22-33 and par.; Jn 6:16-21). This event happened after the feeding of the five thousand. In the night after the feeding miracle as the disciples were rowing back to the western shore of the Sea of Galilee, Jesus came to them walking on the water. The allegation of the rationalists--that Jesus was walking on the shore or in shallow water and so fooled his disciples--is patently ridiculous. They were in the middle of the sea (which is about 600 feet deep in the middle) and laboring hard at their oars against a strong wind.

The response of the disciples when they saw Jesus was terror. All three Gospels (Mt, Mk, Jn) indicate the spine tingling fear that the disciples felt when they saw a man walking in this wind on the sea. Jesus tried to reassure them by saying, "Don't be afraid. It's me."

Here Matthew adds a short narrative about Peter. In one other place in Matthew (16:17-19) there is also material about Peter that no other Gospel records. Luke (22:31-32) has special tradition about Peter as well. It is interesting that Mark's Gospel, which according to ancient testimony was written under the direction of Peter, has so little in it about Peter. We surely should explain this fact out of Peter's modesty in recalling events about himself.

Peter wants to walk on the water like Jesus. Jesus invites him to join him but when Peter begins to think about the deep water and high winds, he panics and sinks. Jesus rescues him with the rebuke, "You of little faith!" When the boat reached the shore again the disciples were overwhelmed by fear and awe of Jesus the miracle worker. They still did not understand him as he was. They still could only think of him in terms of a worldly wonder worker.

Feeding Miracles (Aland 146)

We considered one of Jesus' feeding miracles in chapter 8 when there we commented on the changing of the water into wine (Jn 2:1-10). Four other miracles are in this category: the catches of fish (Lk 5:1-11 when Jesus was first calling his disciples; and again in Jn 21:1-11 after his resurrection); the feeding of the four thousand (Mk 8:1-10 and par); and the miracle we will discuss here, the feeding of the five thousand (Mk 6:32-44 and par.; Jn 6:1-15).

The miracle of the feeding of the five thousand men (not counting the women and children present) made a great impression on the early church. We can tell this because this miracle alone is recorded in all four

Gospels. In addition, the feeding of the five thousand was depicted in some of the most ancient Christian art on the walls of the catacombs of Rome.[6] Thus this event was remembered widely by the early church.

All four Gospels agree that 5000 men were fed; that five loaves and two fish were used to feed them; that the people sat down in orderly fashion in order to be fed; that Jesus blessed the bread in prayer and then distributed it to them; and that they afterwards picked up twelve baskets full of scraps and leftovers (In other words, there were more leftovers than they started with.).

Mark and John both note that one of Jesus' disciples responded, when Jesus told them to feed the crowd, that not even 200 denarii (almost a year's earnings for a day laborer) could buy enough bread for that crowd; and that the miracle took place in the spring of the year (Mk says the grass was green which only happens in the spring; Jn says the event took place at Passover time).

Matthew and Mark use the Greek term *eremos*, "desert", to describe the place along the shore of the Sea of Galilee where the miracle took place. Since there is no actual dry desert there, they must have meant that it was a lonely place or uninhabited place, but the use of that word calls to the mind of the reader the wilderness wandering of Israel described in Exodus through Deuteronomy.

Matthew and Luke note that Jesus first healed the sick before doing the miracle of multiplying the loaves.

Luke alone indicates that the place of the miracle was in the general vicinity of Bethsaida.

John alone informs us that after this miracle some people in the crowd believed that Jesus was the eschatological prophet like Moses (Deut 18) and therefore tried to take Jesus by force and make him their king. The eschatological prophet was expected by Jews in this period as the Dead Sea Scrolls show (see 1QS 9:11; 1QSa; 4QTestamonia). That some people would become so religiously excited at this miracle is understandable when we consider: 1) Herod Antipas had put John the Baptist to death partly out of fear that just such a crowd would start a revolution with John at the head (see above, Chapter 7). Thus there were certainly people in Galilee that were willing to start a revolution, given the right leader. 2) Jesus' feeding the crowd in the desert with bread is strongly reminiscent of Moses--the ancient deliverer of the Israelites--who fed them in the wilderness with manna. Making the crowd sit in organized groups is also reminiscent of the Mosaic camp (Ex 18:21 and Lane). 3) The event like many of Jesus' fellowship meals is certainly a foretaste and harbinger of the Messianic banquet (see chapter 8 and Isaiah 25:6-8; Ezek 39:17-20; Rev 19:17-18).[7] 4) As Lane points out Jesus is acting the role of the Good Shepherd in Psalm 23 who is Yahweh ("Yahweh is my shepherd" Ps 23:1). Thus Jesus makes his followers to sit down in green pastures (Mk 6:39) and feeds them.

Jesus got word of the designs of these fervent Jews who wanted to force him to be their king (were they a group that would someday become Zealots?) and eluded them by going into the hills to pray. He knew that they misunderstood his mission. One other element of this miracle should be noted here. This event is not only a foretaste of the Messianic banquet but also a prelude to the Lord's Supper. Jesus explicitly says so in the sermon in John delivered the next day (Jn 6:32-58, esp. vv. 53-54). Thus just as Jesus nourished these people physically with the bread, so he would nourish them spiritually with the bread of his word.

What is interesting is that just as in virtually all of the other miracles there is no actual description of the miracle. We are simply told that Jesus broke off parts of the bread and fish and continued to distribute these until all had been feed to satisfaction. The miracle is both witnessed by thousands of people and attested by all four Gospels and early Christian art and at the same time shrouded in mystery.

The Interpretation of Jesus' Miracles

We have already noted that there were others in Judaism that allegedly performed a few miracles. We referred above to Eleazar the exorcist and Rabbi Hanina ben Dosa who purportedly not only cured the boy from a distance but also was once bitten by a poisonous snake but did not die (t. Beracoth 2:20). In addition there was the famous Honi the Circle Drawer who prayed for rain in a time of drought and his prayer was heard(*Antiquities* 14.22-24; m. Taanith 3:8).

That there were miracle workers--charismatic figures called *hasidim* by the rabbis--in ancient Judaism is clear. God may have empowered certain Jews just as he did in the Old Testament era. We should point out, however, that the sources attesting to these miracles are from 200 to 500 years after the miracle worker lived. The Gospels, on the other hand, were written only a few decades after Jesus lived.

But the difference between Jesus and these other Jewish wonder workers is in both the number of miracles and in the purpose. Jesus must have done hundreds of healings and other miracles. We listed above in a table the recorded miracles but this is not to mention the numerous times when the text of the Gospels simply says, "And he healed their sick," or something similar. But the other miracle workers are said to have done only a handful of miracles.

Second, Jesus' miracles were signs pointing to his message and validating his message. The exorcist, Eleazar, practiced by his assumed knowledge of secret roots, knowledge the Jews thought had been passed down from generation to generation from Solomon. Jesus' exorcisms meant the kingdom of God was breaking into this age and Satan was being bound. Thus the purpose of Jesus' miracles was quite different.

Jesus' miracles are for the most part continuations of the ministries of Moses and Elijah-Elisha. But in Jesus was something greater than Moses and Elijah. God through Moses (Ex 14:15-31) overpowered the sea by dividing it so the Israelites could pass through. Jesus calmed the sea (Mk 4:35-41) during a raging storm and walked on the water (Mk 6:45-52). God fed the hungry through Moses (Ex 16:4), Elijah (1 Kings 17:7-26), and Elisha (2 Kings 4:1-7; 7:38-44). Jesus fed at least 5000 and later 4000 by multiplying a few small loaves (Mk 6:35-44; 8:1-9). Elisha healed a leper (2 Kings 5:1-14) but Jesus healed many lepers (Lk 17:11-19; Mk 1:40-45). Jesus also went beyond even the great Moses, Elijah and Elisha. He performed many other healing miracles and even overcame demons, the emissaries of the Evil One (Mk 5:11-20). Jesus was a healer and miracle worker like Moses, Elijah, and Elisha, but he was far greater than they.

It is true that Jesus performed miracles because of his compassion for the suffering and needy. He healed diseases (Mk 1:41; 6:34; Lk 7:13), cast out demons (Mk 9:22) and miraculously fed the hungry (Mk 8:2) because he felt *splanchna* ("strong compassion") when he saw their plight. His mighty acts, therefore, were acts of mercy and love to help the unfortunate.

But Jesus mainly performed his miracles as "signs" (*semeia*, Jn 2:11; 3:2) that the kingdom of God was breaking into history in his person. The kingdom of God brings about Satan's downfall and with it, his power to inflict suffering through demon possession. Thus Jesus' ministry was to "bind the strong man" (Satan) so that Jesus might plunder his house (i.e. release those held captive by demon possession, Mt 12:29). Jesus therefore affirmed, "But if it is by the Spirit of God that I cast out demons, then the kingdom of God has come upon you (=God now reigns in your midst; Mt 12:28). Jesus made a similar statement to John the Baptist when asked if he was the Messiah (Mt 11:4-5). Jesus' miracles, therefore, were an integral part of his message and ministry.

Notes

1. For the categories of miracles in general see Betz and Grimm who posit four categories: apocalyptic signs, healings from disease, deliverance from danger or death, and theophanies.

2. Actually there was no cure for genuine leprosy apart from miraculous divine intervention. It continued until it hideously took the life of the sufferer. But many skin rashes and diseases would be diagnosed in a preliminary way as leprosy. See D.P. Wright and R.N. Jones, "Leprosy" in *ABD*; E.V. Hulse, "The Nature of the Biblical Leprosy and the Use of Alternative Medical Terms in Modern Translations of the Bible" *Palestine Exploration Quarterly* 107 (1975) 87-105; and J. Zias, "Death and Disease in Ancient Israel" *Biblical Archaeologist* 54/3 (1991) 146-159. Lepers seem to have been very numerous in ancient Palestine: Mk 14:3, Lk 17:12; m. Megillah 1:7; m. Moed Katan 3:1; m. Sotah 1:5; m. Zebahim 14:3; Qumran Damascus Rule (CD) 13; Qumran Temple Scroll (11QT) 46, 48-49; Pseudo Philo 13:3; Apocryphal Syriac Psalm 155 (see OTP, II). For another (non-canonical) text of this miracle, see the Egerton Papyrus in Hennecke.

3. See *Biblical Archaeologist* 90 (1946) 18 and R. Brown.

4. Matthew reports that there were two demoniacs just as he will report that there were two blind men healed at Jericho (see chapter 14). Undoubtedly Luke and Mark who followed him focus on the most vocal of the demoniacs.

5. Just how small the fishing boats were has been recently discovered when the hull of a two thousand year old boat was found in the muddy shores of the Sea of Galilee. This boat is now being preserved in a long process but will eventually be made available for viewing. See the anonymous publication entitled: *An Ancient Boat Discovered in the Sea of Galilee* (Jerusalem. Israel Department of Antiquities and Museums, 1988); S. Wachsman, "The Galilee Boat" *BAR* 14/5 (1988) 18-33; and C. Peachey, "Model Building in Nautical Archaeology: the Kinneret Boat" *Biblical Archaeologist* 53/1 (1990) 46-54.

6. See E. Syndicus, *Early Christian Art*; and Foster.

7. The Messianic banquet was also much talked about in the intertestamental Jewish literature and in the rabbinic literature: 1 Enoch 62:14; 2 Baruch 29:3-4; 1QSa; 3 Enoch 48A:10; b. Baba Bathra 74b; Pesiqta de Rab Kahana 29.

CHAPTER 12

THE TEACHING METHODS OF JESUS

Bibliography: F.F. Bruce, *The Hard Sayings of Jesus*; C.F. Burney, *The Poetry of Our Lord*; R. Bultmann, *The History of the Synoptic Tradition;* M. Connick, *Jesus, the Man, the Mission, and the Message;* J.D. Crossan, *In Fragments: The Aphorisms of Jesus*; G. Dalman, *The Words of Jesus*; W.D. Davies and D. Allison, *The Gospel According to St. Matthew*; J. Fitzmyer, *The Gospel According to Luke*; B. Fletcher, *The Aramaic Sayings of Jesus*; J. Jeremias, *New Testament Theology*; T.W. Manson, *The Teaching of Jesus*; W. Neil, *The Difficult Sayings of Jesus*; R. Pearson, *The Hard Commands of Jesus*; W.A. Piper, *Wisdom in the Q Tradition*; A. Schweitzer, *The Quest of the Historical Jesus;* W.D. Stroker, *The Extracanonical Sayings of Jesus.*

Jesus was a master teacher. Not only was the content of his teaching innovative, his ethics demanding, but also his method made him a model teacher. In this chapter we will examine some of his teaching forms and look at some of his more significant--and in some cases more difficult--sayings. Two of Jesus' teaching forms we have already examined: parables and beatitudes/woes. Now we look at hyperbole, riddle, prophetic sayings, dominical sayings, and poetic parallelism.

Hyperbole

Hyperbole is an obvious exaggeration for emphasis which produces humor or surprise. Jesus said to those inclined to judge others: "Why do you see the speck in your brother's eye but do not perceive the wooden beam in your own eye?" (Mt 7:3). Also he said, "It is easier for a camel to go through a needle's eye than for a rich man to enter the kingdom of God" (Mk 10:25). Both of these statements would have evoked laughter from Jesus' hearers. But they would not have forgotten his point. The point of the first statement is that we often are oblivious of our own faults--even project them on others--while being experts on the faults of others. Such blindness can lead us to ignore faults in ourselves many times more grievous than those in people of whom we are critical.

The point of the second statement is that rich people have a difficult time in general in accepting that they need God and in loving God above their riches. It is easier to thread a camel through the tiny hole of a needle[1] than for a rich person to enter the kingdom of God in humility and complete commitment.

Another hyperbole is the statement Jesus uttered in reference to sexual lust: "If your right hand causes you to stumble (i.e. to sin), cut it off and cast it from you", and the same with ones right eye (Mt 5:29-30). Jesus' admonition to remove offending body parts is an example of hyperbole which must have shocked his audience. Certainly no one can actually do this literally since we would soon become so amputated as to be unable to move about and function. Yet sin would still remain within us. No, this is hyperbole and was intended to shock the listener even though surely no one took it literally. (As Bruce notes, there is no clear example of anyone ever taking this statement literally and thus having parts amputated.) The effects of sin are horrible and eternal life is more important than the physical body. Thus the hyperbole makes vivid and emphatic Jesus' message.

Luke 14:26 is another case of hyperbole: "If anyone comes to me and does not hate his own father, mother, wife, children, brothers, and sisters, still more even his own life, he cannot be my disciple." Since Jesus elsewhere commands us to love everyone, even our enemies (Mt 5:44), he cannot have meant it literally when he said to hate our family members. This is a case of comparison. Compare, for example, Genesis 29:31 where, "Leah was hated" means, "Leah was not favored like

Rachel." Our love for Christ and his kingdom must be so great that even the love we have for our family members--great as that may be and should be--will seem like hate in comparison. This is a hyperbole that shows that nothing and no one must be given priority to Christ (cf. Mt 10:37). Another way of saying this without hyperbole is, "If anyone comes to me and does not love his own father, etc. *less* than he loves me and my kingdom. . . ."

Our final example of hyperbole is from Mark 11:23: "Indeed I say to you that whoever says to this mountain, 'Be uprooted and cast into the sea.' and does not waver in his heart but believes that what he says will come to pass, it will happen for him." Since we have not seen any mountains moved in such a way--Jesus himself did not demonstrate this either--we must conclude that Jesus was using hyperbole to show the awesome power of faith and prayer. God can of course move mountains and anything else he desires to move. Thus we should always believe that God the omnipotent who holds all things in his hands can do great things for us when we believe and pray. But Jesus was not really inviting anyone to do strip mining through prayer.

The reader should not conclude that hyperbole is exaggeration that no one need take seriously. It was precisely by means of these exaggerations that Jesus meant to impress upon us the importance of taking the message seriously. Thus I am not commanded literally to move mountains, but I am commanded to have a serious life of believing prayer.

Riddles

Jesus often teaches in short pithy sayings or *logia* much like the wisdom of teachers of the book of Proverbs. Many of these sayings in Proverbs are like riddles. That is, they require thought to solve their meaning. This process actually helps the listener/reader to remember the saying.

One kind of riddle is the oxymoron or apparent contradiction. The listener/reader must reflect on why this is not a contradiction and what it means. Thus one can scarcely disregard the message after one has had to wrestle with it to understand it. For example, some Pharisees asked Jesus on one occasion when Jesus was speaking on spiritual blindness: "We are not blind too are we?" Jesus replied, "If you were blind you would have no sin. But now you say, 'We see'--your sin remains" (Jn 9:40-41). Jesus meant if they could admit that they were spiritually blind and in need of teaching, they would have no sin (or be on the way to forgiveness), but since they maintain that they see or understand clearly, their sin remains. To receive salvation we first must admit that we need it.

Mark 10:31 contains another oxymoron: "But many that are first will be last and the last first." (cf. Mt 19:30; 20:16; Lk 13:30). This saying which appears several times in the Gospels and in different contexts was undoubtedly uttered many times by Jesus. The point is that the kingdom of God brings a reversal, "it turns upside down all human calculations" (Fitzmyer). Those that appear to be first now in the eyes of the world will be last at the second coming. This can be both a warning to those outside the church, the unsaved, and a warning to the saved. Even within the church we may hold in high esteem those whom God does not and devalue those whom God greatly esteems.

Among other riddles is Mark 4:25: "Whoever has (something), (more) will be given to him, and who does not have (anything), what he has will be taken from him." (Aland 125, 299; Lk 19:26). This saying which is found also in several contexts in the Gospels means that we can only grow spiritually when we make use of the gifts and lessons that God gives us. To fail to use these gifts means we lose them. There is responsibility in being blessed by God.

"Do not give what is holy to dogs, and do not throw your pearls to the pigs lest they trample on them and turn around and attack you" (Mt 7:6). "Dog" was a term of reproach among Jews because it represented an amoral lifestyle and uncleanness (1 Sam 17:43; 2 Sam 9:8; Psalm 22:20; Prov 26:11). Dogs were in the ancient near east more scavenging pests than pets (1 Enoch 89:42-49; S-B I, 722-726). They roamed the streets of the ancient cities looking for food. Evidently there were dogs running around the temple area for one of the scrolls from Qumran (4QMMT; cf. m. Temurah 6:5) condemns the practice of allowing dogs in there. They would have been eating the bones left over from the sacrifices, or "the holy" (Ex 29:33; Lev 2:3). Thus the first part of Jesus proverbial saying may have been a reference to something being done in the temple area. Pigs were also unclean (Lev 11:7; *Apion* 2.137) and became a symbol of Gentiles or heathen (Aboth d' Rabbi Nathan 34; S-B I, 449-450). The pearls are of course a treasure and came to represent fine wisdom (Davies and Allison; see Aboth d' Rabbi Nathan 18; b. Beracoth 33b; b. Yebamoth 94a). Most interpreters see a chiastic arrangement:

A. Do not give dogs what is holy

B. Do not throw your pearls to the pigs

B. Lest they (the pigs) trample on them (the pearls)

A. And (the dogs) turn around (after eating the sacrificial meat) and attack you.

Davies and Allison are correct when they affirm that this saying probably refers to evangelism. That is, it is an "admonition about the necessity to limit the time and energy directed towards the hard-headed" (I, p. 676). We invite everyone to salvation but we must not waste excessive time among the unrepentant and unyielding. Jesus commanded his disciples elsewhere to shake the dust off their shoes if they were not received (Mt 10:14). This may in addition be a warning against making the deep things of God known to non-Christians. As Davies and Allison remark (ibid.): "Not everything should be set before everybody." Non-Christians should be told about salvation but the profounder theological topics should be for the mature Christians.

Poetic Parallelism

It is a characteristic of Hebrew poetry to place side by side synonymous or contrasting statements (see Burney). This technique is well known from the Old Testament. An example of synonymous poetic parallelism may be found in Psalm 19:2: "Day unto day uttereth speech, and night unto night sheweth knowledge" (AV). And an example of antithetical poetic parallelism is in Proverbs 15:1: "A soft answer turneth away wrath, but grievous words stir up anger" (AV).[2]

Jesus also used these poetic forms. For example Mark 4:22 is synonymous parallelism: "For there is nothing hidden but will be manifest; there is nothing secret but will be made known." By these words Jesus means that his teachings, specifically in this case his Parable of the Sower, will be understood by those pursuing learning from him.

Luke 6:27 (par. Mt 5:441 is another case of parallelism: "But I say to you who hear:

Love your enemies,

Do good to those who hate you."

Jesus repeats the idea of his command but uses different words. We must love and do good things for our enemies. Such literary techniques besides appealing to the Semitic tastes, give emphasis to the command and make it more memorable.

Jesus used synonymous parallelism sometimes but he especially was wont to utilize antithetical parallelism. Jeremias has counted no less than 108 instances of such usage. Manson and Jeremias believed that such statements were especially characteristic of Jesus. For example, Jesus affirmed, "The Sabbath was made for man, and not man for the Sabbath" (Mk 2:27). The Sabbath was given by God to humankind as a day of rest and as a day to contemplate God as creator. It is a gift to us. But God did not create men and women just in order to make them keep the Sabbath. We do not exist for the day, the day exists for us. Thus Jesus meant to emphasize that people who have needs are more important than keeping the Sabbath.

"When the eye is clear the whole body is illuminated, but when the eye is bad the body is in darkness" (Lk 11:34; par. Mt 6:22-23). The clear eye or sound eye (cf. Testament of Issachar 4:6 in OTP) represents a spiritual state, attitude or relationship to God.[3] Those who are spiritually open to the teachings of Jesus will be illumined (=have a clear eye), but those who are not will be in darkness (=have a bad eye).

Another important saying in antithetical parallelism, which in this case is also an oxymoron, is Mark 8:35: "Whoever wants to save his life will lose it but whoever wants to lose his life for my sake and the gospel's will save it." That is, whoever tries to keep his life in this age to the neglect of the kingdom will lose his life in the age to come. But whoever freely gives his/her life to God in this age will gain eternal life in the age to come. The more we cling to things in this life, the more we lose them (both in this life and) in the next one.

Matthew 6:24 also is antithetic parallelism: "No one can serve two masters. For either he will hate the one and love the other, or he will be devoted to the one and be contemptuous of the other. You cannot serve God and *mamona*" (Aramaic word for "riches"). We will serve something or someone says Jesus. We will have a master. But we get to choose who that master will be. We may choose almighty God or some substitute, some idol such as riches (which he named in this instance), fame, career, drugs, power, and so forth. But we cannot serve two at once. Only one of them will truly be our master. Perhaps some believe they can serve God and one other, but they are wrong.

One final example we will cite here[4] is found in Luke 6:43: "For a good tree does not produce bad fruit and a bad tree does not produce good fruit." The antithetic saying contrasts the fruit or lifestyle of different people. On the one hand we should not be judgmental people (Lk 6:37-42), but we can know what people are like by their "fruits" just as we know what kind of tree we have by the fruit it produces. A person really dedicated to the Lord will not consistently do harmful things to others, neglect his/her devotional life, refuse to grow spiritually. On the other hand, a person that is only feigning spirituality may fool us for a while but will not ultimately produce good fruit such as influencing others for the Lord, growth in humility, love, peace, etc., and faithfulness to God's word and his church.

Dominical Sayings

We are using this term to refer to the sayings of Jesus not based on any scripture of the Old Testament but entirely on his lordship. He does not explain or interact with the scriptures but rather gives his command. He speaks as one having authority. Of course many of the sayings in the other categories in this chapter are also dominical sayings. Our first example is found in Matthew 6:25:

> "Therefore I say to you, do not be (unduly) worried (or have great anxiety) about your life, (fretting over such things as) what you will eat or drink or about your body (fretting over) what you will wear. Isn't there more to life than food and isn't there more to your body than its clothes?"

Jesus calls his disciples to absolute trust in God to take care of their needs. We must bear in mind that the people, for the most part, to whom Jesus spoke would have been of very modest means. Many of them would have been extremely poor, even destitute and homeless. Yet he calls on all of them to trust in God for their needs (Recall the model prayer: "Give us today our daily bread", only asking for today's needs.). If Jesus could demand such simple trust of such poor people, surely he wants Christians in the twentieth century western societies to learn this as well.

"Ask and it will be given you. Seek and you will find. Knock and it will be opened to you" (Mt 7:7). This saying should not be interpreted as God's giving the Christian everything he/she prays for as if God were only a cosmic gopher or heavenly Santa Claus. This is rather a statement of God's great love and compassion for his people. God will not grant us things we ask for in the wrong way and with the wrong motives (James 4:3). He will give us all good things, however (Philippians 4:19).

One of Jesus' best known sayings is the Golden Rule: "Whatever you wish that people do to you, thus you also do to them" (Mt 7:12; cf. Lk 6:31). This idea can be found stated negatively among the Greeks as well as in Buddhist and Confucian texts.[5] That is, "Whatever you do *not* wish that people do to you, do *not* do it to them." It is then one which had a large dissemination. The concept is behind Leviticus 19:18 and later Jewish texts often repeat it, again in negative form, (e.g. Tobit 4:15; Ben Sirach 31:15; Testament of Naphtali 1:6; Epistle of Aristeas 207; Didache 1:2; Gospel of Thomas 6; Palestinian Targum on Lev 19:18). The reader may remember that the great Hillel is alleged to have said this to a Gentile who asked him to teach him the whole Torah while the Gentile stood on one foot (b. Shabbath 31a; see Chapter 3). Thus the idea had a universal appeal. Jesus seems to have been the first, however, to make it the foundation of his ethics.[6] This is the Law and prophets, says Jesus, or it summarizes and encapsulates the Old Testament commands concerning dealing with our fellow man/woman. To treat people with the same respect that you wish and need is the basis of the social part of the Ten Commandments. Jesus required an absolute demonstration of love. The content of that love or the definition of that love is that which we would wish for ourselves.[7]

Prophetic Sayings

These sayings concern future events in salvation history such as the founding of the church, the destruction of the temple in Jerusalem, and of course the second coming of Christ.

We will first consider a group of three sayings which have a common element: they appear to have made an incorrect prediction that the end of the age would come soon.

> 1. When they persecute you in that city, flee to another. Truly I say to you, you will not complete the cities of Israel before the Son of man comes (Mt 10:23).

> 2. And he said to them, "Truly I say to you that there are some of those standing here that will not taste of death until they see the kingdom of God coming in power" (Mk 9:1).

3. Truly I say to you that this generation will by no means pass away until all these things come to pass (Mk 13:30).

A. Schweitzer concluded concerning Saying 1 that Jesus incorrectly thought that the Son of man would come in power while he and the disciples were conducting their missionary tour of Galilee. Others have maintained (e.g. R. Bultmann) that either Jesus or some unknown Christian prophet uttered Saying 3 again incorrectly believing that the second coming would be in only a few years. Some try to avoid an apparent problem by making the word "generation" mean "race", that is the Jewish race or even the human race. Thus Jesus would be saying that the Jewish race will not pass away until all comes to pass.

We would answer that the contexts are very important for these texts. Saying 1, the commissioning of the disciples, refers to the second coming and means, as Bruce points out, that the evangelization of Israel will not be completed before the end of the age (cf. Mt 24:14; Rom 11:25-27). Thus the gospel will be preached in all the world, including Israel before the end comes. Exactly when this preaching or evangelism of the world has reached its fullness we do not know. Only God can decide that.

Saying 2, said in the context of Jesus' challenge to his discples to take up their cross and follow him, concerns the coming of the Holy Spirit on the day of Pentecost. Then the kingdom came with power to enable the apostles to carry out their ministries. Thus Jesus assures them that some of them will remain alive, in spite of the dangers involved in discipleship (especially in discipleship committed to martyrdom), to witness that day of God's outpouring.

Saying 3 is Jesus' answer to the disciples question, "When will these things be?" (Mk 13:4) or when will the temple be destroyed? Thus Jesus' statement--that the generation alive then will see these things--means that they would see the temple destroyed. The temple was destroyed about 40 years later.

The next group of sayings has to do with the woes of the eschaton or the end-time. The end-time is accompanied by judgment and woe (Joel 2:1-3). Now the kingdom of God brings about the eschaton. Thus in one way Jesus' presence inaugurated the eschaton but it will be fully consummated at his second coming.

1. I came to cast fire on the earth, and I wish it already were here (Lk 12:49).

2. Do not think that I came to cast peace on the earth. I did not come
to cast peace but a sword (Mt 10:34).

Saying 1 refers to the fire of judgment as John the Baptist also did (Mt
3:10). Saying 2 refers to the persecution that will follow those committed
to him. They will suffer at the hands of unbelievers both now and
especially at the end-time.

Our next saying also concerns the second coming and its harbinger, the
ministry of Jesus: "And he said to them, 'I saw Satan like a star fallen
from heaven'" (Lk 10:18). Jesus said this in response to his disciples
astonishment that they could cast out demons. Jesus' presence initiates the
downfall of the prince of this world, Satan. He began to conquer him in
his ministry of healing and demon exorcism, he conquered him by his
death-resurrection, and he will cast him into the lake of fire at his second
coming. Although the words are in the past tense (Greek imperfect tense)
we should not view this as a statement about Satan's being cast out of
heaven before the creation of the earth. Old Testament prophets
sometimes used the past tense in prophecy to indicate assurance of its
coming about. Thus this is a prediction about the second coming.

Our final prophetic saying is from Jesus' trial before the High Priest at
which he was condemned to death:

> And the High Priest said to him, "I adjure you by the living God to tell
> us if you are the Messiah, the son of God." Jesus said to him, "You
> said that but I say to you from now on you will see the Son of man
> sitting on the right hand of Power and coming on the clouds of heaven."
> (Mt 26:63-64).

Jesus was referring to his own second coming. He stood there then
apparently broken and defeated but he will come again in power. That
same High Priest who now judges him will be judged by Christ some day
as Christ sits on the right hand of the Father (=Power).

Jesus was a master teacher. His words made a profound impression on
his disciples and were therefore remembered and recorded. He is not only
the one who died and rose for us but our teacher as well. As Peter said,
"Lord to whom will we go? You have the words of eternal life" (Jn 6:68).

Notes

1. The oft cited gate into Jerusalem allegedly named "the needle's eye" probably never existed. The sources describing this gate are medieval and evidently based only on imagination. Thus we should not maintain that Jesus was saying e.g., "A camel can pass through the needle's eye (the alleged gate) only if it gets on its knees' or the like. Jesus meant literally an eye of a needle. The picture is striking and ludicrous, which is exactly the point.

There are also some very late Greek mss of this passage which read instead of *kamelos* "camel", *kamilos* "rope". Thus they make Jesus refer to threading a rope through a tiny needle's eye, also difficult if not impossible. This idea is based obviously on the attempt of late copyists to soften the hyperbole.

2. Hebrew poetry also exhibits synthetic parallelism, e.g. Ps 90:2.

3. Cf. the m. Aboth 2:13-14, 16 where the bad eye or evil eye means envy (T. Herford, *The Ethics of the Talmud*).

4. See the long list of examples of antithetic parallelism among Jesus' sayings in Jeremias, p. 15.

5. See Sextus, *Sent.* 89; Herodotus 3. 142; Isocrates, *Nicocles* 61; Diogenes Laertius 5.21; Confucius, *Analects* 15.23. For further parallels see S-B and Davies and Allison on this verse.

6. It is debated whether Jesus was the first one or indeed the only one to state this principle in positive form. See the discussion in Davies and Allison and in Connick.

7. Jesus' statement of the Golden Rule can be found not only in Mt and Lk but also in the Gospel of Thomas 6; Oxyrhynchus Papyrus 654; and Didache 1:2.

Chapter 13

THE EARLY JUDEAN MINISTRY

Bibliography: C.K. Barrett, *The Gospel According to St. John*; R. Brown, *The Community of the Beloved Disciple*; idem., *The Gospel According to John*; R. Bultmann, *The Gospel of John*; J.H. Charlesworth, *The Beloved Disciple*; M. Connick, *Jesus, the Man, the Mission, and the Message*; C.H. Dodd, *The Interpretation of the Fourth Gospel*; E.E. Ellis, *The World of St. John*; R. Fortna, *The Gospel of Signs*; M. Hengel, *The Johannine Question*; E. Kaesemann, *The Testament of Jesus*; G. McRae, *Invitation to John*; L. Martyn, *History and Theology in the Fourth Gospel*; L. Morris, *Studies in the Fourth Gospel*; J.A.T. Robinson, *The Priority of John*; idem., *Redating the New Testament*; D. M. Smith, *Johannine Christianity*; B.F. Westcott, *The Gospel According to St. John*

We will discuss in this chapter Jesus' ministry in Judea, especially Jerusalem, as it is narrated in the Gospel of John. Before we begin the narrative, however, there are a few things we must say about the fourth Gospel itself.

The Author of the Gospel of John

Who wrote this Gospel? It was usually considered to have been written by John the son of Zebedee and the brother of James. But in the last one hundred years or so this view has been challenged by some. We present the main views below:

R. Bultmann's view

Bultmann has been so influential that we must begin by summarizing his view concerning the author of the Gospel of John. Bultmann postulated three sources for the Gospel: 1) a sign source; 2) a discourse source; 3) and a passion source (i.e. a source about Jesus' death).

The sign source is found dispersed throughout John 1-12. Originally it simply enumerated Jesus' signs (miracles) and briefly described each one (e.g. 2:11, 4:54, 12:37). There are seven signs or miracles in John. Since Bultmann did not believe in miracles, he found very little historical value in the sign source.

According to Bultmann, the discourse source was originally a Gnostic (that is, pre-Christian Gnostic) text in Aramaic. In other words the long sermons of Jesus (e.g. Jn 6:26-59; 14:1-17:26) were not uttered by him, maintained Bultmann, but were Gnostic texts that were put in his mouth in the Gospel of John.

The passion source (about Jesus' suffering and death; Jn 18-19) is more historical and is rather similar to that of the Synoptics.

Bultmann alleged that an editor/author--himself a convert from Gnosticism to Christianity--had molded these three sources into something approximating our present Gospel of John. Later, another editor rearranged the Gospel--causing some things to be out of place, cf. 14:31 which is yet followed, wrote Bultmann, by three more chapters of discourse--and also "cleaned up the theology"' a bit, adding references to the sacraments (3:5, 6:51-58) and eschatology or the end-time (5:28f, 12:48).

R. Brown has rightly criticized Bultmann's analysis. Bultmann said that the author did not believe in the sacraments or in eschatology so a later editor must have added them. But this begs the question. Bultmann first decided what he wanted the author to believe, then gave the rest to the editor. The most obvious conclusion is that since these verses are in the Gospel of John, the author wrote them and believed them.

Brown also criticizes Bultmann's source hypothesis. Often the signs and discourses are so closely woven together it is hard to see two sources. The sermon on the bread of life, for example (Jn 6:26-59), flows naturally out of Jesus' miracle of multiplying the loaves to feed the five thousand (Jn 6:1-25). Second, Brown notes that many of the sayings in John are very similar to those of the Synoptics[1], thus ruling out the idea that the author in a rather empty-headed moment simply took a Gnostic sayings-source and attributed it all to Jesus.

Browns View.

Brown himself posits five stages in the composition of the Gospel:
1. An oral tradition independent from the Synoptics but parallel to them. This stage lasted from A.D. 40-60.
2. A community which molded and preached this tradition headed by one outstanding evangelist. This phase was from A.D. 60-75.
3. After a time, the evangelist collected the materials and published them (sometime between 75 and 85).
4. Later the evangelist re-edited the Gospel--perhaps several times--to speak to a new situation (85-95).
5. A member of the evangelist's community about A.D. 100 collected and inserted all material from stage 2 not already in the Gospel.

Originally Brown concluded that stage one was based on the eye-witness testimony of John the apostle who was also the Beloved Disciple. Brown has lately changed his mind, however, on the identity of the Beloved Disciple.

The advantages of Brown's hypothesis are he is much more sensitive to the historicity of John than Bultmann and he is less dependent on unproven assumptions such as the existence of a document like the signs-source or a pre-Christian Gnostic discourse-source. The problem with Brown's hypothesis is he gives too little weight to the external testimony on the identity of the author of John.

Robinson's View

Robinson argues for an early date for the fourth Gospel. Like Brown, he posits stages:
1. AD 30-50 The Formation of the Johannine tradition and the proto-Gospel in Jerusalem.
2. AD 50-55 The first edition of the Gospel of John appears in Asia Minor (Ephesus)
3. AD 60-65 The Johannine Epistles were written.

4. AD 65+ The Final form of the Gospel with the prologue and epilogue appears.

Although Robinson suggests a development in the Johannine literature, he does not appeal to a later disciple or evangelist as the developer. He suggests that "one large mind" is behind all of this. Who was the author? He argues in favor of John the son of Zebedee (=the Beloved Disciple) as the author.

M. Hengel's View

Hengel's construction of the author's background is as follows: Behind the Johannine literature--the Gospel, Letters, and Revelation--stands an outstanding teacher who founded a school in Asia Minor sometime between A.D. 60-70. The school existed until around 100 to 110. This teacher, named John, was a disciple of Jesus (but is not the apostle John) and was thus originally a Palestinian Jew. He lived to an advanced age in Asia Minor and was there known as "the elder." The elder died around A.D. 100 and thereafter his Gospel and letters were edited by his school. After his death, the school quickly dissolved.

Hengel's view is more compelling than the others because of his exhaustive analysis of the ancient sources that give evidence about the identity of the author. Although we may disagree with him in some points, we will basically accept his conclusions below. But first we must survey the evidence.

Evidence for the Identity of the Author

The place to begin in examining the evidence for the authorship is with the references to the Beloved Disciple. There are two types of references in John to an anonymous disciple. He is called the "other disciple" in at least one passage, possibly two (Jn 20:2-10 and maybe 18:15-16) and the "Beloved Disciple" in six places (Jn 13:23-26, 19:25-27, 20:2-10, 21:7, 21:20-23, 21:24). That the two are the same is clear at least in John 20:20 where; he is called "the other disciple whom Jesus loved".

The Beloved Disciple was a close and valued disciple of Jesus. He was seated closest to Jesus at the last supper (Jn 13:23) and it was to him that Jesus committed the care of his mother (19:25-27). He is closely associated with the apostle Peter in the fishing trade in Galilee (21:1-14, 21:20-23) and it was he and Peter that ran first to the empty tomb of Jesus

(20:2-10).

The statement in 18:15 has caused much debate. There we read that "another disciple" who accompanied Peter to the courtyard of the High Priest to see how Jesus' trial was proceeding was "known to the High Priest". In other words this anonymous disciple in John 18:15 was a friend of the High Priest. Historians ask how a disciple of Jesus could have been also a friend or even a friendly acquaintance of the High Priest for surely he would have therefore been recognized as Jesus' disciple and arrested (as Peter evidently feared he himself would). Thus some have suggested that this "other disciple" was not the Beloved Disciple but Nicodemus (see Jn 3:1-4, 7:45-52, 19:38-40) a secret disciple. Others have suggested that the "other disciple" was Judas Iscariot. Either of these suggestions is possible since the other reference to the "other disciple" in John 20:2 has the definite article--"*the* other disciple whom Jesus loved"--but in John 18:15 there is no definite article--"another disciple".

Furthermore, the Beloved Disciple is clearly the eyewitness behind the Gospel of John. In 19:35, after narrating the death of Jesus and the piercing of his side with the soldier's lance, the author writes, "And he who has seen has testified and his testimony is true and he knows that he speaks the truth that you may believe." Thus either the author or the witness behind the author was present at Jesus' crucifixion. He was probably then a disciple of Jesus.

This conclusion is even firmer with respect to 21:24-25. Here the text clearly says that the Beloved Disciple, the one who was present at the last supper (13:23-26), ". . . is the disciple testifying concerning these things and writing them." Thus the material in the Gospel of John comes from the Beloved Disciple.

Who was the Beloved Disciple? The following have been suggested:[2]

1. Lazarus. John 11:3,5,11, and 36 say Jesus loved him.

2. John Mark. This is more a guess than a conclusion based on evidence.

3. An unknown disciple.

4. John the Elder (see below).

5. Thomas (Charlesworth) who confessed Jesus as Lord and God after seeing him resurrected (Jn 20:28).

6. The apostle John, son of Zebedee. He was clearly one of the elite three disciples (i.e. Peter, James, and John) in the Synoptics and he is often associated with Peter in both the Gospels and Acts. Further, John was a Galilean fisherman as was the Beloved Disciple. Therefore, John,

the son of Zebedee, is the best choice.

We conclude, therefore, that the witness to the life and words of Jesus comes from the apostle John. But was he the author of the Gospel or did he stand in relation to it as Peter was to Mark's Gospel, as the living witness for another author?

To answer the above question we must consult later church testimony. First, we refer the reader to the statement of Papias (quoted in part in Chapter 15) about his preference for living testimony as opposed to written. In his statement he listed the names of several Christian notables:

> Andrew. . . Peter. . . Philip. . . Thomas or James. . .
> John or Matthew. . . Aristion and John the elder. . .

The striking thing is that in this list there are two people named John: John--obviously the apostle--and John the elder. From this statement Eusebius (AD 320) argued that there were two great teachers named John in Asia Minor. He also pointed to two tombs in Ephesus which supposedly contained a person named John (*H.E.* III. 39). The same argument was advanced by Dionysius of Alexandria (A.D. 240; in Eusebius, *H.E.* VII.25).

Irenaeus (A.D. 180) wrote that John, the disciple of the Lord, who reclined on his breast, gave out the Gospel of John while living in Ephesus (*Against Heresies* II.22). He indicated that John came to Ephesus sometime after Paul left there (c. 55) and lived there into the reign of Trajan (A.D. 98-117; see *Against Heresies* III.3). Further, the Muratorian Canon, a document from around A.D. 180, states, "The fourth of the Gospels was written by John, one of the disciples" (Trans. in Stevenson, *A New Eusebius*, p. 145).

Which John wrote the Gospel and the epistles of John (for the epistles were undoubtedly from the same author)? 2 and 3 John were written by someone who signed his name "the elder" (2Jn 1; 3 Jn 1) and Papias clearly regarded a "John the elder" as an outstanding teacher. Ellis maintains that John the apostle wrote the Gospel and letters and that John the elder and John the apostle were the same person. But this reading of Papias is hardly possible. Hengel, on the other hand maintains that John the elder wrote the Gospel; and the epistles.

We prefer to see the composition of these documents as paralleling the writing of the Gospel of Mark. John is the apostolic eyewitness who stands behind the Gospel tradition in the Gospel of John--as did Peter for the Gospel of Mark--but John the Elder was the actual writer. Such a conclusion best explains all the evidence, both internal and external. Since the elder signed his name to 2 and 3 John and the style and content is virtually the same also in 1 John and the Gospel, we should conclude that he wrote all four documents, giving them his distinctive vocabulary and theological style. But since an eyewitness, called the Beloved Disciple, stands behind the Gospel accounts, we should also conclude that John the apostle is the source of the tradition narrated by John the elder.

John and the Synoptics

We must consider the similarities and differences between the Gospel of John and the Synoptics on the one hand and the Gospel of John and the epistles of John on the other hand. Scholars have noted for centuries that John stands apart from the Synoptics. It is true that John has basically the same narrative structure as the Synoptics. We have the ministry of John the Baptist, the calling of the disciples, the Galilean ministry, the early abundance of miracles, Jesus' teaching and debate with Jews, his arrest, trial, death, and resurrection. There are also many of the same stories in John that are in the Synoptics such as the cleansing of the temple, feeding of the five thousand with five loaves, calming the storm , the anointing of Jesus before his death, the triumphal entry, and of course the Passion Narrative (from the arrest of Jesus through his death). There are even numerous similarities to Jesus' sayings in the Synoptics (see note 1). These similarities must not be taken lightly or underemphasized. Clearly John and the Synoptics are based on the same tradition about Jesus. One has merely to compare the Synoptics with any of the apocryphal Gospels (see Chapter 16) to see how really similar John is to the former.

On the other hand, the differences are striking too. First, the style, vocabulary, and theology of Jesus in the Gospel of John are more like the Johannine epistles than the Synoptics. The vocabulary in the Gospel and epistles is very plain with very few different words. Any first year Greek student knows how easy it is to read the Gospel and letters of John compared with the rest of the New Testament. The Greek is very grammatical but also very simple. Furthermore, everybody's vocabulary--Jesus', John the Baptist's, the author's--sounds the same. In chapter 3 of the Gospel, for example, Jesus speaks (vv. 5-15), the author comments on Jesus' discourse (vv. 16-21), then John the Baptist speaks (vv. 27-30? or

27-36?). But all three use the typical Johannine vocabulary: love, truth, life, light, witness, believe. These are terms used over and over in the Gospel and epistles.

Second, many of the literary forms commonly used by Jesus in the Synoptics are absent from John. Jesus utters no proverbs in John and almost no parables.

Third, many themes which are common in the Synoptics--such as the Kingdom of God--are rare in John (only at 3:3 and 18:36).

Fourth, many events in John are not in the Synoptics (e.g. changing the water into wine, the story of Nicodemus, the story of the Samaritan woman at the well, the raising of Lazarus). The converse is also true. Much material in the Synoptics is absent from John. There are no demon exorcisms in John, no infancy narratives, no account of the transfiguration, and no account of the Lord's Supper.

How do we account for these facts? First, the author of the Gospel and epistles--which we believe was John the elder writing utilizing the testimony of John the apostle--has recast many of the words of Jesus and John the Baptist into the vocabulary of his community or school. One can in relating a story--especially if one is also giving the story in a language (Greek) different from the language (Aramaic) originally used by the characters in the story--put the events and even discourses in his own words. Thus the words of the author, in John 1:1-14 e.g., sound very much like the words of Jesus, as do the epistles of John. Jesus' words are put in the vocabulary of the Johannine community.

Second, the author was obviously trying not to repeat what was in the Synoptics. We should assume he had some knowledge of at least one or two of the Synoptics and that he is writing to supplement them, both in terms of new events and discourses and also in terms of theological interpretation. This conclusion is very much like what Clement of Alexandria (A.D. 200) wrote:

> But John, last of all, perceiving that what had reference to the body in the gospel of our Saviour, was sufficiently detailed, and being encouraged by his familiar friends, and urged by the spirit, he wrote a spiritual gospel. (Eusebius, *H.E.* VI.14; Trans. in Cruse, *Eusebius*)

Exposition of Selected Passages

We saw in chapter 8 that Jesus confined his ministry in Galilee mainly--

but not exclusively--to the Sea of Galilee basin. But in addition to this locus of preaching and teaching Jesus ministered in Jerusalem. Although only the Gospel of John explicitly indicates that Jesus repeatedly went to Jerusalem, the other Gospels imply that he did. As Connick points out, Jesus had friends in and near Jerusalem (Lk 10:38; cf. with Jn 11:1), his lament over Jerusalem (Mt 23:37: "How often would I have gathered you under my wings") indicates that he had been there often, and opposition toward him in Jerusalem was already well advanced when he arrived there just before his crucifixion. Thus the synoptic Gospels support John's explicit references to several trips to Jerusalem and substantial ministerial activity there. In all Jesus made at least six trips to Jerusalem, including his final journey. We will here comment on some of these trips.

The Meeting with Nicodemus   (Aland 27)

Jesus has cleansed the temple for the first time (Jn 2:13-22; Aland   25) and this event has certainly attracted the attention of the Jewish leadership. One of these leaders that has been watching Jesus and perhaps listening to him teach in the temple was Nicodemus. Scholars have debated whether this Nicodemus could be the same as Naqdimon ben Gorion who is celebrated along with others as one of the wealthiest and most influential men in Jerusalem just before the Jewish war of AD 66 began.[3]   If Nicodemus means to say in John 3:4 that he is now an old man, then this identification would be highly improbable since the Jewish war happened about 38 years after the event of John 3. It is possible, however, that Nicodemus was only using a figure of speech but was not that old when he first encountered Jesus. If the two are the same, then Nicodemus was--or became--one of the most important men in Jerusalem.

At any rate Nicodemus came to Jesus by night to question him. Why did he come by night? He probably did not want to be seen by anyone. The Gospel of John points out that there were secret believers in Jesus (12:42). These people were intimidated by Jesus' opposition and wished to follow from afar. But Brown is correct when he points out that "night" in the Gospel of John takes on a spiritual connotation. It symbolizes a state of spiritual emptiness (1:5; 9:4; 11:10; 13:30). The last reference is especially telling. It describes both the physical conditions of the last supper and the spiritual condition of Judas Iscariot.

Nicodemus begins with a flattering remark when Jesus says, "Truly, truly, I say to you , unless a person has been born from above (or born again) he cannot see the kingdom of God." To be born over again is a concept involved in conversion. The Talmud (b. Sanhedrin 19b; b. Yebamoth 22a) refers to proselytes to Judaism as people who have just been born, now without previous parents or a previous life. But Jesus uses the idea and the expression in a different way. The proper way to translate *gennan anothen* is "to be born from above". In John 3:31 and 19:11,23 the Greek word *anothen* must mean "from above". Further, in the Johannine letters (1 Jn 2:29; 3:9; 4:7; 5:1, 4, 18) the idea is that those who accept Jesus as savior are begotten by God or born again spiritually by the agency of God. For Jesus the idea is not just that someone is born all over again but that he/she is born again through God the spiritual begetter.

Nicodemus feigns total incomprehension over Jesus' words. We probably should not believe him when he says he cannot understand what Jesus is talking about (3:4) though Jesus' words are somewhat different from those of the Talmud. Jesus responds to Nicodemus statement of confusion by saying,"Truly, truly, I say to you unless someone is born of water and spirit he cannot enter the kingdom of God." Some maintain that the reference to water means physical birth. There is no evidence, however, that the term ever meant physical birth. On the other hand we have several references to lustral water along with the Holy Spirit as God's way of spiritually cleansing the hearts of men and women (Ezekiel 36:25-26; Titus 3:5). Thus the reference is probably to baptism. Jesus challenges Nicodemus to change radically spiritually, not just to adhere to some additional halacoth (3:6-8).

Did Nicodemus become a believer? John 7:50-51 shows that he was moving in that direction and 19:39 may mean that he was unashamedly a disciple by that time. In the first passage a group of Jewish leaders has assembled to discuss Jesus. Nicodemus argues in favor of giving Jesus a fair hearing. The second text reports that, along with Joseph of Arimathea, Nicodemus participated in the burial of Jesus.

After teaching in Jerusalem for a while, Jesus and his disciples made a preaching tour of Judea (Jn 3:22) and then returned to Galilee.

Healing Lame Man on the Sabbath (Aland 140,141)

There are references in the Gospel of John to six feasts: three Passovers, one Tabernacles, one dedication, and the unnamed feast mentioned in our text here (Jn 5:1). Some scholars speculate that this feast was the feast of

Purim celebrated since the time of Esther and Mordecai in the month of February.

Jesus, as his custom was, went up to Jerusalem to celebrate the feast and to teach the pilgrims. Upon entering the city he went to a pool called Bethzatha.[4] This pool is alluded to also in Josephus (*War* 2.328, 530) and in the mysterious document from Qumran known as the Copper Scroll (3QTreasure or 3Q15 11:12-13).[5] The pool has been apparently successfully identified in the area just north of the temple. This was a pool--or actually twin pools--that was stirred up at intervals by an underground spring. A pagan healing cult had evidently been attached to this pool and later Jews also began frequenting the locality in the hope of being healed by the waters. The belief by some of the folk was that if one entered the water while it was being stirred up by the spring, healing would take place.[6]

Jesus met a lame man who had suffered from his affliction for some 38 years. The man was in desperate straights, he thought, because he could not get into the churning water soon enough when the spring erupted. He was probably wanting Jesus to stand by in order to throw him into the water at the right moment. Jesus, however, commanded him to get up, pick up his pallet and walk (cf. Mk 2:11). The lame man who had been afflicted so long was healed instantly.

The healing, however, took place on the Sabbath. As it was with Jesus' Galilean ministry, so with the Judean. Jesus' activities on the Sabbath infuriated some of the religious leaders of the community (see chapter 8). Thus some began to resent Jesus deeply and to desire his death (Jn 5:16-18). In the course of their guestioning him Jesus declared that he was the Son of God. This declaration only angered his detractors all the more. Thus early in Jesus' ministry in Judea there were people that desired and perhaps even plotted his death.

Jesus Preaching at the Feast of Tabernacles (Aland 238-247)[7]

The Feast of Tabernacles or Feast of Booths was celebrated in September or October (see Chapter 2). This was a harvest feast like the Feast of Pentecost. But it was also a feast remembering the forty years' wandering in the wilderness. Therefore each participant made himself a small booth out of branches in which he would sleep and eat for seven days. Celebrants also carried a *lulab* or bundle of willow branches and an *etrog* or citrus fruit of some kind. These were waved around as they recited the Hallel Psalms (Pss 113-118) at ceremonies. The priests accompanied by pilgrims would proceed to the Pool of Siloam to fill a golden container with water. This water would be used each day to pour libations on the altar in a solemn ceremony (m. Sukka 4:9). In addition at night they would light four giant menorahs whose wicks were made of the worn-out garments of the priests. The celebrants would dance in front of them with torches in their hands, singing songs while the Levites played instruments (m. Sukka 5:3-4).

Jesus' brothers who are unbelievers (Jn 7:5) urged him to go to the feast to show off his miraculous power. Jesus refused saying, "My time has not yet come." Yet as soon as they had gone Jesus did leave. Did he change his mind? His point was that he would not go up in the manner that they-- tauntingly--had suggested. He went up privately and quietly not for show and not to provoke a confrontation.

The discussion about Jesus among the pilgrims in Jerusalem indicates that they were saying the same things about him that we saw were being said in Galilee (see Jn 7:13, 25-27, 31-32, 40-52; cf. Mk 8:28). He was much on their minds and in their thoughts. Further, some were saying that he was in league with the devil or demon possessed as they had said in Galilee (Jn 7:20; cf. Mk 3:22).

Jesus delivered two sermons during this feast both of which were based on Tabernacles themes. The first one began (Jn 7:57): "If anyone is thirsty, let him come to me and drink." This is an obvious reference to the water procession. The second one is based on the lighting of the giant menorahs (Jn 8:12): "I am the light of the world." These sermons reveal Jesus as the replacement of the feast of Tabernacles even as he is also the replacement of the Passover (Jn 6:35). The light symbolizes both revelation and the presence of God.

In the responses to Jesus' preaching we get interesting hints that the author of the Gospel of John knew the other Gospels. At one point some critics maintain that Jesus cannot be the Christ since the Christ must be born in Bethlehem (7:42). Surely John knows that that is exactly where Jesus was born even though he does not say anything about it; indeed he has no birth narrative at all.

There are several references to certain people who want to kill Jesus (7:19, 25, 37). Thus the animosity has reached an intense level already in Jerusalem. Small wonder then that by the following spring during the Passover they would take action to have him executed. Jesus' Judean ministry like the Galilean gained not only followers and admirers but vicious enemies. His way to the cross was becoming obvious.

Notes

1. For examples of the many similarities of Jesus' sayings in the Synoptics and John see R. Brown, *John* Vol. II, p. 694. Some of the similarities cited are:

John	Matthew	Mark
15:18	10:22	
15:20	10:23, 24	
16:1	24:10	
16:2		13:9

2. See Charlesworth for a more complete list of suggestions on the Beloved Disciple's identity.

3. B. Gittin 56a; Lamentations Rabbah 1.31; Aboth d'Rabbi Nathan Recension A 6, Recension B 13; Ecclesiastes Rabbah 7.12; Genesis Rabbah 42.1.

4. This pool is named variously in the mss: Bethzatha, Bezatha, Belzatha, Bethsaida, and Bethesda (the spelling found in the Authorized Version).

5. See J. Jeremias, *The Rediscovery of Bethesda.*

6. This is the statement in the verse (Jn 5:3b-4) not found in the oldest and best mss: "They (the lame people) were waiting for the churning of the water. For an angel of the Lord at a certain time descended into the pool and stirred it up. Therefore the first one entering the bubbling water would be healed of whatever disease he had." See B. Metzger, *A Textual Commentary on the Greek New Testament*, p. 209. The verse is "a gloss" writes Metzger. We would presume that the verse was originally a comment written in the margin of a ms to explain what people were doing at the pool. Later, a copyist mistakenly inserted the comment into the text of John. But the overwhelming majority of the mss--especially the oldest ones--do not have this verse. Its presence in the Authorized Version only demonstrates that that version is based on late and poor mss.

7. Pericope 242 of Aland is also problematic textually. Only one major Greek ms before the eighth century AD contains the story of the woman caught in adultery. This ms (Codex Bezae or ms D) is well known for its interpolations. Further, where the story does appear--in late mss--it is found in various places. It is placed in some late mss here at the beginning of John 8 but in other mss at the end of the Gospel. One group of mss has the story after Lk 21:38 and one ms has it after Lk 24:53. Thus the story was put in many different places, even in different Gospels. How do we explain this? In chapter 4 we noted that there were probably some authentic sayings and stories about Jesus which are nevertheless not in our Gospels. Some of these were added in a few of the late New Testament mss, usually as interesting stories or sayings to read in addition to the canonical ones. Later these may have been mistaken included in the Gospel text by a few copyists. That seems to have been the case with this story. I hold it to be an authentic narrative of an actual event in Jesus' life. The narrative bears all the characteristics of what Jesus would do. Yet it probably was not originally in the Gospel of John or any other Gospel. It floated orally until a copyist mistakenly

included it.

Chapter 14

The Lucan Travel Narrative

Bibliography: J.H. Charlesworth, ed., *Jesus and the Dead Sea Scrolls*; H. Conzelmann, *The Theology of Luke*; F. Danker, *Luke*; E.E. Ellis, *The Gospel of Luke*; J. Fitzmyer, *The Gospel According to Luke*; I.H. Marshall, *Commentary on Luke*; J. Neusner, *From Politics to Piety*; A. Plummer, *The Gospel According to Luke*; C.H. Talbert, ed., *Perspectives on Luke-Acts*.

The outline of Luke is as follows:
1. Introduction- Chapters 1-4:13
2. Jesus in Galilee- Chapters 4:14-9:50
3. Journey to Jerusalem- Chapters 9:51-19:27
4. Jesus in Jerusalem- Chapters 19:28-24:53

The third section of Luke will concern us in this chapter. At some point in Jesus' ministry in Galilee he began a long and slow journey to Jerusalem (Aland 174; Lk 9:51). Matthew and Mark indicate that he traveled through the territory of Perea (Mt 19:1-2) and the Gospel of John also supports this geographical information (Jn 10:40). Thus Jesus would have left Galilee, preaching in villages as he traveled, crossed briefly into Samaria (Aland 175), moved on a preaching and teaching tour through Perea, crossed the Jordan river at Jericho (Aland 264-265), and from there ascended to the hills of Jerusalem.

But this journey was not just an actual historical journey for Jesus and his disciples; it is also a spiritual journey for the readers of the Gospel of Luke. Both Matthew and Mark also record a similar journey but place far fewer pericopes in it. That is, they do not narrate as many events taking place on this journey. It receives much less emphasis in their Gospels. Luke has stressed it not just as a report of an actual historical event but as a theological and spiritual journey for the reader. As Oswald Chambers wrote, "Jerusalem, in the life of our Lord, represents the place where He reached the culmination of His Father's will." Can we follow Jesus all the way to the cross? Can we make God's will supreme in our life?

Events Early in the Journey
(Aland 174, 175, 184)

"And it came to pass when the days of his being taken up were accomplished that he resolutely set his face to go to Jerusalem" (Lk 9:51).[1] So reads literally Luke's statement about Jesus' determination to go to Jerusalem. The point is that Jesus knew how much opposition, even hatred, there was toward him in Jerusalem. He knew that his going there would mean death but he was determined to carry through his mission. We might paraphrase this verse as follows: "When Jesus knew that the time of his life's work was getting closer, he decided with determination to journey to Jerusalem and to death." So begins this travel narrative. We must keep in mind then that as Jesus encounters these people and interacts with them, he is on his way to die.

Josephus informs us that one can reach Jerusalem in three days from Galilee if one goes through Samaria (*Vita* 269). Because of this pilgrims often cut through Samaria much to the ire of the Samaritans. There were numerous clashes between the pilgrims and the local Samaritans (see Chapter 3). At some point Jesus and his disciples--although they seem to have been in no hurry--pass through part of Samaria. Jesus had a missionary interest in the Samaritan people (Jn 4:1-30; Lk 17:11-19) and may have intentionally passed through this region to preach and teach. He and his disciples were received at one point with the rudeness that may often have characterized the Samaritan treatment of religious pilgrims. The disciples, James and John, the sons of thunder (Mk 3:17), want to call down fire from heaven to consume them like the days of Elijah of old (2

Kings 1:5-12). But Jesus rebukes them for such anger and merely travels to another village where they presumably were accepted.

Not every story narrated by Luke in this section of his Gospel actually happened chronologically at this time. This section is also telling of a spiritual journey as we noted above. The story about Mary and Martha (Lk 10:38-42) is out of place chronologically but not thematically. We know that Mary and Martha lived in Bethany near Jerusalem with their brother Lazarus (Jn 11:1-46; 12:1-11, see chapter 11). Thus this story happened sometime during one of Jesus' visits to Jerusalem. Luke places it here because in the story Martha is worried about and busy about many trivial things while Mary focuses on the one thing that is needful. True disciples need to set priorities. Jesus had resolutely set his face toward Jerusalem in complete dedication to the will of God. We too as his disciples must have as our priority the will of God

Jesus and Table Fellowship (Aland 194, 215, 216)

In the course of Jesus' final journey he was often asked to dine with the Pharisees and others. Table fellowship was an important part of religious life for Jesus and his community of disciples. He was a guest often (Mk 2:15-16; Lk 7:36; 10:39; 11:37; 14:1; 19:5-7) but he even seems to have hosted banquets (Lk 15:2; 24:30). He did not eat the ascetic meals of John the Baptist (Mt 11:19) but was eager to partake of great meals with friends. Further Jesus' teaching about the end-time age and the blessedness of the kingdom of God in its fullness is often framed in terms of a heavenly banquet (Mk 2:19; Mt 8:11; 22:1-14; 25:10; Lk 14:16-24; 22:30). He even talked about the Lord's Supper or Communion in terms of an eschatological banquet (Mt 26:29; Lk 22:18). Therefore, we conclude that table fellowship was an important act of worship and sharing with believing friends in the ministry of Jesus.

As J. Neusner has shown table fellowship was also very important to the Pharisees. Of the 341 individual legal rulings of the early Pharisees that are preserved in the Mishnah and Tosephta, 678 concern table fellowship. The Pharisees wanted to eat their meals in a state of ritual purity like the priests who served in the temple. Their numerous rulings were concerned with the cleanness of the food, of the people, and of the dishes and implements.

But J.D.G. Dunn (in Charlesworth) has also pointed out that the Essenes were very concerned with ritual purity in table fellowship. To eat at the same table with fellow Essenes was the highest honor and one which could only be obtained after a period of probation. At the common table the Essene priest would bless the food both before and after the meal (*War* 2.129-33; 1QS 6:2-5). The Essenes too wanted to live and eat their meals in the same state of ritual purity as the temple priests. But they applied the rules of community worship to community in general. That is the rules in Leviticus 21:17-21 prohibiting people crippled and blind from offering sacrifice in the temple were applied by the Essenes to prohibit these people from sharing their common table in the Messianic age:

> No man smitten with any human uncleanness shall enter the   assembly of God. . . . No man smitten in his flesh, or paralyzed in his feet or hands, or lame or blind or deaf, dumb, or smitten in his flesh with a visible blemish. . . let him not enter among [the congregation], for he is smitten. (1QSa 2:3-10; Trans. G. Vermes, *Dead Sea Scrolls in English*)

Jesus in contrast to the Pharisees and Essenes dined with a wide assortment of people. Here he is in these pericopes dining with Pharisees (Lk 11:37; 14:1). His relationship with the Pharisees was complex. They criticized him, often severely, for eating with and receiving as disciples publicans and sinners (Lk 5:30; 15:2), for not fasting (Mk 2:18), for plucking grain on the Sabbath (Mk 2:24), for healing on the Sabbath (Mk 3:6), and for failing to wash his hands properly in order to maintain ritual purity (Mk 7:1). Jesus in turn accused the Pharisees and their scribes of abandoning the commandment of God in order to hold to the traditions of men (Mk 7:8), of being hypocrites (Mk 7:6; Mt 23:13), and of being vainglorious (Mk 12:38-39). Indeed Jesus' denunciation of the scribes and Pharisees here in Luke 11:37-54 and in Matthew 23 is about as scathing as one can find of any group in antiquity.

Yet here Jesus is dining with Pharisees! The picture is not as simple as many commentators have painted it. There was no widespread hostility between Jesus and all of the Pharisees. He was apparently often invited to dine with Pharisees (see in addition Lk 7:36), something a Pharisee would not do for just anyone since they ate their meals in a state of ritual purity. Jesus must have been regarded in some sense as acceptable by at least some of them. When he was invited, he accepted the invitation to dine. Thus Jesus did not shut out the Pharisees either. Once Pharisees seem to have tried to save Jesus' life when they warned him that Herod Antipas wanted to kill him (Lk 13:31).

Some--perhaps many--of the Pharisees were interested in hearing Jesus but there were still those differences we outlined above. So when Jesus dines at the home of one of the Pharisees he is immediately criticized for not washing his hands first in the Pharisaic way. This criticism leads to Jesus' denunciation of the Pharisaic legalistic tendency and subsequently to anger and hostility toward Jesus on the part of some of those present. This may have been a recurring pattern: Pharisees are fascinated with Jesus' teaching; Pharisees see or hear something that scandalizes them; Jesus denounces their legalism; Pharisees react with hostility.

In addition to dining with Pharisees Jesus dined with tax collectors, "sinners", and the physically handicapped. In Luke 14:7-14 Jesus recommends two things to his Pharisaic host and the other guests. First he reminds them of the teaching of the Old Testament (Prov 25:6-7) that one should seek the lower seat at a banquet and perhaps be later elevated. It is shameful to seek a chief seat and be demoted. For Jesus, however, this bit of wisdom is based on the basic valuation of humility. Humble yourself and let God exalt you; do not seek the exaltation of men (see Mk 10:35-45; Lk 20:45-47).

Second, Jesus recommends that when someone throws a banquet he should not invite so much only his rich friends but rather also, "the poor, the crippled, the lame, and the blind" (Lk 14:13). Thus Jesus was explicitly disagreeing with the Essenes. He ate with all of the undesirables of Jewish society. He embraced not only the popular and respected Pharisees but also the despised sinners and the shunned people with physical handicaps. (Compare Jesus' admonition with the similar one in the m. Aboth 1:5: "Let the poor be the guests of your house.")

Jesus' advice to his Pharisaic host leads to the parable of the banquet. Matthew has a similar parable about a wedding feast. Although the two parables (Aland   216) are similar in many ways they are surely two variations of the same theme and told on different occasions. Jesus could adapt his parables for the situation and the sermon. The point of the parable is that some of the rich are invited to a banquet but make excuses and do not come. But the poor (Luke uses the exact words in 14:21 as in 14:13) do accept the gracious invitation. The rich represent the leaders of Jewish society who in many cases have rejected Jesus' message while the poor and outcasts have accept him. The banquet represents the heavenly banquet of the eschatological age. Thus as Jesus journeys to his death he notes that the wealthy people of his generation have for the most part rejected him but the poor have followed him.

Heavenly Treasures
(Aland 199, 200, 202, 254)

As Jesus is journeying, someone asks him to settle an inheritance dispute between him and his brother. Jesus refuses to be an earthly judge and then adds a warning about the sin of avarice. He adds, "For a person's life is not (measured or valued) from his abundant possessions" (Lk 12:15).

This warning leads to one of Jesus' most moving parables, the Parable of the Rich Fool. This story is about a man that had reaped a bumper crop. His barns and storage bins could not hold his surplus. Instead of thinking about helping the poor from his abundance (or as a good Jew of tithing his crop) the avaricious man built bigger barns so he could hoard his excess. Oblivious to human suffering he would live off the stored up grain for years. He could pay for one continuous party. These were his plans. But God has his hand on history and God said, "On this night they are demanding your life (i.e. your life is demanded) of you" (Lk 12:20). The point of the parable is the futility and vanity of riches. Death cancels any ultimate value to wealth. Only the 'riches toward God" or those acts of service of God really matter. The avaricious man was, says Jesus, a fool.

Jesus admonishes his disciples to store up treasure in heaven by giving alms (Lk 12:33). This idea is also found in the rabbinic literature (t. Peah 4:18) where it is said that one can store up treasure in heaven by giving to charity. Jesus, however, says an unrabbinic thing here when he urges his disciples to sell their possessions in order to be able to give alms.

This saying brings us to one of the most difficult passages in the Gospels: the story of the rich young ruler. As Jesus journeyed he encountered a wealthy young man who approached Jesus to ask him what he yet lacked to inherit eternal life. This question reminds one of the one John Hyrcanus asked of the Pharisees. Hyrcanus asked what, if anything, he yet lacked to be completely righteous. One surly Pharisee replied that Hyrcanus should surrender the High Priesthood (*Antiquities* 13.288-298; b. Kiddushin 66a). The rich young ruler liked Jesus' answer about as well as Hyrcanus appreciated the Pharisee's response to him. Jesus at first replied that (as a good Jew) he should keep the Ten Commandments. The young man objected that he had already mastered these. "Give me something that is really a challenge" he seems to have been saying. Jesus responded, "You still lack one thing. Sell everything you own, distribute it to the poor and you will have treasure in heaven, and come and follow me (to Jerusalem)" (Lk 18:22). Here we see the vital difference between keeping the commandments and being a disciple of Jesus. The one requires performance; the other demands surrender. The young man thought he could impress Jesus or the disciples or both by his obvious piety and performance of the commandments. But what it takes to be a genuine disciple of Jesus is total surrender. That the young man was not ready to offer. His wealth was still too important to him.

What are we to make of Jesus' demand that the young man sell his possessions in order to be a disciple? Some early Christians did that literally (Acts 2:44-45; 4:32-34). But most retained possession of their property and gave contributions to the poor or to the apostles (Acts 11:27-20; 2 Cor 8, 9). Indeed Jesus can not only command to sell one's possessions but he can also command the giving of alms (Mk 12:41-44; Mt 6:2-4; 25:31-46; Lk 19:8). The latter for a peasant farmer is possible on a continuous basis only if he keeps his land. Thus Jesus usually did not require the total renunciation of possessions. There was not just one appropriate response to the message of the kingdom as far as the handling of one's possessions was concerned, but several responses. In the case of the young man, who was clearly a pious Jew, total renunciation and a life of selfless poverty were what Jesus called for. God calls different people to different lifestyles.

Sadly, however, although Jesus is marching to the cross, the young man, because he still loved his things more than he loved God, refused to follow.

The ox in the Pit
(Aland 208, 214)

These two pericopes narrate Jesus' encounters with leaders because of his healing on the Sabbath. In his argument about the justification for healing on the Sabbath (especially Lk 14:5; cf Mt 12:11) he makes reference to a person having "a donkey[2] or an ox in a well". Who would not even on the Sabbath pull them out to save their lives?

We should conclude that the Pharisees probably would not have pulled out a farm animal from a pit or ditch if it were stuck there on the Sabbath:

> R. Judah (c. AD 299) said, Rab (AD 247) said, "If a farm animal fell
> into a ditch (on the Sabbath), one brings blankets and padding and lays
> them under it. If it comes out, it comes out. Others say if a farm animal
> falls into a ditch one cares for it by feeding it in that place (in which it
> is stuck) so it will not die" (b. Shabbath 128b; Trans. S-B).

Thus the Pharisees would have ruled that one could try to save the
animal with blankets and food.

The Essenes, if anything, were even more rigid about the Sabbath:

> No man shall assist a beast to give birth on the Sabbath day. And if it
> should fall into a cistern or pit, he shall not lift it out on the Sabbath.
> (CD 11:13; Trans. Vermes, *Dead Sea Scrolls in English*)

Jesus seems to be intentionally refuting the Essenes (see Charlesworth)
and perhaps the Pharisees on their interpretation of the Sabbath. People
are suffering. Not even the law of the Sabbath important as that may be
can take preference over human need. Ritual takes third place in Jesus'
teaching to devotion of the heart to God and loving ones fellow man.

True Discipleship
(Aland 264, 265)

Jesus' journey is now almost ended. He has crossed the Jordan river
and enters Jericho. As he is leaving one part of the city and entering
another, he encounters two blind men. Mark and Luke mention only one
blind man and only Mark gives the name of the most outspoken one,
Bartimaeus. Compressing two individuals into one is often done by the
Gospel writers. Luke, for example says that there were two angels at
Jesus' tomb but Matthew and Mark refer to only one (Aland 352; Mt
28:1-8 par.). The blind men call out to Jesus to help them and address
him as the Son of David. Son of David is a messianic title (Isa 9:7; Jer
23:5; 30:9; 33:17; Ezek 34:23-24; 37:24-25). Thus the blind men were
confessing Jesus as the Messiah.

The blind men ask to be healed and Jesus, moved with compassion (Mt
20:34), touched their eyes and restored their sight. The blind men
immediately began to follow Jesus. That is, they became disciples and

went with him up to Jerusalem. They responded to God's mercy by surrendering themselves to his will.

Another event that occurred in Jericho was the conversion of Zaccheus the wealthy chief tax collector. He was probably in charge of collecting revenue over several districts in Palestine. We should liken him to John of Caesarea (*War* 2. 287), another wealthy tax collector, who once offered the Roman procurator a bribe of eight talents of silver (=80,000 denarii), an enormous sum. Tax collectors, especially chief tax collectors, could be very wealthy. But they were notoriously dishonest and greedy. They had a reputation not unlike our mafia.

Zaccheus was probably already on his way to repentance because he was eager to see Jesus. His small stature prevented his easy access to Jesus and so he did an undignified thing: he climbed a tree. Jesus apparently passed right under the tree and when he saw Zaccheus in it, called his name and requested to dine at his house. The crowd and presumably some Pharisees (perhaps also some Essenes?) complained of course that Jesus would share a meal with a sinner like Zaccheus. Jesus taught at the table for perhaps several hours. Finally, Zaccheus rose and announced that he was indeed repenting of his life of dishonesty and greed. But his repentance was no mere statement. He gave definite fruits of repentance. He could give half of his goods to the poor. Anyone he has defrauded he would recompense fourfold. Josephus (*Antiquities* 16.3) writes that a thief was required to repay his victims a fourfold fine according to Jewish law.[3] Exodus 22:1 does require repaying four sheep for one stolen but five oxen for one ox. A text discovered in Wadi Murabaat (near Qumran) mentions payment fourfold for damages done (Mur 19:10; see Fitzmyer). Thus Zaccheus was basing his exact payment of restitution on Jewish law.

Evidently paying back money illegally exacted was understood as a requirement of repentance. The Tosephta (t. Baba Metzia 8:28) refers to tax collectors who wished to repent but could not pay back the money illegally gotten. Here Zaccheus not only pays it back but with a fourfold penalty.

Notice Zaccheus did not give all of his possessions away nor did Jesus require that he do so. His case was different from the rich young ruler's. Yet certainly we must assume that Jesus urged Zaccheus to give generously to the poor.

Jesus responds to Zaccheus' statement that he is now a true son of Abraham, that is a spiritual descendant of Abraham. Salvation has come to his house. Zaccheus was once again under the grace and forgiveness of God. "For the Son of man came to seek out and to save the lost" (Lk 19:10. No one was so sinful that Jesus would not offer him the grace of God.

Jesus is on his way to the cross. Some will follow him; others will fail him. It has been a spiritual journey and one which Luke intended for you and me to take as well.

Notes

1. The expression "set his face" is also found in the Hebrew Old Testament (e.g. Gen 31:21). It means to start a journey toward some specific destination.

2. Some mss here read "donkey" and some read "son". Both groups of texts have excellent mss in them. The RSV and NIV have accepted the reading "son".

3. But other texts mention other sums of restitution. Lev 6:5 and Num 5:6-7 require an added fifth. Philo, *Spec Leg* 4.2, says a double restitution was required.

Chapter 15

The Synoptic Gospels

The first three Gospels, Matthew, Mark and Luke, are usually studied together because of their many similarities. Hence they have come to be known as "synoptic" from the Greek word meaning "seen together." The precise relationship of these three Gospels to each other has been the focus of intensive study and debate for well over 200 years. The Gospel of John on the other hand is much less similar to the Synoptics and thus is usually studied by itself or in comparison with the epistles of John (see Chapter 13).

Bibliography: B.C. Butler, *The Originality of St. Matthew*; D. Catchpole, *The Quest for Q*; W.D. Davies, *The Setting of the Sermon on the Mount*; D.L. Dungan, "Mark-The Abridgement of Matthew and Luke" in D.L. Butterick, ed., *Jesus and Man's Hope*; R.A. Edwards, *A Theology of Q*; W.R. Farmer, *The Gospel of Jesus*; idem., *The Synoptic Problem*; P. Feine, J. Behm and W.G. Kuemmel, *Introduction to the New Testament*; ; A.M. Farrer, "On Dispensing with Q" in D.E. Nineham, ed., *Studies in the Gospels*; L. Foster, "The Q Myth in Synoptic Studies" *Bulletin of the Evangelical Theological Society* (1965); R.C. Foster, *Introduction and Early Ministry*; B. Gerhardsson, *Memory and Manuscript*; D. Guthrie, *New Testament Introduction*; P. Hoffmann, *Studien zur Theologie der Logienquelle*;

H.C. Kee, "Synoptic Studies" in E.J. Epp and G.W. McRae, ed., *The New Testament and Its Modern Interpreters*; J.S. Kloppenborg, *The Formation of Q*; E. Linnemann, "Is There a Gospel of Q?" *Bible Review* (1995) 18-23, 42-43; T.R.W. Longstaff, *Evidence of Conflation In Mark? A Study In the Synoptic Problem*; D. Luehrmann, *Die Redaktion der Logienquelle*; B. Mack, *The Lost Gospel: The Book of Q and Christian Origins*; F. Neirynck, T. Hansen, and F. van Segbraeck, *The Minor Agreements of Matthew and Luke against Mark*; J.B. Orchard, *A Synopsis of the Four Gospels in Greek*; S.J. Patterson, "Q The Lost Gospel" *Bible Review* 9.5 (1993) 34-41; S. Petrie, "Q is What You Make It" *Novum Testamentum* 3 (1959) 29-33; R. Riesner, *Jesus als Lehrer*; J.M. Robinson, "The International Q Project: Work Sessions 12-14 July, 22 November, 1991" *Journal of Biblical Literature* 111 (1992) 500-508; E.P. Sanders, *The Tendencies of the Synoptic Tradition*; S. Schulz, *Q, Die Spruchquelle der Evangelisten*; idem , *Griechisch-deutsch Synopsis der Q Ueberlieferung*; R.T. Simpson, "The Major Agreements of Matthew and Luke against Mark" *New Testament Studies* 12 (1966) 273-284; R.H. Stein, *The Synoptic Problem*; B.H. Streeter, *The Four Gospels*; V. Taylor, *The Formation of the Gospel Tradition*; C. Thiede, *Jesus Life or Legend?*; H.E. Toedt, *The Son of Man in the Synoptic Tradition*; L.E. Vaage, *Galilean Upstarts: Jesus First Followers According to Q*; W.O. Walker, Jr., ed., *The Relationship Among the Gospels*; J. Wenham, *Redating Matthew, Mark, and Luke*; R.D. Worden, "Redaction Criticism of Q: A Survey" *Journal of Biblical Literature* 94 (1975) 532-546.

Scholars have asked themselves for centuries why the Synoptic Gospels are so much alike. They have many of the same stories and sayings. The order of these pericopes (sections or paragraphs) is usually identical in at least two of the Gospels and often in all three. Much of the vocabulary and phraseology is similar. Why are these similarities present in the Synoptics but not in John?

For the past 200 years scholars have proposed numerous theories basically under two categories: a non-interdependence among the Synoptics and a definite literary interdependence. That is, some scholars have believed that none of the authors had seen the other Gospels before writing his own Gospel (a non-literary interdependence). Others concluded, however, that two of the authors of the Synoptics knew and copied from at least one other (a definite literary interdependence).

Hypotheses of Non-Interdependence (see Feine, Behm, Kuemmel)

The Primitive Gospel Hypothesis.

The Synoptics, according to this view, are varying copies and translations of one very old Aramaic Gospel, called the Gospel of the Nazarenes. The similarities among the Synoptics are because they copied or quoted this primitive Gospel. The differences are due to translation differences, abridgments and editing on the part of the authors.

Fragment Hypothesis.

The Gospels were compiled from notes and memoranda made by those who had been with Jesus. His disciples jotted down isolated sayings and deeds. These were later collected and used to compose the Gospels.

Tradition Hypothesis.

There was a primitive oral Gospel transmitted at first in Aramaic and later in two different Greek translations.

Literary Interdependence Hypotheses

Augustine's View

As early as Origin (A.D. 220) some declared that Matthew wrote his Gospel first and in the Aramaic language, Mark wrote his Gospel second, and Luke third (see Eusebius, *H.E.* 6.25). Augustine (A.D. 400) also affirmed this order (see *The Harmony of the Gospels* 1.3). Each succeeding Gospel after Matthew knew and used the preceding one(s).

Griesbach's Suggestion

J.J. Griesbach in 1789 proposed the order as follows: Matthew, Luke, then Mark. Again each succeeding Gospel knew and utilized the preceding one(s). Griesbach's hypothesis has been given new life recently by W.R. Farmer and his school of followers (e.g. Longstaff, Sanders,

Dungan).

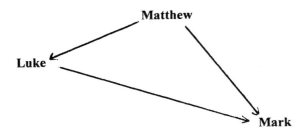

Table 15.1
Griesbach's Hypothesis

The Two Source (Four Source) Hypothesis

The Two-Source (and subsequently Four-Source) Hypothesis was
advanced in the nineteenth century. This hypothesis suggested that Mark
wrote first.   Matthew and Luke used Mark plus a second source
containing mostly Jesus' sayings. This second source--which is purely
hypothetical itself since no such source has been found--eventually came
to be known as "Q", probably from the German word *Quelle* ("source").
To find the alleged Q materials in the Gospels simply locate pericopes
found only in Matthew and Luke (e.g. Aland 108, 224). For two versions
of the Greek text of Q see Schultz or Robinson.

B.H. Streeter's Defense of the Two-Source (Four-Source) Hypothesis

Although the Two-Source hypothesis was advanced in the early
nineteenth century, its definitive statement was made by Streeter in 1924.

By then this hypothesis had pretty well prevailed anyway and Streeter's well written monograph seemed to settle the issue once and for all. He maintained that the priority of Mark was certain: "How anyone who has worked through those pages with a synopsis of the Greek text can retain the slightest doubt of the original and primitive character of Mark I am unable to comprehend." (p. 164) Those who disagreed with Streeter were accused of having "eccentric views of what constitutes evidence." Further, he believed the existence of the hypothetical document, Q, was almost certain. Streeter wrote that the assumption that there had been a Q and that it was used by Matthew and Luke: "though highly probable, falls just short of certainty" (p. 184). Thus, he left little room for nay-sayers to theTwo-Source hypothesis.

Streeter's main arguments for the priority of Mark were as follows:

1. There is much common material between Mark and the other two. Matthew reproduces" 90% of Mark and Luke reproduces over 50% of Mark.

2. There is a common order of events. Mark's order is always supported by either Matthew or Luke.

3. There is much common vocabulary between Mark and the other two. Matthew has 51% of the words of Mark; Luke less. But where the words and expressions are different, Matthew and/or Luke have often "improved" them. That is, they have used purer Greek. (For example, compare Mk 4:6 with Lk 8:6)

Streeter allowed that there were some "meagre" agreements between Matthew and Luke which are not in Mark. Compare, for example, the story of Jesus' cleansing of the temple. Matthew and Luke seem to say that Jesus cleansed it on the same day as his triumphal entry into Jerusalem. But Mark explicitly says he did so on the next day (see Mt 21:10-17, Mk 11:1-19, Lk 19:45-46 or Aland 273). Now of course Matthew and Luke were compressing events in their narration. But the question is why did not at least one of them follow Mark's way of telling the story if they both indeed had used Mark as a source? Streeter said such agreements against Mark were of no consequence but others are not so sure (for a complete list of these passages see Neirynck, Hansen and Segbraeck).

Streeter established the existence of Q as follows:

1. The narrative material common to Matthew and Luke (the double tradition) occurs in different contexts and different order.

2. The degree of resemblance between the parallel passages varies considerably.

There are three explanations for the above two observations. First, one of the Gospels might have used the other. Second, the authors might have shared an oral tradition. Third, the authors could have used a common written source. To accept the first explanation, wrote Streeter, one would have to believe that the author was a "crank" since he would have so radically rearranged the material of the other Gospel. The second solution Streeter considered more probable than the first. However, because there are such close verbal resemblances between Matthew and Luke, it must be more likely that the authors have used a written source, argued Streeter.

Streeter's line of argument raises some questions. Is it not a subjective conclusion that only a crank could rearrange the material of one Gospel to produce his own? Second, how dissimilar must the words of the common tradition be to allow for the probability of an oral source rather than a written one?

Streeter's version of the source hypothesis has become the most popular and for all intents and purposes the standard. Most graduate schools doing Gospels' study operate under the assumption that the Two-(Four) Source hypothesis is proven (the exception is the W.R. Farmer school, see below).

Streeter refined the hypothesis by adding two more main sources (and some other less important ones) to Mark and Q as the sources of Matthew and Luke. These two additional sources he called M (for the material found only in Matthew) and L (for the material found only in Luke). His source theory is as follows:

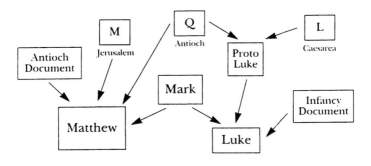

Table 15.2
Streeter's Four Document Hypothesis

The Q Hypothesis

We must emphasize that Q is entirely hypothetical. No one has found such a document or even a reference to such a document. In spite of scholars such as A. Farrer who argued that it is an unreasonable supposition and the more recent school of Farmer, this hypothesis remains the accepted approach to the Synoptic Gospels. How can one analyze a document that does not even exist? As Petrie observed, the danger is that one will describe a document of ones own making.

Yet this problem has not hindered scholars from writing large tomes on all aspects of this document. The older view of Q was that it was a didactic work meant to instruct catechumens or those preparing for baptism. W.D. Davies and H.E. Toedt over thirty years ago, however, thought they could argue that Q was really a document full of crisis because of the (assumed) imminent second coming. Several German scholars such as Schultz and Luerhman were sure that they could identify not one community that produced Q but two. There were two "Q communities" that produced actually two Q's or two redactions (editions) of Q. The first was a Palestinian Jewish Community and the second was a Hellenistic Gentile one. Kloppenborg, however, finds three stages or phases to the composition of Q: phase one which collected Jesus' wisdom sayings, phase two which collected judgment sayings; and phase three which added the temptation story of Jesus. Jesus was little more than an eschatological prophet to the hypothetical Q community according to Kloppenberg. Most recently some scholars (Mack, Vaage) have sought to characterize the Jesus followed by the Q community or the community itself as much like the Cynic philosophers, those wandering ascetic moralists.[1] Mack even makes the absurd claim that the Q community did not regard Jesus as the Messiah: "The remarkable thing about the people of Q is that they were not Christians. They did not think of Jesus as a messiah or the Christ" (p. 4). All of this from a document we do not even possess and whose exact shape and extent scholars cannot even agree upon!

But the most ridiculous claim made by some proponents of the Q hypothesis is that the Q community or communities knew little and cared less about the death and resurrection of Jesus. How could anyone arrive at such a conclusion when everything we have from earliest Christianity shows that the death-resurrection was central? The conclusion is actually a classic case of *petitio principii*, "question begging" or assuming the proposition to be proved. By definition they rule out the death-resurrection from Q then explain this as a singular characteristic of this hypothetical community. First one maintains that Q is the material found only in Matthew and Luke. Since there is very little material common to *only* Matthew and Luke in the accounts of Jesus death and resurrection--indeed all four Gospels are remarkably united in telling about these events--one then concludes that Q did not know about or care about his death and resurrection.

But even if one wishes to accept the totally unproven hypothesis of Q, this conclusion does not follow. Maybe Q had references to Jesus death-resurrection but they are so similar to Mark and John that one cannot now discern them. To draw a picture of a community based first on a hypothesis and then on question begging is probably a waste of time and ink. Further, even if we should accept for the sake of argument propositions one and two (1. Q really did exist. 2. Q did not have any references about Jesus' death or resurrection in it.) these propositions would not prove that the Q community did not care about these events. That would be an argument from silence. One would have to prove that all that the Q community cared about was a part of the Q document. Perhaps this community had several different documents to instruct its members. Perhaps it had one written document of the sayings of Jesus but reserved the death-resurrection stories for oral narration and proclamation. There are many other possibilities. The proponents of Q pile one unsupportable premise on another.

Farrer was correct many years ago to plead for the abandonment of this hypothesis.

Farmer and His School

The most thorough criticism of the two document hypothesis has been that of W.R. Farmer. Farmer not only attempted to discredit the existence of Q, but the priority of Mark, reviving the Griesbach hypothesis. Griesbach had proposed the priority of Matthew and the subsequent use of both Matthew and Luke by Mark. Farmer's emphasis is that there were prior to Streeter--and there certainly have been since--valid reasons offered for doubting the Two-Source hypothesis. Yet, due to the prevailing intellectual climate, the Two-Source theory has gained supremacy. Marcan priority was accepted because Mark, more than any of the other Gospels supported the philosophical presuppositions of the liberal theologians of the early twentieth century. With no birth narratives (and their stories of virginal conception), Mark was seen by many scholars as emphasizing the humanity of Jesus. Thus, it was desirable to have Mark as the earliest source of Christian teaching.

Regarding the Q hypothesis, Farmer maintained that since Luke has inserted his material common to Matthew in several large sections rather than dispersing it throughout his Gospel (as Streeter erroneously maintained), it is not incredible that Luke has used Matthew. Because Streeter's description of the arrangement of the "Q" material (i.e. the double tradition) in Luke was erroneous at this point, his conclusion that Luke would had to have been a "crank" to use Matthew was also in error.

Farmer's view of the Synoptic interrelationship is not without its problems either but at least it does not rely on the existence of a hypothetical document.

Recent Developments

The W.O. Walker Essays

In 1978 a group of New Testament scholars met to hear experts from other disciplines--oral literature, classics, rabbinics, and modern literature--discuss the Gospels. Their conclusions in general challenged the prevailing notions concerning both the literary relationship of the Gospels and the historicity of the Gospel material.

A.B. Lord--who had changed the course of Homeric studies by demonstrating that the *Iliad* and the *Odyssey* were originally oral poetry (see his *Singer of Tales*)--concluded that the Synoptics "have the appearance of three oral traditional variants of the same narrative and non-narrative materials" (p. 90 in Walker). By that statement, Lord--an expert in the study of oral literature--was indicating that he thought Matthew, Mark, and Luke had each written his Gospel from his own oral sources, not from copying from one another.

Even more fascinating was the conclusion of G. Kennedy, the classicist. Kennedy pointed to two phenomena in antiquity that most New Testament scholars seem unaware of. Gospel critics often assume that the materials in the four Gospels were passed on by word of mouth for decades and that these materials were often altered. Some even affirm that new materials were created by Christian communities so that much--some might even say most--of the Gospel narratives and sayings material is not authentically from Jesus.

But Kennedy pointed out that the ancients were wont to make notes on important people. Several of Socrates followers went around taking notes on his sayings. This practice was followed, says Kennedy, not just by the intelligentsia either, for a common cobbler also made notes of everything he could remember that Socrates said to him and he ended up with 33 dialogues (p. 131 in Walker). Note taking was a very common practice in antiquity thus we should expect that some of Jesus' disciples had notes of his sayings.

A recent publication by C. Thiede, a papyrologist, confirms Kennedy's suggestion. Thiede affirms that note taking by shorthand was quite common in antiquity. Plutarch informs us that shorthand was used in the Roman senate. Titus, the son of emperor Vespasian, was reportedly a fast and accurate stenographer. Thiede speculates that Matthew as a tax collector would have known shorthand. At any rate, we should reasonably expect that some of Jesus' disciples had notes of his sayings.

Furthermore, it was not uncommon for ancient people to display prodigious memories. Kennedy again cites the example of the philosopher Seneca who memorized speeches he heard and years later wrote them down. Kennedy adds:

> It would have been a much less demanding task for regular hearers of Jesus or of the apostles to hold in memory a significant part of the teaching they had repeatedly heard and to recite it or write it down at any time there was reason to do so (p. 143 in Walker).

B. Gerhardsson.

Gerhardsson published his work on the Gospels in 1961. His thesis was that just as the rabbis had transmitted their teaching about the Law orally--now preserved at least partially in the Mishnah--so Jesus transmitted his new Torah orally. Now the rabbis spent many years memorizing the oral Torah and later teaching it to students. They had a careful system to preserve the words of the sages. We should expect Jesus and his disciples to have done the same, maintained Gerhardsson. More recently, R. Riesner has argued similarly.

Although most New Testament scholars have not been convinced by all of Gerhardsson's arguments (see Kee), he did remind us of one important fact. Memorization of important teachings in Palestine was very common-place. Therefore, it is highly probable that Jesus' words and deeds were carefully remembered and recited--and of course taught to others--until some decades later they were written down.

Conclusions Concerning the Synoptic Relationships

In reaching any conclusion in this area one must consider the evidence of the ancient Christian author, Papias. Papias was bishop if Hierapolis in Asia Minor in the early second century A.D. and wrote a treatise on the *Sayings of the Lord* in A.D. 133. Papias claimed to possess the oral teaching of Jesus' disciples and he was, according to the Christian historian, Eusebius (4th cent. A.D.), a hearer of John the elder, of Polycarp, and of one Aristion, all important late first century to early second century Christian leaders. Papias himself evidently did not know any of the twelve apostles but knew those who did. He wrote of his oral learning in one of the few fragments of his we have left:

> I will not hesitate to set down for you, along with my interpretations, everything I carefully learned then from the elders and carefully remembered, guaranteeing their truth. For unlike most people I did not enjoy those who have a great deal to say, but those who teach the truth. Nor did I enjoy those who recall someone else's commandments, but those who remember the commandments given by the Lord to the faith and proceeding from the truth itself. And if by chance someone who had been a follower of the elders should come my way, I inquired about the words of the elders--what Andrew or Peter said, or Philip, or Thomas or James, or John or Matthew or any other of the Lord's disciples, and whatever Aristion and the elder John, the Lord's disciples, were sayings. For I did not think that information from books would profit me as much as information from a living and abiding voice.

(quoted in Eusebius, *H.E.* 3.39. Trans. in J.B. Lightfoot and J.R. Harmer, *The Apostolic Fathers*, p. 314)

Thus Papias sought out information about Jesus, the apostles and the "elders" from those who had known them. He valued living witnesses over written documents.

Papias describes the composition of the Gospels, Mark and Matthew as follows:

> And (John) the Elder used to say this: Mark having become Peter's interpreter, wrote down accurately everything he remembered, though not in order, of the things either said or done by Christ. For he neither heard the Lord nor followed him, but afterward, as I said, followed Peter, who adapted his teachings as needed but had no intention of giving an ordered account of the Lord's sayings. Consequently Mark did nothing wrong in writing down some things as he remembered them, for he made it his one concern not to omit anything which he heard or to make any false statement in them.

> So Matthew composed the oracles in the Hebrew language and each person interpreted them as best he could. (quoted in Eusebius *H.E.* 3.39. Trans. in Lightfoot and Harmer, *The Apostolic Fathers*, p. 316)

Thus Papias indicates that Mark wrote from his memory of Peter's eyewitness testimony concerning the events of Jesus' life. This is much like the process described by Kennedy and the Fragment and Oral Tradition hypotheses described above.

Matthew, according to Papias, wrote his "oracles" (Gk: *logia*) in the Hebrew (that is, probably Aramaic) language. Furthermore Irenaeus (A.D. 180), Origen (A.D. 220), Clement of Alexandria (A.D. 200), and Augustine (A.D. 400) wrote also that Matthew composed his Gospel first and in Aramaic.[2]

Thus the testimony of the ancient Christian authors is that Matthew wrote his Gospel first and in the Aramaic language. Further, Papias indicates--as does Irenaeus and Clement of Alexandria--that Mark's Gospel is based on Peter's preaching. Mark wrote down--either while Peter was yet alive (Clement) or after his death (Irenaeus)--what Peter had taught and preached about Jesus's life and deeds.

Luke, the author of the third Gospel, gives us some idea of his process in writing his work in the prologue (Lk 1:1-4):

Since many have taken it in hand to compose a narrative about the events fulfilled among us, even as the eyewitnesses and ministers of the word taught them to us orally from the beginning, it seemed good to me also, most excellent Theophilus, to write for you (an account) correctly and in order since I have followed (these events) from the beginning. That way you will know the certainty of the words you were taught.

From Luke's statement we learn the following: First, there were already several accounts of Jesus' deeds and words by the time Luke wrote. Some of these accounts may have been nothing more than the published notes of eyewitnesses. But it is equally possible that Luke knew about Matthew. Second, Luke has gotten his material from the "eyewitnesses" and "ministers of the word" (possibly those who memorized and taught the sayings of Jesus) who taught these materials orally. Third, Luke's purpose is to help his readers--and his patron, Theophilus--know with certainty that the words and deeds attributed to Jesus in his Gospel are accurate. Thus Luke was concerned to repeat only accurate descriptions of Jesus' life.

From such ancient evidence one should conclude that probably Matthew wrote his Gospel first. He perhaps published it in Aramaic and later in Greek. Mark wrote his Gospel from his recollection of Peter's eyewitness testimony about Jesus. Luke wrote based on the testimony of numerous eyewitnesses and perhaps from others' notes. Luke and Mark knew and read, Matthew. They usually follow his order of events but not always.

J. Wenham's recent work probably best describes the process of Gospel composition. The Synoptics are three independently written documents, based on oral teaching and notes of eyewitnesses. But Mark probably was familiar with Matthew as was Luke. Mark and Luke were influenced by Matthew as far as the general outline of events. Wenham accepts the Augustinian order of composition (see above). But we would conclude that Luke wrote before Mark. Thus we would favor the Griesbach order. We adapt Wenham's diagram as follows:

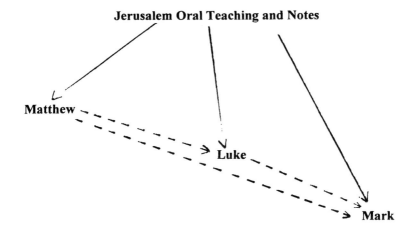

Table 15.3
Synoptic Origins
(Adapted from Wenham)

Notes

1. For the Cynics see D.A. Fiensy, *New Testament Introduction*, pp. 193f.
2. Cf. C. Thiede and M. D'Ancona, *The Eyewitness of Jesus* who maintain that the Magdalen Papyrus of a tiny portion of Matthew dates to before AD 70. If correct, this would support the argument of Matthean priority (although Thiede seems still to accept the Marcan priority). For a rebuttal of Thiede's conclusion, see G. Stanton, *Gospel Truth?*

Chapter 16

The Apocryphal Gospels

Bibliography: B. Altaner, *Patrology*; R. Camron, "The Gospel of Thomas" in *ABD* ; idem., *The Other Gospels*; J.H. Charlesworth, *New Testament Apocrypha and Pseudepigrapha*; J.D. Crossan, *Four Other Gospels*; idem., *The Historical Jesus*; S. Davies, "Christology and Protology of the Gospel of Thomas" *Journal of Biblical Literature* 111 (1992) 663-682; Idem., "Thomas, the Fourth Synoptic Gospel" *Biblical Archaeologist* (1983) 6-14; J.K. Elliott, *The Apocryphal New Testament*; R.W. Funk and R.W. Hoover, *The Five Gospels*; E. Hennecke, W. Scheemelcher, and R. McL. Wilson, *New Testament Apocrypha*; M.R. James, *The Apocryphal New Testament*; H. Koester, *Ancient Christian Gospels*; idem., *History and Literature of Early Christianity*; H. Koester and S.J. Patterson, "The Gospel of Thomas, Does it Contain Authentic Sayings of Jesus?" *Bible Review* 6.2 (1990) 28-39; R.J. Miller, *The Complete Gospels*; idem., "The Gospels that Didn't Make the Cut" *Bible Review* 9.4 (1993) 14-25; E. Pagels, *The Gnostic Gospels*; J. Quasten, *Patrology*; Q. Quesnell, "The Mar Saba Clementine: A Question of Evidence" *Catholic Biblical Quarterly* 37 (1975) 48-67; J.M. Robinson, *The Hammadi Library*; W.D. Stroker, *Extracanonical Sayings of Jesus*; H.E.W. Turner and H. Montefiore, *Thomas and the Evangelists*; P. Vielhauer, *Geschichte der urchristlichen Literatur*; idem., "ANAPAUSIS: Zum gnostischen Hintergrund des Thomasevangeliums" in W. Etester and F.H. Kettler, eds. *Apophoreta*.

The word apocrypha is a Greek word meaning "hidden things". We apply the term to certain books found in the Bible of the Catholic and Eastern

Orthodox churches. These are the so-called Old Testament apocrypha (e.g. 1 Maccabees, Wisdom of Ben Sirach, and 4 Ezra). These writings come from the intertestamental period, that time span between the writing of the Old Testament and the writing of the New Testament. Many Bibles such as the *Oxford Annotated Bible* include the apocrypha for comparison.

In addition, there are writings called pseudepigrapha ("false writings") which are falsely attributed usually to great Old Testament heroes such as Moses, Abraham, Ezra, and Solomon. A standard collection can be found in J.H. Charlesworth, *The Pseudepigrapha of the Old Testament.* Some examples of these books are the Book of Enoch, the Testaments of the Twelve Patriarchs, and the Book of Jubilees Both the apocrypha and pseudepigrapha are helpful to the student of the New Testament in understanding the literary and theological world of Judaism during the time the New Testament was written.

There is also a body of literature known as the New Testament Apocrypha. These books include apocalypses or revelations (books purporting to give information about the end of time), apocryphal Acts which detail information allegedly about the apostles (including information about apostles not much referred to in our New Testament Acts of the Apostles) and some apocryphal letters. But most numerous among the New Testament Apocrypha are the apocryphal Gospels. The standard collection of Hennecke quotes or discusses around 60 different texts. We will devote most of this chapter to a description and analysis of some of these Gospels.

The obvious questions one has of these texts are: Why were they not included in the New Testament? Is there anything of historical value in them? How should a believer read these texts?

Preliminary Issues

We must make three points before we begin our description of the apocryphal Gospels. First all of the New Testament Apocrypha are late, from the second century and following. The New Testament is predominantly a first century book. These texts stand outside it chronologically.

Second, these texts have no legitimate claim to apostolic authority. The

Gospel of Matthew has a valid claim to coming from the apostle Matthew. Mark has a traditional connection with the apostle Peter. Luke was an associate of Paul. The Gospel of John stems from the apostle. But the apocryphal texts are late and have no supporting internal or external evidence for apostolic origins.

Third, these texts were not universally accepted. They were read in certain regions with pleasure much the way we might read a historical novel, with a basis in history but with many fantastic details thrown in to maintain interest. In addition these apocryphal Gospels often add invented stories about Jesus' boyhood, for example, to fill in the gaps of the New Testament. The canonical Gospels--that is, our New Testament Gospels--on the other hand did have universal acceptance. The following chart presents this evidence:

	Ir	**Ter**	**Cl**	**Mur**	**Or**	**Eus**
4 Gospels	x	x	x	x	x	x
Acts	x	x	x	x	x	x
13 Pauline Letters	x	x	x	x	x	x
Hebrews	?	?	x	0	?	x
1 Peter	x	x	x	0	x	x
2 Peter	?	0	x	0	?	?
James	?	0	x	0	?	?
Jude	?	x	x	x	0	?
1 John	x	x	x	x	x	x
2 John	x	0	x	x	?	?
3 John	?	0	x	0	?	?
Revelation	x	x	x	x	x	x
Epistle of Barnabas	0	0	x	0	0	*
Apocalypse of Peter	0	0	x	?	0	*
Gospel of the Hebrews	0	0	?	0	0	*
Gospel of Egyptians	0	0	?	0	0	0
1 Clement	0	0	x	0	0	0
Didache	0	0	x	0	0	0
Shepherd of Hermas	0	0	x	?	0	*

Epistle to Laodiceans	0	0	0	*	0	0
Epistle to Alexandrians	0	0	0	*	0	0
Acts of Paul	0	0	0	0	0	*

Table 16.1
Early Christian Literature Accepted as Canonical

(Ir=Irenaeus; Ter=Tertullian; Cl=Clement of Alexandria; Mur=Muratoriam Fragment; Or=Origin; Eus=Eusebius)

(KEY: x=included in canon; ?=undecided or disputed; 0=Not mentioned; *=Considered spurious)

Thus the apocryphal texts cannot stand up against the measuring stick ("canon") applied to our New Testament. Yet we still may learn something from them. At least one should be informed about these texts since so much is being written about them lately. Every Christian leader should know what the issues and facts are.

Introduction to the Main Apocryphal Gospels

The Infancy Gospels

A. The Protevangelium of James. This text, written probably about AD 150 (Hennecke) purports to give us more of the background of Jesus' birth. The story begins with Joachim and Anna who are lamenting that they have had no children. Both are greatly pained by their childlessness when an angel announces to Anna that she will conceive a child. The child she gives birth to is Mary. At three years of age Anna and Joachim present Mary to the temple priests where she will be raised as one of the servants of the Lord (notice the similarity thus far to the story of Samuel). At age 12 Mary is given to the care of an elderly widower, Joseph the carpenter, who has sons that are already grown. Joseph takes Mary to his house and goes immediately to build his buildings. Mary is one of those pure virgins of the tribe of David selected to help sew a new veil for the temple. Later she is told by an angel that she will conceive by the power of the Holy Spirit. The trouble that comes thereafter is predictable since first Joseph and then the priests do not believe at first that Mary is really a virgin. Mary's virginity is confirmed, however, through various ways. Eventually Jesus is born and a woman is healed from touching the infant Jesus.

B. The Infancy Story of Thomas. This text which was written toward the end of the second century A.D. (Hennecke) must be distinguished from the sayings Gospel of Thomas which we will discuss later. The Infancy Gospel of Thomas is a bizarre account of Jesus' boyhood which represents Jesus as an *enfant terrible*. Jesus at age five is represented as able to do all sorts of wonders. He makes some birds out of clay then turns them into real sparrows. He causes a boy to wither up and die because the boy destroyed a dam in a brook. He causes another lad to die because the boy bumped against him. When the parents of the dead boys protest, they become blind.

A teacher named Zacchaeus is horribly embarrassed by Jesus in this tale because Jesus is so much wiser than the teacher. Of this teacher and two subsequent ones Jesus keeps asking the hidden meaning of the letters of the alphabet.

Jesus also does miracles at age six in the Infancy Gospel but these miracles seem more helpful and benign. He raises a few people from the dead, heals a terrible wound on the foot of a lad, carries water for his mother in the folds of his garments, plants one seed of wheat and reaps bushels, and corrects his fathers bumbling carpentry work by lengthening a beam that Joseph had cut too short (adults in general are portrayed as incompetent). The story ends when Jesus is twelve and the family goes to the temple for the Passover (see Lk 2 and Aland 12). Even this weird text's last scene which is obviously adapted from the Gospel of Luke grossly exaggerates Jesus' display of wisdom and intelligence. Jesus is a mere show off. Such an account contrasts markedly with the restrained account of Luke.

The author of the Infancy Story of Thomas had a marked taste for crude and startling miracles. These miracles have a definite offensive and foreign feeling to them. One cannot imagine the Jesus of the New Testament even as a boy acting in such a selfish and destructive manner. Further, the constant harping on the meaning of the alphabet in the Infancy Gospel is pure Gnosticism.

The Fragmentary Jewish Christian Gospels

The Christian authors of the second century through the fifth centuries often refer to Gospels used by Jewish Christians. These are variously named the Gospel of the Ebionites, the Gospel of the Nazaraeans, and the Gospel of the Hebrews.

A. The Gospel of the Ebionites. The Ebionites were an early Jewish Christian heretical sect that denied the virgin birth of Jesus, regarded him merely as a prophet, and observed the Jewish law including circumcision. Their name, *Ebionaioi* (Gk) or *'ebionim* (Heb) means the "poor ones" and may indicate a connection with the Essenes since the Qumran texts often refer to their members as the poor (4QpPs37). They were said to use only the Gospel of Matthew of our canonical Gospels but had in addition a Gospel of their own which was probably an adaptation of some of the stories in our canonical Gospels. This Gospel is extant only in a few quotations which indicate that it was composed originally in Greek probably in the middle of the second century AD. Among other items of interest these quotations have Jesus and John the Baptist reject the eating of meat (cf. the controversy in Rom 14:1-23) and affirm a vegetarian diet.

The example we quote below is an example of the adoptionist heresy. That is, that Jesus was not eternally the Son of God but was adopted as son at his baptism:

> When the people were baptized, Jesus also came and was baptized by John. And as he came up from the water, the heavens were opened and he saw the Holy Spirit in the form of a dove that descended and entered into him. And a voice (sounded) from heaven that said: Thou art my beloved Son, in thee I am well pleased. And again: I have this day begotten thee. (Epiphanius, *Haer.* 30.13.7f; trans. by P. Vielhauer in Hennecke).

The last alleged statement from heaven, "I have this day begotten thee", is a quotation of Psalm 2:7 and was often applied at Jesus baptism by the adoptionists. None of the New Testament Gospels, however, say that this scripture was heard at Jesus' baptism.[1]

B. Gospel of the Hebrews. The Christian authors of the second century and later also refer often to a Gospel of the Hebrews. It was only a little shorter than our Gospel of Matthew according to ancient statements. It was composed probably in the mid second century AD possibly in Egypt for use by Jewish Christians. The Gospel of the Hebrews does not seem to be merely an adaptation of the four New Testament Gospels as does the Gospel of the Ebionites. Rather it is probably a separate, though very late, account of the life of Jesus. There is nothing grossly heretical about the few fragments that have been preserved but James the Lord's brother does play a more prominent part than in the New Testament. James was the leading figure in most Jewish Christian circles in the first and second centuries. This Gospel was also composed in Greek. We quote here an account of Jesus' appearance to James after his resurrection:

> And when the Lord had given the linen cloth to the servant of the priest, he went to James and appeared to him. For James had sworn that he would not eat bread from that hour in which he had drunk the cup of the Lord until he should see him risen from among them that sleep. And shortly thereafter the Lord said: Bring a table and bread! And immediately it is added: he took the bread, blessed it and brake it and gave it to James the Just and said to him: My brother, eat thy bread, for the Son of man is risen from among them that sleep. (Jerome, *vir. inl.* 2; trans. by P. Vielhauer in Hennecke).

Narrative Gospels

A. Secret Mark. In 1941 M. Smith was staying in the Mar Saba desert monastery in Israel when he discovered a partially preserved manuscript purporting to be a letter from Clement of Alexandria (c. AD 200) to one Theodore. The letter alleged that there were three versions of the Gospel of Mark: a) Public Mark (our present canonical Mark) b)Heretical Mark, a perversion of our canonical Gospel by Gnostics, and c) Secret Mark, a new version of Mark made by Mark himself for the spiritually elite. The letter quotes two of the stories of Secret Mark.

This document has sparked furious controversy. There has even been speculation that M. Smith composed this text himself and has tried to push this hoax on the scholarly world (see the discussions in Quesnell and Crossan).[2] One problem is that the original manuscript has never been examined scientifically and there is lack of good photographs of the original manuscript. Another is Smith's claim that the heretical version of the Gnostics is the correct one. Smith obviously had an ax to grind.

Secret Mark adds nothing to our understanding of the New Testament in general or to the life of Jesus in particular but it does illustrate something of the nature of the debate over these extracanonical documents.

B. The Gospel of Peter. The Gospel of Peter was referred to in the ancient Christian sources but no text of it existed until 1886 when a Greek fragment of it was found in Akhmim in Egypt. This work was produced in the second century AD since it was mentioned by sources around AD 200.

The Gospel of Peter, at least the fragment of it which we possess, is concerned with the death and resurrection of Jesus. It begins with Pilate's washing of his hands and ends with resurrection appearances. It is mainly a conflation of our four canonical Gospels with a few embellishments. We quote one example:

> And they brought two malefactors and crucified the Lord in the midst between them. But he held his peace, as if he felt no pain. And when they had set up the cross, they wrote upon it: This is the King of Israel. And they laid down his garments before him and divided them among themselves and cast the lot upon them. But one of the malefactors rebuked them, saying, "We have landed in suffering for the deeds of wickedness which we have committed, but this man, who has become the saviour of men, what wrong has he done you?". And they were wroth with him and commanded that his legs should not be broken, so that he might die in torments. (Trans. by C. Mauer in Hennecke).

Nag Hammadi Texts

A. The texts in general. In 1945 two Egyptian farmers while looking for a naturally occurring fertilizer in the cliffs near Nag Hammadi discovered an ancient clay jar. Inside the jar were thirteen books with over 50 individual tractates. These documents were written in Coptic, the ancient language of Egypt. A later inventory of their contents showed that most of the documents were Gnostic, some were Jewish, and one was a part of Plato's *Republic*. Among the 50 odd texts are several works called Gospels. There are the Gospel of Truth, the Gospel of Philip, the Gospel of the Egyptians and the Gospel of Thomas. The first three of these Gospels are nothing more than rambling discourses on Gnostic themes[3] and quite different from our canonical Gospels both in content and in literary form. The Gospel of the Egyptians, for example, deals with the origin of the heavenly world and the origin of the race of Seth, typical Gnostic obsessions.

B. The Gospel of Thomas. This Gospel is quite different from the other Gospels found at Nag Hammadi. It contains 114 sayings each introduced with the words "Jesus said". This Gospel was known before its discovery in Egypt by a quotation in Hippolytus of Rome (AD 200; see *Haer*. 5.7.20), and in three Greek papyrus fragments also found in Egypt: Papyrus Oxyrhynchus 1, 654, and 655. But these sources were only fragmentary. Therefore the discovery of the complete text of the Gospel of Thomas, albeit in the Coptic language, was a boon in historical investigation.

The Gospel of Thomas has been dated from AD 50 to 140. The early date (see Crossan) is highly speculative and suspect. The better suggestion is somewhere between AD 100 and 140. The work was probably composed in Syria where Thomas was a favorite apostle.

According to Camron, of the 114 sayings in this text 68 have Biblical parallels. Is Thomas then a rehash of the canonical Gospels or does it represent an independent tradition of Jesus' sayings? The debate is sharply divided. Scholars cannot even agree if there is a consensus on this issue. On the one hand one can read statements like the following from S. Davies: "The consensus of scholarship at present date is that the Gospel of Thomas. . .was *not* made by persons who were simply picking and choosing sayings from the gospels and adding others" (p. 9). But then the balanced and sober survey of scholarship by Camron concludes: "The question of the relationship of the Gospel of Thomas and the Gospels of the New Testament is still to be resolved" (*ABD* 6.537).

Yet the members of the so-called Jesus Seminar[4] seem to have accepted that Thomas represents an independent tradition of Jesus' words. They call Thomas the Fifth Gospel and have granted it a status just short of canonical. There is no hint of the unresolved issue of the relationship between Thomas and the canonical Gospels in the publication by Funk and Hoover.

The same puzzling conclusions of some recent scholars are evident concerning the nature of the theology of the Gospel of Thomas. Camron clearly lays out the Gnostic character of many of the sayings of this text (see especially sayings 18,19, 49, 50). He maintains: "A majority of scholars have concluded that the Gospel of Thomas is a gnostic gospel. . . ." (*ABD* 6.539; similarly in Turner and Montefiore). Yet again S. Davies affirms: "The Gospel of Thomas is quite frequently said to be a gnostic document. But the Gospel of Thomas is *not* a gnostic document" (p. 6). Probably the best statement is that in Funk and Hoover: ". . .it is best to describe Thomas as reflecting an incipient gnosticism" (p. 501).

The student should then be critical when he/she reads that these issues concerning the Gospel of Thomas have been decided. They have not. In spite of the efforts of some to grant Thomas a nearly canonical status we still suspect that Thomas is mostly a Gnosticizing rehash of the New Testament Gospels.

The reader will recall that in Chapter 4 we quoted one saying from the Gospel of Thomas. Here we add to that a few more examples. We will use the results of the Jesus Seminar (see Funk and Hoover) which concluded that 37 of the 114 were genuinely from Jesus. Most (but not all) of the sayings that the Jesus Seminar concluded were authentic sayings of Jesus are paralleled in our New Testament Gospels.

Saying 2: Those who seek should not stop seeking until they find. (cf. Mt 7:7-8)

Saying 10: I have cast fire upon the world and look, I'm guarding it until it blazes. (cf. Lk 12:49)

Saying 14: When you go into any region and walk about in the countryside, when people take vou in, eat what they serve you. . . After all, what goes into your mou:h will not defile you; rather, it's what comes out of your mouth that will defile you. (cf. Lk 10:7; Mk 7:15)

Saying 20: It's like a mustard seed. (It's) the smallest of all seeds, but when it falls on prepared soil, it produces a large plant and becomes a shelter for birds of the sky. (cf. Mt 13:31-32)

Saying 63: There was a rich person who had a great deal of money. He said, "I shall invest my money so that I may sow, reap, plant, and fill my storehouses with produce, that I may lack nothing." These were the things he was thinking in his heart, but that very night he died. (cf. Lk 12:16-21)

Saying 97: The (Father's) imperial rule is like a woman who was carrying a (jar) full of meal. While she was walking along (a) distant road, the handle of the jar broke and the meal spilled behind her (along) the road. She didn't know it; she hadn't noticed a problem. When she reached her house, she put the jar down and discovered that it was empty. (no parallels in the New Testament) (All translations are from Funk and Hoover.)

The Gospel of Thomas probably represents an amalgam of some independent traditions about Jesus and a retelling of the sayings of the canonical Gospels.

Concluding Remarks

As we surmised in Chapter 4 there probably are genuine sayings and events of the life of Jesus that exist today in sources outside the New Testament. Certainly our canonical Gospels could not have included everything of note that Jesus did or said and for that matter they never claimed to do so (see Jn 20:30-31; 21:25). This material is of interest to the historian but has little to offer faith. Although the sources may contain authentic sayings of Jesus and genuine historical events, these materials are not authoritative for Christians.

The apocryphal Gospels, even those with no authentic Jesus traditions-- which is the case for the overwhelming majority of them--are still valuable to us, however, because they reveal much about the Christian circles that produced them. We can see in them the wide diversity in second century and third century Christianity. It ranged from the Jewish Christians on one side to the Gnostic heresies on the other. These centuries were the crucial era when the orthodox faith, tried by the fire of persecution, gained the victory over those extremes on the fringes. The apocryphal Gospels are in their way a record of that struggle.

Finally, it is helpful to compare and contrast these Gospels with our canonical Gospels. Both the theological content and the literary form can contrast markedly from the New Testament. The philosophical rambling of some of them are set off more sharply when we read the simple prose of the Jesus story in the canonical Gospels. The silly accounts of some of the infancy Gospels appear even more ridiculous with placed alongside our reserved and restrained Gospels of Matthew and Luke. Even the sayings Gospel of Thomas seems tedious and cold when viewed from the perspective of the moving drama within the four New Testament Gospels. To read the apocryphal Gospels is to appreciate the grandeur and eloquence of the canonical Gospels. R.C. Foster wrote:

> The survey of the entire field of sources of the life of Christ sends us
> back with renewed reverence to the New Testament. . . The astounding
> differences between these (apocryphal) stories and the beautiful and
> reserved accounts of the New Testament offer striking evidence of the

divine inspiration of the latter (pp. 31, 289).

Notes

1. New Testament Greek manuscript D, Codex Bezae, a manuscript known for unusual additions to the Gospels, does add Psalm 2:7 at Luke 3;22.

2. See the exchange also between Smith and Quesnell in *Catholic Biblical Quarterly* 38 (1976) 197-203; and the more recent (and negative) assessment of the manuscript by A.H. Criddle, "On the Mar Saba Letter Attributed to Clement of Alexandria" *Journal of Early Christian Studies* 3 (1995) 215-220.

3. For a summary of Gnostic beliefs see D.A. Fiensy, *New Testament Introduction*, pp. 188-190.

4. The Jesus Seminar is a group of scholars (reports of the total membership vary) from North America that meets twice a year to discuss and vote on whether they accept sayings or actions of Jesus as recorded in the New Testament as genuine and historical. For a popular report and assessment of this group see: "Jesus Christ, Plain and Simple", *Time* January 10, 1994; "A Lesser Child of God", *Newsweek* April 4, 1994; "Five Gospels, No Christ", *Christianity Today* April 4, 1994. More scholarly assessments (negative) can be found in : M.J. Wilkins and J.P. Moreland, eds., *Jesus Under Fire*; G.A. Boyd, *Cynic, Sage or Son of God?*; B. Witherington, III, *The Jesus Quest*; and L.T. Johnson, *The Real Jesus*. A defense of the Jesus Seminar by one of its members can be found in: M.J. Borg, *Jesus in Contemporary Scholarship*. The results of the first series of meetings by the Seminar are published in Funk and Hoover, *The Five Gospels*.

Chapter 17

Jerusalem: Geography and Sociology

Bibliography: N. Avigad, *Discovering Jerusalem*; N. Avigad and H. Geva, "Jerusalem" in E. Stern, ed. *New Encyclopedia of Archaeological Excavations In the Holy Land*; M. Avi-Yona, *The Holy Land*; D. Bahat, *The Illustrated Atlas of Jerusalem*; F. J. Bliss and A.C. Dickie, *Excavations at Jerusalem*; M. Ben-Dov, *In the Shadow of the Temple*; D. Bahat and M. Broshi, "Excavations in the Armenian Garden" in Y. Yadin, ed., *Jerusalem Revealed*; M. Broshi, "Estimating the Population of Ancient Jerusalem" *Palestine Exploration Quarterly* 106 (1974) 33-51; Idem., "Excavations in the House of Caiaphas, Mt. Zion" in Yadin, ed., *Jerusalem Revealed*; L. Finkelstein, *The Pharisees*; M. Hengel, *The Hellenization of Judaea in the First Century After Christ*; J Jeremias, *Jerusalem in the Time of Jesus*; Idem., *The Rediscovery of Bethesda*; S. Krauss, *Talmudische Archaeologie*; R.M. Mackowski, S.J. *Jerusalem, City of Jesus*; B. Mazar, *The Mountain of the Lord*; G. Mussies, "Greek in Palestine and the Diaspora" in S. Safrai and M. Stern, *The Jewish People in the First century*; E.P. Sanders, *Judaism: Practice and Belief 66 B.C.E.-66 C.E.*; G. Sjoberg, *The Pre-Industrial City*; E.M. Smallwood, "High Priests and Politics in Roman Palestine" *Journal of Theological Studies* 13 (1962) 14-34; M. Stern, "Aspects of Jewish Society: The Priesthood and Other Classes" in S. Safrai and M. Stern, *Judaism in the First Century*; J. Wilkinson, *Jerusalem as Jesus Knew It*.

A Tour of Jerusalem

When Jesus entered Jerusalem to the shouts of "Hosanna" by onlookers (Mt 21:9), he was entering the "most illustrious city in the east" (Pliny, *Natural History* 5.70) Jerusalem, with 60,000 inhabitants, is described by Josephus as mainly consisting of two parts: the Lower City and the Upper City (see Map 17.1). The Lower City consisted of the Ophel, the City of David, and the Tyropoeon Valley. The Upper City was on the hill to the west (*War* 2.422). Josephus also writes of an area just north of the Lower and Upper Cities which he calls New Town (*War* 2.530; 5.331). By the time of the war in AD 66 this last area was encompassed by the third north wall. But at the time of Jesus' ministry only a small part of that suburb was enclosed--by the second north wall. The fourth important district in ancient Jerusalem was the Temple Mount.

We begin our tour of ancient Jerusalem in the northeast corner of the city. The twin pools of Bethesda were the location of a healing cult that is referred to both in the New Testament and in the Copper Scroll of the Dead Sea Scrolls (see Jeremias, *Rediscovery*). Jesus healed the lame man here while the lame man waited for someone to throw him into the churning waters (Jn 5:1-9). Moving south we come to the Temple Mount. We have already described the function and architecture of the temple (see chapter 2). The temple was constructed on one of the two main hills of Jerusalem (the other one is where the Upper City lay). To build such a large structure in a steep hill Herod the Great had to construct a large platform for it. Jesus taught daily in the temple during the final week of his life (Mt 26:55; Jn 18:20). Extending from the mountain on which the temple stood was a raised spur called the Ophel. At the southern end of the spur was the location of the ancient City of David.

Just to the east of the Temple Mount was the Garden of Gethsemane, or Garden of the Olive Press where Jesus often went to pray (Lk 22:39). At the southeast corner of the city stood the Pool of Siloam near which Jesus healed a blind man then told him to wash his eyes in the pool (Jn 9:1-12). The Essene Gate at the southwest corner indicates that there were Essenes in Jerusalem and that they probably would have heard Jesus teach. The Upper Room was where Jesus ate the Last Supper with his disciples (Mt 26:17-20; Acts 1:13). Not far from the Upper Room was the palace of Caiaphas, the High Priest. Here Jesus was kept until morning and here he was interrogated by Caiaphas (Mt 26:57-68). Herod's palace, a magnificent construction second only to the temple itself, was in Jesus' day the Praetorium. This was the residence of the Roman procurator,

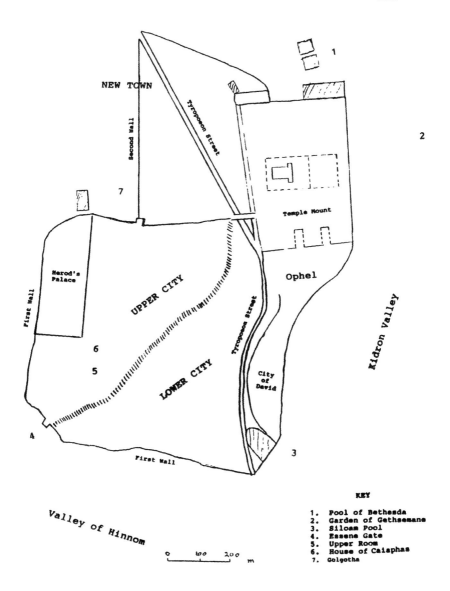

KEY

1. Pool of Bethesda
2. Garden of Gethsemane
3. Siloam Pool
4. Essene Gate
5. Upper Room
6. House of Caiaphas
7. Golgotha

Map 17.1
Jerusalem in the Time of Jesus

Pontius Pilate, and the place of Jesus' trial (Jn 18:28). Finally we come
to Golgotha (where the Church of the Holy Sepulchre now stands), place
of Jesus' crucifixion and near here his tomb (Mt 27:33; Jn 19:41).

The Social Classes of Jerusalem

There were three classes in ancient Jerusalem: the upper class which
resided mostly in the Upper City, the lower class which lived in the Lower
City and the New Town, and the submerged class which lived on the
outskirts of the city or whose members were homeless.

The upper class lived mainly in the Upper City and consisted of the
temple nobility and the lay nobility. Most of these, even the wealthy
priests, were probably large estate owners though some may have been
wealthy merchants.

Literary and archaeological sources have identified many medium to
large estates in Judea and even around Jerusalem itself. Since large land
owners tended in antiquity to live in the city as absentee landlords and
leave the administration of their estates to bailiffs, these land holdings
may well have belonged to the members of the Jerusalem upper class.

The sources certainly testify that wealthy families lived in Jerusalem
before the first Jewish war. The rabbinic sources tell of three wealthy
men who lived in Jerusalem before and during the first Jewish war. They
were allegedly capable of supplying Jerusalem for twenty-one years. One
of them could supply wheat and barley, one oil and wine and the third,
wood. These men were either large estate owners whose estates produced
these crops or merchants. Even allowing for obvious exaggerations, the
three must have possessed great wealth.

Probably the most significant class of wealthy landowners was the
group of aristocratic priests and especially the High Priestly families. The
most obvious example is the family of Josephus. He states that he has
come from a wealthy and influential priestly family of the Hasmonean
line *(Vita* 1f; *Antiquities* 16.187) and that he owned lands near Jerusalem
(probably just west of the city) before the war *(Vita* 422). Since,
according to his autobiography, he is never seen residing on his farm, we
can assume that he had a bailiff to oversee his tenants or slaves and that
he lived for the most part in Jerusalem.

Other priests, especially the High Priests, were also wealthy. Ananias son of Nebedaeus (High Priest in AD 48) was wealthy enough to pay bribes to Albinus the Procurator and the current High Priest, Jesus son of Damascus, so that he could continue a campaign of extortion against both the peasants and the poorer priests (*Antiquities* 20.205-207) to extract forcibly the tithes for himself and his servants.

Wealth was especially prominent in the main High Priestly families, that is the houses of Boethus, Hanan, Phiabi and Kathros (see Smallwood and M. Stern). The Talmud represents these families as powerful and ruthless:

> Woe is me because of the house of Boethus, woe is me because of their staves! Woe is me because of the house of Hanan, woe is me because of their whisperings! Woe is me because of the house of Kathros, woe is me because of their pens! Woe is me because of the house of Ishmail the son of Phabi, woe is me because of their fists. For they are High Priests and their sons are (Temple) treasurers and their sons-in-law are trustees and their servants beat the people with staves.[1]

That these priestly houses were wealthy can hardly be doubted. The wealth of the house of Boethus, for example was legendary (b. Gittin 56a; b. Yebamoth 61a) as was that of the house of Phabi (b. Yoma 35b). Annas and Caiaphas of the house of Hanan apparently owned large mansions (Jn 18:15, 18; Mk 14:53). Some of their riches may have been acquired by extortion and violence but such practices could not produce sustained wealth. They must have owned lands in Judea and perhaps elsewhere which brought them such large fortunes.

Thus the literary evidence indicates that a wealthy, aristocratic class lived in Jerusalem in the first century AD, many of whom, but not all, were from one of the influential priestly families. In this context we must add the testimony of Josephus. He writes of a significant group of wealthy citizens living in the Upper City of Jerusalem at the outbreak of the war who became the targets of the Sicarii and other revolutionary factions (*War* 2.428, 652; 4.140f). Here Herod had built his palace as we noted above and Agrippa II and several chief priests had mansions there also (*War* 1.402; 2.422, 426, 428). In this district is also the traditional location of Caiaphas' house (see Broshi).

The archaeological excavations of the Jewish quarter of Jerusalem confirm the impression we get from the literary sources that a significant wealthy class resided in Jerusalem before the war. The excavation team of N. Avigad discovered in the Upper City large mansions owned obviously by very rich people. The "Herodian house" from the first century BC, the "Palatial Mansion" from the first century AD, and the "Burnt House" from the first century AD are architectural testimony of this class. But just as interesting for our purposes are not only the huge mansions but the rows of slightly more modest houses which still, according to Avigad "belonged to upper class families." These houses are not only distinguished by their size from other houses of the same period, but by their furnishings and decorations. The costly pottery, the wine imported from Italy, the elaborate frescoes and floor mosaics and the many water installations, among other items, point to the wealth of the occupants. That these people were Jewish is evident from the *mikvaoth* (ritual baths) found in many of the houses. This evidence, then, fits hand-in-glove with the literary evidence.

These aristocratic priests were strongly opposed to Jesus. He preached scathing sermons against the rich, especially those who oppressed the poor. He taught the doctrine of the resurrection of the dead, a belief unacceptable to these Sadducean priests. He had already (Jn 2:13-17) challenged their base of power in cleansing the temple and would do so again (Mat 21:10-17). Thus Jesus and his followers appeared to these wealthy members of the high priestly family to be a threat. Jesus predicted that it would be they who killed him (Mk 10:33). Later they would also persecute the early church (Acts 4:1,6; 5:17).

The lower classes consisted of the poorer priests and Levites, the small merchants, the craftsmen, and the unskilled laborers. The lower class priests, divided into twenty-four weekly courses (*Antiquities* 7.3651, lived in villages throughout Judea and Galilee. They served in the temple approximately two weeks a year. But many priests resided in Jerusalem. The priests in Jerusalem at the time of Nehemiah numbered 1,192 (Neh. 11:10-14; but cf. 1 Chron. 9:13). E.P. Sanders surmises reasonably from this figure in Nehemiah's time that by the first century AD there were probably "a few thousand priests and Levites" in Jerusalem.[2]

The poorer priests worked at a trade such as stone cutting, the sale of oil, or in agriculture. Sanders' contention that many priests were scribes, teachers of the law and judges has some support also (Ben Sirach 45:17; *Vita* 9,196-198; *Apion* 2.187).

Priests also received tithes, at least theoretically, but it is difficult to know how much income they actually received from them. Not all peasants paid the tithes (m. Demai; Philo, *On the Special Laws* 1.153-155). Further the more powerful and the wealthier priests on occasion seem to have robbed the poorer ones of their dues. In the time of Agrippa

II the High Priestly families sent their slaves to claim forcibly the tithes while the poorer priests went hungry (*Antiquities* 20.179-181; cf. b. Pesahim 57a). This text from Josephus may hint at on-going class animosity between the wealthier and poorer priests.

Likewise Levites formed a subgroup in the lower class. They were considered beneath the ordinary priests in station. In the main they must have been of rather modest means. M. Stern remarked on the relative lack of references to Levites in the second temple sources. Nehemiah 11:18 gives the number of Levites as 460 in his day, less than half his figure for priests. We may assume that the same proportion existed in the first century AD.

Jeremias conjectured that the Levites' two subgroups, the singers and the door keepers were of unequal rank (b. Arakim 11b; *Antiquities* 20.216-218). The singers were, he maintained considered to be higher in social standing. Each desired in the time of Agrippa II to be given greater honors.[3]

Apparently Levites like priests found employment as scribes or craftsmen. One of the temple singers, Joshua ben Hananiah, for example, was a nailsmith (see Jeremias).

The lower class also included craftsmen and small merchants. One of the main sources of income was the temple which required bakers, weavers, goldsmiths, washers, merchants of ointments and money changers. Further, the temple was still in the process of being built. This labor force employed a large number of carpenters and stone masons. Josephus reported that when the temple was completed in the procuratorship of Albinus (AD 62-64), it put 18,000 workers out of a job (*Antiquities* 20.219). Thus the temple required a large force of craftsmen throughout most of the first century AD.

But in addition there were markets both in the Upper and Lower Cities where wares were sold (*War* 2.305, 315). Jerusalem was famous for jewelry, spinning, weaving, dying, tailoring, shoemaking, perfume and incense but also produced oil, pottery, ossuaries, stoneware, and woodwork. In the Lower City was the Tyropoeon Valley (or "valley of the cheese makers") with a main street running through it lined by shops on both sides of the street. The name suggests that a cheese market stood there but we should expect that other goods were found there as well. Archaeologists have found remains of the street, its large drain, and some shops from the temple all the way south along Tyropoeon street.

In addition there was a market center in the New Town district, north of the first wall. Josephus writes that metal workers, tailors, fullers, wooldealers, and timber merchants had a market in the New Town district (*War* 2.530; 5.147, 331; cf. Lamentations Rabbah I.1).

Also in the lower class were the unskilled day laborers. Laborers could work in the fields or olive groves around Jerusalem ploughing, weeding, harvesting, threshing, picking fruit and doing other seasonal jobs. Most often the laborer worked as a burden bearer who carried wood, reeds, harvested crops, and other kinds of burdens. Some even carried around other people. Many unskilled laborers were watchmen. They were paid to watch over animals, fields of crops, children, the sick, corpses, and the city gates. But laborers also performed functions such as bathhouse attendants, messengers, manure gatherers, and thorn gatherers (m. Baba Metzia 6:1, 7:5-8).

The unskilled worker was apparently paid on average one denarius per day (Mt. 20:2; Tobit 5:14). But many were certainly paid less. Hillel worked as a wood cutter in Jerusalem earning one half denarius a day (b. Yoma 35b). Another poor man of Jerusalem made a living by trapping doves and lived on about one fourth denarius a day (Leviticus Rabbah 1.17).

We should expect that most of the craftsmen and small merchants lived near the Tyropoeon market and thus in the Lower City or in the less populated New Town near those other markets. Archaeologists have discovered the ruins of some houses in the Lower City. M. Ben-Dov describes the area in the Lower City known as the City of David as "slums" and terms it "run-down."

The City of David (the southern part of the Ophel spur) was of course the oldest inhabited area in Jerusalem. Even in the Hellenistic period the evidence is that most residents lived there. Only in the first century BC did people begin moving up the slope toward the Upper City. Thus most of the lower class lived in the older district of the city. As we shall see below, however, Jews from the diaspora and proselytes were also drawn to this area.

At the very bottom of the social and economic scale was the submerged class or the class of outcasts. This class included slaves, beggars, those from unapproved occupations, and the diseased.

According to the Talmud, the occupations which were scorned were prostitutes, dung collectors, donkey drivers, gamblers, sailors, tanners, peddlers, herdsmen, and usurers among others (m. Kiddushin 4:14; m. Sanhedrin 3:4). Jesus was often among such people (Mk 2:15; Lk 15:1).

With regard to the diseased we should think especially of the lepers who seem to have abounded in Palestine. Jesus also healed many of them

(Mk 1:40; 14:3; Lk 17:12). Such people were declared unclean by a priest (Lev 13:11, 25) and had to remain apart from everyone else crying out from a distance "Unclean!" (Lev 13:45f). Lepers lived then a life of social ostracism.

Beggars also appear frequently in first century Palestine. They are lame (Acts 3:2; Jn. 5:3; m. Shabbath 6:8; Lk. 16:20) or blind (Jn. 9:1; Mt. 21:14; Mk. 10:46) and sit along the roadside in the country (Mk. 10:46) or along the streets and alleys in the city (Lk. 14:21). Jeremias suggested that beggars were especially numerous in the temple precincts.

Slaves in Jerusalem were mostly domestics of the wealthy. A Jew could become a slave as punishment for stealing, out of poverty or from indebtedness. The Hebrew slaves would presumably be liberated in the Sabbatical year (Deut 15:12). Gentile slaves or "Canaanites" were slaves for life. Jeremias and Krauss note that slaves were sold on a special platform in Jerusalem.

The royal courts of the Herodian family had many domestic slaves (*War* 1.511, 673; *Antiquities* 17.199). The High Priests also had numerous slaves (Mk. 14:4-7; Jn. 18:18, 26; *Antiquities* 20.181, 206f). Thus the wealthy elites could own scores or even hundreds of slaves which served as household servants, body guards, eunuchs in the harem (*War* 1.511; m. Yebamoth 8:4) and other uses. But other well-to-do residents could also own a few slaves (cf. m. Eduyoth 5:6) such as the physician of Jerusalem (m. Rosh HaShanah 1:7) or Mary the mother of John Mark (Acts 12:13).

In the ancient cities the submerged class, especially the destitute, the beggars, and the terribly ill usually lived on the outskirts of the city (Sjoberg). The farther one was from the center socially and economically, the farther one lived also from the center geographically. Thus the wealthy lived mainly in the Upper City, the lower class in the Lower City and the New Town, and the outcasts lived on the fringes of the city if indeed they had residences at all.

The Cultural Groups Among Jerusalem's Jews

The predominantly Jewish city of Jerusalem was bicultural. Most of the residents spoke and understood only Aramaic; some were bilingual; still others could probably speak only Greek.

Certainly the mother tongue of most Palestinian Jews was Aramaic: "The prominence of Aramaic at every level as the main language of Palestinian Jewry is now solidly backed by evidence. . . ." (SVM II, p. 26). Even in Jerusalem Aramaic was predominate. The inscriptions on stone boxes (ossuaries) which held the bones of the deceased in Jerusalem are mostly in a Jewish script (Aramaic or Hebrew). The native languages tended to remain strong even under the cultural assault of Greek in the eastern part of the empire and Latin in the west.

Yet many, especially the educated and merchants, did learn Greek either out of an interest in Greek literature, a desire to appear sophisticated, or for business reasons. The incursion of the Greek languages and culture into Jewish Palestinian society is quite evident on many fronts. Coins were minted in Palestine with Greek inscriptions; the Hebrew and Aramaic languages adopted numerous Greek loan words; many Palestinian Jews had Greek names; the architecture of the residences and the pottery show Greek influences; the government--as far back as Herod the Great--was Hellenized; there was a gymnasium; and there have been found numerous inscriptions, papyri and ostraca in Greek (see Mussies). N. Avigad writes from his experience excavating the houses of the wealthy: "The pursuit of things Hellenistic was then not uncommon in Jerusalem, particularly among the ...nobility" (p. 120).

But others were Greek culturally because they grew up in Greek centers of the diaspora. Even their tomb and ossuary inscriptions were chiseled in Greek. Hengel reports on an on-going project of collecting all the known epitaphs from Jerusalem. So far, of all the ossuaries with inscriptions (many ossuaries are not inscribed) the Greek inscriptions make up 39% of the total. Most of the rest are in a Semitic language only, but some are bilingual. Hengel concludes that those people inscribed their ossuaries in Greek whose family used Greek as the vernacular. Thus he suggests (conservatively) that the Greek speaking population of Jerusalem was 10% to 20% of the total population. Based on our figure for the total population of Jerusalem (60,000 residents) the Greek speaking Jews numbered 6,000 to 12,000.

There is evidence that many if not most of these Jews grew up in the diaspora. There are ossuary and epitaph inscriptions in Greek of people which indicate they are from North Africa, Alexandria, Capua in Italy, Asia, and Macedonia. Josephus says that Ananel the priest came from Babylonia (*Antiquities* 15.22,34,3951) and Boethus the priest came from Alexandria (*Antiquities* 15.319-22; 17.78,339; 18.3; 19.297f). The New Testament refers to other Jerusalem residents that came from the diaspora:

Simon of Cyrene (Mk. 15:21), Barnabas of Cyprus (Acts 4:36), and Nicolas a proselyte from Antioch (Acts 6:5).

There were also proselytes in Jerusalem, former non-Jews who had grown up in Greek culture. One of the Seven in Acts was as noted above Nicolas the proselyte from Antioch (Acts 6:5). The ossuaries tell of others: "Judas, son of Laganio, the proselyte" (in Greek).[4] In addition, the royal family of Adiabene, which had converted to Judaism, had palaces and tombs in Jerusalem. Queen Helena, her son Menobazus, and Grapte, another relative, had residences (*War* 4.567; 5.55, 119, 252f; 6.355; *Antiquities* 20. 17-37, 75-80). These palaces were located in the lower city not far from the Siloam pool. B. Mazar believes that a large building excavated in this area was one of these palaces. He suggests that this area was the popular place of residence for the highly placed Jewish proselytes from abroad

Therefore, we conclude that a considerable number of diaspora Jews had immigrated to Jerusalem by the first century AD. As Hengel maintains, we have to assume that these Jews living in Jerusalem for the most part knew only Greek and therefore worshiped in their own synagogues and socialized only with other people who could speak their language.

In addition to the residents of Jerusalem that spoke Greek, there were thousands from the diaspora that came to the feasts. Estimates vary as to the number of pilgrims that came to Passover and the other feasts. J. Jeremias concluded that 125,000 pilgrims arrived on average at Passover. E.P. Sanders arrived at the figure of 300,000 to 500,000. Of these tens of thousands were from the diaspora and the rest from Palestine. If we assume that 30,000 of the pilgrims were from the Greek speaking diaspora, then we have at various times of the year an even larger number of Greek speaking Jews in Jerusalem.

These pilgrims had to stay somewhere and it appears they stayed in community centers built especially for them. Archaeologists have discovered several buildings south of the temple mount with a large number of rooms, ritual baths and many cisterns. These could have been used to house pilgrims. In addition, a most significant inscription, the Theodotus Greek inscription, was found in the City of David. Theodotus, the "ruler of the synagogue", donated a building for studying Torah and included guest rooms to house pilgrims and ritual baths to prepare them to enter the temple.[5] Thus pilgrims were housed in the synagogue.

Thus the Lower City, especially the City of David and the Ophel, was the locus for Greek speaking Jews. Jewish pilgrims, who speak Greek, undoubtedly staying in this locality, will approach Philip, Jesus' disciple, and request to speak with Jesus (Jn 12:20-21). Thus even the Greek segment of Jerusalem knew about Jesus. It also shows that Jesus and many of his disciples could speak at least some Greek.

Where did Jesus teach and preach when he made his trips to Jerusalem? Where did he and his disciples stay? On the one hand he has a friend in the Upper City who lets him use the Upper Room. He is known among the Greek speaking Jews in the City of David. We know that he taught in the temple. He healed invalids near the pool of Bethesda and the pool of Siloam. He has friends also in Bethany, a village near Jerusalem, as we will see next. It appears then that Jesus' acquaintances in Jerusalem could be quite as diverse as those in Galilee. He ministered to all classes of people.

Notes

1. Translation in Epstein, *The Babylonian Talmud* (b. Pesahim 57a).

2. Jeremias (p. 200) estimated the total number of priests in Palestine was 7200 and the total number of Levites was 9600. Sanders (p. 78) writes that 20,000 total for both groups is probably correct (see *Apion* 2.108).

3. But see L. Feldman, *Josephus* (LCL) Vol. X. p. 117 who maintains the door keepers were the upper ranking Levites and the singers were of lower rank.

4. The inscription is found in J.B. Frey, *Corpus Inscriptionum Judaicarum* Vol. II, number 1385.

5. Ibid., Vol. II, number 1404.

Chapter 18

The Triumphal Entry and Temple Cleansing

Bibliography: C.K. Barrett, "The House of Prayer and the Den of Thieves" in E.E. Ellis and E. Graesser, eds., *Jesus und Paulus*; R. Brown, *The Gospel According to John*; M. Connick, *Jesus, the Man, the Mission, and the Message*; V. Eppstein, "The Historicity of the Cleansing of the Temple" *Zeitschrift fuer die Neutestamentliche Wissenschaft* 55 (1964) 42-58; C.A. Evans, "Jesus' Action in the Temple: Cleansing or Portent of Destruction?" *Catholic Biblical Quarterly* 51 (1989) 237-70; J. Finegan, *Archaeology of the New Testament*; J. Fitzmyer, *The Gospel According to Luke*; J. Fleming, "The Undiscovered Gate Beneath Jerusalem's Golden Gate" *BAR* 9/1 (1983) 24-37; R.C. Foster, *Studies in the Life of Christ*; M. Goguel, *The Life of Jesus*; M.D. Hooker, "Traditions about the Temple in the Sayings of Jesus" *Bulletin of the John Rylands University Library of Manchester* 70 (1988) 7-19; W.L. Lane, *The Gospel According to Mark*; I.H. Marshall, *Commentary on Luke*; O. Michel, "*onos, onarion*" *TDNT*; E.P. Sanders, *Jesus and Judaism*; E. Schweizer, *The Good News According to Mark*; idem., *The Good News According to Matthew*; V. Taylor, *The Gospel According to Mark*.

The Triumphal Entry (Aland 269-270)

Jesus will now enter Jerusalem one last time. He has been here on several occasions before: as a youth to attend the Passover, perhaps before his ministry as a carpenter, certainly at least four earlier times to preach and teach.

Jesus' journey from Galilee to Jerusalem has caused a great deal of excitement. Messianic fervor is increasing, not only because Jesus is approaching the holy city but because it is the time of Passover which celebrates God's deliverance of his people under Moses. We might expect then that Messianic expectations would be higher during the feast.

Jesus prepared for his entry by securing a suitable animal to ride. He sent some of his disciples ahead to secure a donkey and her foal. If the owner asked about their taking the donkey they were simply supposed to say, "The Lord needs them". Was all of this prearranged (as Marshall affirms) or is Jesus showing his foreknowledge here (see Fitzmyer). Probably the latter.

Why does Jesus ride a donkey?[1] We must first point out what Jesus did not ride. He did not ride in a war chariot. Rather he rode the common beast of burden, the animal used by peasants to carry their wares and themselves. In the prophecy of Zechariah (9:9), riding the donkey is a sign of humility and poverty: "Behold your king is coming to you, poor and riding a donkey." We must allow for the fact that Jesus deliberately rode on the donkey in fulfillment of Zechariah 9:9 to show that he was the Messiah. This prophecy is quoted both by Matthew (21:24) and John (12:15). Since few scholars would claim any literary relationship between these two Gospels, we must ask where the two of them would have gotten the idea that Jesus fulfilled Zechariah 9:9 with his triumphal entry into Jerusalem? The Holy Spirit of course may have given them both the same insight. But we should probably reckon with the idea that Jesus made this connection himself and informed his disciples that he was purposely performing a messianic action.

The rabbis often expounded on this text in Zechariah to describe the coming of the Messiah:

> Rabbi Jehoshua b. Levi (AD 250) has contrasted Daniel 7:13: "Lo, with the clouds of heaven came one like a son of man," with Zechariah 9:9: "Poor and riding on an ass." If they (Israel) have merits, (the Messiah) comes with the clouds of heaven; if they have no merits, (he comes) poor and riding on an ass. (b. Sanhedrin 98a; trans. by O. Michel).[2]

As Fitzmyer points out, the rabbinic reflections on Zechariah 9:9 are much later than Jesus' time. Yet they may be based on older tradition. At any rate whether other Jews were making the connection between the passage in Zechariah and the coming Messiah or not, Jesus did. He purposely chose a donkey upon which to enter the city.

Jesus approached the city by passing through the villages of Bethphage ("the house of figs") and Bethany, a village referred to earlier as the home of Lazarus (=Simon the leper) and his sisters, Mary and Martha. These villages lay on the Mt. of Olives (see Finegan). The Mt. of Olives was already associated with the coming of the Messiah because of Zechariah's prophecy (14:4):

> And Yahweh will go out and will do battle against those nations as he fights in the day of battle. And his feet will stand on that day upon the Mt. of Olives which is before Jerusalem on the east. And the Mt. of Olives will split into two with a fault to the east and to the west, a great valley. And half of the mountain will be moved to the north and half to the south.

The Jewish false prophet, the so-called Egyptian, gathered his followers on the Mt. of Olives where he promised to make the walls of Jerusalem collapse (*Antiquities* 20. 169). Thus, it was probably generally believed in Judaism that the Messiah would declare himself on this mountain. It is interesting that the ancient Jewish cemetery on the Mt. of Olives, one of the oldest in continuous use (see Fleming), is still a highly desirable spot to be buried. Modern Jews and Christians still believe in the connection between this mount and the coming Messiah.

As Jesus descended from the Mt. of Olives he headed toward the Golden Gate, the eastern gate of the Temple. This gate also may have had Messianic connections. That is, the Jews may have expected, from the prophecy in Zechariah and one related to it in Joel 3:2, that the Messiah would pass through this gate. There are later references to the gate in this way (see J. Fleming).

One can see from inside the walls of Jerusalem and especially within the Temple precincts the top of the Mt. of Olives. Thus people could see Jesus descending into the city. When they began to realize that it was Jesus heading for the Golden Gate, many of the pilgrims rushed out of the city to meet him and to lay before him both their cloaks and their garments. All of this is a way of acclaiming someone as king or conqueror. An interesting account is given by Josephus of Titus' entry into Antioch after his victory in the Jewish war:

When the citizens of Antioch learned that Titus was near, they were far
too delighted to stay within their walls, and rushed out to meet him,
proceeding over thirty furlongs (4 miles), not only men but crowds of
women and children as well, pouring out of the city. And when they
saw him approaching, they lined both sides of the road and greeted him
with extended arms and, calling down every kind of blessing on him.
they escorted him in his train. (*War* 7.100-102; Trans. in G. Cornfeld,
Josephus)

Thus the people of Jerusalem were hailing Jesus as a king, as the
Messiah. Laying down garments in front of a king is referred to in 2
Kings 9:13. To lay down palm branches and other leafy branches is also
highly meaningful. A cuneiform tablet records that when Cyrus entered
Babylon (586 BC) the crowd threw down green twigs in front of him (text
in J.B. Pritchard, *Ancient Near Eastern Texts*). When the Maccabees
regained the temple and cleansed and rededicated it the people carried
palm branches, ivy wreathes, and other ornate branches (1 Macc 13:51;
2 Macc 10:7). When Bar Kosiba minted his coins, he stamped the image
of a palm branch on one side. Thus the palm branch--and perhaps tree
branches in general--represented liberation and deliverance.

As Jesus proceeded toward the city, the crowd shouted parts of Psalm
118:25-26: "We beseech you, Lord, save us now. We beseech you, Lord,
deliver us now. Blessed is he who comes in the name of the Lord." This
psalm was recited by pilgrims coming up to the feasts and is still a part of
the Passover recitation done by Jews (see Birnbaum, *Daily Prayer Book*).
It is interesting, however, that people often used language similar to this
in asking for help from a monarch (2 Sam 14:4; 2 Kings 6:26). The
words, "Save us!', surely must have had a political significance to many
of these religious pilgrims as they sang them on their way to the Passover.
They must have thought of Moses who delivered their ancestors from
Egyptian bondage so long ago. Each Passover must have brought a
yearning for God to raise up another deliverer like Moses to give his
people freedom.

But intermingled with these scripture quotations were shouts like:
"Blessed is the coming kingdom of our father David!" (Mk 11:10); and:
"Blessed is . . . the king of Israel!" (Jn 12:13). Thus the crowd was hailing
Jesus as the Messiah, as another King David.

Jesus, of course, was the Davidic king, the Messiah, but he had no
intention of fulfilling the expectations of the crowd: to lead a revolution
and establish again the earthly kingdom of David. Yet it is important to

point out that he accepted this demonstration and even encouraged it with his entry. He was clearly declaring his Messiahship, though he was defining Messiahship by riding on a donkey and entering in a lowly fashion (Mt 21:5; cf. 11:29-30).

Luke records that some of the Pharisees demanded that Jesus silence the crowd and reject their acclamation. Jesus replied: "If these people will be silent, the rocks will cry out" (Lk 19:40). This was the time to declare his Messiahship. Nothing could stop it. As one frustrated Pharisee exclaimed: "Just look! The whole world has gone after him" (Jn 12:19).

The triumphal entry, then, was an outburst of enthusiasm and excitement partly generated by the spirit of the feast of Passover and partly by Jesus' own person since he was becoming well-known by Palestinian Jews, especially after his raising of Lazarus (Jn 12:17-18).

Jesus paused upon entering the city to lament its coming destruction (Aland 270). Lament is a common oriental practice seen often in the Old Testament (e.g. the book of Lamentations). Jerusalem could have learned the way of peace but the city will reject Jesus' message and will therefore be destroyed as it was in the days of Jeremiah.

The Temple Cleansing (Aland 271-275)

Jesus descended the Mt. of Olives, passed through the Golden Gate, and entered the temple. Here Matthew and Luke describe events a bit differently than Mark and John. Matthew and Luke seem to say that the cleansing of the temple took place on the same day as the entry. Mark states that Jesus entered the temple, looked around, and returned the next day for the cleansing. John mentions no cleansing at all at this time but has an account of a temple cleansing in 2:13-17, that is during the first Passover of his ministry.

Foster is correct; Mark has the proper order while Matthew and Luke are compressing events for the sake of the narration. Jesus then entered the Temple to look around on the day of his entry but cleansed the Temple on the following day.

What about John's account? Jesus undoubtedly did the same thing at his first Passover as at his last. It is possible that the Gospel of John, as many commentators affirm, simply moved this event from the final week of Jesus' life to an earlier time. The author would have done this for theological reasons. Yet no really good theological motive has been offered for such a literary liberty. Why would moving this event to the early part of Jesus' ministry have served the Gospel of John theologically? Actually very little interpretation of this is found in John. Thus we conclude that Jesus cleansed the Temple twice. The first time he took the authorities by surprise. They hardly knew what to make of this prophet from Galilee that ousted the money changers. But the last time they were more familiar with him. His growing popularity, especially after the demonstration the day before during his entry into the city, made it clear that he was making Messianic claims to authority, even over the Temple service. Thus they moved to have him executed.

Jesus entered the Temple--actually the court of the Gentiles--and cast out or drove out those who sold sacrificial animals such as pigeons and those who exchanged money. Further, he prohibited people from carrying anything through the temple area (also prohibited in the Talmud, m.Beracoth 9:5; b.Beracoth 54a; and alluded to by Josephus ,*Apion* 2.106). He quoted Isaiah 56:7 and Jeremiah 7:11: "My house will be called a house of prayer for all the nations or Gentiles) but you have made it the lair of robbers."

The Temple tax could only be paid in Tyrian coins; thus foreigners coming to the city would need to exchange their currency (Ex 30:11-16; m. Bekhoroth 8:9; m. Shekalim 1:3). Likewise, people traveling long distances would not bring animals with them; thus they would need to buy one. Why then did Jesus drive these people out and claim that the Temple had become a den of robbers?

There are at least five suggestions as to what Jesus was doing in his "cleansing" of the Temple:

1) Jesus' action was entirely prophetic. He wished to show that the Temple would someday be destroyed and disappear (Connick, Sanders). In the manner of many of the Old Testament prophecies by symbolic action (cf. Ezekiel 4:1-3 and see below on the cursing of the fig tree) Jesus acted out what would take place regarding the temple in AD 70.

2) Jesus objects to making the court of the Gentiles a place of business and thus from prohibiting Gentiles from praying there (Lane, Eppstein). Eppstein argued that only under Caiaphas' high priesthood did they begin to sell sacrificial objects in the court of the Gentiles.

3) Jesus was showing his condemnation of the corrupt high priesthood (Evans). There is evidence that the High Priests were greedy, resorted to extortion and bribery, and were worldly and unholy (Testament of Moses 5:3-6:1; t. Menahin 13:21; *Antiquities* 20. 181, 206-207; b. Yebamoth

6 1a; *Antiquities* 20. 213). Thus Jesus was giving his judgment on the high priestly families.

4) Jesus was condemning the "robbers", that is, the Zealots who were at that time using part of the Temple area for their plans of violence (Barrett). Josephus often calls robbers (*lestai*) those who many consider to have been Zealots or freedom fighters.

5) Jesus was making a Messianic statement. There was expectation that the Messiah would manifest himself in the Temple, would purge the Temple and city of unholiness, and even set up a new and glorious Temple (Zech 14:20-21; Ezekiel 40-48; Malachi 3:1; 1 Enoch 90:28-29; Psalms of Solomon 17:26-18:7). The passage in the pseudepigraphical book, 1 Enoch[3], is especially significant:

> Then I stood still, looking at that ancient house (i.e., the Temple) being transformed: All the pillars and all the columns were pulled out; and the ornaments of that house were packed and taken out together with them and abandoned in a certain place in the South of the land. I went on seeing until the Lord of the sheep brought about a new house, greater and loftier than the first one, and set it up in the first location which had been covered up--all its pillars were new, the columns new; and the ornaments new as well as greater than those of the first, (that is) the old (house) which was gone. All the sheep were within it. (Trans. E. Isaacs, OTP)

We would judge suggestions 1, 2, and 4 improbable. Jesus indicates nothing about the Temple's destruction in this action. Why would he quote the texts from Isaiah and Jeremiah if this were his purpose? Further, Eppstein's contention that Caiaphas had only recently introduced the market in the court of the Gentiles is based on speculation. Barrett's assertion that the "robbers" were actually Zealots assumes that there were Zealots in AD 30--a position that many now reject--and assumes that Jesus used the same term for Zealots as Josephus.

We view this action as a messianic act. He is announcing as the Messiah his judgment on the corrupt high priesthood. Thus we prefer a combination of 3 and 5. The Old Testament clearly predicted such a function for the Messiah and the intertestamental literature shows that this messianic expectation remained strong.

If we accept Mark's narration of the sequence of events as the actual chronological one, then Jesus and his disciples after looking around in the Temple on the day of the triumphal entry returned to Bethany for the night. On the next day as he was on his way to cleanse the Temple he was hungry and spotted a fig tree. But when he approached to pick some figs for breakfast, he found that the tree was barren. Mark adds that it was not even the season for figs (11:13). Jesus therefore commanded: "Let no one ever again eat your fruit!" Matthew's Gospel says that the tree withered up immediately (21:19) but Mark says that Jesus and his disciples continued on to the Temple and only as they were proceeding back to Bethany that evening, after cleansing the Temple, did they notice that the tree had withered. Again Matthew is compressing the narrative.[4] Mark is probably giving us the step by step account here.

Whatever the exact sequence of events we are left wondering why Jesus responded so angrily to the tree when it was not even the season for figs. Clearly this is a prophetic symbolic action. Prophets in the Old Testament were wont to act out coming events (1 Kings 11:30-39; Jerk 27-28; Isaiah 20:1-6; Hosea 1-3; Ezek 5:1-4).[5] This was then an intentional action on Jesus' part to indicate his displeasure with unfruitful Israel (cf. Jer 8:13; Joel 1:7).

The miracle impressed Jesus' disciples and so as they continue walking Jesus uses the occasion, as he often did, to teach them about prayer. We must pray believing in the power of God. Jesus' words: "Whatever you ask in prayer you will receive" must be understood as a prayer not uttered for selfish ends. We must truly believe in the power of prayer but never use prayer as a magical means to satisfy our worldly desires. Further, prayer is ineffective if we have anger and bitterness in our hearts. We must forgive others--even if they do not ask for our forgiveness--so that our prayer life may be sincere and so that God may forgive us.

These two events, the triumphal entry and the cleansing of the temple, sealed Jesus' fate of death. The first event would have caused great concern on the part of the Roman procurator, Pontius Pilate. Here was someone hailed as a new king, a possible revolutionary leader--at least in the procurator's eyes. The second event pitted Jesus against the power base of the chief priests, who had long sought to remove Jesus from his ministry (Jn 5:18). The chief priests comprised one of the most influential and one of wealthiest groups within the aristocracy. Clearly the two-- Pilate and the high priestly family--conspired together to have Jesus killed.

Notes

1. Since Matthew writes (21:7), "Jesus sat on them", some commentators

maintain that Matthew pictures Jesus riding both the donkey and the colt at the same time, in the manner of a circus rider. But as R.C. Foster points out, the "them" Jesus sat on probably refers to the garments that his disciples placed on the donkey.

2. See also Pisikta Rabbati 34, b. Beracoth 56b, Canticles Rabbah 1 and S-B.

3. 1 Enoch is a composite of many sections which date from the second century BC to the first century AD. This section is according to E. Isaacs, from the second century BC.

4. The chronology of events surrounding the cleansing of the Temple as narrated by Matthew, Mark and Luke give problems for the advocates of the two source hypothesis. Why would Matthew and Luke have so freely ignored Mark's sequence of events?

We must also note, however regarding the cursing of the fig tree that it is quite possible that Matthew is giving us the literal version of the event. Perhaps Mark separated the cursing of the tree from the recognition that the tree had withered in order to frame the cleansing of the Temple with it. In other words, Israel as represented by its Temple, is barren and will be destroyed.

5. See H.E. Freeman, *An Introduction to the Old Testament Prophets.*

Chapter 19

The Disputes in the Temple
(Aland 276-286)

Bibliography: R.H. Charles, *The Apocrypha and Pseudepigrapha of the Old Testament*, II; J.H. Charlesworth, *Jesus within Judaism;* D.A. Fiensy, *Social History of Palestine in the Herodian Period*; L. Finkelstein, *The Pharisees*; J. Fitzmyer, *The Gospel According to Luke;* R. Gundry, *Matthew;* M. Hengel, "Das Gleichnis von den Weingaertnern Mc 12:1-12 im Licht der Zenonpapyri und der rabbinischen Gleichnisse" *Zeitschrift fuer die neutestamentliche Wissenschaft* 59 (1968) 1-39; idem., *The Zealots*; D. Hill, *The Gospel of Matthew;* R. Horsley, *Jesus and the Spiral of Violence;* J. Jeremias, *Jerusalem in the Time of Jesus*; idem., *The Parables of Jesus*; W. Lane, *The Gospel According to Mark*; I.H. Marshall, *Commentary on Luke;* E. Rivkin, *A Hidden Revolution*; R.L. Rohrbaugh, "The Pre-Industrial City in Luke-Acts: Urban Social Relations" in J.H. Nehrey, ed. *The Social World of Luke-Acts*; L. Schiffman, "New Light on the Pharisees" *Bible Review* (June 1992) 30-33, 54; E. Schweizer, *The Good News According to Mark;* idem., *The Good News According to Matthew;* W. Stenger, *Gebt dem Kaiser was des Kaisers ist*; V. Taylor, *The Gospel According to Mark.*

Jesus entered the temple the next day and was immediately challenged by the chief priests, the scribes and the elders. These were the religious, scholarly and socio-political leaders respectively. "By what right or authority do you do these things (i.e. cleanse the temple)?" (Mt 21:23). The scribes or sages that are represented in the Talmud were very emphatic about the importance of honoring only the authority of a seasoned scholar. One Talmudic passage (b. Sota 22a; cf. also b. Avodah Zara 19a) intones that only a scholar who is at least 40 years old should be listened to. Those who have not been properly schooled and yet insist upon teaching are like those that slay a mighty throng say the rabbinic sages.

The leaders demand that Jesus give his pedigree to prove that he has the right to teach and especially to make pronouncements on the validity of the temple. The content of Jesus' response is typical of a prophet. He says in effect that his authority comes directly from God not from any school or human agency.

But the way Jesus answers is typical of the rabbis. He answers their question with another question. Such an answer was considered doubtless a good teaching method and a good method of debate (see e.g. Pesiqta 40a; b. Taanith 7a; b. Sanhedrin 65b; and S-B). Jesus' question, however, catches the chief priests in a dilemma. First they must answer by what authority John the Baptist had baptized. The leaders realize that if they say that John did so by only human authority, the crowd will become angry because John, who is now a martyr, was very popular and respected by the masses as a prophet. If they concede that John spoke from God, however, they will condemn themselves because they did not submit to his baptism. Thus Jesus' first encounter with these leaders ends in their inability to press him further to check his credentials.

Jesus then told a parable that described the Jewish authorities. A man had two sons (Mt 21:28) and told both to work in the vineyard. One flatly refused but later decided he would work; the second said he would work but changed his mind and did not. The first son represents the Jewish authorities who initially said "Yes" to God but did not do what God asked (i.e. accept Jesus as the Messiah). The publicans and prostitutes, however, had reversed the situation. They are represented by the second son.

The next parable, the Parable of the Wicked Husbandmen, is found in all three synoptic Gospels (see Mt 21:33-46 and par.) and in the Gospel of Thomas 65.[1] The parable has the highest claim to historicity both because of its multiple attestation and because of its accurate representation of the historical situation. The parable is about a large estate owner that planted a vineyard. Jesus probably fashioned this parable after Isaiah 5. All the details are here which one would expect in a vineyard: a wine press, a tower[2], a fence made of thorny hedges, and tenant farmers. Even the animosity displayed by the tenants toward the land owner is an accurate detail as Hengel has shown. There were often tensions when it came time for the tenants to pay their rent since the rents were usually quite high.

The large estate owner sent his servants to collect the rent from the vineyard but the tenants beat them and even killed some of them. The patient land owner finally decided to send them his son hoping they would have respect for the heir and thus would pay what they owed. They did not respect the son, however, but killed him hoping that they could now claim the land as their own. The land owner is now full of grief over his murdered son and coming to his vineyard, executes the criminals.

The parable is of course ful of allegorical elements. The servants that came to collect the rent are the prophets of old. They were mistreated just as are these servants in the story. The son who is finally sent represents Jesus himself. Notice that Jesus here predicts his death to the Jewish leaders but not that he will be crucified. Jesus only told his closest disciples ahead of time that he would suffer crucifixion (see Mt 20:19). He knew from biblical and more recent history that messengers of God were often persecuted. The Old Testament prophets Isaiah, Jeremiah, and Ezekiel were mistreated (according to the pseudepigraphical Lives of the Prophets, *OTP* Vol. II, they were sawed in two, stoned, and murdered respectively). An outstanding Jewish hasid named Honi the Circle Drawer (see chapter 11) had been stoned (m. Taanith 3:8; b. Taanith 23a; *Antiquities* 14.22; see Charlesworth). Most recently John the Baptist had been beheaded (see chapter 7). Thus Jesus would have naturally expected to meet martyrdom. His knowledge that he would be crucified, however, was supernatural.

This parable is then a summary of salvation history. God has sent his prophets repeatedly to his people and they have mistreated them and rejected their message. Now in the latter days he has sent them his son (cf. Hebrews 1:1-4) and they will also mistreat him and reject his message.

The chief priests, scribes and Pharisees who were present understood the parable. Some people in the crowd (Mt 21:41) even pronounced the fate of the wicked tenants. Therefore, they became even more angry and bitter toward Jesus and even more determined to end his life. They would have had the temple guards arrest him on the spot but they were afraid of a riot.

The next parable, the Parable of the Great Supper, appears in both Matthew and Luke in the New Testament as well as in the Gospel of Thomas 64. These three texts indicate that they are different versions of the same basic story. The parable in the Gospel of Thomas is as follows:

A person was receiving guests. When he had prepared the dinner, he sent   his slave to invite the guests. The slave went to the first and said to that one, "My master invites you." That one said, "Some merchants owe me money; they are coming to me tonight. I have to go and give them instructions. Please excuse me from dinner." The slave went to another and said to that   one, "My master has invited you." That one said to the slave, "I shall have no time." The slave went to another and said to that one, "My master invites you." That one said to the slave, "My friend is to be married, and I am to arrange the banquet. I shall not be able to come. Please excuse me from dinner." The slave went to another and said to that one, "My master invites you." That one said to the slave, "I have bought an estate, and I am going to collect the rent. I shall not be able to come. Please excuse me." The slave returned and said to his master, "Those whom you invited to dinner have asked to be excused." The master said to his slave, "Go out on the streets and bring back whomever you find to have dinner."[3]

The parable in Thomas is closest to that in Luke but is not exactly like it. What we have here--if indeed the Gospel of Thomas' parable is from an independent tradition and not a later reworking of Luke--is a record of how Jesus could adapt the same general story for use in several situations. He surely told parables more than once to more than one kind of audience and with more than one point to make. These three versions of the same basic narrative indicate his mastery in story telling.

The parable in Matthew concerns a wedding banquet that a king gave for his son. To give a banquet for ones son was evidently a sign of devotion in the orient for the rabbinic literature speaks often of a father's doing so (b. Beracoth 31a; Genesis Rabbah 3; Deuteronomy Rabbah 9; b. Gittin 68b and S-B). This king is showing his love for his son by sponsoring a feast and inviting all of the important people. But those invited either made light of the invitation and refused to accept or actually became violent and beat or killed those servants sent to invite. To refuse an invitation to a meal in this culture was not rare. Often people would not attend until they knew exactly who else would be there and by whom they would be seated (b. Sanhedrin 23a). In other examples of refusing invitations it is difficult to tell why those invited did not accept (t. Baba Bathra 6:14; m. Nedarim 8:7). For some reason these people seem often to have refused dinner invitations. What is unusual in this parable, however, is the violent reaction. They were being invited to something enjoyable, yet they responded angrily. The king became angry and sent his army to destroy their city. Jesus had been very familiar with one such destroyed city. Sepphoris, which lay only three or four miles from his native village of Nazareth, was completely destroyed in 4 BC and its inhabitants were sold into slavery. (*Antiquities* 17.289; *War* 2.68). Surely stories of such a horrible ordeal were commonplace in Jesus' village. He now uses this event to color his parable. It is possible, also, that he gives here a veiled prediction of the destruction of Jerusalem.

Once again the servants go out to make invitations to the banquet for his son, but this time they invite not the notables of the community but those in the streets. Now the wedding hall is full. Those who refused the invitation have been cast off and those who accepted, even though they are not people that society would ordinarily call desirable, are a part of this celebration.

Thus the parable up to this point is about God's inviting all people to his feast (=the Kingdom of God). He begins with the leaders of his people but they decline the invitation and even respond violently in some cases. Here the parable is parallel to the previous one, the Parable of the Wicked Tenants. Therefore, God punishes these unrepentant people and invites the outcasts of society. They accept and enter his kingdom.

Now the parable takes a new turn. This is actually, as J. Jeremias pointed out, a double edged parable. It makes two points. At the wedding feast the king notices that someone has come without the proper wedding garment. He commands that this person be cast out of the banquet room "into the outer darkness and there will be weeping and gnashing of teeth." (Mt 22:13). This probably is a reference to Hell. Jesus concludes by saying, "Many are called, but few are elected". That is, many (actually everyone) are invited into the kingdom but not everyone accepts the conditions for entrance and for remaining in the kingdom.

That guests were supposed to be cleaned up and in bright and shining clothes is clear enough. Johannan ben Zakkai (c. AD 80) told a parable with some similarities to this second part of Jesus' parable.[4] His point was that a person should repent now and not put it off because one never knows when his life will end. Jesus' point is that one cannot remain in the kingdom of God without meeting moral conditions. There must be a change in lifestyle. Thus the wedding garment represents the robe of righteousness.

The Lucan parable (14:15-24) is different from Matthew's in several ways: First of all the context is different. It is not uttered in the temple during the final week of Jesus' life but in the long travel narrative (see chapter 14). Second, this is not a double edged parable but it makes only a single point. Third, the banquet is not a wedding banquet but simply a feast. In Luke's parable after the guests are invited three of them make excuses. The householder then orders his servants to invite the poor and crippled people in the streets and back alleys of the city. This group accepts the invitation. Finally a third invitation is given to yet another group of people: those along the roads going out of town. They too accept the invitation. As Rohrbaugh has shown this parable accurately reflects the situation of the urban poor.

The point of the parable in Luke is that the invitation given to the leaders of Israel to enter the Kingdom of God is being declined. Therefore, the invitation will be given--indeed is being given--to the outcasts such as tax collectors and harlots. Further, the invitation will even be given to Gentiles (those on the roads outside the city).

At some point during this week of teaching and debate in the Temple some Pharisees and Herodians (that is members of the Herod family and their wealthy associates) came to Jesus to try to entrap him with a question (Mt 22:15-22 and par.). They began by flattering him and declaring their admiration for him as one who speaks his mind without regard for popularity or for gaining favor with wealthy and powerful men. After thus attempting to weaken Jesus' defenses, they asked the question: "Is it right to pay taxes to Caesar or not?"

The paying of taxes to Caesar began on a regular basis in AD 6 when Archelaus, the son of Herod the Great, was deposed from his ethnarchy (rule over Judea, Samaria, and Idumea) and sent into exile. Henceforth Rome ruled these territories directly by sending a procurator. Rome always took a census upon acquiring new territories to size up the amount of taxes it could count on. During the census of AD 6 one Judas of Galilee (or Gamala) began a rebellion. Josephus describes him as follows:

> . . .A Galilean, named Judas, incited his countrymen to revolt, upbraiding them as cowards for consenting to pay tribute to Romans and tolerating mortal masters, after having God for their lord. (*War* 2.118; trans. by Thackeray, LCL)

But Judas, a Gaulanite, from the city of Gamala, taking Saddok, a Pharisee, as his partner, pressed for a rebellion. These two maintained that the census was nothing but outright slavery and they challenged their nation to counter with an assertion of freedom. Should they succeed, it would offer economic gain. If on the other hand they were frustrated in their effort, they would make for themselves honor and fame for pursuing their noble cause. The Almighty would also (they affirmed) do nothing else but assist them in the successful prosecution of their plan. . . (*Antiquities* 18.4-5; Trans. by the author).

Thus Judas of Galilee believed to pay taxes to Caesar was the same as disobeying, even denying, God. His strict either/or interpretation of taxes (either pay them to God or to Caesar) led to a full rebellion which was put down by the procurator Coponius (see chapter 1). It is this volatile issue which is still on the minds of people some 24 years later. Should a devoted follower of God--to whom all the land of Israel belongs--pay taxes to a human ruler whom many claim as a god? The taxes were of two kinds (see Stenger and Fiensy): taxes on the produce of the land and the poll tax or head tax. The former tax was a percentage (probably around 12%) and the latter was a flat amount (probably one denarius) paid for every adult.

Jesus gives a clever response. He asks for a coin (probably a one denarius coin) and asks whose picture is on it. The image of the emperor was, of course, imprinted on the coins. Thus he replied, "Hand over to Caesar that which belongs to Caesar and to God that which belongs to God." This response then did not directly answer their question. If he had simply said to pay the taxes to Caesar, he would have incurred the wrath of those still loyal to Judas of Galilee (who had been martyred in the rebellion) and who as ardent Yahwists (followers of God) saw any payment of tribute to Caesar as apostasy. If he had said not to pay the taxes, the Romans could have arrested him as a revolutionary. It was then a brilliant response to a clever trap.

But what did Jesus mean? Most commentators have concluded that he counseled for paying the due tribute to the government, even the cruel and godless Roman government. But some lately, such as Horsley, read the enigmatic answer of Jesus as just the opposite. "Give over to Caesar what belongs to Caesar. . ." means that one should give nothing to Caesar since nothing belongs to him. But Horsley's interpretation seems to ignore the fact that Jesus asked for a coin and demanded to know whose picture was on it. That action would seem to indicate that he was advising them to pay the tax.

The Sadducees next approach Jesus to debate the issue of the general resurrection of the dead at the end of the age (Mt 22:23-33 and par.). Josephus writes that the Sadducees did not believe in any survival of the soul after death:

> As for the persistence of the soul after death, penalties in the under world, and rewards, (the Sadducees) will have none of them. (*War* 2.165; trans.by Thackeray in LCL).[5]

That the issue of the resurrection was a major point of dissension between Pharisees and Sadducees (there were other differences of course; see Rivkin and SVM) can be seen in the Mishnah (Sanhedrin 10:1) where those who deny the resurrection will not be saved in the age to come:

> These are they that have no share in the world to come: he that says that there is no resurrection of the dead prescribed in the Law, and [he that says] that the Law is not from Heaven, and an Epicurean. (Trans. in Danby).

The Sadducees have what they think is a good argument against the possibility of the resurrection. According to the Law (Deut 25:5-10) if a man died without a child, his brother would take his wife to have a child for him in his name. Now the Sadducees concoct a story[6] in which a woman has had seven husbands in such a manner, all of which have died. Finally, she died. Now, ask the Sadducees, in the resurrection whose wife is she?

Jesus responds in a way typical of rabbinic argumentation. He used midrash or exposition of scripture to attack their claims. In the first place, in the resurrection, says Jesus, we are like the angels and do not marry. It was evidently the belief of the common folk that in the age to come the righteous would live in abundance with many wives and beget children.[7] Given that belief, the Sadducees would have had Jesus in a theological corner. But Jesus espoused the view of the resurrection found in a few of the apocalyptic texts: We will be like the angels (cf. 1 Enoch 104:2-6; 2 Enoch 22:8; 2 Baruch 49-51). Thus one cannot speak of whose wife the woman will be. We will not have that kind of relationship after the resurrection.

But more importantly, Jesus argues from the Torah, perhaps the only part of the Old Testament accepted by the Sadducees as authoritative. Since God said to Moses at the burning bush (Exodus 3:6), "I **am** the God of Abraham, Isaac, and Jacob" then they must have still been alive at the time or they would be alive again. That is, God was still their God; thus they had not ceased to exist. Once God establishes a relationship with someone, nothing can break it, not even death. Jesus' appeal to the Torah to establish the resurrection by the interpretive method of midrash is similar to the arguments of many of the famous rabbis such as Gamaliel II (AD 90) and Joshua ben Hanania (AD 90).[8] Thus Jesus argues in a typically rabbinic (and Pharisaic) way against the Sadducees.

But notice that Jesus chides the Sadducees for failing to appreciate the power of God (Mt 22:29). Those that have difficulty with the resurrection or afterlife in general for that matter are also those that do not appreciate seriously enough God's power. In the final estimation of the problem, it is difficult not to believe in life after death if one believes in the all powerful God of creation.

One of the scribes of the Pharisees approved of Jesus' debate with the Sadducees and thus brought to him his own question: "Which commandment in the law is the great one?" (Mt 22:36 and par.). The rabbinic texts speak often of the numerous commandments (248 positive commands, 365 prohibitions, thus 613 in all)[9]. They also debated which were the light commandments and which were the heavy commandments. Some said honoring father and mother was the heaviest (j. Kiddushin 1.58) others that the prohibition against taking the name of Yahweh in vain was the heaviest (b. Shebuoth 39a) or keeping the Sabbath (j. Nedarim 3.4). Most seem to have listed three general categories as the heaviest: the prohibitions against idolatry, sexual sin, and murder.[10]

So it was not unusual for a scribe to ask Jesus this question. What is unusual is Jesus' answer. He quotes (Mk 12:29) the *Shema* (Deut 6:4), that Jewish creed recited both morning and evening in the temple and the synagogue. To love God with all one's being is the heaviest commandment. The second to it is to love ones neighbor as oneself (Lev 19:18). Thus the greatest or heaviest commandments are to love. Motivation was always at the heart of Jesus' teaching. If we begin with purity of heart, we conduct our actions accordingly. But to love our fellow man properly we must first begin with love for God. God must be to us a heavenly father.

The scribe, who had come at least in part to test Jesus' knowledge (Mt 22:35), was quite impressed with his answer. He agreed with Jesus by affirming that love is more important than any ritual or offering. Jesus in turn responded that the scribe had properly understood the will of God and thus was not "far from the Kingdom." That is, he was well on the way to becoming a disciple.

One final debate occured when Jesus asked the Pharisees concerning the Messiah (Mt 22:41-46). Whose son will he be? They answer that the Messiah will be the son ⸱f David since there are several Old Testament prophecies that indicate that (Isaiah 9:7; Jeremiah 23:5, 30:9; Ezekiel 34:23f, 37:24f). Jesus responds with another question that puts them in a dilemma. How then can David call his son "Lord" in Psalm 110, an acknowledged Messianic psalm. Would a man call his son, if the son were a mere man, Lord?

The Psalm reads literally from the Hebrew: "A psalm of David. An oracle of Yahweh to my Lord." But if David is writing the psalm about the Messiah, that means he is calling him Lord. Thus the Messiah is more than a mere man, more than a mere military hero (the typical Jewish idea). He is a heavenly figure.

At some point in this last week of Jesus' earthly life he began to attack the Pharisees and scribes (Mt 23:1-36). They like to be seen in their piety, wearing phylacteries and long fringes.[11] They are hypocrites; they are legalists and they lay heavy legal burdens on people.

Evidently Jesus denounced these people more than once. In Luke there are two contexts for these denunciations: Here in the section parallel to Matthew 23 (i.e. Lk 20:45-47) and in an earlier section (i.e. Lk 11:42-52). Mark also records these denunciations but in a terser form.[12] Thus clearly Jesus did denounce the scribes and Pharisees, probably on more than one occasion.

It is sometimes alleged that Matthew is antisemitic because of the scathing words in his Gospel against this group. Indeed he has more of this attack than the others. But we must carefully consider the facts: First, Jesus himself clearly did bluntly criticize this group. Matthew is not manufacturing but collecting and reporting words. There are too many sources with similar words attributed to Jesus to conclude that Matthew concocted most of this chapter.

Second, this denunciation is not out of character with others like it which may also refer to the Pharisees. Several scholars have noted a similar passage in the so-called Assumption of Moses (or Testament of

Moses):

> And in the time of these, destructive and impious men shall rule, saying that they are just. And these shall stir up the poison of their minds, being treacherous men, self-pleasers, dissemblers in all their own affairs and lovers of banquets at every hour of the day, gluttons, gourmands. . . . Devourers of the goods of the [poor] saying that they do so on the ground of their justice, but in   reality   to   destroy   them, complainers, deceitful, concealing themselves lest they should be recognized, impious, filled with lawlessness and iniquity from sunrise to sunset: saying: "We shall have feastings and luxury, eating and drinking, and we shall esteem ourselves as princes." And though their hands and their minds touch unclean things, yet their mouth shall speak great things, and they shall say furthermore: "Do not touch me lest thou shouldst pollute me in the place [where I stand"]. . . (Trans. in Charles).

Jeremias (*Jerusalem*) and Finkelstein argued that this passage referred to the Pharisees or at least to one branch of the Pharisees. Charles and J. Priest (in *OTP* I) have affirmed that it alludes to the Sadducees or temple priests. It would seem to the present author more clearly to describe the Sadducees than Pharisees, but the point is that such blunt denunciations were common fare in the ancient Jewish world. This is a Jewish text saying these things about other Jews. There is certainly no antisemitism here.

Even more interesting in this connection are the comments about the Pharisees contained in the Dead Sea Scrolls from Qumran. L. Schiffman has collected some of these to indicate what at least one other Jewish group thought about the Pharisees. These texts do not refer to the Pharisees by name but it is becoming a growing consensus that the group alluded to in the scrolls was the Pharisees. The Essenes call this group "the builders of the wall" (CD 4:19-20, 8:12-18; cf. m. Aboth 1:1, 3:17). The wall was the extra laws created by the Pharisees to insure that they would not transgress the Torah. This group has, according to the Essenes, corrupted the Torah and preach falsehood. They are "seekers after smooth things." (1QH 4:10-11; 4Q169 1 [the commentary on Nahum]). They interpret false laws, choose falsehoods, seek out opportunities to violate law, choose luxury, declare innocent the guilty and guilty the innocent. They violate the covenant and annul the law, and band together to do away with the righteous (CD 1:18-20 see Schiffman, p. 33). Thus one can see that

Disputes in the Temple

Jesus was not the only one to criticize the Pharisees nor was he the only one to polemicize against a Jewish group. There is nothing antisemitic about such a thing. Further, we can see that the Pharisees, or more precisely, some of the Pharisees, exhibited qualities that left them open to criticism.

Nor was Matthew's detailed report of Jesus' verbal attack on the scribes and Pharisees out of any animosity or antisemitism on his part. Matthew was a preacher. His concern in writing the Gospel was to meet the spiritual needs of the Christian community in which he lived. If he goes into greater detail about these matters, it is because his own congregation(s) were exhibiting some of these same tendencies. He is then preaching to his Christian congregation(s) not polemicizing against Jews, Pharisaic or otherwise.

The last scene from these disputes in the Temple is that of witnessing the contributions to the Temple treasury (Mk 12:41-44; Lk 21:1-4). Many wealthy people dropped in large amounts of money; a poor widow gave only two small coins. Yet Jesus commended her and said that she had actually given a greater gift since she had given all that she had. Her gift was one of pure devotion to God and sincerely given. This brief narrative summarizes well Jesus' differences with those leaders (Sadducees, chief priests, scribes, Pharisees) with whom he debated in the Temple: It is sincerity of heart and fervent devotion to God that counts, not ritual correctness, wealth, or knowledge.

Notes

1. See Chapter 16 for a description. This apocryphal gospel is probably an amalgum of independent oral traditions of Jesus' words and sayings harmonized from our canonical Gospels.
2. See D.A. Fiensy, *Social History of Palestine in the Herodian Period*, pp. 31-35 for towers and pp. 80-85 for tenant farmers. See also Hengel, "Gleichnis".
3. Translation in R.W. Funk and R.W. Hoover, *The Five Gospels*.
4. B. Shabbath 153a: "A king invited his servants to a banquet but did not set a definite time for the banquet. The wise ones cleaned up and sat at the entrance to the palace. They said , 'Should there be any shortcomings in a king's palace?' But the foolish went away to their work. They said, 'Is there any banquet without arduous preparations?' (And so there will be plenty of time to clean up later.) Suddenly the king demanded that the servants be

present. The wise ones came before him cleaned up; but the foolish were soiled and dirty. The king was pleased with the wise and upset with the foolish. He said, 'These who have cleaned themselves up for the banquet may sit and eat and drink, but those who did not clean themselves up must stand and watch.'" (Translation in S-B)

5. B. Sanhedrin 90a also represents the Sadducees as denying the resurrection. One rabbinic tradition (Aboth de Rabbi Nathan 5) says that the students of a scribe named Antigonus of Soko (c. 150 BC) first began to deny the resurrection. Most likely, however, the Sadducees simply did not find clear statements in the Old Testament, especially the books of Moses, that supported the resurrection. See chapter 3 for a description of the Sadducees.

6. The story is vaguely reminiscent of the story of Sarah in the apocryphal book of Tobit 3:8.

7. Cf. the Christian heretic, Cerinthus, who taught that "after the resurrection the kingdom of Christ will be on earth, and that the flesh, dwelling at Jerusalem, will once more serve lusts and pleasures". (Eusebius, *H.E.* 3.28.2). See also the following rabbinic texts that speak of having wives in the physical, human way in the age to come: b. Sanhedrin 92b; Midrash on Psalm 73; b. Shabbath 30b.

8. For an explanation of midrash see J. Neusner, *Invitation to Midrash*. For the texts indicating the arguments of Rabban Gamaliel II and Rabbi Jehoshua ben Hanania see S-B. For example Gamaliel II argued against the Sadducees by quoting Deut 11:9 in which God promised to give the land of Israel to the patriarchs. Since he actually gave the land to their descendents, he must raise them from the dead in the future. See b. Sanhedrin 90b and 91b.

9. See Exodus Rabbah 33; Pesiqta 22, 101a; b. Makkoth 23b; Sifra on Deuteronmy 12:23.

10. See j. Nedarim 3.12; Sifra on Deuteronomy 19:11; b. Arakhin 15b; t. Peah 1:2. See S-B.

11. Phylacteries (Gk:*phulakteria*; or *tephilin*Heb) were leather boxes worn on the forehead and right forearm. Inside the boxes were bits of writing with the following verses: Ex 13:1-10; 11-16; Deut 6:4-9; 11:13-21. Both the Mishnah (Shebuoth 3:8,11) and Josephus (*Antiquities* 4.213) refer to phylacteries. Archaeologists have found in recent years actual phylacteries from antiquity. They were discovered at Qumran (1st cent. AD) and at Wadi Murabaat (c. AD 135), both sites on the western shore of the Dead Sea. See S.T. Fagen, "Phylacteries" in *ABD*. Fringes (Heb: *tzitzit*) were commanded in Num 15:37-41. See S. Sandmel, *Judaism and Christian Beginnings*.

12. The Gospel of Thomas 39 and 89 also contain parallel sayings.

Chapter 20

The Eschatological Discourse

(Aland 287-300)

Bibliography: L. Boettner, *The Millennium*; J. Bright, "The Date of the Prose Sermons of Jeremiah" *Journal of Biblical Literature* 40 (1951) 15-29; R. Bultmann, *The History of the Synoptic Tradition*; M. Connick, *Jesus the Man, the Mission and the Message*; G. Dalman, *Arbeit und Sitte in Palaestina*; E.E. Ellis, "How the New Testament Uses the Old" in I.H. Marshall, *New Testament Interpretation*; J. Fitzmyer, *The Gospel According to Luke*; R.C. Foster, *Studies in the Life of Christ*; R. Gundry, *Matthew*; J. Jeremias, *The Parables of Jesus*; L. Hartman, *Prophecy Interpreted*; M. Hengel, *The Charismatic Leader and His Followers*; W. Lane, *The Gospel According to Mark*; H. Lindsay, *The Late Great Planet Earth*; J.R. Lundbom, "The Book of Jeremiah" in *ABD*; T.W. Manson, *The Sayings of Jesus*; I.H. Marshall, *Commentary on Luke*; E. Schweizer, *The Good News According to Mark*; idem., *The Good News According to Matthew*

Preliminary Considerations

Upon leaving the Temple one day during this final week of Jesus' public ministry, the disciples remarked on the beauty of the edifice and the magnificence of its stones. The Temple was certainly a wonder of the ancient world with foundation stones weighing hundreds of tons. To those unaccustomed to seeing large buildings this would have been very impressive. Yet when this statement is uttered, Jesus responds with a prediction of the Temple's destruction. Not one stone will be left standing. This came to pass in the Jewish War of AD 66-73 (*War* 7.1).

The disciples later ask him. "When will these things come to pass and what is the sign of your coming and the end of the age?" (Mt 24:3). Thus they ask both about the destruction of the Temple and about the final consummation or the last day (Gk: *eschaton*). There follows a lengthy discourse that has been debated, cut up, and often overly emphasized by modern interpreters.

We may categorize the views concerning the interpretation of the eschatological discourse as follows: I. Those understanding the discourse as being intact. In other words, they conclude that Jesus uttered all of these things on this occasion. II. Those considering the discourse as not being intact. They argue that other sayings and teachings have been added to an original apocalyptic sermon.

Sermon Intact

A. Most premillennialists (e.g. Lindsay; and see the summaries in Boettner) would maintain that all of the sermon refers to the end of the world. This is a "little apocalypse" which summarizes Revelation 4-19. The "desolating sacrilege" or "abomination of desolation" as it is called in the King James Bible (Mk 13:14 and par.) will be an idol which will be placed in the (rebuilt) Temple during the reign of the Antichrist.

B. Amillennialists and Postmillennialists (Boettner) say that none of the sermon refers to the final consummation. It all refers to the Jewish war of AD 66-73 and the destruction of the Temple in AD 70. The desolating sacrilege would be the desolation of the Temple at that time.

C. R.C. Foster combines the two above views. The discourse or sermon was delivered by Jesus on this occasion but Jesus, in typical Old Testament fashion (see below), intermingled predictions about the end of the world with those of the Jewish war. Thus the content of the discourse is as follows:

Mk 13:5-23	The fall of Jerusalem and the Jewish war.
Mk 13:24-27	The second coming.
Mk 13:28-31	The fall of Jerusalem and the Jewish war.
Mk 13:32-37	The second coming.

Sermon Not Intact

A. E. Schweizer attributes very little of the eschatological discourse to Jesus. He maintains that Mk 13:5-13 and 13:24-27 are from the early church's reading of the Old Testament. Later, a Christian prophet added 13:14-20. These latter verses refer to Emperor Caligula[1] or later in the 60's. Only 13:21-23 is "from the tradition" (i.e. perhaps from Jesus).

B. M. Connick's analysis is somewhat similar to Schweizer's. He affirms that Mk 13:6-8, 14-20, and 24-27 have been added (c. AD 40, the time of Caligula) to the original words of Jesus.

C. The work of L. Hartman (followed by Ellis) is the most intriguing of those we will give in category II. Hartman maintains that the sermon is Jesus' midrash on certain passages in the book of Daniel (e.g. Dan 7:13, 9:27). A midrash was a Jewish commentary on the Old Testament (Heb verb *darash*: "to search"). Jesus' original midrash was Mk 13:5b-8, 12-16, 19-22 and 24-27. Jesus' midrash, maintains Hartman, has been supplemented by other sayings of the Lord and reshaped by the Gospel writers and the church before them.

How shall we conclude concerning this discourse? We should probably learn both from Foster's and Hartman's contributions. We should not assume that the eschatological sermon or discourse is about only one theme (thus only about the fall of Jerusalem or only about the second coming). Nor should we assume that Jesus uttered all of these words on the same occasion.

The Old Testament prophetic books often seem to be chronologically displaced. That is, the oracles are not in proper chronological order. As J.R. Lundbom writes about the book of Jeremiah, "The book of Jeremiah bears ample witness to the claim that people in antiquity compiled spoken and written discourse differently than we do today." (Lundbom III, 711; cf. Bright). The reader may also note this with the case of the book of Isaiah where we first read about his call to prophetism in chapter 6. Obviously the first five chapters are out of place chronologically. We may then have here a composite of several sermons in no particular chronological order. The Gospel writers seem to tack on thematically similar materials to a discourse. We can see no reason to conclude, however, that some parts of this discourse come from any other source than Jesus, himself.

Further, it is also typical of Old Testament prophecy to intermingle oracles having to do with the historical circumstances of their day with oracles about the end of the age (often termed in the Old Testament "the Day of the LORD"). See, for example, Joel 2:1-27, compared with verses 28-32; Micah 2:12-3:12 and 4:1-5; Daniel 11:1-45 and 12:1-4. In these texts the authors speak of events and persons that are clearly from their own time but then add oracles about a universal kingdom of peace and about the end time resurrection of the dead. Thus it is not unusual to have oracles of Jesus about both the Jewish war and the end of the age set side by side in a discourse with no clear demarcation of content.

Brief Analysis of the Discourse in Mark (Aland 287-295)

Mark 13:3-23 refers to the Jewish war. First Jesus lists some signs that the end of the city and Temple are coming: False Messiahs, wars and rumors of wars, earthquakes, famines, persecutions and the abomination that brings desolation or desolating sacrilege.[2] The last sign that Jesus gives, the abomination of desolation, is based on Daniel 9:27, 11:31, and 12:11. Many scholars, conservative and liberal alike, understand this to have been fulfilled by the sacrilege committed by Antiochus IV Epiphanes in the days of the Maccabees (1 Maccabees 1:54-59, 6:7) in 168 BC when the king erected an altar to the pagan god Zeus upon which he sacrificed pigs. Jesus is saying that that sacrilege was not ultimately fulfilled by that event. There will be yet another act of profaning the Temple.

Jesus' point is that when that final sign is seen, the faithful should flee (13:14). Eusebius, the Christian historian of the fourth century AD records that the believers did exactly that:

> The whole body, however, of the church at Jerusalem, having been commanded by a divine revelation, given to men of approved piety there before the war, removed from the city, and dwelt at a certain town beyond the Jordan, called Pella. (*H.E.* 3.5.3; Trans. in Cruse)

Thus the Christians heeded Jesus' warning and command. They fled when they saw the final sign approaching Jerusalem and their lives were saved.

The next section (13:24-27) must refer to the end of the age. Jesus combines teaching on this subject (or the Gospel authors combine Jesus' teachings on this subject) with teaching on the destruction of Jerusalem. This is not unusual for Old Testament prophets as we saw above. The "in those days" of verse 24, however, as W. Lane correctly observes, is a stereotypical Old Testament expression (Jer 3:16, 18; Joel 2:28; Zech 8:23) and "has no temporal value." That is, we must not think that Jesus was setting a date for the end of the age. When the age does end, however, it will be accompanied by cosmic woes: the sun is darkened, the moon turns to blood, and the stars fall.

Verses 28-31 refer again to the fall of Jerusalem. Verse 30 indicates that the generation of Jesus' time will not pass away until it sees the horrible events of the Jewish war.

Verses 32-37 have to do with the second coming and the end of the age. Although many of those alive in Jesus day will see the destruction of Jerusalem and God's judgment on Israel, no one knows (v. 32) the day or hour of the consummation of the age. Lane is correct that Jesus makes a contrast between verses 30 and 32.

The Parables in Matthew
(Aland 296-300)

Matthew has in addition to the discourse also found in Mark and Luke, five parables illustrating the end of the age. One of these is found in summary form in Mark (the parable of the talents) and all of them but two are found in Luke but in different locations (i.e. not connected with this sermon). Thus we conclude that Matthew has added teachings of Jesus with similar theme to this sermon. The five parables are:

1. The parable of the householder (also in Lk).
2. The parable of the good and wicked servant (also in Lk).
3. The parable of the ten virgins.
4. The parable of the talents (also in Lk).
5. The last judgment.

The parable of the householder (Mt 24:43-44),[3] if Jeremias was correct, is based on an actual event. Someone's house was broken into during the night while the family slept. Now the whole village is buzzing about this happening. Jesus used the theft to create a parable. Just as the family was caught unaware when the thief came, so will the unbelieving and unfaithful be caught when Christ comes at the end of the age. Christ represents the thief and the unprepared, the sleeping family. The

comparison of our Lord with a thief--one that he himself first made--
seems improper, but we must remember (see Chapter 9) that parables
often make only one point and so unusual elements necessary for the story
to work may be used. The metaphor of the thief coming in the night
became a common one in early Christian teaching (1 Thess 5:2; 2 Pet
3:10; Rev 3:3; 16:15).

The next parable (Mt 24:45-51) concerns a servant entrusted with his
master's household (probably a large agricultural estate). The master
delays in coming (v. 48), that is the Lord does not come again as soon as
some think he will. Now the servant can respond one of two ways. He
can continue to be faithful in all things or he can become wicked and
lapse into immorality and fail to keep faithfully his commitment. Christ's
church can do the same. It can wait patiently and faithfully for the Lord
to come to redeem it or it can lapse into unbelief, immorality, and
lukewarm commitment. But when the Lord comes, he will exact
judgment on his church.

The third parable (Mt 25:1-13), the Ten Virgins, concerns the delay in
the second coming. The ten virgins=the expectant Christian community;
the tarrying bridegroom=the delay in the second coming; and the rejection
of the foolish virgins=final judgment (Jeremias). We saw in a rabbinic
parable (b. Shabbath 153a, quoted in chapter 19 of this volume) that
guests could be suddenly expected to be ready for a banquet. In this case
the guests, the ten virgins, are awaiting the arrival of the groom to the
banquet room. Probably the wedding customs varied from village to
village. E. Schweizer notes that Palestinian maidens as late as the turn of
this century carried torches and danced at weddings until their torches
went out. Here the custom seems to have been that they waited at the
door of the banquet hall with their lamps lit and then perhaps
accompanied the groom into the festivities.

The point of the parable is that some were ready for the coming of the
groom and some were not. Likewise, some will be ready--because they
live expectantly and faithfully--for the second coming of our Lord and
some will not. Verse 13 carries the warning: Watch because you do not
know the day or hour. Not knowing, as Schweizer points out, can lead
some to fanatical enthusiasm but others to negligence. But we must avoid
both extremes by waiting patiently and faithfully.

The parable of the Talents (Mt 25:14-30) is found also in Luke 19:11-
27 and in summary form in Mark 13:34. In addition there is a version in
an apocryphal Gospel called the Gospel of the Nazarenes.[4] Once again
(cf. the parable of the Great Supper discussed in chapter 19) we probably

should see here Jesus' adaptation of this theme on several occasions. Thus the parables in Matthew and Luke are not the same one but two different parables.

Matthew's parable tells of a man who upon embarking on a long journey leaves with three servants differing amounts of talents. A talent was a weight of silver equal to 10,000 denarii or drachmae. Thus it was a huge sum of money when we consider that the average day laborer could earn about 200 denarii a year. The first servant was given five talents to invest, the second was given two, and the third, one. "After much time" (note the delay of the second coming) the estate owner returned and demanded a reckoning. The first two servants doubled their investments but the third, fearing to take a risk only maintained his one talent. The third servant knew that his master was a very demanding one and would not tolerate failure. The estate owner rewarded the first two servants but rebuked the timid man and took from him his one talent because he had not used it wisely.

What does the parable mean? Jeremias maintained that originally Jesus addressed this parable to the Jewish scribes. Or we might say that Jesus addressed the parable on one occasion to the scribes. Much had been entrusted to them (learning, scholarship) and much was therefore expected of them.

But the parable was applied also to the disciples of Jesus. The estate owner then=Christ; the servants=the disciples; the journey=Christ's ascension; the talents=the abilities and responsibilities given to each disciple; the return of the estate owner=the judgment. The point is we must not be devoted more to our own personal security than to Christ. We must be ready to take action even if it involves risk to our financial, professional, and personal well being. A faith concerned only with doing nothing wrong ignores the will of God (Schweizer).

Luke's parable is placed within the historical context of Archelaus, the son of Herod the Great, who in 4 BC journeyed to Rome to claim his throne and was opposed by a Jewish embassy (see *War* 2.80; *Antiquities* 17.299-300). Further, the amount of money given to each was a *mina* (=100 denarii or drachmae) and thus a much smaller amount of money. Each servant was given the same amount of money unlike the Matthean parable. Finally, there were ten servants instead of three.

Again we notice that an element in the parable must not be pressed. In both parables (Mt 25:24; Lk 19:21) the estate owner is said to be a harsh or austere man. We must not apply this literally to Christ at judgment. This is only scenery necessary for the story to work.

The last parable we consider is the lofty vision of judgment (Mt 25:31-46). Jesus begins this pericope on the final judgment by comparing it to gathering and separating sheep from goats. As G. Dalman pointed out, sheep and goats graze together during the day but must be separated at night since goats want warmth but sheep fresh air. Sheep are more valuable than goats and have a traditional identification with the people of God (2 Samuel 24:17; Psalm 77:20; Isaiah 63:11; Jeremiah 13:20, Ezekiel 34:2-31). Therefore in the parable they represent the righteous and the goats the unrighteous.

After the brief parable, Jesus gives us a glimpse of what the judgment will be like. In the parable itself, the Son of man acts as a shepherd who separates sheep from goats. But then at verse 34 the story shifts somewhat and Christ is referred to as "the King". He speaks to his people and commends them for their righteous life. They are invited into the eternal kingdom which has been waiting for them since the beginning of time. What has characterized their life? They fed the hungry, gave drink to the thirsty, showed hospitality to strangers, clothed the naked, and cared for the sick and the imprisoned. What is especially striking in this scene of judgment, however, is that Jesus represents the righteous as having done all of these things for him personally. When they ask when they could have done any of this for Christ, he responds: "Truly I say to you, Whenever you did it to anyone of the least of my brothers, you did it to me." (verse 40). Thus Christ identifies with his disciples.

To the unrighteous Christ says the opposite. They are commanded to depart to the eternal fire prepared originally only for the devil and his minions. Hell was never intended for the descendants of Adam and Eve. But through unrighteous living they have been judged worthy of it. What had they done or failed to do? They had not fed, clothed, etc. the King who is Christ. But when had they failed to do these things for Christ? When they failed to do them to anyone of the least of his brothers.

We must note here that R. Bultmann and (more recently) R. Gundry have argued that Jesus never uttered these lofty words at all but they were created by Matthew out of Jewish tradition. Gundry maintains that Matthew used Isaiah 58:7 to fashion this pericope:

> Is it not to divide to the hungry your bread, to bring poor wanderers
> to a house, when you see the naked to clothe him, and not to hide
> yourself from your kinsmen?

Bultmann quotes the following rabbinic parallel:

In reference to Deuteronomy 13:5 it is asked: How can a man walk after God? . . . But the meaning is that you acquire his properties. Just as God clothes the naked (Gen 3:21), so must you clothe the naked; as God visits the sick (Gen 18:1) so do you; as God comforts the mourners (Gen 25:11) so must you; as God buries the dead (Deut 34:6) you must do likewise. (b. Sota 14a; trans. in Bultmann).

These and other[5] citations convinced Bultmann that this pericope could not be from Jesus himself but was rather "derived from Jewish tradition" (p. 124).

But the logic behind this argument is difficult to accept. Jesus was a Jew also. If Matthew could compose this section based on Isaiah 58 and other Jewish tradition, why could not Jesus? Bultmann and Gundry are really only begging the question. On the other hand T.W. Manson (followed by Jeremias) has declared that this pericope contains features difficult to credit "to anyone but the Master himself."

Note finally two elements in this section. First Jesus identifies himself with the needy as he does elsewhere in the Gospels (Mt 10:40-42=Lk 10:16; Mk 9:37) and Acts (9:4 and par.). Thus helping the oppressed and needy is an act of devotion and worship of the living Christ. Second, the righteous are not aware of their righteousness (even as the wicked are not aware of their selfish preoccupation that led to neglect of the needy). This is not then works righteousness or righteousness which is earned. This is rather spontaneous love and sympathy that flows out of a soul that has truly experienced forgiveness and redemption. As Schweizer adds, the truly righteous person knows of no works to his credit. We might add that the truly wicked person also knows of no evil works to his credit. Goodness and evil flow naturally from what we are and from what we believe and value.

Thus the emphasis in these teachings on the second coming is on being patient and faithful. This is a time of testing and waiting. While the people of God wait and watch, we must use what abilities and opportunities God gives us and we must care for the needy of our world. We cannot know the day or hour of our Lord's coming but we do believe that his coming is certain.

Notes

1. On Caligula's antics see: Philo, *Legatio ad Gaium*; Josephus, *Antiquities* 18. 261-301; Tacitus, *Histories* 5.9.

2. Josephus lists many such signs that later supposedly warned people of the city's doom (*War* 6.288-299; cf. b. Yoma 39b) though his signs are more the silly speculations and imagination of the ignorant masses.

3. The parable is also in Luke 12:39-40 and Gospel of Thomas 21 and perhaps 103.

4. The text is as follows: "But since the Gospel [*written*] in Hebrew characters which has come into our hands enters the threat not against the man who had hid [*the talent*], but against him who had lived dissolutely--for he [*the master*] had three servants: one who squandered his master's substance with harlots and flute-girls, one who multiplied the gain, and one who hid the talent; and accordingly one was accepted (with joy), another merely rebuked, and another cast into prison--I wonder whether in Matthew the threat which is uttered after the word against the man who did nothing may refer not to him, but by epanlepsis to the first who had feasted and drunk with the drunken." (Eusebius, *Theophania* on Mt 25:14-15; trans. by P. Vielhauer in E. Hennecke, W. Schneemelcher, and R. McL. Wilson, *New Testament Apocrypha*). An epanlepsis is a revision or correction. Thus Eusebius, on the basis of the Gospel of the Nazarenes, wanted to understand Matthew's parable somewhat differently that it reads now.

5. Jeremias quotes the Egyptian Book of the Dead: "I have given satisfaction to God by doing that in which he delights: I have given bread to the hungry, water to the thirsty, clothed the naked. . ." See also parallels in Testament of Joseph 1:5-6; 2 Enoch 9, 42:8, 63; and Midrash Tanhuma 15.9.

Chapter 21

From The Plot To Kill Jesus To The Arrest (Aland 305-329)

Bibliography: H. Andersen, *The Gospel of Mark*; C.K. Barrett, *The Gospel According to John*; S.G.F. Brandon, *Jesus and the Zealots*; R. Brown, *The Death of the Messiah*; idem., *The Gospel According to John*; R. Bultmann, *The Gospel of John*; J.M. Creed, *The Gospel of Luke*; J. Fitzmyer, *The Gospel According to Luke*; S.M. Gilmour, "The Gospel of Luke" in *Interpreter's Bible*; D. Hill, *The Gospel of Matthew*; A. Jaubert, *The Date of the Last Supper*; J. Jeremias, *The Eucharistic Words of Jesus*; M.-J. Lagrange, *Evangile selon Saint Jean*; W. Lane, *The Gospel According to Mark*; T.W. Manson, *The Sayings of Jesus*; A.H. McNeil, *The Gospel According to St. Matthew*; I.H. Marshall, *Commentary on Luke*; E.P. Sanders, *Jesus and Judaism*; E. Schweizer, *The Good News According to Mark*; idem., *The Good News According to Matthew*; V. Taylor, *The Gospel According to Mark*; B.F. Westcott, *The Gospel According to St. John*.

From the Plot to the Upper Room (Aland 305-307)

Jesus has been teaching in the Temple in Jerusalem for some days. Exactly how long this period of teaching was we do not know. Some scholars, assuming that Mark has intentionally given a careful chronology, have maintained that Jesus entered Jerusalem triumphantly on Sunday and taught in the Temple only two days before the Jewish leaders plotted his death (see Mk 11:12; 11:20). But Matthew and Luke do not have the same chronological references and Mark does not actually say that only a few days have elapsed. Mark is usually rather loose about chronological references. The events and controversies given to us only in summary form in the previous chapters seem rather to have taken several days or weeks. Thus the triumphal entry may have been several weeks before Jesus' death.

At any rate, the time is now only two days before the Passover (Mt 26:2; Mk 14:1) and the chief priests, elders, and scribes have gathered to discuss the situation with Jesus.

E.P. Sanders is probably correct that the cleansing of the Temple, done sometime after Jesus' entry, has been the last straw for these Jewish leaders. That objectionable (for them) event has been followed by several days of Jesus' teaching in the Temple in an authoritative manner. They fear a mass following and opposition to the accepted leadership and authority. They want to arrest him and have him executed. They fear the populace, however, especially during the coming Passover (cf. Josephus, *Antiquities* 20. 106-107) and so must do all they plan in secret.

They explicitly plan not to arrest Jesus during the feast (Mt 26:5) but then arrest him within a day or two. Did they change their plans? Jeremias maintained that this statement meant that they planned not to arrest Jesus in front of the crowd gathered at the feast. That is, that they planned to arrest him in secret. But we must also reckon with the part played by Judas Iscariot. His volunteering to betray Jesus may have changed their time table. Thus perhaps at first they planned to wait until the feast was over to arrest Jesus but when the unexpected help of Judas came they may have decided to go ahead immediately.

John's Gospel informs us that an earlier council was held regarding Jesus (Jn 11:47-53). As a matter of fact we should not be surprised if there were several such councils. In this earlier meeting they are clearly anxious about the large following that Jesus has. They fear that the Romans will interpret this as a rebellion and send an army to destroy the Temple and the whole nation. The High Priest, Caiaphas[1], exhorts them to take courage and do the necessary thing, that is to kill Jesus. In his speech before the assembly, however, Caiaphas made an unwitting prediction: "It is fitting that one man should die on behalf of the people and that the whole nation should not perish" (Jn 11:50). John says that Caiaphas said more than he knew for Jesus as a matter of fact did die for his nation, indeed for the whole world that we might not perish.

Jesus resided in Bethany each evening while teaching in the Temple (Mt 21:17). On one occasion[2] while he was eating a meal a woman came to him with a container of precious ointment and anointed him. This anointing is placed in Matthew and Mark right after the plot of the Jewish leaders but in John sometime before the triumphal entry. John says that this happened six days before the Passover (12:1). We are inclined to say that John is giving the actual chronology while Matthew and Mark place the event here to contrast the woman's devotion to Jesus with Judas' perfidy. Thus Matthew and Mark place the event based on theme not chronology.

Matthew, Mark and John agree in saying that this took place in Bethany, that the ointment was nard (Gk: *myron*), that someone objected to the waste of such an expensive ointment, that it could have been sold for about 300 denarii, and that Jesus said "The poor you always have with you". Matthew and Mark name the owner of the house where this took place as Simon the leper; John says it is in the village of Lazarus (see Jn 11:1-44). It is possible if Lazarus and Simon are the same person that Lazarus had dual names as men sometimes did. It is also possible that his name Lazarus (Heb for "God has helped") was given to him after his being raised from the dead by Jesus. Some commentators have speculated that Lazarus died of leprosy and was thus raised and cured by Jesus. But it is also possible that these are two different people. The event may have taken place in the house of Simon but in Bethany the village where Lazarus also lived. John's Gospel merely says: "Jesus six days before the Passover came to Bethany where Lazarus was'" (Jn 12:1). He does not clearly indicate that the anointing took place in Lazarus' house. Even though Mary, Lazarus' sister, anointed Jesus, it does not necessitate that this took place in her house. At any rate the anointing took place in Bethany and Lazarus was present whether he was the same person as Simon or not.

Matthew and Mark agree that the anointing was on Jesus' head while John has the ointment poured on his feet. We would naturally expect the feet to be washed and anointed at a dinner (see Jn 13; Lk 7:46) but the head was often anointed before going out into the public (Psalm 23:5; 141:5). Thus we see no problem in concluding that both his head and feet were anointed. Matthew and Mark do not give the woman' s name but John informs us that she was Mary, Lazarus' sister. Matthew and Mark also do not give the name of the objector (s) but John says that at least one of them was Judas Iscariot who was a thief and merely wanted to steal the proceeds from the precious ointment.

Why did Mary do this? Three hundred denarii were about one and one half year's wages for a day laborer in those times. Thus the ointment was very expensive. She did it out of pure devotion. This action is in character with what we know of Mary, the sister of Lazarus and Martha (Lk 10:38-42). Jesus says that devotion to him must take precedence to everything, even works of charity (Mt 26:10-11). Mary did not perhaps know it but she was actually anointing Jesus' body ahead of time for his burial (Mt 26:12). That sort of commitment in the context of so much hatred and jealousy toward Jesus was truly remarkable and therefore would be told again and again as an example for later followers of the Lord (Mt 26:13).

The Jewish leaders have taken counsel about apprehending Jesus and executing him without arousing the ire of the masses. They seem to have been troubled about how this could be done until an unexpected conspirator came forward. Judas Iscariot or Judas son of Simon Iscariot was one of the original twelve disciples (Mk 3:16-19). The word Iscariot[3] has been variously interpreted and its interpretation influences the conclusion as to why Judas betrayed Jesus (see Brown, *Death*):

1. Man of Kerioth. Most historians see the name as a designation of geographical origin. As Brown points out, however, we have no clear evidence that such a village existed in Judea or Galilee.

2. The Sicarius. The Sicarii (from the Latin word for dagger) were assassins that arose in the mid-first century AD (*War* 2.254-257, 425; *Antiquities* 20.186). These ruthless men wanted to oppose the Roman hegemony over Palestine. There are problems with this identification also as Brown points out since the spelling is unusual (How did *sicarius* become *iskarioth*?) and there is no indication elsewhere that Judas was a political revolutionary.

3. The name is based on the Semitic root *skr* which means "to give over, surrender to". Again Brown points to linguistic difficulties.

4. The name means "the deceiver" and is a literal transliteration of the Semitic expression: *ish seqarim* "man of lies". The problem with this interpretation is that we have no evidence that Judas lied about anything.

Which one[4] is correct? The most plausible one is still the first one. That explains the epithet "Iscariot" as applied both to Judas (Mt 26:14) and to Judas' father Simon (Jn 13:2; 6:71). It is most simply understood as a designation of origin. That we have no known village in Judea or Galilee by that name is not decisive. There are indications that villages by that name stood in the Transjordan region and in the Negev (see *MacMillan Bible Atlas*). Thus the name was an ancient one. Further, this linguistic expression is found elsewhere (cf. m. Aboth 1:3,4: "Antigonus Ish-Soco"; and others designated this way, 3:7, 8).

Thus we can get no help in understanding Judas' actions or his motives from the title Iscariot. What did Judas actually do? Some say Judas merely revealed Jesus' whereabouts. To know where to arrest him away from the crowds would be a great help to the chief priests and others. Other scholars say that Judas revealed Jesus' Messianic intentions. But this seems to have been unnecessary. Both Caiaphas and Pilate seem to have been fully aware or at least suspicious of this. Still others say that Judas merely identified Jesus. The arresting guards probably would not have known what Jesus looked like in that age of no newspapers or television. Probably then Judas betrayed both the best place and then identified Jesus to the arresting party. Such help made it possible to arrest and try Jesus in relative secrecy although the size of the arresting group may have been rather large (see Chapter 22) and may have created a bit of a disturbance. Still it was done quickly, unexpectedly and at night. This precluded a reaction by a mob.

But why did Judas do this? What he did of course fulfilled scripture (see Mk 14:18-21; Mt 27:9; Jn 13:18) but that does not tell us of his own motive. The Gospels teach us that Satan entered his heart ((Lk 22:3; Jn 13:2, 27) and led him to do this act but what went on before this, what was Judas thinking that he would allow Satan to enter his heart? We might suppose that greed was his motive since in Matthew's account he asks for money to betray Jesus (Mt 26:14-15; cf. Mk 14:11) and in John's Gospel we are told that Judas was a greedy thief (Jn 12:4-6). Yet 30 shekels of silver or 30 silver denarii, though desirable to be sure, were not by any means a fortune. Would a loyal disciple betray his master for such a sum? Something happened within Judas before he ever thought about the money.

The motives usually assigned to Judas (see Brown, *Death*) fall into three categories:

1. Judas was actually a spy and had been working for the Sanhedrin for some time. There is no evidence for such a scenario, however.

2. Judas' motives were pure. Either a) Jesus instructed him to betray him so he could be crucified or b) he himself thought of it in order to force Jesus to show his power. But the Gospels do not indicate any such righteous intentions on Judas' part. Further, the second suggestion--that Judas wanted to force Jesus to show his power--would not really be a

good or pure motive. That was the very thing Jesus intentionally rejected: "My kingdom is not of this world' (Jn 18:36).

  3. Judas was disappointed in Jesus. Either a) he grew impatient that Jesus did not inaugurate the kingdom of God on earth (thus he was a Zealot or nationalist), b) or he was scandalized with Jesus' claims to be the Messiah and Son of God and thought that he was blaspheming, c) or he simply for some unknown reason lost faith in Jesus. We should probably look to the last suggestion. We have no evidence that Judas was a nationalist or that he was religiously scandalized by Jesus' claims. We can easily understand, however, that someone whose zeal for a teaching master had grown cold would lose faith in him, even grow to despise him. We often carry with us certain worldly expectations as to what God must do for us and when these expectations are not met we may become resentful, even angry. We will not be able to ascertain the exact reason for Judas' loss of faith and subsequent resentment of Jesus but we may be reasonably sure that such an event preceded his decision to betray him.

From the Upper Room to the Farewell Discourses (Aland 308-316)

  The Passover is drawing near and Jesus and his disciples prepare for its celebration. Jesus gives two of his disciples, Peter and John (Lk 22:9) instructions to go into Jerusalem (probably through a certain gate) where they would meet a man carrying a jar of water (perhaps usually done by women). This man would provide them with the upper room for their Passover meal. These instructions are similar to those Jesus gave to his disciples before the Triumphal Entry concerning the animal he was to ride on (Mk 11:1-10). Jesus demonstrates again his command of the situation.

  The problem we encounter here is the chronology. The Synoptics seem to say that this is already the first day of the Unleavened Bread (Mt 26:17) but the Gospel of John says that Jesus ate the meal before the feast of the Passover (13:1). The feast of Unleavened Bread began in the evening of the 15th of Nisan and ended on the 21st of Nisan. On the afternoon of the 14th of Nisan the lambs were slaughtered in the Temple. In the lunar calendar system a new day began at sundown. Thus our Thursday evening, for example, would be the beginning of Friday for them. The question is then did Jesus eat a Passover meal with his disciples or merely a fellowship meal? Second, was Jesus crucified on the 14th of Nisan or on the 15th of Nisan, or on the day they slaughter the lambs for the

Passover (the 14th) or on the day they eat the Passover (the 15th)? Almost everyone agrees that Jesus was crucified on Friday of that week but was that Friday the 14th or the 15th of Nisan that year?

J. Jeremias has argued strongly that the meal Jesus and his disciples ate was a Passover meal. They ate it in Jerusalem (where the Passover had to be eaten in those days, see m. Pesahim 7:9); they sang a hymn during the meal (Mt 26:30 and par.); they ate it at night (1 Cor 11:23; Jn 13:30; see Ex 12:8, Jubilees 49:12); and they drank wine, something not often done at meal times (Lk 22:17, 20; see m. Pesahim 10:1). On the other hand scholars such as E. Schweizer have noticed problems with concluding that this happened on Passover evening (15th Nisan). Would they crucify Jesus on the Passover? Would Simon of Cyrene be coming in from his farm on the Passover day (Mk 15:21)?

Several attempts at harmonizing John and the Synoptics have centered on different calendars. Thus A. Jaubert has argued that Jesus ate the Passover according to the Essene calendar but this was actually one day earlier than the official calendar. Lagrange suggested that Jesus used a Galilean reckoning of the Passover that was a day earlier than the Judean. P. Billerbeck (in S-B) offered that there were Pharisaic and Sadducean calculations that were a day apart. The problem with the last two suggestions is that there is no evidence that such different calendars existed. We do know, however, that an Essene calendar existed which was somewhat different from the official Jerusalem one.[5] Nevertheless, since Jesus was not an Essene why would he be following the Essene calendar? All such attempts to harmonize John with the Synoptics seem misguided.

The best solution is that of R. Brown (*John*). Brown suggests that Jesus simply ate a Passover-like meal with his disciples a day early. Probably he knew that his time was short and he wanted to eat this meal of such spiritual importance before he was crucified. Thus John was correct; it was eaten before the Passover, but the Synoptics were also correct; it was a Passover meal.[6]

Both the Gospel of John (13:1-20) and the Gospel of Luke (22:24-28) record that the disciples had trouble with pride. Luke says this explicitly, John implicitly in his narration of the foot washing story. Foot washing in the orient was a necessity due to the hot and dusty climate (Gen 19:2; Judges 19:21) but it was always done--when not performed by oneself--by a social inferior. Hebrew slaves should not be compelled to wash anybody's feet, only non-Hebrew slaves (or "Canaanite" slaves) should have to do that (Mekilta on Exodus 21:2). Women usually performed this task whether wives for their husbands (b. Ketuboth 4b; 61a; 96a) or female slaves for the master and the guests (Sifre on Deuteronomy 33:24; 1 Samuel 25:41; cf. Aboth de Rabbi Nathan 16). Children were obligated to wash their father's feet (t. Kiddushin 1:11) and disciples their master's feet (b. Ketuboth 96a). Washing the feet of people would become an act of piety and service for Christian women (1 Tim 5:10). Thus the overwhelming impression one gets from all of these texts is that only socially inferior people (slaves, children, and women) washed the feet of others.

In Luke's narrative he indicates that the disciples were disputing who was the greatest disciple. Jesus began to teach them verbally and probably at this point gave his object lesson in humility. He performed the task of slaves and women: He washed his disciples' feet. This was both an example of humility and humiliation. The truly great people in the Kingdom of God are servants not those that dominate (Lk 22:26-27; Jn 13:13-16). Peter is shocked and appalled that Jesus would stoop to do such a thing (cf. his shock when Jesus predicted his death [Mk 8:32]). He refuses to allow Jesus to wash his feet but Jesus demands it. He too must be shamed for he too was among those arguing about who was the greatest. He must accept the rebuke.

Only John's Gospel narrates the actual foot washing although Luke's Gospel has the same general theme as we noted above. Likewise, John's Gospel does not report the institution of the Lord's Supper during this meal. The Lord's Supper teaching is rather connected to the feeding of the 5000 in John (see 6:53-58). Why did John leave out the Lord's Supper account and substitute rather the episode of the foot washing? As we noted in chapter 13, John tended to supplement the Synoptics in places. That is, he includes material not in the Synoptics often as a substitute of well-known materials from the Synoptics.

The supper was punctuated not only by the selfishness of the disciples in general but by two troublesome predictions made by Jesus. First he predicted that someone would betray him. Jesus knew what Judas had done. Exactly when this prediction came in the Passover meal is unclear. Matthew and Mark put it before the institution of the Lord's Supper and Luke after it. John, who also narrates that Jesus predicted Judas' betrayal, of course did not narrate the institution of the Lord's Supper but places Jesus' prediction after the foot washing. It is possible that the prediction of betrayal came during the Supper. Thus while Jesus was explaining the meaning of his coming death ("This is my blood, shed for you") he showed Judas that he knew of his treachery.

Jesus' announcement of his knowledge of the betrayer was actually a plea for repentance. The disciples want to know "Is it I?" Peter whispers to the Beloved Disciple (whom we identified in chapter 13 of this volume as the apostle John) to ask further. Jesus responds that the one dipping with him in the *haroseth* (the jelly-like dip) is the man. Jesus gives Judas a piece of bread with the dip on it. When Judas brazenly takes the bread and eats it, Satan enters his heart (Jn 13:27), that is, he fully commits himself to the murder of Jesus. The insignificant--to the rest of the disciples--act of taking the morsel of bread was the final step in Judas' decision to reject Jesus. The offer of the morsel, however, was an offer of repentance and forgiveness on Jesus' part. It was a token of fellowship and trust. The other disciples do not exactly understand what is happening. The language "hand me over" (Greek: *paradidomi*; Hebrew: *masar*; Syriac: *sh^elem*) can be confusing. They think he is leaving to buy more food when Jesus says to him, "What you do , do it quickly" (Jn 13:27). Judas accepts the morsel, abruptly leaves the Upper Room, and seeks out his fellow conspirators. John writes after he tells us that Judas leaves: "And it was night." (Jn 13:30). That is, it was both literally nighttime and it was darkness for Judas' soul.

The second troublesome prediction that Jesus made was that Peter would deny him three times. In Matthew and Mark this story is placed after they had sung a hymn while in Luke and John it is told during the Passover meal. Again we cannot be sure exactly when Jesus made this prediction but only that it was sometime during the evening. Peter brags that even though the others might leave him, he never would ((Mt 26:33); he will even go to prison and death for Jesus (Lk 22:33; Jn 13:37). Jesus answers that it will be quite the contrary. He will fall even further than the others. He will actually verbally deny him. It will be a time of terrible testing and temptation by Satan. He will sift him like wheat but Peter will later repent. The later repentance will come when Peter sees the risen Lord (see Chapter 24).

Jesus gives apparently mysterious instructions in the Gospel of Luke (22:35-38). He refers to the sending out of the seventy (10:1-12) in which they were instructed not to take an extra pair of sandals, knapsack, or money bag. Now they must get these things because a persecution is coming. They must prepare for opposition; they can no longer depend on the charity of the villagers. To emphasize his point Jesus adds: "And let him not having a sword sell his cloak and buy one." The disciples say, "Look! Here are two swords." Jesus responds, "That is enough."

Brandon, who wanted to insist that Jesus was a Zealot plotting to overthrow the Roman hegemony in Palestine, argued that this passage proves his thesis. Here is Jesus urging his disciples to get a sword. This understanding of the words of Jesus is unlikely, however, in light of Jesus' command for Peter to put away his sword in the garden of Gethsemane and his admonition for his disciples not to live by the sword (Mt 26:51-52). Fitzmyer is correct when he suggests that the reference to a sword is symbolic. Just as a sword would be taken in preparation for a conflict in military life, the disciples must prepare for a battle against the principalities of Satan. They must arm themselves for a spiritual battle. The disciples misunderstand, however, and show Jesus their two swords. Jesus, frustrated at their misunderstanding, says, "Enough of that!" Manson captures well the moment: "This short dialogue throws a brilliant light on the tragedy of the Ministry. . . it is full of bitter disappointment. The grim irony of (verse) 36 is the utterance of a broken heart" (p. 341).

It was in the midst of this posturing, disputing and misunderstanding that Jesus instituted the Lord's Supper. There are four accounts of the Lord's Supper in the New Testament: the three in the Synoptic Gospels, plus that in 1 Corinthians 11:23-25.

Matthew and Mark are very similar. Luke and Paul also bear similarities to one another not in the other two sources: ("This is my body [given] for you"; "Do this for my remembrance"; "The cup after supper"; "The new covenant".).[7]

We have already agreed above with Jeremias that this meal was a Passover meal. The Passover was divided into four parts around the four cups of wine (m. Pesahim 10:1-7).

1. At the first cup one eats the *haroseth* or dip, and other hors d'oeuvres.

2. The second cup is accompanied with the roasted lamb (*pesah*) the unleavened bread (*matsah*) and the bitter herbs (*maror*).

3. The third cup is the time of the blessing of the meal or the benediction.

4. The fourth cup is done with the singing of the Hallel Psalms (118-120).

Since Luke and Paul write that the cup of the institution of the Lord's Supper was after the meal (Lk 22:20; 1 Cor 11:25) we may conclude that this was the third wine cup of the Passover celebration. The breaking of the bread to symbolize Christ's body took place during the meal itself.

All accounts of the Lord's Supper stress three common elements:

1. This action anticipates the future fulfillment of the kingdom of God (Mt 26:29; Mk 14:25; Lk 22:16, 18; 1 Cor 11:26).

2. This meal represents the present covenant relationship between God and his people (Mt 26:28; Mk 14:24; Lk 22:20; 1 Cor 11:25).

3. This celebration recalls Jesus' death (Mt 26:28 "blood . . . poured out for many for the forgiveness of sins"; Mk 14:24 "blood. . . poured out for many"; Lk 22:20 "the cup poured out for you is . . . my blood"; 1 Cor 11:25 "this cup . . . is my blood"). Matthew adds the phrase "for the forgiveness of sins" (26:28). In other words, Jesus' death was a sin offering (Hebrew: *hat'at)* like the offering of animals for sin in the Old Testament (Lev 4:3-35; 5:9, 11-12; 6:18, 23; 8:10-14; 10:1-13; etc.). The guilt of the "many" (a Semitism for "all") was transferred to him (cf. Lev 1:4; 3:2). He became a sin offering for us by his death, by his poured out blood (2 Cor 5:21); he accepted our curse of guilt (Gal 3:13). Thus his death was an atoning sacrifice and the Lord's Supper is meant to recall this act of grace and forgiveness.

The Farewell Discourses in John (Aland 317-329)

The Johannine discourses exhibit many of the typical themes of the Gospel of John and the epistles of John (love, truth, peace, fellowship, remaining faithful, the Holy Spirit). On the other hand many of the sayings in these discourses are parallel to sayings in the Synoptics (cf. 16:32 with Mt 26:31; cf. 16:23 with Mt 7:7-8, and for others see chapter 13, note 1). It is sometimes difficult to tell if we should locate these discussions in the Upper Room or on the way to Gethsemane. John 14:31 ("Rise, let us go") suggests that the fourteenth chapter belongs to the Upper Room and the rest to the walk to Gethsemane. But we must also allow that some of the material is from other times and has been placed here because of a compatible theme.

Jesus begins his discourse in John with the admonition to resist the anxiety of the moment. He will go ahead of them like Yahweh into Canaan to prepare an eternal home for them and will then take them to be with him (14:1-3). He describes heaven in terms readily understandable to Jews of Palestine. In the Old Testament, especially during the Iron age period, many Jewish extended families lived in compounds. They called these compounds in Hebrew *Beth Av*, the house of the father. They consisted of an edifice with a large courtyard in the middle. The patriarch of the extended family was the leader and his word was final. The closeness in living arrangements as well as in family ties made for a secure environment. You always knew that someone would be there to help you in case of need.[8] Jesus describes heaven in those terms. God is the patriarch. The "house of the father" is large with many rooms (or with many family quarters). Heaven will be a place of fellowship and love like the *Beth Av*.

Thomas questions where Jesus is going, what the way is. This leads to one of Jesus' most important statements in the Gospel of John: "I am the Way, the Truth, and the Life" (14:6). The self-designation "Way" is similar to that used by the Qumran community to designate itself (1QS 9:17-21; CD 1:3). Both Jesus and the Qumran community appropriated the term from Isaiah 40:3: "The voice of one crying in the wilderness; prepare the way of Yahweh". This was also the scripture that John the Baptist quoted of himself (Jn 1:23; cf Mk 1:3). Later the Christians would designate their group as the Way (e.g. Acts 9:1). For the Qumranites the Way means the manner of interpreting and obeying the Old Testament Law that is peculiar to them. But Jesus applies this term not to a manner of action but to himself. He as a person is the Way to please God. Devotion to him, following him constitutes the Way.

He is also the Truth. That is, he is the complete truth. While there is some truth is philosophy and some truth in every sort of religion, he and he alone is the full truth about God and his will. To comprehend Jesus' message is to know all that one needs to know in this life about the truth of salvation. He is also the Life. He created life (Jn 1:4) and will sustain life for eternity by the resurrection (Jn 11:25). To follow him leads to life.

Jesus now begins to teach about the Paraclete (Greek: *paracletos*). The Greek word can mean advocate, mediator, comforter, counselor, or exhorter. The Paraclete is clearly the Holy Spirit or "Spirit of Truth" (14:17; 14:26; 15:26). The Holy Spirit will come upon the disciples to take Jesus' place among them. He is *another* Paraclete (14:16). That is, Jesus is now among them as their Paraclete but the Holy Spirit will carry on the earthly ministry of Christ after Christ's ascension and the assumption of his heavenly ministry: The Paraclete will keep them from being orphaned (14:18); he will teach them all things and bring to their memory what Jesus taught them (14:26, 16:13); he will bear witness of Jesus (15:26); he will convict[9] the world of sin, righteousness, and judgment (16:8 [or that it has sinned in failing to believe in Jesus, that Jesus is righteous, and that judgment awaits if the world does not repent; see Brown, *John*]); and the Holy Spirit will glorify Christ (16:14). Thus the Holy Spirit is one who is "called alongside" (the literal meaning of *paracletos*) to help the people of God.

Jesus in these discourses borrows a metaphor from the prophets Isaiah and Jeremiah who compared Israel to a vineyard (Isa 27:2-6; Jer 5:10; 12:10-11). In these passages Israel the vineyard will become wasteland if it does not repent and individual Israelites will be broken off the vine if they continue in their sinful lifestyle. Jesus has the same warning (15:2, 6) but seeks to emphasize that his disciples must remain in him as a branch that receives life giving sustenance from the trunk (15:4). We need the spiritual communion with the living Christ to maintain our faithfulness. As Brown notes, this metaphor certainly sounds like a reference to the Lord's Supper. The phrase "I am the vine" is very similar to "This cup (of wine) is my blood."

One of the important themes in these discourses is the importance of love both for ones neighbor and for God. Jesus gives his disciples a "new commandment" (13:34) that they love one another. He means by this not actually that he is giving them a new commandment but rather that he is giving them a commandment for the new covenant since loving ones neighbor and God were of course already an important part of the Old Testament. Love for Christ involves keeping his commandments (14:15, 21). The commandments are to believe on him (6:29) and to love ones neighbor (15:12). Keeping these commandments will insure that the disciple remains in Christ's love (15:10).

The discourses end with the prayer of Jesus. In John there is no narrative of Jesus' prayers in the Garden of Gethsemane. Rather this prayer replaces the Gethsemane prayers of the Synoptics (see chapter 22). Brown argues that the prayer of John 17 bears certain affinities with the so called Lord's Prayer (Mt 6:9-13). First, he addresses God as "Father" in John 17:1. "Hallowed be your name" of the Lord's Prayer is similar to John 17:1 where Jesus wants to glorify God. "Your will be done on earth" is like John 17:4 where Jesus wishes to complete the work that the Father has given him. "Deliver us from the evil one" is almost verbatim in John 17:15. Thus this is a typical prayer of Jesus.

The prayer is mostly about Jesus' disciples both those living at that time and those to come later. He prays that God will keep them in his name and protect them from Satan. They will suffer persecution but he prays that they will be guarded from unfaithfulness. He prays for all future disciples, that they might have the kind of unity that he enjoys with the Father, unity of mission and love. Our unity as Christians comes from our commonality of union with Jesus Christ. If I am united with Christ, I am also spiritually one with all others that are united with Christ.

Thus Jesus closed his discourses in the Upper Room and on the way to Gethsemane. Some of his most important teachings occurred in that setting. How these events and sayings must have been etched on the minds of his disciples. They were his last words to them before his death.

Notes

1. Has his tomb been discovered? See Z. Greenhut, "Burial Cave of the Caiaphas Family" *BAR* 18/5 (1992) 28-36.

2. The anointing story given in Luke 7:36-50 is undoubtedly an entirely different event. The details are too dissimilar and the context is different. Nor should one assume, as has often been done, that the sinful woman in the story in Luke is Mary Magdalene. The woman is unnamed in this story and there is never any reference to Mary Magdalene as a former harlot or adulteress. In addition, of course, the Mary (of Bethany) mentioned in John's Gospel as the one that anointed Jesus was not the same as Mary Magdalene for Magdala (Mary Magdalene's home town) was in Galilee but Bethany was in Judea just outside of Jerusalem. Thus these two cannot be the same person either.

3. The name occurs in the Gospels as *Iscarioth, Iscariotes, Skarioth* (Codex Bezae), *Skariotes* (Codex Bezae), *apo Karyotou* (both Codex Bezae and Codex Sinaiticus). See Brown, *Messiah*; and BAGD. The last title is an attempted translation of the possible Semitic phrase: *ish kerioth* "man from Kerioth".

4. Brown lists several more possibilities for the word Iscariot but considers them "minor explanations". *Death* II, 1413-16.

5. See G. Vermes, *The Dead Sea Scrolls* (pp. 175-77); J. C. Vanderkam, *The Dead Sea Scrolls Today* (pp. 61-62).

6. For a different (and unconvincing) suggestion see Lane.

7. Because Codex Bezae (ms D) omits Lk 22:19b-20, some commentators, e.g. Gilmour, argue that this is an interpolation. But the overwhelming number of manuscripts have these verses. Thus Creed and Fitzmyer rightly argue to retain them.

8. See D.A. Fiensy, *The Social History of Palestine in the Herodian Period.* Several Jewish texts describe different parts of heaven or different resting places of the dead (e.g. 1 Enoch 39:4; 41:2; 45:3; 4 Ezra 8:80, 101) but these texts express a much different idea than that of Jesus.

9. Does the Holy Spirit convict the world only in the minds of the believers (Brown) or does he convict unbelievers and turn them to Christ as well as strengthen believers (Westcott)? It is more likely the latter.

Chapter 22

The Arrest and Trial of Jesus (Aland 330-340)

Bibliography: D.W. Amram, "Blasphemy" *Jewish Encyclopedia*; H. Andersen, *The Gospel According to Mark*; C.K. Barrett, *The Gospel of John*; O. Betz, "Jesus and the Temple Scroll" in J.H. Charlesworth, ed., *Jesus and the Dead Sea Scrolls*; H.W. Beyer, "*blasphemeo*" in *TDNT*; J. Blinzler, *The Trial of Jesus*; R. Brown, *The Death of the Messiah*; idem., *The Gospel According to John*; R. Bultmann, *The Gospel of John*; idem., *History of the Synoptic Tradition*; H. Cohn, *The Trial and Death of Jesus*; J.M. Creed, *The Gospel of Luke*; S.J. De Vries, "Blasphemy" in *IDB*; M. Dibelius, *From Tradition to Gospel*; J. Fitzmyer, "Abba and Jesus' Relation to God" in *A cause de l'evangile*; idem., *The Gospel According to Luke*; S.M. Gilmour, "The Gospel of Luke" in *Interpreter's Bible Commentary*; J. Jeremias, *The Central Message of the New Testament*; idem., *The Eucharistic Words of Jesus*; W. Lane, *The Gospel According to Mark*; S. Langdon, "The Release of the Prisoner at the Passover" *Expository Times* 29 (1918) 328-330; J.W. McGarvey, *Commentary on Acts*; J.S. McLaren, *Power and Politics in Palestine*; H. McNeile, *The Gospel of Matthew*; A. Saldarini, "Sanhedrin" in *ABD*; E. Schweizer, *The Good News According to Mark;* idem., *The Good News According to Matthew*; G.S. Sloyan, "Recent Literature on the Trial Narratives of the Four Gospels" in T.J. Ryan, ed., *Critical History and Biblical Faith*; V. Taylor, *The Gospel According to Mark*; V. Tcherikover, "Was Jerusalem a 'Polis'?" *Israel Exploration Journal* 14 (1964) 61-78; P. Winter, *On the Trial of Jesus.*

Arguments for a Pre-Gospels Passion Narrative

Several scholars have posited that a coherent narrative of Jesus' death existed, probably in written form, before the first Gospel was penned. J. Jeremias noticed that the nature of the Gospels of John and Mark change with the retelling of the final week of Jesus' life. The Gospel of John seldom narrates the same material as the Synoptics but from the Triumphal Entry on there is much more agreement in content. Further, Mark's Gospel until the Entry consists of separate blocks of material or pericopes that could for the most part be given in any sequence. But from here on his story flows as a coherent narrative. Thus Jeremias posited that there was an earlier Passion Narrative beginning at Jesus' arrest (since there is even closer agreement between John and the Synoptics from the arrest on) and a later and longer Passion Narrative beginning at the Triumphal Entry.

V. Taylor suggested that there were two layers or strata to the Passion Narrative: an original non-Semitic stratum which was a unified narrative and a later Semitic stratum which consisted of vivid, self-contained episodes. The latter were inserted into the former, wrote Taylor. The non-Semitic stratum consisted, according to Taylor, of the narratives of the plot to kill Jesus, Judas' offer to betray Jesus, Jesus' prediction that the disciples would deny him, his arrest, his trial before the Sanhedrin, his trial before Pilate, his crucifixion, his burial and the story of the empty tomb. The Semitic episodes--which exhibit grammatical signs of being translated from Hebrew or Aramaic--were the narratives of Jesus' being anointed by Mary, the Passover preparation, the Lord's Supper, the agony in Gethsemane, Peter's denial and the mockery of Jesus.

It is also clear that Luke has followed a separate tradition for his Passion Narrative. Thus we seem to have at least three very similar versions of the ancient Passion Narrative: one followed by Matthew/Mark; one followed by Luke; and one followed by John. Thus the history of the pre-Gospels' Passion Narrative can be diagramed as follows:

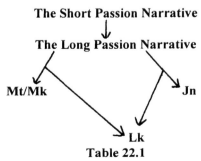

The Short Passion Narrative

The Long Passion Narrative

Mt/Mk   **Jn**

Lk

Table 22.1

The Pre-Gospels Passion Narrative

R. Bultmann, M. Dibelius, and others also accepted that such a narrative existed long before the Gospels were penned. R. Brown has most recently accepted this view though he notes that not as many follow it today as in the past. If, however, this suggestion is correct--and the evidence given by Jeremias and Tayor seems compelling--then we may be even more confident of the events narrated in the Passion Narrative. It was put together at a very early stage under the influence of eye-witnesses.

The Arrest
(Aland 330-331)

After Jesus' farewell discourse to his disiciples and the prayer that followed (Jn 14-17), he led them out to an olive garden called Gethsemane (Aramaic for "oil press"). This garden lay just east of the walls of Jerusalem and at the foot of the Mt. of Olives (see map in chapter 17). Luke indicates that Jesus and his disciples had often gone there (Lk 22:39). This was a familiar place of refuge and prayer for Jesus and his disciples when they were in Jerusalem.

The Synoptic Gospels next report Jesus' struggle in prayer concerning his coming death. The Gospel of John omits this struggle. In addition to the three Synoptics, we have a text in the Epistle to the Hebrews that probably refers to this event:

> (Jesus) in the days of his flesh offered up prayers and supplications with strong cries and tears to the one who had the power to save him from death. He was heard because of his piety. Although he was a son, he learned obedience through that which he suffered. Having become perfected, he became the cause of salvation to all who are obedient to him. (Heb 5:7-9)

The passage from Hebrews seems to describe Jesus' spiritual agony in the Garden of Gethsemane and thus confirms the accuracy of the Synoptic accounts and gives another theological perspective. Jesus had to learn obedience experientially in order to be the savior who also demands our obedience. Thus his suffering in part was to show us how to obey.

Jesus entered the garden with his disciples and told them to sit while he prayed. He took with him as he walked off a little distance Peter, James and John. These three seem to have been his special disciples (cf. Mt 17:1; Lk 8:41). Jesus apparently needed the support of his closest friends. Mark informs us (14:36) that as Jesus prayed he used the Aramaic familiar name for father, *Abba.*[1] He was addressing his loving father in his hour of terrible need. Luke relates that an angel appeared in order to strengthen him (22:43). He began to pray, asking God to let the "cup" pass (i.e. the cup of suffering[2]) if it is possible. "Yet", he prayed, "not as I will but as you will." (Mt 26:39). Jesus wanted to avoid the suffering if possible, but he wanted even more for God's will to be done.

The emphasis of this narrative is on the intense emotional agony that Jesus experienced. Unlike the Greek philosopher Socrates who went to his death by drinking poison without tears and without any plea to save his life, in cool resolve, Jesus is found in soul wrenching distress over his coming death. In Matthew's Gospel it says, "And he began to be upset and in deep anxiety. Then he said to them, 'I am intensely grieved, almost to the point of death' (26:38)". In the Gospel of Luke we read, "And since he was in such agony, he prayed more fervently. And his perspiration became like blood drops flowing down on the ground" (22:44).[3] The Epistle to the Hebrews, quoted above spoke of Jesus' strong crying and tears. Thus Jesus was under enormous emotional stress and felt as if the stress itself would kill him. His torture began even before he was arrested. One is inclined to think that this was not the only time Jesus agonized over his coming death. How many sleepless nights had he spent during his three years' ministry troubled about what was to come?

Why was Jesus in such horrendous distress? He knew he was about to be executed by crucifixion. The pain, the torture, the agonizing delay in death were enough to unnerve anyone. Jesus certainly did not crave suffering; but he wanted to do God's will. As Oswald Chambers has written devotionally:

> Choosing to suffer means that there must be something wrong with you, but choosing God's will--even if it means you will suffer--is something very different. No normal, healthy saint ever chooses suffering; he simply chooses God's will, just as Jesus did, whether it means suffering or not. (*My Utmost for His Highest*)

Second, Jesus suffered not just physically but because of the terrible burden of bearing the sins of the world. His cry of anguish on the cross (see chapter 23) was not just from pain but also from separation from God, the most horrible state imaginable. To have that experience before him was distressful in the extreme.

To Jesus' physical suffering and spiritual separation from God as the sacrifice for sin was the added burden of being rejected by his own people. As the Gospel of John says, "He came into his own creation and his own people did not receive him" (Jn 1:11). He had come to offer salvation but many of his own people would plot and carry through his death.

Finally, Jesus suffered from the intense temptation of the moment. Surely Satan did not tempt him only immediately after his baptism to gain the world by sinful means (see chapter 7). Now the temptation must have been excruciating to avoid the cross and become an earthly, military Messiah.

Jesus returned to his close friends only to find them asleep. The support he had needed and wanted from them was not to be there. He urged them to stay awake and pray with him and to pray that they too could overcome temptation, but they were perhaps weary from the emotion of the hour. Jesus went off again by himself to pray. The second prayer quotes Jesus' model prayer of Matthew 6:10 (cf. Mt 26:42): "May your will be done." Again Jesus returned to find his disciples asleep and urged them to remain awake. He separated from them a third time to pray the same prayer: He wants to avoid the cross but he wants more to do the will of God.

Why does the Gospel of John represent this event in a different fashion? Commentators have noted that in John 12:27 and 18:11 Jesus seems to be referring to the agony in the Garden of Gethsemane because he says there that he will certainly drink the cup that the Father has given him and that he will not ask to be saved from this hour. Bultmann maintained that John knew about the Gethsemane story but did not want to tell it because he wanted to present Jesus as already glorified and not as human. Barrett affirms that John intentionally omitted the Gethsemane narrative because he did not want to represent Jesus as doubtful about going to the cross. But this is not a very nuanced view of Jesus' personality. Surely anyone could have ambivalent feelings about something as horrible as Jesus would have to endure. He would at one moment express strong resolve but at others question whether it was really God's will that he do it. The statements in John's Gospel do not indicate anything more than that Jesus wrestled with his destiny. But this we already knew.

The real question is why did John leave out entirely any reference to the Garden of Gelthsemane agony? Jesus' last prayer in John is in John 17 (see Chapter 21 of this volume). Here he struggles not with his destiny but with the destiny of his disciples. He prays that they may be protected from disunity and apostasy. Thus the Gospel of John also represents Jesus as struggling in prayer just before his arrest although the content of the struggle is different. Yet both topics--concern for his disciples' welfare after he is gone and concern about his own death--would seem historically appropriate. John's goal often in his Gospel is to supplement the Synoptics (see Chapter 13). He wants here to present Jesus' struggle of worry over his disciples even as the Synoptics have already presented Jesus agony over his coming crucifixion. Both were sources of terrible distress.

Jesus returns the third time from his prayer struggle but now he seems to be at peace about the answer God has given him. He says, "It is enough" (Mk 14:41). Now he is ready. He has received angelic help; he has received an answer from his heavenly father; he is strengthened. At this point Judas arrives with the Temple police and Roman soldiers to arrest Jesus.

As we concluded in Chapter 21, Judas' task was probably to indicate where Jesus could be arrested with a fair degree of privacy (in order to avoid a riot) and also actually to identify Jesus to the soldiers and Temple police. Thus he led the arresting band to Gethsemane, a place Jesus and his disciples were accustomed to go, and there pointed him out to the arresters by a kiss.

The Synoptics say that Judas had a crowd or mob from the chief priests, scribes and elders (i.e. from the Sanhedrin) with him. John uses the word *speira* or cohort which is literally 600 soldiers and could even refer to Roman soldiers. These, says John, were accompanied by some assistants to the chief priests and Pharisees. Thus all four Gospels agree that the Sanhedrin sent men to arrest Jesus (probably the Temple police) but John adds mention of soldiers, quite a large number of soldiers, and these soldiers could be Roman (18:3). The number of a cohort could vary somewhat, however, and perhaps John uses the Greek term *speira* rather loosely. So we may not necessarily need to conclude that so large a force arrested Jesus although that would have precluded any attempt on the part of loyal crowds to release him forcibly. That Romans may have participated in the arrest leads to intriguing questions. Did Pilate cooperate with the chief priests in plotting Jesus' death? Was Pilate's later attempt to have Jesus freed merely an act, mere dissembling?

The arresting band arrived and Jesus went forward to meet them. When they told that they were seeking Jesus, he responded *ego eimi*, "I am (he)". At that point the crowd fell back, evidently because Jesus in epiphany revealed his glory to them (Jn 18:6). Judas kissed Jesus and then the crowd laid hold of him.

A ruckus ensued with at least one of Jesus' disciples, Peter, drawing a sword and striking Malchus, the High Priest's servant and slicing off his ear. Jesus ordered his disciples to desist from violent actions: "All who take the sword will die by the sword. Do you not suppose that I could not beseech my father and he would assign to me more than twelve legions of angels?" (Mt 26:52-53). Jesus modeled his teaching in the Sermon on the Mount in his non-violent arrest (cf. Mt 5:38-42).

Only the Gospel of Luke informs us that Jesus healed the assaulted servant's ear (22:51). In general Luke emphasizes Jesus' compassion in the Passion Narrative (cf. 23:34).

When Jesus stopped the fighting, his disciples ran. One unusual story, narrated by Mark, is about a young man who happened to be present with nothing on but a linen cloth wrapped around him. The arresting crowd tried to seize him but he too ran away leaving the cloth behind (Mk 14:50-51). Evidently, as Dibelius maintained, this was an eyewitness--some have suggested it was Mark himself--who happened to be present for the arrest but whose identify is now unknown to us. Either the young man was Mark, and so he left out his name out of modesty, or Mark did not know the young man's name when he wrote his Gospel.

The Jewish Trial
(Aland 332-335)

The four Gospels give seemingly varying accounts of the trial before the Sanhedrin. (For the function and character of the Sanhedrin, see chapter 2.) Both Matthew and Mark report two meetings of the Sanhedrin (one at night and another one in the morning) followed by one trial before Pontius Pilate. Luke narrates one morning meeting of the Sanhedrin followed by a trial before Pilate and a trial before Herod Antipas. Luke is the only canonical Gospel to report the hearing with Antipas.[4]

John records a hearing before the former High Priest, Annas, one before the current High Priest, Caiaphas, followed by the trial under Pilate's command.

Obviously there were several sessions during the night and the following day. The motives of the participants are not entirely clear but the sequence of events was probably as follows:

1. Jesus was first interviewed by Annas, the father-in-law of Caiaphas.

2. Next Jesus was tried and condemned during a night session of a hastily gathered portion of the Sanhedrin.

3. The Sanhedrin consulted the next morning about the strategy for delivering Jesus to Pilate then sent him on to the procurator.

4. Pilate interrogated Jesus and wanted to execute him but wished, perhaps in order to avoid trouble, to have a Jewish authority condemn and sentence Jesus.

5. He therefore sent him to Antipas. Antipas, however, wanted nothing to do with Jesus' execution for some unknown reason and sent him back to Pilate.

6. Pilate received Jesus back and feigned helpless consent with the wishes of the Jewish populace, even washing his hands in public to symbolize his innocence in Jesus' death.

Was the session with Caiaphas an actual, legal trial? Much ink has been spilled over this question. If we rely on the Mishnah as our authority of Jewish law for this period, there are questions. The main passage of relevance is m. Sanhedrin 4:1[5] which delineates the rules for cases in which one could be executed.

The illegalities of the trial of Jesus are obvious if indeed these regulations were in force at the time of Jesus. Blinzler cites some scholars who maintain that no less than 27 laws were broken by the Sanhedrin in condemning Jesus. That allegation is probably, however, an exaggeration. In the main three regulations were broken. First, the Gospels indicate that only witnesses against Jesus were interviewed, but the Mishnah states that there must also be witness for the defendant and that these witnesses must begin the hearings. Second, his trial was at night but a capital case was not to be tried at night. Third, they reached a verdict on the same day as his trial but a capital case required a day to deliberate if the verdict were to be guilty.

Would the Sanhedrin have acted so illegally? Various answers have been given:

1. Some (e.g. Gilmour) suggest that the trial narratives in the Gospels are inaccurate. Thus the Sanhedrin did not do what the Gospels claim it did.

2. Others (see the survey in Blinzler, p. 138) maintain that in fact the Sanhedrin did act illegally from beginning to the end of the trial.

3. Older Jewish scholars (e.g. A. Buechler) said there were two Sanhedrins: a religious and a political one. The regulations in the Mishnah were for the religious body; Jesus was condemned by the political Sanhedrin.

4. Some maintain (e.g. F.E. Meyer cited in Brown, *Death*; cf. Cohn) that there was never a real trial before the Sanhedrin but only an informal investigation or inquiry. Thus they did not have to adhere to the regulations.

5. Finally, others maintain (Blinzler, Winter, Brown) that the Mishnaic regulations were not in force in Jesus' day. Thus we cannot say that the Sanhedrin acted illegally.

Most scholars today would accept the last position. The evidence indicates that these regulations in the Mishnah were Pharisaic and from second century AD. But the Sanhedrin was probably under the control of the Sadducees. Further, studies by Tcherikover and McClaren show that the Sanhedrin was an evolving body with changing membership and procedures (cf. Saldarini) and functioned in an *ad hoc* manner. Thus the passage from the Mishnah that puzzles so many historians does not really come into play. Some of these regulations may have been followed generally, but were not necessarily binding.

But it is also possible that this was not an official trial but only an interrogation or inquiry in order to fix charges and hand Jesus over to Pilate. That a Roman procurator would consent to the wishes of the Jewish authorities can be seen in the case of Jesus son of Ananias who under the procurator Albinus kept pronouncing woes on the Temple until the leaders delivered him over to the procurator for flogging (see below).

According to the Mishnah (m. Sanhedrin 4:3-4), which again may be unreliable for our period of concern, the Sanhedrin sat in a semicircle. Two scribes sat in front of them taking notes. Further in front of the judges sat facing them three rows of disciples of the sages to observe. Witnesses would be brought in to be examined separately. We may assume that Jesus' trial went something like this in light of no conflicting evidence. Thus Jesus probably stood somewhere between the semicircle of judges and the three rows of disciples of the sages. The full Sanhedrin would have consisted of 71 jurists but often only 23 judges heard capital cases (m. Sanhedrin 1:6). Since this may not have been an actual trial, we may suppose that even fewer were present. Finally, the location of the trial/interrogation was at Caiaphas' house that night, although it is possible that the morning session took place in the hall of hewn stone next to the temple (m. Middoth 5:4; cf. *War* 5.144, 6.354).

At first the accusing witnesses contradicted one another and thus were useless in supporting the plan of the Sanhedrin to condemn Jesus. Finally, two were found that agreed that Jesus claimed he would or could destroy the Temple and rebuild it in three days (Mt 26:61/Mk 14:58; cf. Jn 2:19 and Gospel of Thomas 71). Such a charge was not trivial. Jeremiah was severely dealt with for prophesying the destruction of the Temple and city (Jer 26:1-19). Furthermore, years after Jesus' days on earth another man named Jesus, Jesus ben Ananias, went about predicting the destruction of the Temple and was beaten within an inch of his life by the authorities (*War* 6.300-309).

Jesus had answered nothing to any of the witnesses. He stood silent like a lamb led to the slaughter (Isaiah 53:7). Yet the High Priest seems to have had little interest in any of the charges, even the one about the Temple. He finally made his own allegation.

"Are you the Messiah, the son of God?" asked Caiaphas (Mt 26:63). This was the High Priest's real concern. Was Jesus claiming to be the Messiah? Jesus seems to answer yes in Matthew and Luke but in a rather vague way. Mark indicates clearly that Jesus said in effect, "I am." to Caiaphas' question. When Caiaphas heard Jesus' answer, he tore his garments (as the Mishnah prescribes, m. Sanhedrin 7:5) and shouted, "Blasphemy!" Why was this blasphemy and why was Jesus condemned to death by the Sanhedrin?

Leviticus 24:10-16 is the main biblical text describing blasphemy (Heb. *nqb*). But there are numerous references to cursing God or his people in the Old Testament and later Jewish literature.[6] The Mishnah as was its inclination[7] narrowly delineated what the blasphemy of Leviticus 24 meant. It comes to mean in the Mishnah only pronouncing the name

"Yahweh" or using some circumlocution for Yahweh (the Blessed One, Heaven, or the like) in a degrading or disrespectful way. But during the time of Jesus blasphemy was not so neatly defined. It is a rather vague concept but involves denigrating or cursing God, his agent, or his people (1 Kings 21:10). Regarding the last category the Temple Scroll, commenting on Deuteronomy 21:23 says:

> If a man slanders his people and delivers his people to a foreign nation and does evil to his people, you shall hang him on a tree and he shall die. (11QT 64; trans. in Vermes).

Thus O. Betz argues that Jesus was condemned for blasphemy because he claimed, falsely in the eyes of the Sanhedrin, to be the Son of God[8] and the Messiah. God would surely protect his Messiah (see 1 Samuel 7:12-15) but here stood Jesus in mortal danger. This to the Sadducean Sanhedrin was making a mockery of God. W. Lane's assessment of the charge of blasphemy is similar. Since Jesus stands there a broken prisoner, it is blasphemous for him to claim to be the Messiah in the eyes of Caiaphas and others expecting a worldly kingdom.. (Recall that many Jewish leaders embraced Bar Kosiba [see Chapter 1] the would-be military Messiah in AD 132.) Of course Caiaphas and others had already predetermined the verdict but this verdict had seemed to them obvious for some time. There was no question for them; Jesus must be executed.

Thus Jesus was judged guilty of death. The Mishnah prescribes four kinds of execution (burning, beheading, stoning, and strangling; m. Sanhedrin 7:1) but if the Temple Scroll reflects Sadducean thought, he was sentenced to death by crucifixion or "hanging" on a tree. He was sent to Pilate to carry out the sentence since the Jewish court no longer had the *ius gladii* or the right of enforcing the death penalty (Josephus, *War* 2.117; *Antiquities* 18:2; John 18:31).

While Jesus was being tried, Peter and one other disciple were out in the courtyard of the High Priest waiting and hoping to get some news. It is during this time that Peter denies Jesus three times as Jesus had predicted he would do. Matthew and Mark have him denying Jesus at the end of the trial; Luke narrates the denial before the trial; John has one denial then the interrogation before Annas followed by two more denials and finally the trial before Caiaphas. Probably the denials were taking place simultaneously with the trials/interrogations. While Jesus is

298 The Arrest and Trial of Jesus

confessing his mission and identity in grave peril, Peter is lying and cursing to save his neck. Thus John's narration is literarily more skillful. When Peter hears the rooster crow, he remembers Jesus prediction and he leaves in bitter tears (Mt 26:75 and par.)

Another disciple that failed Jesus, Judas Iscariot, did not handle his sin well. Rather than repent and change his behavior, he returned the betrayal money to the chief priests and committed suicide by hanging himself (Mt 27:3-10). The chief priests took the money, "blood money", and purchased a burial ground for strangers, fulfilling a prophecy from Jeremiah (32:6-15, 18:2-3; cf. Zechariah 11:12-13). This event was, of course, as Schweizer correctly maintains, after Jesus' trial and execution. Matthew places the event here for theological reasons: Jesus has just been condemned by the Sanhedrin and marked for execution but his betrayer realizes that Jesus is innocent and that he himself is condemned for betraying him.

Actually there are three accounts of Judas' death. In addition to the one in Matthew's Gospel, there is one in Acts 1:18-19 in which it says that Judas purchased a field with his bribe money and fell headlong into it bursting open. A third account is attributed to Papias, the early second century Christian writer that claimed to have known those that were close to the apostles.[9] Papias described an illness in which Judas swelled up in loathsome fashion and eventually succumbed.

The classic harmonization of Matthew and Acts on the death of Judas is that Judas hanged himself and after decomposing for some days--no one would touch the body of the betrayer--fell from his rope and burst open (see McGarvey). It is even possible that the version told by Papias developed out of this harmonization: A body hanging for several days in the heat of Palestine would swell. It is also possible that his suicide came after an illness developed. At any rate, all three sources indicate that Judas died soon after Jesus' crucifixion. Though we do not know exactly how soon this happened, it must have happened sometime between Jesus' death and ascension for Peter talks about it in Acts 1.

The Roman Trial
(Aland 336-340)

Pilate now presided over the trial of Jesus. We narrated briefly three incidents in Pilate's administration of Judea that are in Josephus.[10] These incidents show that Pilate sometimes had difficulties understanding and dealing with Jewish sensitivities. He had threatened both the peace of the region and his own career already by this time with the riots in Jerusalem over the standards with images on them (breaking the second commandment, Ex 20:4) and over the appropriation of Temple funds to build an aqueduct. Thus by the time Jesus' case comes to him he is uncertain of his standing among the Jewish leaders and probably determined to do something to gain their favor.

The third incident--that of the slaughter of Samaritans and the execution of their leader who had promised to show his followers the sacred vessels--also demonstrates Pilate's fear of leaders of mass movements. Thus Pilate would have received Jesus with an existing sense of concern since he had surely heard something about him. Perhaps he had even heard of the demonstration at Jesus' triumphal entry into Jerusalem a few days before this. If we are to understand the words of the Gospel of John (see above) as saying that a cohort of Roman soldiers participated in the arrest of Jesus, then he was involved in the plot to execute Jesus.

Did Pilate conduct his own separate investigation and trial or did he merely confirm the Sanhedrin's decision? That is not clear. At a regular trial there would have been attendants and minor legal experts but we read about none of these at Jesus' trial. But Brown (*Death*) points out that the trial of a non-Roman citizen could be conducted in a much more informal way.

All four Gospels have Pilate asking Jesus if he is the king of the Jews (Mt 27:11 and par. ; Jn 18:33). Anyone claiming to be king would breech the *Lex Julia maiestatis* (Julian law of majesty) which was established by Julius Caesar and confirmed by Augustus. The offense (*crimen laesae maiestatis*) was injuring the majesty of the emperor by claiming to be king instead of him (see Cohn). The laws preserved in the *Digest* of Justinian some centuries after Jesus (but believed to contain ancient laws) read that those who are authors of sedition and upheaval in the empire are liable to crucifixion (*Digest* 48.8.3-4).

The Gospels picture Pilate as wanting to release Jesus but being constrained by the crowd to crucify him. As Brown points out, there is nothing implausible about such a story. We can see from the historical situation that Pilate was in that he must have felt it necessary to placate the Jewish mob and especially the leaders.

But it is also possible that Pilate was not really so keenly interested in releasing Jesus as he pretended. Luke's Gospel points out that Pilate said three times ,"I find no crime in this man." But is that really a sincere attempt to release an innocent man? Would Pilate have worried that much about the life of a Galilean carpenter? Given Rome's usual paranoia concerning leaders of movements in the provinces--and we have seen Pilate was typical in this regard as the Samaritan incident proves--it would have been unusual if Pilate had really wanted to release Jesus. More likely is it that he only feigns disinterest in him in order to allow the crowds to make the decision. That way he can avoid incurring their displeasure later.

The decision by the voice of the crowd (*acclamatio populi*) was done from time to time but especially in the east as Brown points out. Herod the Great acceded to the wishes of the crowd on a couple of occasions (*Antiquities* 16.393-94; 17.157-64) and at the trial of Polycarp in Smyrna in Asia Minor the wish of the crowd was followed (Martyrdom of Polycarp 11-12). Thus when the leaders of the Jews stirred up the crowd to demand that Jesus be crucified and Barabbas be released, Pilate gave in to their wishes.

While Pilate is dallying with the crowd and interrogating Jesus, his wife sent word that she had had a dream about Jesus in the night and that he should have nothing to do with Jesus' execution. This is a favorite feature of Matthew's Gospel. In the birth narratives other pagans, the wise men, have dreams about Jesus and are told not report to Herod the Great. God's revealing his will to pagans in dreams is also typical of the Old Testament: Pharoah (Genesis 41:1-8); Nebuchadnezzar (Daniel 2, 4).

Pilate at some point in the proceedings seeks to divert responsibility to Antipas, the tetrarch of Galilee when he hears that Jesus is a Galilean. So he sends Jesus to Antipas for an inquiry. Antipas had long sought to meet Jesus, perhaps even to arrest him as he had John the Baptist (Lk 9:7-9; 13:31). He had heard of Jesus' miracles and wanted in a cynical way to see one. Jesus refused, however, to speak even a word to the tetrarch. After some mockery and mistreatment by his guards, Antipas sends Jesus back to Pilate.

It had become the custom to release during the Passover a prisoner to show the good will of Rome to the masses. Such actions during feasts were by no means uncommon in the ancient world. Langdon has noted that these amnesties were done in Assyria and Babylonia. The Roman historians, Livy (5.13.7-8) and Dionysius of Halicarnasus (12.9.10) refer to such actions. The Greek feasts of Thesmophoria, Panathenae, Kronia, and Dionysia (see Brown, *Death*) often were accompanied by the release of prisoners. Rulers were constantly being importuned by the masses to free prisoners (see *War* 2.28; *Antiquities* 20.215; Suetonius, *Tiberius* 47). One papyrus text (Florentine Papyrus 61) from Egypt, dating from AD 85 is relevant:

"Thou hadst been worthy of scourging. . . but I will give thee to the people." (Trans. in Deissmann, *Light from the Ancient East*, p. 269). Evidently the ruler surrendered a prisoner to the crowds.

A text from the Mishnah is especially interesting. In the tractate Pesahim 8:6 it states: "They may slaughter (a lamb) for one whom they have promised to bring out of prison. . ." (Trans. in Danby). Evidently one was allowed to slaughter a Passover lamb in the expectation that a prisoner would be set free.

All this evidence plus other texts referred to in Brown *(Death)* and Blinzler combine to convince that this practice referred to in the Gospels is quite plausible. Prisoners, even hardened criminals guilty of horrible crimes, were often released to pacify the mob, especially at festivals.

The prisoner that Pilate compared with Jesus was one Barabbas. Some of the Greek manuscripts of Matthew call him "Jesus Barabbas" as if his name were really Jesus the son of Abbas.[11] If this was Barabbas' name, then Pilate chose him purposely for the name and because he too was a leader of a mass movement. Thus the choice was Jesus Barabbas or Jesus of Nazareth. The chief priests and others, however, have incited the mob to demand Barabbas' freedom and to crucify Jesus. The sad end was that a murderer and perhaps would-be worldly ruler was liberated while the innocent one suffered in his place. Barabbas becomes the type and symbol of us all.

Jesus was condemned to be crucified. What was his charge? It was that he was the king of the Jews. This was the issue that Pilate questioned him about and this will be the accusation fastened to his cross. Thus Pilate condemned Jesus for the same crime as the Sanhedrin. They condemned him for the blasphemy of claiming to be the Messiah and Pilate for the injury to the emperor's majesty in claiming kingship.

Notes

1. Whether *abba* meant anything like "daddy" is now debated. Jeremias (*Central Message*) had maintained that it was the word for intimate, family relationship between father and child. Fitzmyer, however ("Abba") now disputes this claim. At least it shows that Jesus regarded God as a loving father, whatever the precise philological distinctions.

2. The metaphor "cup" is a semitic way of referring to the experience of strong emotion: In the Old Testament it usually refers, when used metaphorically, to the cup of God's wrath. Isaiah 51:17; Jeremiah 16:7; Ezekiel 23:33; Revelation 14:10. Jesus often used this figure of speech to describe his suffering and death: Mt 20:22, Jn 12:27.

3. Luke 22:43-44 are absent from many of the earliest and best manuscripts. They are not in papyrus 75, in the first corrected hand of Sinaiticus, in Vaticanus, or in Alexandrinus. The verses are, however, in the original hand of Sinaiticus as well as in the second corrected hand of Sinaiticus. They are also in Codex Bezae. Many want to omit the verses from Luke (see the United Bible Society Text), but other commentators (e.g. A. Harnack, B.F. Streeter, A. Loisy (see Creed), and most recently Brown, *Death.*) have argued to retain it. We will also consider it genuine.

Did Jesus sweat blood or does verse 44 only use blood in comparison, i.e.: He sweat as profusely as blood flows? Although many have envisioned the former, the language of Luke probably indicates the latter.

4. The apocryphal Gospel of Peter does refer to the trial before Antipas, even seeming to make Antipas the one that condemned Jesus to death: "And then Herod the king commanded that the Lord be taken, saying to them, What things soever I commanded you to do unto (Jesus), do." Trans. in J.A. Robinson, *ANF.*

5. "Non-capital cases may begin either with reasons for acquittal or for conviction, but capital cases must begin with reasons for acquittal. . . In non-capital cases all may argue either in favour of conviction or of acquittal; but in capital cases all may argue in favour of acquittal but not in favour of conviction. . . In non-capital cases they hold the trial during the daytime and the verdict may be reached during the night; in capital cases they hold the trial during the daytime and the verdict also must be reached during the daytime. In non-capital cases the verdict, whether of acquittal or of conviction, may be reached the same day; in capital cases a verdict of acquittal may be reached on the same day, but a verdict of conviction not until the following day. Therefore trials may not be held on the eve of a Sabbath or on the eve of a Festival day." (Trans. in Danby)

6. See 2 Kings 19:4, 6, 22; Isaiah 52:5; Ezekiel 35:12; 1 Maccabees 2:6; 2 Maccabees 8:4, 15:24; CD 5:11-12; Sifre on Numbers 15:30f; b. Pesahim 93b and the articles by Beyer, De Vries, and Amram. There are other Hebrew words for blaspheming and cursing: *gdph, n ts, shlh, qll.*

7. Cf. m. Sanhedrin 8:1-4 with Deuteronomy 21:18 and 11QT 64.

8. Caiaphas asked Jesus is he was the son of God not in the Christian sense (i.e. God of very God, the metaphysical sense) but in the Old Testament sense that the king of Israel is called a (ethical) son of God. See 2 Samuel 7:14.

9. The account is quoted by Apollinaris of Laodicea (fourth century AD) and is as follows: "Judas was a terrible, walking example of ungodliness in this world, his flesh so bloated that he was not able to pass through a place where a wagon passes easily, not even his bloated head by itself. For his eyelids, they say, were so swollen that he could not see the light at all, and his eyes could not be seen, even by a doctor using an optical instrument, so far had they sunk below the outer surface. His genitals appeared more loathsome and larger than anyone else's and when he relieved himself there passed through it pus and worms from every part of his body, much to his shame. After much agony and punishment, they say, he finally died in his own place, and because of the stench the area is deserted and uninhabitable even now; in fact, to this day no one can pass that place unless they hold their nose, so great was the discharge from his body and so far did it spread over the ground." (Trans. in J.B. Lightfoot, J.R. Harmer, M.W. Holmes, *The Apostolic Fathers*).

10. These events are recounted in *War* 2.169=*Antiquities* 18.55-59; *War* 2.175-77=*Antiquities* 18.60-62; *Antiquities* 18.85-89. Brown *(Death)* lists three other events in Pilate's rule: Lk 13:1-2, the bloodied Galilean sacrifices; Philo, *Ad Gaium* 299-305, the golden shields incident; and the minting of coins with pagan symbols that is known from archaeology (see *Israel Exploration Journal* 5[1956] 54-57 and 9 [1959] 193-95).

11. See Metzger, *Textual Commentary*. He states that many text critics accept that Barabbas was also named Jesus.

Chapter 23

The Death and Burial of Jesus (Aland 341-351)

Bibliography: H. Andersen, *The Gospel of Mark*; C.K. Barrett, *The Gospel of John*; O. Betz, "Jesus and the Temple Scroll" in J.H. Charlesworth, ed., *Jesus and the Dead Sea Scrolls*; J. Blinzler. *The Trial of Jesus*; R. Brown, *The Death of the Messiah*; idem., *The Gospel of John*; J.M. Creed, *The Gospel According to St. Luke*; R. Delbrueck, "Antiquarisches zu den Verspottungen Jesu" *Zeitschrift fuer die Neutestamentliche Wissenschaft* 41 (1942) 124-145; A. Edersheim, *Sketches of Jewish Social Life*; J. Finegan, *Archaeology of the New Testament*; J. Fitzmyer, "Crucifixion in Ancient Palestine, Qumran Literature, and the New Testament" *Catholic Biblical Quarterly* 40 (1978) 493-513; idem., *The Gospel According to Luke*; H. Fulda, *Das Kreuz und die Kreuzigung*; N. Haas, "Anthropological Observations on the Skeletal Remains From Givat ha-Mivtar" *Israel Exploration Journal* 20 (1970) 38-59; R. Hachlili, "Burial" in *ABD*; M Hengel, *Crucifixion*; D. Hill, *The Gospel of Matthew*; H.-W. Kuhn, "Der Kreuzesstrafe waehrend der fruehen Kaiserzeit" *Aufstieg und Niedergang der Roemischen Welt* II.25.1 (1982) 648-793); W. Lane, *The Gospel According to Mark*; K. Latte, "Todesstrafe" in *Pauly-Wissowa*, Supplement, Vol. 7, 1599-1619; R.M. Mackowski, *Jerusalem, City of Jesus*; W. McNeil, *The Gospel According to Matthew*; B. Malina, *The New Testament World: Insights from Cultural Anthropology*; I.H. Marshall, *The Gospel of Luke*; E. Meyers, "Tomb" in *IDB* Supplement; G. O'Collins, "Crucifixion" in *ABD*; J. Schneider, "*stauros*" in *TDNT*; E. Schweizer, *The Good News According to Mark*; idem., *The Good News According to Matthew*; W.H. Stephens, *The New*

Testament World In Pictures; J. Strange, "Crucifixion" in *IDB* Supplement; V. Taylor, *The Gospel According to St. Mark*; V. Tzaferis, "Jewish Tombs at and Near Giv'at ha-Mivtar, Jerusalem" *Israel Explorations Journal* 20 (1970) 18-32; J. Wilkinson, *Jerusalem as Jesus Knew It*; P. Winter, *The Trial of Jesus*; J. Zias and E. Sekeles, "The Crucified Man from Giv'at HaMivtar: A Reappraisal" *Israel Exploration Journal* 35 (1985) 22-27.

Crucifixion in the Ancient World

> Punished with limbs outstretched, they see the stake as their fate; they are fastened (and) nailed to it in the most bitter torment, evil food for birds of prey and grim pickings for dogs. (*Apotelesmatica* 4.198f; trans. in Hengel).

Thus is described in an ancient source the horrible punishment by crucifixion, an end described by Josephus as "the most wretched of deaths" (*War* 7.203).

Crucifixion was practiced by barbarian peoples generally in antiquity, such as in India, Assyria, and Scythia. But the Greeks also used a form of this execution as well as the Carthagenians and thus in turn the Romans.

The execution began with the pre-crucifixion torture:

> (A man) is put to the rack and mutilated and has his eyes burnt out and after himself suffering and seeing his wife and children suffer many other signal outrages of various kinds is finally crucified. . . (Plato, *Gorgias* 473bc; trans. in Hengel).

Ancient sources regularly refer to beatings, scourgings, and mutilation of the eyes and tongue (Plato, *Republic* 361e-362a; Seneca, *Epistle* 101; Lucian, *Piscator* 2). The scourging alone must have been horrible. Josephus tells that one Jesus son of Hanan was scourged until his bones were showing beneath the gashes in his flesh (*War* 6.304; cf. 2.612). In addition the victim would be compelled to carry his cross or cross beam through the city, doubtless to the taunts and rocks of the crowds on the streets (Plautus, *Carbonaria* fr. 2; Plutarch, *Moralia* 55A4; Artemidorus, *Oneirokritika* II.56). These tortures could end a person's life before he ever came to the cross, but usually some care was taken to prevent that from happening. The intention was to prolong the torture. A person could be crucified in various ways according to the sadistic delight of the tormentors. Many were nailed to the cross upside down or in other positions (Seneca the Younger, *Dial* 6; Josephus, *War* 5.449-51). The victim was crucified naked (Melito, *Passion* 96f; Artemidorus II.61; Dionysius of Halicarnassus 7.69) and the genitals were often impaled (Seneca the Younger, *Dial* 6). Often the condemned were fastened on crosses low enough that dogs and wild beasts could chew on their legs (Philo, *Ad Flaccum* 2.84-85; Ps. Manetho 4.198f; Horace, *Epistles* 1.16. 46-48).

The condemned were usually crucified beside well traveled roads: "Whenever we crucify the guilty the most crowded roads are chosen where the most people can see and be moved by this fear" (Quintilian, *Decl* 274; trans. in Hengel). Crassus the Roman triumvir and general crucified the slaves in the Sparticus rebellion (6000 in number) along the Appian Way (Appian, *B. Civ* 1.120). Jews were crucified within view of the walls of Jerusalem during the Jewish rebellion (*War* 5.449-51).

Most cruel was the practice of torturing the families of the condemned criminals. The Athenians crucified Artayctes by nailing him to a wooden plank instead of a cross and while he was thus fastened, they stoned his son in front of him (Herodotus 9.120; see also 4.202). Alexander Janneus, the Jewish High Priest and prince, crucified 800 Pharisees and had their wives and children slaughtered in front of them as they hung from the crosses (Josephus, *Antiquities* 13.380-83). Recall also the text from Plato quoted at the beginning of this section (and see also Diodorus, Siculus 18.16.3; cf. b. Aboda Zara 18a).

Finally, we should mention the shame and stigma that went with crucifixion. It was not lightly that the author of Hebrews (12:2) referred to the "shame" of the cross that Jesus endured. Ancient sources routinely refer to the cross as the "infamous stake" (see Hengel, p. 7). Cicero, the Roman orator and lawyer who lived in the first century BC, argued that one should never even mention the word cross in reference to a Roman citizen, so shameful and reproachful was it (*Perd.* 16). In crucifixion every effort was made to mock, taunt, humiliate, and shame the victim. In a society so sensitive to honor and shame (see Malina), to be so reproached was considered emotionally unbearable.

Jesus' Death
(Aland 341-349)

Pilate finally gave in to the wishes of the Jewish chief priests and the mob. Whether he had been hesitating out of concern for doing the right thing or simply as a pretense we cannot now ascertain. At any rate, to disavow any blame for this action, he ordered a basin of water to be brought and washed his hands in public. Washing the hands in such a way was a symbol of innocence among the Greeks (Herodotus 1.35; Virgil, *Aeneid* 2.719; Sophocles, *Ajax* 654). Jews also understood this action in this way because of Deuteronomy 21:6-9 (see m. Sota 9:6; S-B).

Thus Pilate, either sincerely or dissemblingly, avowed his innocence in this matter. When he did so, some of the Jews present proclaimed, "May his blood be on our heads and on the heads of our children!" (Mt 27:25). This was a common Semitic way of indicating guilt or blame for a deed, especially a deed in which someone was killed (Deut 22:8; 2 Sam 1:16; Jer 51:35; b. Avodah Zarah 12b; b. Yoma 21a; see S-B). Thus they were accepting the guilt for Jesus' death. These words, uttered by a crowd of fanatics, should not, however, be taken as a condemnation of all Jews, then or now.

Pilate had Jesus scourged, then turned him over to be executed. The whipping was done most likely by leather thongs fitted with pieces of bone or metal so that the flesh would be lacerated (Brown, *Death*). It would have been a bloody and violent sight. What is striking is how little is said of it in the Gospels. This contrasts with other depictions of sufferers such as the pious Jews, Eleazar (4 Maccabees 6:1-23), and Hanina ben Teradion (b. Aboda Zara 18a) whose tortures are described in gory detail. Every effort was made on the part of the authors of these texts to evoke pity for the sufferers.. But the Gospel writers avoid trying to arouse pity or sympathy. They prefer to emphasize the spiritual reason for Jesus' death.

Jesus was mocked by soldiers at least three times. The first time was when he stood before the High Priest (Lk 22:63). The second time was in the presence of Herod Antipas (Lk 23:11). The third time was by Pilate's Roman soldiers. Matthew and Mark have the mocking of the Roman soldiers after Pilate's sentence of death; John places the mocking before the sentence. John was apparently compressing events.

Mocking a condemned prisoner or some other figure of contempt was certainly known in antiquity (see Delbrueck). The soldiers of Vespasian mocked emperor Vitellius in AD 69 before his execution (Dio Cassius 65. 20-21). In AD 38 in Alexandria, Gentiles, to show contempt for the visiting Jewish king, Agrippa I, selected a homeless, retarded man named Carabas for mockery. They dressed him up in mock royal garments: a papyrus crown, an old rug for a robe, and a discarded stick for a scepter. Some pretended to be his body guards, others hailed him as king, still others pretended to approach him for judgments (Philo, *In Flaccum* 36 39).[1] In Persia in the first century AD a condemned prisoner was mocked for several days and given royal vestments to wear before his execution (see Schweizer, *Mark*). Further the game of mock-king was played often among Romans and Greeks alike in which someone was dressed up as a king and ridiculed, especially during a festival. Sometimes the one mocked would even be sacrificed (i.e. killed) to the gods (see Brown, *Death*). Thus Jesus' mocking was certainly not out of character with the base and depraved standards of that time.

Consequently they put a mock crown of thorns on Jesus' head, both as a joke and as a further means of torture (for the exact identification of the plant from which the crown was made see Brown, *Death*). They put on a purple robe (Mt says a scarlet robe, 27:28) and put a reed in his hands as the cruel mob did to Carabas in Alexandria. They struck him on the head with their fists, spat on him, and pretended to salute him as king.

Now Jesus was led out of the city toward his place of execution. It was part of the torture to compel the condemned to carry his own cross or cross beam (Latin: *patibulum*) through the city (see above) past jeering mobs and certainly receiving blows and stones. Jesus was evidently unable to complete this task because of weariness and loss of blood from the scourging. Therefore they compelled Simon from the city of Cyrene in north Africa to carry Jesus' cross. If this Simon is the same one mentioned in Acts 13:1, then Simon was a black man and later a great prophet in the church (see F.F. Bruce, *Acts*). Since Mark mentions the names of his sons (Mk 15:21), we might suppose that they too became important Christian leaders, perhaps in the church at Rome where Mark's Gospel was written (cf. Rom 16:13).

A group of people, especially women, following Jesus were uttering loud laments over his fate. Jesus turned to them and, quoting from Hosea 10:8, warned them rather to lament for Jerusalem. "For if they do this when the wood is wet or green, what will happen when it is dry?" (Lk 23:31). As Fitzmyer concludes, this proverbial saying probably means: If they kill me, a righteous man (=burning the green wood), what will happen to Jerusalem which rejects God's Messiah (=burning the dry wood)?

The executioners, their victims, and the mob now reached Golgotha.

Golgotha is an Aramaic word meaning head or skull. The Greek and Latin equivalents are: *kranion* and *calvaria* respectively. Evidently something about the place reminded people of a skull or head. In 1885 General Gordon identified a hill with two small holes or caverns that from a distance look like a skull with two eye sockets. This he maintained is the place of Jesus' crucifixion. Since there is a first century tomb nearby, as John's Gospel indicates Jesus' tomb was (Jn 19:41), Gordon was sure he had found the site of Jesus' death.

But most modern archaeologists (see Finegan, Mackowski, and Wilkinson) place more credence in the traditional site known by the populace of Jerusalem at least from before the time of Constantine (in AD 325). According to Eusebius' *Life of Constantine* 3.25-40 there had been a tradition that Jesus was crucified and buried in the vicinity on which the Church of the Holy Sepulcher now stands. The details seem to fit better with this site than with Gordon's.[2]

The place of execution was of course outside the city walls as Hebrews 13:12 remembered and as we would have surmised anyway from Numbers 15:35 (cf. b. Sanhedrin 42b). Both of these sites would have been outside the city walls at the time of Jesus' death. Following Roman practice it would have been along a busily traveled road.

Before Jesus was actually fixed on the cross he was offered a mixture of wine and myrrh. Matthew (27:34) indicates that he was offered wine and a bitter substance which some translators render "gall". P. Billerbeck is correct, however, that this is merely Matthew's way of referring to myrrh which was a bitter tasting spice (see Midrash on Song of Songs 3:6; S-B). The practice of offering to condemned criminals this pain killing mixture or one similar to it is well attested in the rabbinic sources. Evidently because of Proverbs 31:6 Jews thought such a humanitarian gesture necessary: "Rab Chisda (died AD 309) said, 'One gave to him who went out to be executed a piece of frankincense in a glass of wine in order to take away his consciousness'" (b. Sanhedrin 43a; cf. Semahot 2; Numbers Rabbah 10. See S-B). When Jesus tasted the mixture, he refused to drink it down either because of the bitter taste or, more probably, because he did not want anything to interfere with his free choice in going to his death.

Again we are struck with how briefly the Gospel writers refer to the fact that Jesus was crucified. It must have been extremely painful and torturous to have large nails--the spike nail in the skeleton of the crucified man discovered in the tomb at Givat ha-Mivtar was 4 ½ inches long (see Tzaferis and Strange)--driven through ones wrists and ankle bones. Yet, though this was "the most bitter torment" (recall the quotation at the beginning of this chapter) the writers barely mention Jesus' actual crucifixion. This is because evoking mere emotions of sympathy for a suffering man was not enough. Jesus was no mere martyr to the Gospel writers, no mere Jobian figure. His suffering was for the sin of the world.

As Jesus was being nailed to his cross he uttered a prayer: "Father forgive them. They do not know what they are doing" (Lk 23:34).[3] Jesus, then, modeled his teaching for us about loving our enemies (Mt 5:43-44). Even in his death he prays for his torturers. This was Jesus' *first saying* (of seven sayings) from the cross.

It was evidently the custom to tack a placard on the cross somewhere to indicate what the charge was against the criminal. Carrying a placard with the charge against one was known elsewhere. The brutal emperor Caligula (Ad 38-41) made a slave accused of stealing carry around both a placard tied to his neck and his own severed hands (Suetonius, *Caligula* 32). During the persecutions of Christians one Attalus was fed to the wild beasts in the arena with a placard around his neck that read: "This is Attalus, the Christian." (Eusebius, *Ecclesiastical History* 5.1). Even in Palestine criminals on the way to execution wore a sign that detailed their crimes (m. Sanhedrin 6:1; 11:4).

Pilate ordered that the charge against Jesus be attached to his cross: "The king of the Jews." (Mk 15:26). John's Gospel adds that the charges were published in Aramaic, Greek, and Latin (19:20). Some of the quibbling chief priests demanded that Pilate not say he was the king of the Jews but that he claimed to be the king of the Jews. Pilate dismissed them, evidently weary of their demands.

Jesus' clothes were confiscated by his executioners who, not wanting to rip the garments into so many pieces, cast lots for them (Mk 15:24). Casting lots or shooting dice was a favorite sport among Roman soldiers (see "Dicing" *OCD*; Stephens, p. 292). This fulfilled an Old Testament prophecy (Psalm 22:18).

There were many people watching this gruesome and probably sickening scene from afar (Mk 15:40). Jesus' mother, however, was standing directly beside the cross (Jn 19:25) with John the son of Zebedee to support her. Mary was probably compelled to be present. The reader will recall that we pointed out above that the family of executed persons would often be compelled to be present at the cross for torment themselves. Perhaps Mary herself suffered some indignities on this occasion. Or, more likely--since none of the Gospels indicate any such thing --she was simply compelled to watch Jesus' death. One cannot imagine that she would have chosen to witness the horrible torture and humiliation of her son.   At any rate, when Jesus saw her standing there, he indicated that she was to be cared for from then on by John: "Woman behold your son" (Jn 19:26). This was the *second saying* from the cross. Now those passing by on the road joined the sadistic game of humiliation. They made insulting gestures with their heads and taunted him, daring him to come down from the cross if he really be the son of God (Mt 27:39-40). If he can destroy the temple and rebuild it, he should be able to come down; if he could save other people, he should be able to save himself; God could save him if he wanted to. These people behaved like the wicked ones described in the intertestamental book, the Wisdom of Solomon (2:10-20) who taunt and revile the righteous man and dare God to save him. More importantly, their words echo the words of Satan during Jesus' time of intense temptation (Mt. 4:1-11): "If you are the Son of God". Then Satan tried to coax Jesus into achieving his messianic mission by using worldly means. Thus Satan comes back to tempt him one last time in the words of these mockers.

Now the two criminals, the robbers, who were crucified alongside Jesus speak. They would have been among the bandits spoken of so often by Josephus. They were hardened criminals who had preyed on rich and poor alike, living in gangs and attacking people as they traveled, perhaps sometimes raiding villages.[4] One of them began to revile Jesus, either out of pure meanness or because of his desperation. But the other robber rebuked the first one and asked Jesus to remember him when he comes into his kingdom rule. In other words, the second bandit indicated that he had faith in Jesus' messianic claims. Jesus promised: "Today you will be with me in paradise" (Lk 23:43). This was Jesus' *third saying* from the cross. The Greek word paradise was a Persian loanword. It meant in Persian, a zoological or botanical park. In the intertestamental period, Jewish texts use the word to refer to the place of the righteous dead. That is, they exist in a blessed and beautiful place like a park or like the Garden of Eden (1 Enoch 32:3; Testament of Levi 18:10; *Antiquities* 1.37). Thus the robber was saved by his faith.

At the sixth hour, or at about noon, the land about Jerusalem was covered with darkness. This darkness cannot have been from an eclipse since eclipses cannot happen during a time of full moon (which characterizes the Passover). It might have been caused by some severe storm from the desert but these storms are not frequent in the hill country. The darkness was rather a supernatural event. The significance of the darkness would have been understood by Jews and pagans alike: It was

God's judgment on the world. The prophet Amos spoke of God's darkening the sun at noon in his judgment (8:9). Joel (2:2) also wrote of the day of the Lord, his day of judgment, as a day of darkness (cf. b. Sukkah 29a; Philo, *de Providentia* 2.50). Pagans also seem to have regarded darkness as a sign of judgment.[5]

Now Jesus uttered his *fourth saying* from the cross: "My God, my God, why have you forsaken me?" (Mt 27:46). What did he mean? Was this merely a cry of physical anguish. Blinzer notes, surely correctly, that crucifixion often was accompanied with gruesome screams: ". . . the screams of rage and pain, the wild curses and the outbreaks of nameless despair." Yet Jesus' shout was not exactly like that. He did not rage at his executioners but rather prayed for their forgiveness. His outcry is one of great agony, but it is both physical and spiritual agony. Lane has best described the horror for Jesus:

(Jesus' outcry) must be understood in the perspective of the holy wrath of God and the character of sin which cuts the sinner off from God. . . Jesus offered himself to bear the judgment of God upon human rebellion. . . Now on the cross he who had lived wholly for the Father experienced the full alienation from God which the judgment he had assumed entailed. His cry expresses the profound horror of separation from God. (p. 573)

But Jesus cry is not just one of pain and anguish. Jesus quoted Psalm 22, probably not just the first line which we have given for us in the texts of Matthew and Mark, but the whole psalm. The psalm begins with lament and pain but ends affirming faith. H. Andersen therefore says of Jesus cry: It expresses both the horror of the moment and faith in the future. Jesus penetrated the abyss of all men's lostness but he believed in the God of hope.

At about the same time as his cry of horror, Jesus also uttered his *fifth saying*: "I am thirsty" (Jn 19:28). Someone thought his cry in Aramaic[6] sounded like he was calling for Elijah to save him. There are indications that some Jews thought--doubtless based on Malachi 3:23--Elijah would deliver them from the Romans (b. Avodah Zarah 17b, 18b). Lane suggests, however, the unidentified person was only mocking Jesus here. At any rate this person dipped a sponge in some cheap peasant wine (Gk: *oxos*; Lat: *posca*) and put the sponge on a stick to lift it to Jesus mouth.

When Jesus had sipped a little of the soured wine, he uttered his *sixth saying*: "It is finished" (Jn 19:30). He meant by this that his work of vicarious suffering was about over. He felt death coming on.

Just before he died, he uttered his **seventh saying**: "Father, into your hands I commit my spirit" (Lk 23:46). This is also a quotation of a psalm, Psalm 31:6. It is an expression of profound trust in the midst of unspeakable suffering.

Then, succumbing to shock, dehydration, and blood loss, Jesus died.

At Jesus' death, several signs followed: the veil of the temple was torn, the earth shook, rocks were split, and some of the saints who had died were raised (Mt 27:51f). Matthew, Mark and Luke mention the torn curtain in the temple. This veil could be either that covering the entrance to the Holy of Holies or that at the entrance to the Holy Place. Both were elaborate works of art made of red, purple, blue and white materials with rich embroidery (Josephus, *War* 5.212f, 219). What does this signify? Various suggestions have been made: 1) The tearing of the veil showed God's displeasure toward the High Priesthood. 2) It signified the tearing down of the separation between God and man. 3) It signified the end of the temple system. 4) It prophesied the destruction of the temple. Really all of these suggestions seem contained in the rending of the temple veil but numbers 2 and 3 are probably primarily in focus.

The earthquake was also a sign of judgment (Joel 2:10). The splitting of rocks is a sign of the end (Zechariah 14:4). The opening of some tombs seems to have been a foretaste of the second coming when all the dead will rise. Thus Jesus' death, his victory over Satan and sin, was the beginning of the eschatological age, the initiation of the end-time era.

Jesus' death and his last hours on the cross had impressed the centurion in charge of his crucifixion. Upon his death, the Centurion said, "This man was righteous" (Lk 24:47). In other words the centurion could easily tell that Jesus was no criminal but a righteous man.[7] Further, the signs at his death, the darkness and the earthquake--he could not have known yet about the others--indicated to him that Jesus was no ordinary person.

Jews did not leave a criminal to hang on a cross over night (Deut 21:22-23 and 11QT 64:6-13). Thus since it was approaching nightfall and since the next day was an especially holy day, the Jews asked Pilate to hasten the deaths of the three crucified men. We know elsewhere that the victims could be killed by a hard blow to break bones (Cicero, *Phil* 13.12). While the intention was to prolong the condemned person's life in order to prolong the torture (see Josephus, *Life* 420-21; Iamblichus, *Babylonica* 2, 21; Seneca, *Epistle* 101. 10-13) certain circumstances could make this sadistic goal impossible. Interestingly, the legs of the crucified man found in the tomb of Giv'at Ha Mivtar just northeast of Jerusalem at first were said to have been broken by one or two powerful blows (see Tzaferis) but a second examination has cast some doubt on this conclusion (see Zias and Sekeles).

Thus the soldiers broke the legs of the other two victims but when they came to Jesus he appeared to be already dead. He had been tortured all night, doubtless with great loss of blood. The soldier poked and prodded Jesus with his spear to see if there was any response, piercing his side clear to the heart and out flowed blood and a clear liquid (Jn 19:34). John points out that Jesus fits the symbolism of the Passover lamb which takes away the guilt of the world (see Jn 1-29). Just as the Passover lamb was not to have any bones broken, so Jesus was spared broken bones (Exodus 12:16). The soldiers did not know it but they were entirely in the hands of God.

Jesus Burial (Aland 350-51)

Now comes forward a person heretofore unknown: Joseph of Arimathea. He was a disciple of Jesus, say all four Gospels, but had not made himself publicly known as a disciple until now (Jn 19:38). Although crucified victims were ordinarily allowed by the Romans to be eaten by wild beasts and vultures (Horace, *Epistle* 1.16.48), Jews were very sensitive about burying the dead. It was highly offensive for anyone not to be buried. Josephus writes:

> Jews are so careful about funeral rites that even malefactors who have been sentenced to crucifixion are taken down and buried before sunset. (*War* 4.317; trans. in Thackeray, LCL; cf. 11QT 64)

Thus Joseph, the wealthy, respected member of the Sanhedrin, "took courage" (Mk 15:43)--since he too could have been accused of treason-- and asked for the body of Jesus. He put him in his own family tomb, recently hewn in the very vicinity that Jesus was crucified. John adds that he was assisted in this by Nicodemus who also now out of grief and shame was willing to declare his devotion to Jesus (Jn 19:39).

The chief priests now fear further trouble with Jesus' disciples and so request a guard to be posted at Jesus' tomb. They have heard rumors that

Jesus' predicted his own death and resurrection and thus they want to guard against any fraud. In so doing, of course, they only helped to verify that Jesus was truly raised from the dead.

Notes

1. Another mockery of Jews took place after the Jewish uprising of AD 115. See the papyrus text in V.A. Tcherikover and A. Fuks, *Corpus Papyroroum Judaicarum* II, p. 89.

2. One other site for the crucifixion has been suggested by E.L. Martin (see the discussion in Brown, *Death*). Martin has posited the Mt. of Olives as the place of crucifixion. He has had almost no supporters in this view.

3. This verse is absent from an early papyrus copy of Luke, from the Vaticanus uncial (4th cent.), and from the original hand of Codex Bezae (6th cent.). Thus some are less than confident that it was originally a part of the text of Luke. For comment on this see B.M. Metzger, *A Textual Commentary on the Greek New Testament*. For a brief summary of manuscripts, see D A Fiensy, *Introduction to the New Testament*.

4. See R. Horsley and J. Hanson, *Bandits, Prophets and Messiahs* for this group.

5. See e.g. Virgil, *Georgics* 1.463f; Diogenes Laertius 4.64; Plutarch, *Pelopidas* 295a; idem., *Caesar* 69.4; idem., *Romulus* 27.6; Ovid, *Fasti* 2.493.

6. Mark's rendering of Jesus' Aramaic is more like the colloquial Aramaic of the time. Matthew's words contain a mixed Hebrew and Aramaic saying much like the rendering of Psalm 22:1 in the rabbinic Aramaic Targum. See S-B.

7. Cf. the reaction from the tormentor of Hanina ben Teradion (b. Aboda Zara 18a) who was also impressed by the death of this pious man.

Chapter 24

The Resurrection

Bibliography: R. Brown, *The Gospel According to John;* R. Bultmann, *Kerygma and Myth;* M. Connick, *Jesus the Man, the Mission, the Message;* W.L. Craig, *Assessing the Evidence for the Historicity of the Resurrection of Jesus;* C.F. Evans, *Resurrection and the New Testament;* J. Fitzmyer, *Gospel According to Luke;* R. Fuller, *The Formation of the Resurrection Narratives;* N. Geisler, *The Battle for the Resurrection;* H.-G. Geyer, "The Resurrection of Jesus Christ: A Survey of the Debate in Present Day Theology", in C.F.D. Moule, ed., *The Significance of the Message of the Resurrection for Faith in Jesus Christ;* C. Gresham, *What the Bible Says About the Resurrection;* G. Habermas and A. Flew, *Did Jesus Rise from the Dead?;* M. Harris, *From Grave to Glory;* G.E. Ladd, *I Believe in the Resurrection of Jesus;* W. Lane, *The Gospel According to Mark;* W. Marxsen, *The Resurrection of Jesus of Nazareth;* G. O'Collins, *Jesus is Risen;* T. Oden, *The Word of Life;* G. Osborn, *The Resurrection Narratives;* W. Pannenberg, "Did Jesus Really Rise from the Dead?" *Dialog* 4 (1965) 128-35; P. Perkins, *Resurrection: New Testament Witness and Contemporary Reflection;* A. Richardson, "The Resurrection of Jesus Christ" *Theology* 74 (1971) 146-54; W.C. Robinson, "The Bodily Resurrection of Christ" *Theologische Zeitschrift* 13 (1957) 81-101; V.Taylor, *The Gospel According to Mark;* D.A. Walker, "Resurrection, Empty Tomb and Easter Faith" *Expository Times* 101 (1989-90) 172-75.

The Empty Tomb (Aland 352, 354)

The disciples were devastated by Jesus' crucifixion. Of that all the

Gospels testify. They were cowering behind the closed doors of the upper room, wracked with guilt for having forsaken him, and filled now with doubt and despair. They must have had nightmares from having witnessed the horrible torture of their Lord. Yet in their grief some of the women insisted upon performing some of the conventional burial rites, even though they were a few days late.

Early in the morning, just before dawn, Mary Magdalene and some of the other women made their way to the tomb. They knew of course where the tomb was because they had followed Joseph of Arimathea and had seen the location of his garden tomb. The women were bringing spices such as is described in the Mishnah. M. Shabbath 23:5 indicates that a body would be washed and anointed with aromatic oils. This could not be done earlier due to the constraints of time, although Joseph did have at his disposal 100 pounds of myrrh and aloes to wrap in with the burial shroud.

At some point before they arrived at the tomb there was an earthquake-- perhaps only a local shaking--and the tomb was miraculously opened. Jesus' body was raised in a transformed state. Though he was still in his body and it was recognizable to his disciples, his body was now immortal. An angel of the Lord opened the tomb, rolling the stone away whereupon the guard at the tomb collapsed out of shock and amazement (Mt 28:4).

After all of this, the women arrived and saw angels at the tomb. Matthew and Mark mention only one angel and Mark describes him as "a young man" (Mk 16:5), a usual way of describing angels in Jewish literature (2 Maccabees 3:26, 33; Josephus, *Antiquities* 5.8.2). Luke and John refer to two angels (Lk 24:4; Jn 20:12). At any rate, the angels announced to the women that Jesus was no longer in the tomb because he had been raised from the dead. The women were to tell the disciples what had happened. Although they were at first dumbfounded and spoke to no one (Mk 16:8), they later ran to the upper room to inform the disciples, especially Peter.

Both Luke[1] and John note that Peter--John says Peter and the Beloved Disciple--ran to the tomb to verify that it was empty. Peter and the disciple whom Jesus loved reached the tomb and peered in at the shroud. Peter entered the tomb to inspect it and the other disciple followed. When the other disciple saw the grave clothes rolled up, he believed. What was there about the grave clothes that led him to believe that Jesus had been raised? Some affirm that the rolled up or folded up grave clothes indicated to the Beloved Disciple that Jesus' body had not been stolen since robbers would not have taken time to fold up the shroud. But more likely is the suggestion that the clothes were still in their wrapped up shape as if Jesus' body had passed through them at his resurrection. Thus the women's testimony about the empty tomb was supported by the inspection made by Peter and the Beloved Disciple.

The guards at the tomb regained their courage and presence of mind and ran to report the disappearance of Jesus' body from the tomb. The chief priests after offering a bribe, instructed them to claim that Jesus' disciples had stolen his body.

Only Matthew in the canonical Gospels records that the chief priests requested a guard from Pilate in order to guard Jesus' tomb. Likewise, only Matthew narrates the chief priests' telling the guards to fabricate a story about the empty tomb. But the apocryphal Gospel of Peter (see chapter 16), which some think might have independent traditions, does have a parallel account:

> Then (the chief priests) drew near and besought (Pilate) and entreated him to command the centurion and the soldiers to say nothing of the things which they had seen: For it is better, say they, for us to incur the greatest sin before God, and not to fall into the hands of the people of the Jews and to be stoned. Pilate therefore commanded the centurion and the soldiers to say nothing. (Trans. by J.A. Robinson in *ANF*).

Though the Gospel of Peter's account is not exactly like that in Matthew, it does corroborate that there were guards at the tomb and that the guards had to be instructed about what to say when the tomb was discovered to be empty. Matthew's report that they fabricated a story about his disciples' stealing Jesus' body was certainly, however, what actually happened. Matthew reports (Mt 28:15) that this story was in circulation at the time he wrote his Gospel. Further, Justin Martyr (c. AD 140) also noted that Jews in his day made this claim:

> You have sent chosen and ordained men throughout all the world to proclaim . . . that his disciples stole him by night from the tomb, where he was laid when unfastened from the cross. . . . (*Dialogue with Trypho* 108; trans. by A.C. Coxe in *ANF*).

Thus we can see that the Jewish tactic in Justin's day for dealing with the Christian witness about the resurrection of Christ was to send opposing teachers out to claim that Jesus' disciples had stolen his body. This is exactly what Matthew says they did from the very beginning.

Some deny that Jesus' tomb was really empty but maintain that the women went to the wrong tomb or that they never went to any tomb at all and that the narratives of the empty tomb were freely composed (i.e. fabricated) at a later time. M. Harris and W.L. Craig, however, have composed a list of arguments in support of the tomb's being empty. Among their arguments are:

1. The empty tomb narratives are told in all four canonical Gospels (and also in the apocryphal but perhaps independently attested Gospel of Peter).

2. The earliest Christians could not have continued to proclaim in Jerusalem that Jesus had been raised if the tomb had not been empty. An opponent would only have had to take people to the tomb to disprove the disciples' claim.

3. The Jews themselves admitted that the tomb was empty when they went about maintaining that the disciples had stolen Jesus body (see above). Why claim that they stole the body if the body was still in the tomb?

4. The first witnesses to the empty tomb were women, an unlikely story to have made up since women were not considered by Jewish law to be admissible witnesses (S-B 3.217, 559-60). Thus if someone were going to compose an empty tomb story years after Jesus' death, he would not have had women find the tomb empty.

The evidence certainly indicates that Jesus' tomb was empty and that the first witnesses of this fact had seen an angelic vision. Yet as the Gospels indicate, Jesus' disciples still did not believe that Jesus' had been raised even after the women told of their most surprising experience. All the accounts indicate that his disciples were overwhelmed with discouragement and doubt. They were not easily convinced that Jesus had been raised.

The Resurrection Appearances in Jerusalem (Aland 361, 353, 355, 356, 357)

The oldest written account of Jesus' appearances after his resurrection is found in Paul's letter to the Corinthians (15:3-8). This letter was written in AD 54 and thus probably earlier than any of the four Gospels. But even more important is the indication that the references to appearances go back to a very early time. The clause: "What I delivered to you" (v. 3; Gk, *paredoka*), refers specifically to transmitting teaching to students.

Paul also said that this was teaching that he had "received" (*parelabon*), that is, from the earliest Christian community in Jerusalem and Galilee. Thus the terminology Paul used indicates that these accounts came from eyewitnesses.

Paul writes in his epistle to the Galatians (1:18) that three years after his conversion (which took place probably around AD 32 or two years after Jesus' death and resurrection) he went up to Jerusalem to "get to know" (Gk: *historeo*) Peter. He also met with James the Lord's brother (Gal 1:19). Surely much of the information in 1 Corinthians 15 comes from these two Christian leaders. Thus this testimony comes from about five years after the events or AD 35.

Paul lists first Peter as an eyewitness to the risen Christ. Peter's special visitation is also referred to in Luke 24:34.

Jesus' appearance to the twelve apostles is also recorded by Luke (24:36-43) and John (20:19-23). Jesus' appearance to over 500 brothers at one time is not expressly narrated by the Gospels, but it is quite possible that, as W.L. Craig suggests, this appearance is the same as that in Matthew 28:16-20. A large crowd such as this would congregate in the open air, probably on a hill side. The most reasonable place to posit for such a large following would be in Galilee. Thus Matthew's narrative seems to fit well with Paul's reference to the 500.

Nowhere else in the New Testament is there a report that the risen Jesus appeared to James.[2] But even if we did not have this report, we would infer that the risen Christ had appeared to James since he had been an unbeliever before Jesus' resurrection appearances (Mk 3:21, 31-35; Jn 7:1-10). Yet shortly after Jesus' ascension James and the other brothers of Jesus are found in the upper room along with the other believers awaiting the Holy Spirit (Acts 1:14).

Jesus' appearance to "all the apostles" (which seems to be a different group from the twelve) is also not explicitly narrated in the Gospels. These "apostles" or "ones sent out" (as missionaries) could refer to the seventy (Lk 10:1) or the 120 of Acts 1:15.

Finally, Paul writes, the risen Christ appeared to him. Paul says he is like someone "abnormally born". This is an unusual way for Paul to refer to himself and, therefore, many commentators have concluded that he is quoting what his opponents and detractors have said about him. Paul had a way of doing this (cf. 2 Cor 10:1, 10) which said, "Look at what God can do with someone as weak as I." Paul's story is very similar to James's. He too had been an unbeliever and a persecutor of the church (Phil 3:6; Gal 1:13; 1 Cor 15:9) but due to his seeing Christ, the risen Lord, had completely changed his course of life. As George Lyttleton wrote in his *Observations on the Conversion of St. Paul*: "The conversion and apostleship of St. Paul alone, duly considered, was of itself a demonstration to prove Christianity to be a divine revelation."[3]

This very old tradition recorded by Paul is compelling testimony. It relates that Jesus appeared resurrected to both individuals alone and to large crowds of 500 and perhaps to the 120. He appeared both to devoted followers and to bitter enemies, even to his own skeptical family. The change in both his disciples and his former enemies alike is striking.

Jesus appeared first, according to the Gospels, to the women that had visited the tomb. When they found that the tomb was empty, they ran to report it to the disciples. Then they returned with Peter and the Beloved Disciple to inspect the tomb. After Peter and the Beloved Disciple left, they remained behind and thus were the first to see the risen Christ.

The appearance to the women (only Mary Magdalene is mentioned in John) is recorded in both Matthew and John.[4] These are the women that have followed Jesus around in Galilee (Lk 8:5) to assist in ministry in whatever way possible. They were present at the cross to witness the horrible spectacle of Jesus' torture and death (Aland 348, Mt 27:55-56 and par.). These are then faithful disciples who have known Jesus probably almost from the beginning of his ministry. In both narratives the women grasp at Jesus (Mt 28:9; Jn 20:17) and seek to hold him in their presence. They seemed overwhelmed with joy and astonishment. Jesus commands them to go to his "brothers" to tell them what they have seen.

Later in the day two disciples, one of whom was named Cleopas (Lk 24:18), were walking from Jerusalem to their home village of Emmaus.[5] The name of the other disciple is not given but this disciple was probably Cleopas' wife or son. There is mention of a Mary, wife of Clopas, in the Gospel of John (19:25) who was present at the cross. Cleopas was an alternate spelling of Clopas so probably this is her husband. His family figures prominently in later Christian history in Jerusalem. A second century author maintained that Cleopas was the father of a man that would become an important Jerusalem Christian leader (Hegesippus in Eusebius, *H.E.* 3.11).

At any rate, as the two walk, a stranger catches up with them and walks alongside. He asks them what they are troubled about and they explain that they had believed in Jesus of Nazareth but he has been condemned and crucified. They have placed all their hopes in him as the (political) redeemer of Israel from Roman dominance. Now they are depressed after witnessing the horrible death of their Messiah.

The traveler is, of course Jesus, but they cannot recognize him because their eyes are miraculously prevented from doing so. Jesus begins to explain the Old Testament scriptures to the two travelers. That is, he explains what the scriptures teach about the suffering, death, and resurrection of the Messiah. The scriptures he covered were doubtless some of those given in the sermons of the book of Acts (see e.g. Acts 2: Ps 16, 110; Acts 3: Deut 18).

As they reach the village Jesus acts as if he will continue walking. But the two--with typical oriental courtesy--prevail on him to spend the night, share a meal, and continue their conversation. During the meal Jesus takes bread and blesses and breaks it in his usual manner (Mt 14:19; 26:26). At once their eyes are opened and they recognize Jesus who vanishes from them. The two travelers hurry back to Jerusalem to announce that they have seen the risen Christ only to be told that Simon Peter has also seen him (Lk 24:34).

This is a fascinating narrative of an appearance of the risen Jesus. Details such as the name of their native village and the name of one of the (relatively unknown) disciples make this story historically vivid. The allusion to Peter's seeing the risen Christ harmonizes with 1 Cor 15:5. The theological message of the story is that the disciples must reach a new understanding, a Christological understanding, of the Old Testament. Second, Jesus, the Messiah, can only be properly understood through the breaking of the bread, that is, through the Lord's Supper which symbolizes his suffering and death.

Later that day Jesus appeared to the eleven apostles (with Thomas being absent) in the Upper Room in Jerusalem. This appearance is recorded by both Luke and John (Aland 356, 365). The similarities between the two Gospels are striking (although the language is so different as to rule out that one copied from the other): 1) In both of the Gospels Jesus stands miraculously and suddenly in their midst and salutes them, "Peace to you!" 2) Both Gospels refer to the joy of the disciples. 3) In both Gospels the time of Jesus' appearing is in the evening still on the first day of the week, the day of his resurrection. 4) In both Gospels Jesus displays his wounds for his disciples in order to convince them that he was truly raised bodily from the dead and not merely a phantom or ghost. 5) In both Gospels Jesus teaches them about their mission to carry his message and about their receiving power from the Holy Spirit. 6) Both Gospels stress the motif of doubt on the part of the disciples. They do not doubt that it is Jesus in their midst but that he is corporeal. Jesus thus displays his wounds to demonstrate a continuity between himself, the risen Lord, and the earthly Jesus.

The theological motifs in Luke are familiar: Jesus emphasizes that his death and resurrection have fulfilled Old Testament prophecies. Jesus charges his disciples to witness to the truths of the gospel. Jesus promises that the Holy Spirit will come to give them power to accomplish this task.

In John's Gospel Jesus breathes on them to impart the Holy Spirit (20:22), but in Luke's Gospel he promises that the Spirit will come upon them if they wait in Jerusalem (24:49). Jesus' breathing on the disciples in John is a personal gift of the Spirit in order to strengthen the eleven. Luke's promise of the Holy Spirit (which happened on Pentecost) was the promise of a public sign to empower the church.

One week later--again on Sunday-- Jesus appeared again to the eleven, this time with Thomas present. Why are the disciples still in Jerusalem when Jesus commanded them to go to Galilee (Mt 28:7; Mk 16:7)? The Passover feast--that is the time of unleavened bread--lasts one week. Thus they have remained in Jerusalem for the duration of the feast. They were undoubtedly preparing to travel to Galilee when Jesus appeared to them again.

Thomas had expressed a refusal to believe in the resurrection unless he could carefully inspect Jesus' scars (Jn 20:25). Now Jesus shows him his wounds on his hands and side and urges Thomas to believe. Thomas indicated a zeal for martyrdom earlier (Jn 11:16) and a desire to follow Jesus wherever he might go (Jn 14:5). He was a pragmatic zealot. But his hopes and faith have been crushed by the brutal death of Jesus. Nevertheless, upon seeing Jesus and inspecting his wounds, he exclaimed, "My Lord, and my God." His doubt has ended. He is once again ready to follow Jesus anywhere he would lead. But this time he will follow him not as an earthly Messiah, but as the risen Lord and God. Thomas' confession of faith is surely the theological climax of the Gospel of John.

At some point, probably during this first week, Jesus also appeared to James his brother (see above and 1 Cor 15:7).

The Appearances in Galilee (Aland 367, 364)

After the first week of Jesus' resurrection appearances (see the chronology below), the disciples journeyed to Galilee to await further visits from the risen Lord. Seven of them went fishing while waiting (Jn 21:2).[6] They had rowed out on the sea of Galilee and fished all night without catching anything. Early in the morning, Jesus stood on the shore about 100 yards away and called to them. The disciples could not recognize Jesus because of the distance between them. He asked them if they had caught anything. When they responded that they had not, he suggested to them to cast their net on the right side of the boat. This time they caught so many fish they were unable to haul them in.

Jesus had similarly encountered some of his disciples three years earlier (Lk 5:1-11) when he summoned them to follow him. Then he had told them to cast out their nets and when they did, they miraculously caught so many fish that the nets began to tear. The memory of that event now came back and the Beloved Disciple (Jn 21:7) said, "It is the Lord!" When Peter heard that, he jumped into the water to swim to shore.

There on shore Jesus had prepared a charcoal fire and they roasted fish and had some bread with it. Jesus ate in their presence again demonstrating that he had been bodily raised from the dead.

As they ate Jesus asked Peter, "Do you love me more than these?" Who or what were the "these"? Some maintain that Jesus was referring to the other disciples ("Do you love me more than these other disciples?") Better is Brown's suggestion that "these" refers to the fishing boats, nets, etc. That is, "Do you love me more than these fishing boats? Are you willing to leave your occupation to follow me?"

Jesus asked Peter this question three times and each time Peter answered, "Lord you know that I love you."[7] The asking of this question three times was certainly in reference to Peter's denial of Jesus three times (Mk 14:72; Aland 333). Thus Jesus was intending to rehabilitate Peter after his failure. Peter would confess three times that he loved Jesus to help him forget that he had denied him three times.

After Peter confessed his love for Jesus each time, Jesus commanded him, "Feed my sheep." That is, if he truly loved Jesus above everything else, above all the worldly advantages he might achieve, then he should fulfill his apostolic mission of feeding or nurturing the sheep of the flock (the church). We must note carefully what many commentators point out: Jesus says to feed "*My* sheep". The sheep are the Lord's and not the pastor's. Second, the pastor is told to "feed" them. His commission is to feed with the nourishment of the gospel, to live a life of service with the word of God.

Jesus concludes his instructions to Peter by predicting that in his old age he will have to "stretch out" his hands in order to be bound and lead to a place he would not choose. This prediction is surely concerning his future imprisonment, perhaps even his future crucifixion (tradition has it that

Peter was crucified in Rome).

Thus in this appearance Jesus himself became a pastor to lead his disciple Peter back into the fold of forgiveness and to restore him to his apostolic commission. Jesus modeled the seeking shepherd, the very role he wanted Peter to play until his death predicted on this day.

The final post-resurrection appearance in Galilee was on a mountain (Mt 28:16). Mountains are important locations for Jesus' revelations, especially in the Gospel of Matthew (see 5:1). Some would see this appearance as identical to the appearance to the 500 mentioned in 1 Corinthians 15: 6 (see above). Certainly a mountain or hillside would make an ideal location for speaking to such a crowd. We would think that a large crowd of disciples would be more likely in Galilee around the Sea of Galilee where Jesus preached most often. That some people who were present "doubted" (Mt 28:17) would indicate that more than just the eleven apostles were present. They had already seen the risen Lord several times. Even Thomas no longer doubted that he had been raised!

Jesus speaks on this occasion with majesty and regal authority: "All authority in heaven and earth has been given to me." Now he is not concerned to demonstrate his corporeality by eating with his disciples or by showing his wounds. Rather, he acts already as the exalted Lord that he will become at his ascension. In this capacity he commands his disciples to make other disciples for him, to baptize them, and then to teach them further (cf. Lk 24:47f; Jn 20:21; and the longer ending of Mark, see Excursus below). He has finished his ministry on earth of teaching his disciples. Now he looks to the future of his church and makes provision for bringing others into his kingdom. Though he will soon be absent from them in the body, he will remain with them until the close of the age as the exalted ruler of the universe.

The Ascension
(Aland 365, Acts 1:1-11)

On the fortieth day (Acts 1:3) Jesus appeared to his disciples one last time in bodily form. If one had only Luke's Gospel one might conclude that the ascension took place on the same day as the resurrection. But the book of Acts, also written by Luke, makes it clear that Luke was merely compressing events in his Gospel for the sake of literary unity. The resurrection appearances were spread out over a period of 40 days.

The disciples had returned to Jerusalem and he instructed them to remain there until they received power from on high, that is the baptism of the Holy Spirit. Then after leading out to the village of Bethany, he blessed them and departed from them. He was carried into heaven (Lk 24:51) and so passed from his earthly ministry and began his heavenly ministry.

Does the ascension story teach a "three storey universe" (i.e. with heaven above, earth in the middle, and hell below) as R. Bultmann maintained? We should, as T. Oden points out, not assume that either the biblical writers or the ancient people took "up" as the direction of heaven all that literally. Rather, the physicality of direction only symbolizes the metaphysicality of a different dimension.

Conclusion

As Connick points out. The resurrection of Jesus must be accepted as a real event for the following reasons: 1) The existence of the Christian church. It would be very difficult to explain the church if Jesus' ministry had ended with his crucifixion. Harder still is it to imagine that the disciples in their state of depression and confusion could have dreamed up or hallucinated such a conclusion as these resurrection appearances. 2) The existence of the New Testament. The theme of Christ's resurrection permeates virtually every New Testament book. Who would have written these books if he believed that Jesus' had ended with death and humiliation? 3) Sunday as the day of worship. Jews kept Saturday as the sacred day. How can we explain the change to Sunday for Christians apart from the fact that the momentous resurrection of the Lord took place on this day? 4) The Lord's Supper. Who would celebrate the death of a horribly crucified man by reenacting the death symbolically unless that celebrant also believed that the same man had been raised?

Notes

1. This verse is widely attested for Luke's Gospel (24:12) but is absent in a few manuscripts. Yet the oldest and best witnesses (including the Sinaiticus and Vaticanus uncials from the fourth century and Papyrus 75 from the third century) have it and it, therefore, undoubtedly was a part of Luke's original Gospel as

Fitzmyer argues. This is one of the examples of the so-called "western non-interpolations."

2. This is undoubtedly the brother of Jesus (Gal 1:19, 2:9; Mk 6:3) and not James the son of Zebedee or James the son of Alphaeus. The latter two James's never reached the prominence in the Jerusalem church that the brother of Jesus did. Hence when Paul names him without qualification, he seems to be referring to the most prominent and well-known James. It is significant that a brief narrative of Jesus' post-resurrection visit to James appears in the apocryphal Gospel to the Hebrews written in the second century AD. This text is quoted in Chapter 16. According to the Gospel of Hebrews, Jesus appeared to James to encourage him to eat something because James, who according to this apocryphal gospel had been in the Upper Room at the Last Supper, had taken a vow of fasting. It is historically improbable that James, an unbeliever, was in the Upper Room at that time so the story has false elements in it. It probably does, however, contain a kernel of truth. More likely, James, like the apostle Paul, was in a state of shock after having seen the risen Lord and could not eat (cf. Acts 9:9). Later Jesus appeared to him again or sent someone to him like Ananias (cf. Acts 9:10-19) to encourage James to take food. Cf. Also Gospel of Thomas 12.

3. Quoted in F.F. Bruce, *Acts*.

4. The longer ending of the Gospel of Mark also refers to Jesus' appearing to Mary Magdalene (Mk 16:9). See the Excursus below on the longer ending. At least, however, one could say that this longer ending is an old tradition that confirms the appearance to the women.

5. Luke tells us that Emmaus was 60 stades or just under 7 miles from Jerusalem (but a few manuscripts read 160 stades or just under 19 miles). Geographers are, however, uncertain about the exact location of this village since several villages in ancient Palestine were called Emmaus. See Fitzmyer.

6. Arguments that chapter 21 of John's Gospel, the so-called "appendix", was not an original part of his text are not convincing. Likewise, those who maintain that this is the same event as Lk 5:1-11 have failed to demonstrate this conclusion. See the handling of these issues in Craig.

7. In the Greek text of John's Gospel Jesus used the Greek word *agapao* the first two times that he asked Peter this question and Peter responded with the word *phileo*. Some commentators, therefore, want to see a distinction in the kind of love Jesus is asking for and the kind of love that Peter is able to give. That is, they maintain that Jesus was asking for a higher love but Peter could only give a more human love or personal affection at that time. But as Brown points out, the two probably spoke Aramaic between them and these two kinds of love are not expressible in either Aramaic or Hebrew.

EXCURSUS

The Longer Ending of Mark (Aland 363)

Although the King James Version of the Bible contains Mark 16:9-20, most recent versions (e.g. Revised Standard Version, New International Version, Jerusalem Bible) note that there are manuscript problems with these verses. The verses are in some of the oldest manuscripts such as the Alexandrinus (5th cent.) , Ephraemi (5th cent.), and Bezae (6th cent.) texts but are absent from the older and better manuscripts of the fourth century, the Sinaiticus and Vaticanus texts (For a brief description, see D.A. Fiensy, *New Testament Introduction*, pp. 354f). Text critics (that is those who master the discipline of comparing and studying the manuscripts. See B. Metzger, *A Textual Commentary on the Greek New Testament*) of the New Testament almost universally reject these verses from the Gospel of Mark. Some maintain that Mark ended at 16:8; others affirm that Mark had another ending (perhaps similar to Matthew's) but that the ending has been lost.

Even if one does conclude that the longer ending of Mark (that is verses 9-20) should be omitted from the Gospel, one should leave open the possibility that these verses stem from an independent oral tradition that goes back to the earliest Christian community in Jerusalem. The verses form a good summary of many of the resurrection appearances of Jesus and may have therefore been a catechism used for instructing Christian converts. The table below shows that these verses parallel several other narratives in Matthew, Luke and John.

16:9= Jn 20:14-18

16:12= Lk 24:13-35

16:14= Lk 24:36-43 and Jn 20:19-23

16:15= Mt 28:19 and Lk 24:47

16:16= Mt 28:19

16:19= Lk 24:51

Table 24.1

Traditions in the "Longer Ending"

The reader will note that only the verses concerning the accompanying signs--that is, handling serpents and drinking poison--are not represented in this table.

It is possible that if verses 9-20 were not originally in Mark's Gospel, someone composed them based on reading Matthew, Luke and John. But since the vocabulary of these verses is much different from the narratives in the other Gospels, it is more likely that this is an independent, oral tradition that actually confirms and supports the narratives in the other Gospels. For such traditions, see Chapter 4. Thus an oral tradition which summarized Jesus' post-resurrection appearances might have been appended to a manuscript of Mark's Gospel by a copyist in the early second century. Verses 9-20 may not be Marcan but they are then historically reliable.

Appearances in Jerusalem	Appearances in Galilee
First Sunday: 1. Women discover the empty tomb 2. Peter and John inspect the tomb. 3. Jesus appears to the women. 4. Jesus appears to the two on the road to Emmaus. 5. Jesus appears to Peter. 6. Jesus appears to the Eleven (without Thomas). 7. Jesus appears to James . **"After Eight Days"**: 8. Jesus appears to the Eleven with Thomas.	
	Between Ten and 38 Days: 9. Jesus appears to the seven by the Sea of Galilee 10. Jesus appears to the disciples (the 500?) on a mountain in Galilee.
The Fourtieth Day: 11. Jesus appears in Jerusalem, leads disciples out to Bethany, ascension.	

Table 24.2

Jesus' Post-Resurrection Appearances

Epilogue

The Living Lord

Thus ends the story of the earthly Jesus. It began with his laying down his heavenly glory in order to become a man (Jn 1:1; Phil 2:6-8). It involved his ministry of teaching, healing, dying and being raised from the dead in glorious victory. "Wherefore God highly exalted him and gave him a name above every name" (Phil 2:9). Christ's exaltation is the counterpart of his humiliation (i.e. the point when he assumed humanity). He now transcends all earthly categories, all historical realities.[1] He enters his glory, the glory that he had known before his incarnation (Jn 17:5). His earthly mission is complete; now his heavenly ministry of intercession and divine governance begins. "Christ died once for the sinners, the righteous for the unrighteous in order that he might lead us to God, having been put to death in the flesh and made alive in the spirit. . . (and he) is (seated) on the right hand of God, having gone into heaven, with angels, principalities, and powers subjected to him" (1 Pet 3:18, 22). "Worthy is the Lamb that was slain to receive power, wealth, wisdom, strength, honor, glory and praise" (Rev 5:12).

Note

1. T. Oden, *The Word of Life.*

Glossary

Apocalyptic: A term used to describe a type of literature which claims to be revelations of hidden knowledge written by an inspired seer (literally: "revelation").

Apocrypha: A term used by Protestants to denote those books appearing in the Roman Catholic Old Testament which they do not accept as canonical (literally: "hidden").

Canon: A closed body of writings considered to be inspired and authoritative (literally: "a measuring stick").

Catechism, Catechetical: Having to do with instruction given to those about to undergo Christian baptism (literally: "instruction").

Christology: The study of the doctrine of Christ.

Diaspora: The dispersion of Jews from Palestine into the Greco-Roman world (literally: "dispersion").

Eschatology: The study of the end-time, for Christians the second coming of Christ (literally: "study of the end").

Gemara: Commentary on the Mishnah (literally: "completion").

Haggadah: Nonlegal materials in the rabbinic literature (literally: "Narrative").

Halacah: Legal materials in rabbinic literature (literally "walking", hence rule of conduct).

Hasidim: The pious ones.

Hasmonean: The family of Hasmon, the earliest known figure of which is Mattathias, the father of Judas Maccabeus.

Hanukkah: the feast of dedication begun when Judas Maccabeus recaptured and cleansed the Temple (literally: "dedication").

Midrash: Study; also interpretation of the Old Testament (literally: "searching").

Mishnah: A written codification of the Pharisaic oral law, completed in AD 200 (literally: "repetition").

Pericope: A small literary unit such as a narrative or a form of teaching.

Pseudepigrapha: Those ancient Jewish texts not accepted today in any canon (literally: "false writings".

Septuagint: The Greek translation of the Old Testament supposedly done by seventy translators (literally: "seventy").

Talmud: The Jewish oral law in its final form, including both Mishnah and Gemara. Completed by AD 500 (literally: "learning").

Targum: Translation of the Old Testament into Aramaic, originally done orally, later written down (literally: "translation").

Tombs: Either natural caves or hand-hewn ones in which the dead were laid. Tombs could be either *archasolium* (that is vaulted ceiling tombs) or *kokh* tombs (or tombs that looked like ovens or niches also called *loculi*). Often tombs contained *sarcophagi* or stone or wooden coffins or *ossuaries* smaller boxes made of stone or wood in which only the bones of the deceased were placed.

Torah: The Old Testament law; also (for Pharisees) the oral law (literally: "instruction").

Tosephta: A collection of statements and traditions closely associated with the Mishnah (literally: "addition, supplement")

Vulgate: Jerome's Latin translation of both the Old and New Testaments (literally: "common").

Yahweh: The personal name of god in the Hebrew Old Testament (sometimes spelled Jehovah in old English versions).

Index

Index of Aland References (numbers in italics refer to sections in Aland)